Politics in

CHINA

*The Little, Brown Series
in Comparative Politics*

Under the Editorship of

GABRIEL A. ALMOND

JAMES S. COLEMAN

LUCIAN W. PYE

A COUNTRY STUDY

Politics in

CHINA

Second Edition

James R. Townsend

University of Washington

Boston   Toronto
LITTLE, BROWN AND COMPANY

To Matt and Mike

Preface to the Second Edition

Profound changes have occurred in Chinese politics since the first edition of *Politics in China* was completed in 1973. The policies that emerged from the Great Proletarian Cultural Revolution of 1966–1969 became increasingly controversial in 1974–1976, leading to sharp factional disputes accompanied by an economic downturn. There was a historic turning point in 1976, with the deaths of Zhou Enlai and Mao Zedong, another escalation of intraparty conflict, and the purge, late in the year, of the most ardent advocates of the Cultural Revolution version of Maoism. Subsequently, the post-Mao leadership repudiated the Cultural Revolution, embarking on new policies that reversed many precepts associated with the Maoist model and intensified China's interaction with the global system. The adoption of new party and state constitutions, coupled with renewed emphasis on legal principles and organizational stability, initiated a period of political institutionalization. A second edition of *Politics in China* is in order simply to describe these dramatic changes in Chinese political life.

Moreover, the death of Mao was the end of an era in the politics of the Chinese Communist Party and possibly the end of the long revolutionary era that began in mid-nineteenth-century China. The challenge of assessing the Maoist era was an important factor in my decision to undertake a second edition of this book. The first edition presented Maoism largely as a static model whose features were best represented in the objectives, processes, and policies of the Cultural Revolution, which provided the primary context for my interpretation of the Maoist model. In the second edition, with better perspective on the outcome and significance of the Cultural Revolution, I have treated Maoism more as a transitional developmental strategy and have delineated more sharply the Maoist period in which that strategy prevailed. In an effort to explain China's passage through the Maoist period, I have given more attention to international influences on Chinese affairs, although the book remains essentially a study of domestic politics.

One major theme of the book that remains unchanged is emphasis on the fluid character of the Chinese political system. The institutional and policy changes of 1973–1979 were as significant, although not as violent and disruptive, as those of the Great Leap and the Cultural Revolution. They were also equally surprising to most outside observers, suggesting that an open mind and a willingness to abandon one's own preconceptions remain an indispensable asset in the study of Chinese politics.

Events of the winter of 1978–1979 underscored the preceding point. Establishment of diplomatic relations between the United States and the People's Republic of China at the end of 1978, with new agreements on academic exchanges, hopes for greatly expanded economic ties, and Deng Xiaoping's visit to the United States in January 1979, seemed to intensify the Chinese "opening" to the West that had flourished in 1978. Within China, a flood of posters, demonstrations, and public debate on sensitive issues signaled a growing movement for "democratic" reform. But no sooner had Deng returned to China in February than the Chinese invaded Vietnam. Although the People's Liberation Army pulled back after a few weeks of inconclusive fighting, the hostilities were a sobering reminder of the military implications of China's modernization and the global security problems that may accompany it. They seemed, too, to increase tension within the Chinese leadership. There was a tightening up on public debate and criticism, warnings about the danger of uncritical acceptance of foreign influences, admissions of continuing weaknesses in the national economy and the people's standard of living, and a general reassessment of the ambitious goals of the new period. The Central Committee's Third Plenum, in December 1978, had acknowledged the inescapable demands of the agricultural economy. Subsequent cutbacks or delays in plans for industrial development and foreign economic exchange were the other side of this coin, a reminder that the four modernizations entail sharp competition for scarce resources. Chinese politics will reflect these strains and uncertainties, with their potential for policy conflict and reversals, for the forseeable future.

I have benefited greatly in my revisions of *Politics in China* from comments on the first edition by students, colleagues, and reviewers and from the publications of other students of China. My very warm thanks go to Diane Fathi and Arlene McGougan for typing and other assistance, to Philip Wall for his work on many of the tables and charts, and to John Frankenstein for providing *pinyin* versions of Chinese names and a "Note on the Romanization of Chinese." I am also grateful to the following people at Little, Brown and at Cobb/Dunlop Publisher Services, who did so much to improve the manuscript and bring it to completion: Tim Kenslea, Edith Lewis, and Vicki Kaplan. I retain full responsibility, of course, for all errors and shortcomings.

A Note on the Romanization of Chinese

There are several systems, all of them unsatisfactory in some way, for rendering Chinese words in the Roman alphabet. The two most widespread today are the *pinyin* system, used in the People's Republic of China, and the older Wade-Giles system, which until recently was almost universally used in English-language scholarly work on China. This book uses, except as noted, the official *pinyin* system; the more familiar Wade-Giles transcription follows the *pinyin* rendering in parentheses at the first occurrence.

There are, however, a number of cases where familiarity, custom, sheer recognizability, and ease of scholarly access argue for retention of older romanizations, especially in a textbook such as this. Thus, in this book, Peking [Beijing], Canton [Guangzhou], Yangtze [Changjiang], Manchuria [Dongbei], Tibet [Xizang], and Inner Mongolia [Nei Monggul] are given in their non-*pinyin* versions; brackets denote *pinyin* versions of older usages. The names of some individuals (Chiang Kai-shek, Sun Yat-sen) and organizations (the Kuomintang, referred to throughout this text by the standard initials KMT) are not changed.

Finally, we should note that we have retained that word of most uncertain origin, China. Otherwise, the name of this book would be *Politics in Zhongguo.*

Contents

Charts and Tables

Politics in

CHINA

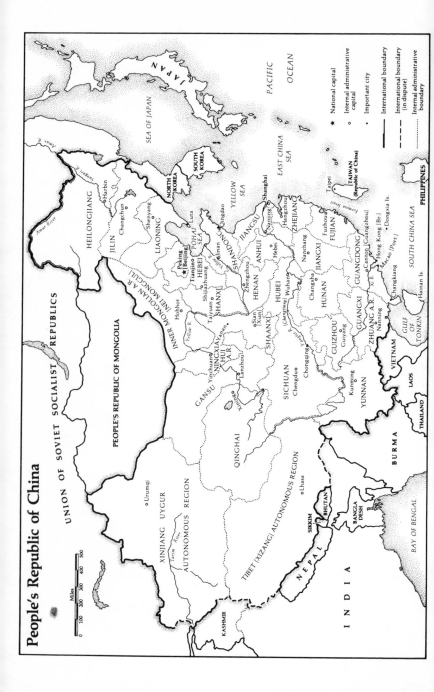

People's Republic of China

UNION OF SOVIET SOCIALIST REPUBLICS

PEOPLE'S REPUBLIC OF MONGOLIA

INNER MONGOLIAN A.R. (NEI MONGGOL)

HEILONGJIANG

JILIN

LIAONING

NORTH KOREA

SOUTH KOREA

JAPAN

SEA OF JAPAN

Amur River

Amur R.

Sungari R.

Harbin

Changchun

Shenyang

Luta

PACIFIC OCEAN

XINJIANG UYGUR AUTONOMOUS REGION

Urumqi

Tarim River

QINGHAI

TIBET (XIZANG) AUTONOMOUS REGION

Lhasa

GANSU

Lanzhou

NINGXIA HUI A.R.

Yinchuan

Yellow R.

HEBEI

SHANXI

Taiyuan

Hohhot

Shijiazhuang

Peking (Beijing)

Tianjin

PO HAI SEA

SHANDONG

Jinan

Qingdao

YELLOW SEA

Yellow R.

HENAN

Zhengzhou

JIANGSU

Nanjing

Shanghai

ZHEJIANG

Hangzhou

EAST CHINA SEA

SHAANXI

Sian (Xian)

Yangtze R.

HUBEI

Wuhan (Changjiang)

ANHUI

Hebei

Nanchang

JIANGXI

FUJIAN

Fuzhou

TAIWAN (Republic of China)

Taipei

Formosa Strait

SICHUAN

Chengdu

Chongqing

Yangtze R.

HUNAN

Changsha

GUIZHOU

Guiyang

GUANGDONG

Canton (Guangzhou)

Hong Kong [Br.]

Macao [Port.]

Dongxia Is.

SOUTH CHINA SEA

YUNNAN

Kunming

GUANGXI ZHUANG A.R.

Nanning

Changkiang

GULF OF TONKIN

Hainan Is.

VIETNAM

LAOS

THAILAND

BURMA

INDIA

NEPAL

BHUTAN

SIKKIM

BANGLA DESH

KASHMIR

BAY OF BENGAL

PHILIPPINES

Xi R.

Miles

0 100 200 300 400 500

★ National capital

⊙ Internal administrative capital

○ Important city

• Important city

——— International boundary

–––– International boundary (in dispute)

·········· Internal administrative boundary

CHAPTER I

The Study of Chinese Politics

THE SETTING OF CHINESE POLITICS

The Revolutionary Setting. Politics in China is the product of a prolonged revolutionary era, spanning at least the period between 1911 and 1949 and including not one but three forceful overthrows of the political system. The first revolution in 1911 displaced an imperial system that had endured for centuries. The second, culminating in 1928 with the establishment of a new central government under the control of the Kuomintang (KMT), replaced the disunited "warlord" rule of early republican China with a more vigorous, organized, and centralized system of single-party domination. The third revolution of 1949 brought the Chinese Communist Party (CCP) to power, inaugurating the present Communist system.

Even this delineation, broad as it is, does not define the scope of China's revolutionary era. Successful efforts to overthrow national political institutions and elites establish the decisive peaks of a revolutionary process, but they do not necessarily mark the limits of the process itself. In the case of the Chinese revolution, it is probably best to date the initiation of the process from the Taiping Rebellion (1850–1864), an upheaval so disruptive in its impact and goals that it may be regarded as "revolutionary in character" and "the beginning of the end of Confucian China."[1] Moreover despite the Com-

---

[1] Franz Michael, in collaboration with Chung-li Chang, *The Taiping Rebellion, Volume I: History* (Seattle: University of Washington Press, 1966), p. 199.

munist victory of 1949, the revolutionary era lasted until the death of Mao Zedong in 1976. The Great Proletarian Cultural Revolution, which erupted in 1966 and was only partially re-solved by the CCP's Ninth Congress in April 1969, was clear evidence of continuing revolutionary features in Chinese poli-tics. Mao and his supporters insisted that this campaign was truly a "revolution"; indeed, their propagandists called it "the greatest of revolutionary mass movements," one which "has no parallel in the history of mankind."[2] Without necessarily accepting the accuracy of this claim, we see in it testimony to Chinese perceptions of their times as revolutionary.

The revolutionary character of Chinese politics is, for the external observer, a source of both fascination and frustration. The richness and power of Chinese civilization have long held a peculiar fascination for outsiders. To that attraction is now added the recognition that one of the most dramatic events of human history has occurred, and is still unfolding, in modern China. The politics of revolution defy easy understanding or generalization, however, regardless of the student's inter-est and enthusiasm. We shall consider later in this chapter some conceptual questions about the study of Chinese poli-tics, but a few more concrete problems deserve mention here.

Political upheaval and social change are, of course, the es-sence of revolution. It is simply recognizing the obvious to say that modern Chinese politics have been unstable, that political and social changes have come so rapidly during the course of the revolution that descriptions at one point in time have seldom held true for long. It is not so obvious, perhaps, to recognize how often these changes have violated preconcep-tions about what was "possible" in China. Consider only a few examples of propositions seriously held by at least some ob-servers during recent decades. At various times it was thought that China could never gain true unity and independence; that Chinese Communism could never become a significant politi-cal force; that China would necessarily develop as a pro-West-ern power; that the Chinese peasant could not be collectivized; that the Sino-Soviet alliance could not be broken; that the

[2] *Peking Review,* no. 42 (October 18, 1968), pp. 26, 31.

authority of the CCP could not be seriously threatened from within. None of these propositions was unreasonable at a particular point in time, but in every case the "impossible" became not only possible but real. The lesson is not that judgments and predictions are useless but rather that analysis of a revolutionary era requires an expanded vision of what is politically possible.

Second, a revolutionary setting raises the stakes of political competition, transforming many differences into struggles for political and human survival. The "agreement to disagree" is not impossible in such a setting, but it may be a luxury and a risk. When the outcome of political struggle is seen as decisive for both personal careers and long-term structuring of society, participants who hold firmly to their ambitions and ideals will not hesitate to extend the "rules" of the game. The use or threatened use of armed force then becomes central in the political process, as it was in China throughout the 1911–1949 period. The army's declining role in Chinese politics between 1949 and 1958 was a concrete sign of the decline of revolutionary politics. Its rising political role after 1959 and into the Cultural Revolution—first symbolic, then as a threat and ultimately in deployment against other organized political groups —was equally concrete evidence of a revolutionary revival.

Finally, the prosaic yet unavoidable problem of source material and corroborative evidence should be raised. It is not easy to acquire knowledge about the dynamics of Chinese politics. Data on contemporary China are drawn largely, although by no means exclusively, from official Communist sources that are subject to severe limitations and restrictions. This is not simply a post-1949 problem, however, a consequence solely of the CCP's effort to maintain a closed communications system. The production and preservation of reliable source material probably suffers in any revolutionary situation. Archives may be lost, destroyed, or sealed; key participants may be silenced; independent sources may be suppressed while official sources become overtly propagandistic; the acquisition of data generally, whether by scholars or officials, assumes low priority and immense difficulty in a society disrupted by internal war and revolution. Gaps and conflicts in sources on modern Chinese politics are, therefore, unavoidable, and not just a function of Communist secrecy. Although there is no useful purpose served by belaboring here the technical aspects of this problem,[3] the reader should remember that the nature of the times justifies a particularly critical approach to interpretations of Chinese politics and to the sources on which these interpretations are based.

The Historical Setting. The enduring aspects of China's prominence include history, size, location, and resources. Generalizations about China's historical greatness—its wealth, its power, and the quality and longevity of its culture—abound in texts of every description. More relevant here are the expectations of greatness that this tradition has left in the minds of Chinese and foreigners alike. Historically derived images have an intangible quality, but their importance with regard to China is unmistakable. Indeed, in modern times they have led repeatedly to exaggerated estimates of China's influence and capabilities. They appeared in a dangerous complacency with which the Manchu emperors responded to intensified Western pressures beginning in the late eighteenth century. Perhaps equally misguided were the Western traders and missionaries on the other side, who foresaw a commercial or religious conquest of China that would alter the shape of world history. The United States in World War II nourished what were at that time illusory visions of China's world status. One wonders to what extent American fears about China's domination of Southeast Asia, its influence in Africa, or its military threat to the North American continent—to mention a few of the concerns voiced in the United States during the cold war years—drew on the image rather than reality of Chinese power. The Chinese, too, have tended to attach global significance to their actions, as in the earlier quote about the Cultural Revolution. Although political rhetoric naturally exaggerates hopes and

[3]A useful discussion is Michel Oksenberg, "Sources and Methodological Problems in the Study of Contemporary China," in A. Doak Barnett, ed., *Chinese Communist Politics in Action* (Seattle: University of Washington Press, 1969), pp. 577–606.

fears, the majesty of China's tradition is an element in the entire world's high expectations about the nation's future.

In more practical terms, the student of Chinese politics must grapple with historical references simply because they pervade Chinese political discourse. The Chinese frame of reference is strikingly self-centered and historical. Comparisons are mainly with the past—with the empire, with the KMT, with "before Liberation" or "before the Cultural Revolution" or "since the Gang of Four"—rather than with other systems. Well-known figures from the past provide analogues for contemporary heroes and villains. Orienting examples and metaphorical images draw heavily from the historical and literary traditions.

This tendency to load contemporary political discourse with references to the past is partly a cultural characteristic, partly a function of the closeness and relevance of the traditional system. Many of the leaders who governed the People's Republic of China (PRC) until recently were born before the fall of the empire in 1911. Mao and his senior colleagues knew imperial society firsthand and received part of their education in the traditional style. Younger leaders were recruited into politics before 1949 and are well aware of traditional ideas and social patterns that persisted after 1911. So long as the theme of revolutionary transformation endures, traditional society will serve as a reference point for measuring the revolution's progress.

The International Setting. The PRC's area of 3.7 million square miles makes it the world's third largest state; its population—estimated at 951 million in 1976—is by far the world's largest, comprising over one-fifth of the global total (see Appendix A).[4] Economic growth since 1949 has been cumulatively impressive, despite important slumps. One analyst has estimated

[4]All figures for the Chinese population are estimates, based largely on projections from the 1953 census and diverging widely because of uncertainty about how rapidly, if at all, the birth rate has been declining. The Chinese have offered few official estimates since the 1950s, preferring to use loose, rounded, rhetorical figures; the one in use in 1978 was 900 million, even though it was less than the total obtained by adding previously released figures for provincial populations. An excellent introduction to the size, distribution, and composition of the Chinese population is Leo A. Orleans, *Every Fifth Child: The Population of China* (Stanford: Stanford University Press, 1972).

average annual growth rates for 1953–1974 as follows: 5.6 percent in GNP; 3.4 percent in GNP per capita; 10.5 percent in industrial production; 2.4 percent in agricultural production; 2.2 percent in population.[5] Given the country's size, this growth has pushed it into the higher levels of global economic power. In 1976, for example, its GNP of $324 billion was 4.7 percent of the total world GNP (the United States accounted for 24.3 percent) and the sixth largest in the world, trailing only the United States, Soviet Union, Japan, West Germany, and France.[6] The PRC's great north-south extent across temperate zones, its varied topography, and its generally rich mineral and energy resources provide a solid base for economic diversification and growth. The skills and industriousness of the massive population are a proven asset. Projections are hazardous, but on balance China seems likely to maintain its vigorous economic growth and to strengthen its place in the global economic order.[7]

The territory of China dominates the East Asian area, sharing borders with the Soviet Union, Pakistan, India, Vietnam, Korea, and other countries and in proximity to Japan and Southeast Asia. It occupies the center of a region of great strategic importance where much of the world's population is concentrated. Diplomatically, the PRC has been a member of the United Nations and its Security Council since 1971; in February 1979 it had diplomatic relations with 118 countries, compared with 21 countries which maintained formal ties with the Republic of China (ROC) on Taiwan. PRC armed forces are close to four million, with over three million in the army. China detonated its first nuclear device in 1964, orbited its first space satellite in 1970; missile delivery capabilities are

[5] Arthur G. Ashbrook, Jr., "China: Economic Overview 1975," in United States Congress Joint Economic Committee, *China: A Reassessment of the Economy* (Washington: Government Printing Office, 1975), p. 24. See also Appendixes B and C.

[6] Central Intelligence Agency, *Handbook of Economic Statistics 1977* (ER 77-10537, September 1977), pp. 1, 18–19.

[7] For a guardedly optimistic view of China's economic prospects, with a good discussion of the necessary qualifications of such predictions, see Robert F. Dernberger, "China's Economic Future," in Allen S. Whiting and Robert F. Dernberger, *China's Future: Foreign Policy and Economic Development in the Post-Mao Era* (New York: McGraw-Hill, 1976).

growing although they remain far behind those of the super-powers. The PRC is a major regional power, a potential global power, and an important actor in international politics. Its diplomatic recognition by the United States in January 1979 removed the last formal barrier to full international participation.

This is an exceedingly simplified view of China's international setting, one that stresses the country's weight in the global scales. It must be qualified by several points. First, the PRC's economic power reflects its size, not its level of development. Despite a strong growth record and three decades of rapid industrialization, China remains unevenly developed and still heavily dependent on its agricultural sector. Its estimated 1976 per-capita GNP of $340 places it among the poorer countries of the world. More to the point, it has a precarious food-population balance that complicates growth strategies. The basic problem is that only about 15 percent of the land is suitable for agricultural use, with most of the rural population—which is about 85 percent of the total population—concentrated on the cultivated sixth of China's land surface. Chinese officials observe that their economy must support over one-fifth of the world's population with only 7 percent of its cultivated land. To support industrialization and feed its population, China must keep agricultural growth ahead of population growth. It has done so, but with very little surplus; grain production per capita, for example, was scarcely higher in 1975 than it had been in 1952 and was below the peak year of 1958 (see Appendix C). Reduced population growth in the 1960s and 1970s has helped; if the annual population growth has fallen below 2 percent, as some experts think, then the total population is less than in the estimates used here, and the picture is correspondingly brighter. But the fact remains that China's long-range economic development requires a technical revolution in agriculture and that the needs of the agricultural sector are a major constraint on economic plans. Moreover, failure to resolve the food-population problem would leave the country vulnerable to serious food shortages.

There are other trouble zones in future PRC development. Rising consumer demands might disrupt a development pattern that has restrained consumption. Transportation facilities have lagged behind the general level of industrial growth. Since 1976 officials have been acknowledging that scientific and technological backwardness, in both military and civilian sectors, is a major obstacle to future development. In sum, continued economic growth will not be easy or automatic. It appears to be increasingly dependent on foreign trade and technology, and possibly capital as well, which will pose delicate political issues for Chinese elites.

Also, China's current international position is somewhat misleading because it is at odds with the insecurities and constraints that have dominated most of the PRC's existence. Throughout the 1950s and 1960s, it perceived the United States as a major threat to its security because of American intervention in the Korean War in 1950–1953 and Vietnam in the 1960s, United States military security treaties with Japan, South Korea, Taiwan, and the SEATO and ANZUS countries, and diverse American efforts to contain and isolate China. American support enabled the ROC to hold the China seat in the UN and to receive diplomatic recognition from a majority of UN members until 1971. A serious territorial dispute with India led to a brief border war in 1962, followed by years of strained relations between these two Asian powers. Chinese fears of Japanese rearmament were strong in the 1960s. Above all, the intensification of the Sino-Soviet conflict after 1960 made China the potential target of both of the nuclear superpowers. Border fighting with the Soviet Union in 1969 underscored the USSR's emergence as China's major enemy and was a major factor leading to Sino-American rapprochement in the 1970s. Recent years, then, have brought reduced tensions with the United States (growing trade and exchange, the establishment of liaison offices in 1973 and embassies in 1979), fuller participation in international organization, and a substantial growth in China's foreign trade, especially with capitalist countries (see Appendix D).

The relative isolation and insecurity of the earlier period remains important, however, since it influenced a Chinese political generation and was thoroughly meshed with Maoist images of self-reliance, war preparedness, and reliance on human over material factors. The PRC has many territorial claims—to Taiwan, Hong Kong, and Macao, to Indian and

Soviet border areas, and to island groups in the East and South China seas—that remain unresolved largely because of post-1949 China's relatively weak position in power politics. The earlier period hangs on, too, in China's absence from arms limitations and nuclear test agreements, and in its relatively low volume of international trade (for example, its 1976 foreign trade total was less than that of either Hong Kong or Taiwan). Most significantly, the PRC has not escaped the acute security threat from the USSR. It is seriously inferior to the Soviet Union in strategic capabilities, not likely to overcome this gap in the foreseeable future, and hence bound to give high priority to this issue in domestic and foreign policies alike.

Finally, to think of the PRC as having "joined the club" is to invert the image of China as a revolutionary force in global politics, an image that acquired considerable currency in the 1950s and 1960s. Increasingly over those years, the PRC presented itself as a self-conscious opponent of the world power structure, as a champion of Third World countries and national liberation movements. The ascendancy of the Maoist model within China, especially in the Cultural Revolution, attracted great interest as a substantive enactment of the Maoist alternative to both Western and Soviet developmental models. This is not the place to assess the validity of the revolutionary image, which has never been wholly true or false,[8] but it is essential to note that the Chinese themselves, and many foreign observers, are accustomed to thinking of the PRC as an opponent of and an explicit alternative to the world of the superpowers, a force for radical change that would necessarily challenge rather than accommodate the existing order. This image complicates the position of current PRC leaders who have, since the death of Mao Zedong in September 1976, intensified China's global interactions in their pursuit of national security and access to the foreign

---

[8]A useful introduction to the range of issues raised by the Maoist model is Michel Oksenberg, ed., *China's Developmental Experience* (New York: Praeger, 1973). For closer analysis of the distinctiveness of Mao's economic development strategy, see the collection of essays by John G. Gurley, *China's Economy and the Maoist Strategy* (New York: Monthly Review, 1976). These questions and many others are probed in a postmortem on Mao's career in Dick Wilson, ed., *Mao Tse-tung in the Scales of History* (Cambridge: Cambridge University Press, 1977).

trade, technology, and capital necessary for continued development.

The revolutionary, historical, and international setting poses formidable challenges to the student of Chinese politics — whether beginner or old hand. That student must try to understand the breadth and rapidity of change in China's revolutionary era while acknowledging the relevance of patterns rooted in an imperial order two milennia old; must take account of the partisanship that pervades both Chinese and foreign sources on the revolution while making use of this substantial and valuable body of literature; must grasp the uneven character of China's development, in which intractable problems and backward sectors coexist with impressive social and economic advances; must puzzle over China's efforts to find security and support within the international order even as it struggles to transform that order and escape its restraints; and must comprehend the dialectics of the PRC's movement toward and away from Maoist, Soviet, and Western concepts of development. These are difficult challenges, but they are also the source of much that is fascinating in the study of Chinese politics.

ISSUES IN THE HISTORY OF CHINESE COMMUNISM

For some time after 1949 the major debates and generalizations about Chinese Communism revolved around questions relating to its historical background, seeking thereby to identify the essence of the new regime. There were many reasons for this historical orientation. History and historians held a special place in Chinese studies, while political scientists in the field were relatively few. The newness of the Communist government and the inadequacy of information about it discouraged a thorough examination of post-1949 events. So far as Americans were concerned, political considerations intruded by cutting off contact with the mainland and riveting American attention on the question of why China fell to the Communists. In time, all these considerations lost some of their force, and studies based directly on post-1949 politics began to grow rapidly. Nonetheless, debate on the character of the Communist Revolution, relying heavily on pre-1949 data for proof and documentation, has influenced strongly efforts to generalize about the present system. This debate divides roughly into three major themes or controversies: Maoist independence versus Marxist-Leninist orthodoxy; Chinese versus foreign influences; the sources of Communist victory in 1949.

Maoism Versus Orthodoxy. The controversy over "Maoism" is the most explicit, controversial, and enduring debate about Chinese Communist politics. When the *China Quarterly* — the foremost Western journal of contemporary Chinese affairs — began publication in 1960, Maoism was the subject of lead articles in the first two issues;[9] the choice was an accurate indication of what seemed to be the most important controversy in the field. Without attempting to present the views of particular writers, the general thrust of the argument can be stated simply. Supporters of Maoism argued that Chinese Communism, as shaped by Mao Zedong's leadership and represented by his writings, contained distinctive, deviant, or heretical forms of Marxism-Leninism and hence was politically and ideologically independent of Moscow. Those who argued for Chinese "orthodoxy" and rejected the "Maoism" label found no significant deviations by Mao from Marxist-Leninist doctrine and strategy, and they saw the Communist Revolution in China as politically and ideologically dependent on Moscow. In reality, of course, the argument has been an exceedingly sophisticated and tortuous one. Still, as suggested by the simplified version stated above, it posed a fundamental political question that was crucial to an understanding of the post-1949 regime: were the Chinese Communists independent revolutionaries who were not tied to Moscow, or were they simply the leaders of the Chinese branch of a movement centered in Moscow?

The Sino-Soviet conflict resolved the question of China's political independence. Despite substantial Russian influence in China during the 1950s, the CCP soon demonstrated its political and ideological autonomy, with Maoism gaining wide acceptance in the West (the word Maoism is seldom used in China) as the most appropriate term for the distinctive Chi-

[9]Karl A. Wittfogel, "The Legend of 'Maoism,'" *China Quarterly,* nos.1, 2 (January-March, April–June 1960), pp. 72–86, 16–34; and Benjamin Schwartz, "The Legend of the 'Legend of "Maoism,"'" *China Quarterly,* no. 2 (April–June 1960), pp. 35–42.

nese brand of Marxism-Leninism. The post-1949 triumph of Maoism naturally strengthened the arguments of those who had emphasized its pre-1949 roots.[10] The Maoism debate continues on two broad fronts, however. First, the exact timing and extent of Mao's early deviation from Soviet doctrine remains in dispute, with arguments focusing on the intricacies of revolutionary strategy and CCP-Comintern relationships in the 1927–1935 period.[11]

Second, and of more current interest, has been an ongoing discussion about who are the orthodox Marxist-Leninists. Granted a significant doctrinal gap exists between Chinese and Russian Communists — the earlier denials of the gap having been silenced — is it Maoism or Soviet socialism that is most true to the parent doctrine? The Russians and some Western analysts, although far from agreement, see Soviet socialism as more orthodox and Maoism as a deviation tending toward some variant of anarchism, subjectivism, bourgeois nationalism, or Trotskyism. The Chinese and other Western analysts — again not in agreement — see Maoism as closer to Marxian values and Leninist revolutionary themes, with the Soviet Union exhibiting a heretical tendency toward bureaucratism, imperialism, and all-round revisionism or capitalist restoration.[12] This is a fascinating debate, infinitely more complicated than these remarks suggest, and now further complicated by post-Mao reversals of some of the Cultural Revolution policies believed to be at the core of Maoism. In this context, earlier assertions about the essential similarity of Chinese and Soviet

[10]For an excellent survey of Mao's thought, especially his "sinicization" of Marxism-Leninism, see Stuart R. Scram, *The Political Thought of Mao Tse-tung,* rev. and enl. ed. (New York: Praeger, 1969).

[11]See, for example, Hsiao Tso-liang, *Power Relations Within the Chinese Communist Movement, 1930–1934* (Seattle: University of Washington Press, 1961); Ilpyong J. Kim, *The Politics of Chinese Communism: Kiangsi under the Soviets* (Berkeley: University of California Press, 1973); John E. Rue, *Mao Tse-tung in Opposition, 1927–1935* (Stanford: Stanford University Press, 1966); Shanti Swarup, *A Study of the Chinese Communist Movement, 1927–1934* (London: Oxford University Press, 1966); and Richard C. Thornton, *The Comintern and the Chinese Communists, 1928–1931* (Seattle: University of Washington Press, 1969).

[12]See Wilson, ed., op. cit; and "Symposium on Mao and Marx," *Modern China,* vol. 2, no. 4 (October 1976), and vol. 3, nos. 1, 2, 4 (January, April, October 1977); this "symposium" contains articles and comments by several scholars holding different views on the question.

socialism may revive, although the distinction between the two when China was under Mao's leadership seems secure.

Chinese Versus Foreign Influence. As the Sino-Soviet split cooled the controversy about the CCP's relationship with the Soviet party, a related but more subtle question came to the fore: did the victory of Chinese Communism represent a conquest by foreign ideas (Western if not Russian) that would destroy the Chinese tradition, or did it represent the beginning of a new "dynasty," foreign in some aspects of its style but faithful to traditional patterns of rule? Despite occasional allusions to a CCP "dynasty" or to Mao as "emperor," serious discussion of this theme has avoided polarization around a literal acceptance of either of the two positions. The view that the Communist Revolution is essentially antitraditional and a vehicle for spreading values foreign to China is more common, although it seldom appears without qualifications; it has strong support, of course, in the self-image that the Chinese Communists project. Arguments on the other side have been presented succinctly by C. P. Fitzgerald, who has pointed out strong similarities between Communist and traditional Chinese patterns of rule. He has emphasized in particular the idea of a "world sovereign authority," state management of a balanced economy, and the establishment of an orthodox doctrine to order society and provide a standard for recruiting elites.[13]

Obviously, contemporary Chinese politics shows a mixture of indigenous and foreign influences. The real value of this debate is not to prove one perspective right and the other wrong but to establish what the mixture is. Since the prevailing tendency is to focus on the changes accomplished and sought by CCP elites, it is healthy to heed the reminders of those who assert the "Chineseness" of China. John Fairbank has been a temperate but persistent spokesman for this view, urging caution in concluding that the tradition is weakened or destroyed, despite what ideology and official directives might imply, and insisting that Chinese history still provides some explanations for Chinese behavior.[14] The analysis in later chapters will

[13]C.P. Fitzgerald, *The Birth of Communist China* (Baltimore: Penguin, 1964), pp. 41–42 passim.

[14]John K. Fairbank, *China: The People's Middle Kingdom and the U.S.A.* (Cambridge, Mass.: Belknap Press, 1967).

identify many areas in which the influence of the Chinese past is still evident.

It is worth noting that debate over the proper role of Chinese and foreign influences is not simply a Western intellectual gloss of no interest to the Chinese themselves. To the contrary, China's intellectuals and politicians have addressed this question explicitly ever since the late nineteenth century, offering different formulae on how to use foreign and Chinese things in the reconstruction of their system.[15] Recent Chinese diatribes against the Gang of Four for irrationally praising things Chinese and opposing things foreign are a striking resurrection of this theme; assertions about China's need to learn from the advanced countries of the West suggest that the subtle balance between the two poles may be shifting toward a stronger foreign orientation after a period emphasizing the Chinese orientation.

Sources of Communist Victory. The third major controversy about the history of the Communist Revolution involves the sources of CCP success in its struggle with the KMT. What conditions and appeals gave the CCP the strength for victory, and what kind of revolution did it lead? The most provocative thesis has been Chalmers Johnson's study of Communist growth during the Sino-Japanese War (1937-1945).[16]Johnson argues that the CCP's leadership of nationalistic peasant resistance to the Japanese invader was responsible for the party's emergence as a contender for national power; the Communist Revolution derived its main strength from nationalist appeals, not from a program for socioeconomic change. It is clear that the Japanese invasion permitted the CCP to strengthen greatly

---

[15]For analysis of Mao's position on this question, see Stuart R. Schram, "Introduction: The Cultural Revolution in Historical Perspective," in Schram, ed., *Authority, Participation and Cultural Change in China* (Cambridge: Cambridge University Press, 1973), pp. 3–27.

[16]Chalmers A. Johnson, *Peasant Nationalism and Communist Power: The Emergence of Revolutionary China, 1937–1945* (Stanford: Stanford University Press, 1962). Criticism of Johnson's thesis is summarized in Elinor Lerner, "The Chinese Peasantry and Imperialism: A Critique of Chalmers Johnson's *Peasant Nationalism and Communist Power,*" *Bulletin of Concerned Asian Scholars,* vol. 6, no. 2 (April-August 1974), pp. 43–56. Johnson responds to his critics in "Peasant Nationalism Revisited: The Biography of a Book," in *China Quarterly,* no. 72 (December 1977), pp. 766–85.

its position relative to the KMT; the nationalist legitimacy that the party acquired during the war was indispensible for the attraction of popular support and neutralization of opposition that led to ultimate victory. Japanese actions and Communist response were probably decisive in the timing and staging of the CCP's conquest of the mainland.

However, there are other factors to be considered in defining the basis of Communist victory. KMT weakness as well as CCP strength, and especially military capabilities on both sides, are directly relevant since the final outcome was settled by force of arms. The Communists' commitment to social and economic change, particularly their promise of land redistribution, was a source of popular support and revolutionary recruitment during many periods of party history. Organizational skills and personal behavior of CCP members played a major role in expanding the party's influence, regardless of the specific issues that made a locality vulnerable to Communist penetration. The CCP's ability to address more traditional peasant economic needs and concepts of social justice illuminates the seeming paradox of a Communist revolution based more on peasantry than proletariat.[17] None of these factors denies the importance of the Japanese presence and the CCP's nationalistic appeals to resist it, but they show that the Communist revolution was a multifaceted phenomenon that cannot be labeled neatly as either a "national" revolution or a "social" revolution. The same can be said of the post-1949 period, in which themes of national independence and reconstruction have continued to blend with themes of radical social and economic change.

[17]For a sample of diverse interpretations of the Communist revolution, see Lucien Bianco, *Origins of the Chinese Revolution, 1915–1949* (Stanford: Stanford University Press, 1971); William Hinton, *Fanshen: A Documentary of Revolution in a Chinese Village* (New York: Monthly Review Press, 1966); Roy Hofheinz, Jr., *The Broken Wave* (Cambridge: Harvard University Press, 1977), and "The Ecology of Chinese Communist Success: Rural Influence Patterns, 1923–1945," in Barnett, ed., op. cit., pp. 3–77; Tetsuya Kataoka, *Resistance and Revolution in China: The Communists and the Second United Front* (Berkeley: University of California Press, 1974); Mark Selden, *The Yenan Way in Revolutionary China* (Cambridge: Harvard University Press, 1971); and Ralph Thaxton, "On Peasant Revolution and National Resistance: Toward a Theory of Peasant Mobilization and Revolutionary War with Special Reference to Modern China," *World Politics,* vol 30. no. 1 (October 1977), pp. 24–57.

These debates about the essence of Chinese Communism have raised important questions about the post-1949 system without providing definitive answers. Neither the questions nor the difficulty of answering them is unique to China, of course; students of the Bolshevik Revolution have grappled with similar issues, without notable success in resolving them. The problem, as suggested in this chapter's introductory paragraphs, is that the essence of revolution defies simple definitions. In the Chinese case, the initial "either-or" questions have yielded, as scholarly studies have multiplied, to recognition of the complexity of the questions posed. This is probably a healthy development. In any case, it helps to explain the inconclusiveness of efforts to classify the PRC's political system, a topic to which we now turn.

MODELS FOR THE CHINESE POLITICAL SYSTEM

During the 1960s, controversy over historical issues began to wane, and a substantial body of literature on post-1949 politics emerged. One striking characteristic of this literature was the absence of a dominant model as a guide for analysis and considerable diversity in efforts to classify the system. Initially, there was an inclination to call the PRC a totalitarian system, or at least to group it with other Communist systems. This gave way to greater interest in treating China as a "developing" system, shifting away from European-centered models and emphasizing China's similarities to Third World countries. There has also been a pronounced tendency to classify the system on its own terms, to identify a Chinese or Maoist model that might or might not stand alone as a type.

The Totalitarian Model. It is not surprising that theories of totalitarianism were attractive to students of Communist China. The theories developed largely from studies of Nazi Germany and Stalinist Russia, leaving the Soviet Union as the principal model of totalitarianism in the postwar years. When China proclaimed its intention of following the Soviet model — while Stalin was still alive — there was a natural tendency to assume that China had incorporated the totalitarian model. Moreover, Chinese Communist political behavior and institutions displayed sufficient "fit" with the model, particularly in the drive for ideological conformity and the monopoly of power by a single party, to defend its assumed applicability. But despite much acceptance of the term and implicit use of the model, no full-scale analysis of "Chinese totalitarianism" appeared. There was reluctance to apply the totalitarian model systematically to all aspects of the Chinese system.

One reason for this reluctance was the emergence of important discrepancies between the People's Republic and the model. The clearest and most representative statement of the totalitarian model laid out six "basic features" of the "totalitarian dictatorship"; an official ideology; a single mass party led typically by one man; a system of terroristic police controls; a technologically conditioned monopoly of communications; a similar monopoly of all means of effective armed combat; central control and direction of the entire economy through bureaucratic coordination.[18] But in China it seemed that Mao Zedong's leadership of the CCP was not comparable to the dictatorships of Hitler or Stalin; controls rested much more on psychological pressures of indoctrination and persuasion and on close personal supervision by cadres than on police terror; central bureaucratic planning and controls were less salient, especially after 1957, than in the Soviet Union. Moreover, theorists of totalitarianism had identified the phenomenon as a reaction against or perversion of the modern Western state, one that "could have arisen only within the context of mass democracy and modern technology."[19]

While the Chinese revolution took place in such a context in the global sense, it was not directly aligned with this particular historical pattern.

The totalitarian model's application to China was also inhibited by questions about its inherent validity that came to the fore in the 1960s.

Working mainly from developments in the Soviet bloc following de-Stalinization, critics argued that the model had been overly influenced by the excesses of particular personalities (e.g., Hitler and Stalin); that it could not account for pluralistic phenomena within the assumed "monolithic" totalitarian state; and that it failed to differentiate adequately among

[18]Carl J. Friedrich and Zbigniew K. Brzezinski, *Totalitarian Dictatorship and Autocracy* (New York: Praeger, 1961), pp. 9–10.

[19]Ibid., p. 3; and Hannah Arendt, *The Origins of Totalitarianism* (New York: Meridian, 1958).

different types of systems (e.g., fascist and Communist states) that might display some of its characteristics. As alternatives, they suggested abandonment of the model, limitation of its application to the few historical examples that approximated it, or major revisions to accommodate variations within highly ideological and authoritarian single-party states.[20] In any case, the growing challenge to the model's credentials made it progressively less attractive as a guide for rigorous analysis of the Chinese system.

As the totalitarian model lost ground, the comparative study of Communist systems began to attract students of China. Although this approach is moving ahead rapidly, particularly in studies of Soviet and East European politics, it has not acquired a dominant place in the China field. Very few scholars have the skills and inclination to carry out a rigorous comparison of European and Chinese Communist systems. Moreover, the Sino-Soviet conflict and the debate over totalitarianism have left a reservoir of skepticism about assumptions of similarities between the two great Communist powers. There is great value in including China in comparisons of Communist systems, but — at least during the Maoist era — that value lies mainly in demonstrating the extent of variations within the category.[21]

"Developing Country" Models. The intensification of the Sino-Soviet conflict in the 1960s coincided with the growth in Western academic circles of a vast literature dealing with problems of development. While neither China nor any other country is typical of what are so loosely called "developing" or "underdeveloped" areas, it is understandable that students of China began to explore this literature for conceptual guidance and possible models. On the face of it, modern China's credentials

---

[20]For a summary discussion of the totalitarian model and its critics, see Robert Burrowes, "Totalitarianism: The Revised Standard Version," *World Politics*, vol. 21, no. 2 (January 1969), pp. 272–94. See also the contributions to a Symposium on Comparative Politics and Communist Systems in *Slavic Review*, vol. 26, no. 1 (March 1967).

[21]See, for example, Chalmers Johnson, ed., *Change in Communist Systems* (Stanford: Stanford University Press, 1970).

for inclusion in this group are substantial. Its experience with Western (and Eastern) imperialism, its preindustrial agrarian economy, and its revolutionary confrontation with traditional institutions have generated most of the problems broadly associated with the developmental process. Of course, there is no single model for a developing political system, nor even agreement on the definition of terms like *development* and *modernization,* but the literature suggests several categories of systems with which China might be grouped and which illuminate important features of Chinese politics.

One category derives from broad historical outlines of the modern era and groups China with a relatively small number of other countries that began modernization under the influence of the Western example but without direct foreign control; their traditional governments were sufficiently effective to resist overt colonization and hence embarked on modernization with significant continuities of national tradition, territory, and population.[22] This continuity provides protection against the crises of personal and national identity that have occurred in other transitional societies but may produce an "authority crisis" when modernizing elites eventually destroy the traditional authority system.[23] Another perspective emphasizes the level of economic development, indicating that China is most appropriately grouped with countries of roughly equivalent economic circumstances. Some proponents of this approach argue that "Communism is a phenomenon of underdevelopment" and that Communist movements "share numerous characteristics with non-Communist modernizing movements."[24] This category, then, includes both Communist and non-Communist systems whose politics reflect similarities derived from common economic problems.

[22]C. E. Black, *The Dynamics of Modernization: A Study in Comparative History* (New York: Harper, 1966), pp. 119–23. The other countries that Black places in this "pattern" are Russia, Japan, Iran, Turkey, Afghanistan, Ethiopia, and Thailand. Black is, of course, aware of the truly formidable differences among these countries in their experiences with modernization.

[23]Lucian Pye, *The Spirit of Chinese Politics: A Psychocultural Study of the Authority Crisis in Political Development* (Cambridge, Mass.: M.I.T. Press, 1968), esp. chap. 1.

[24]John H. Kautsky, *Communism and the Politics of Development: Persistent Myths and Changing Behavior* (New York: Wiley, 1968), pp. 1, 3–4.

China also corresponds to a system that appears in nearly all typologies of developing countries, variously referred to as mobilization system, movement regime, neo-Leninist mass party system, or radical or totalitarian single-party system.[25] The type varies in its definition by different writers but contains the following core elements: a single political party that monopolizes political power and penetrates all other politically significant organizations; an explicit, official ideology that legitimizes and sanctifies revolutionary goals; a determination to politicize and mobilize the citizenry, characteristically through party-led mass movements. The mobilization system, to use Apter's phrase, clearly has something in common with the totalitarian model, but it places the dominant political party in a significantly different context. Whereas the totalitarian model projects an image of an impenetrable, monolithic, bureaucratic, and technologically competent regime, the mobilization system operates in a fluid, unresolved struggle to transform a "transitional" society. The latter seems closer to Chinese reality, identifying the social context more accurately and emphasizing the open struggle to mobilize the population behind the radical, futuristic goals of elites.

The modernization and development literature, like the totalitarian model, has nourished certain assumptions about Chinese politics and development — a point to which we will soon return. In terms of specific models, however, it has had little impact. China scholars have gone window-shopping in it — citing a reference here, testing a hypothesis there — but few have adopted any of the general approaches within it. For one thing, the literature itself is too loose and sprawling to be of much help; by the 1970s, it was also the target of much criti-

[25]On the mobilization system, see David E. Apter, *The Politics of Modernization* (Chicago: University of Chicago Press, 1965), esp. chap. 10. On the movement-regime, see Robert C. Tucker, "Towards a Comparative Politics of Movement-Regimes," *The American Political Science Review*, vol. 55, no. 2 (June 1961), pp. 281–89. On the neo-Leninist mass party, see Clement Henry Moore, *Tunisia Since Independence: The Dynamics of One-Party Government* (Berkeley: University of California Press, 1965), esp. the introduction. *Radical or totalitarian single-party system* are phrases that fall in the public domain, with predictable variation in their meaning.

cism for its ethnocentric biases and empirical weaknesses.[26] Moreover, despite Maoist departures from Soviet Communism, the role of ideology and party in the PRC and its revolutionary origins set it apart from the great majority of non-Communist Third World countries.

One response to this dilemma is to combine the two general perspectives discussed thus far, that is, to classify the PRC with other Communist systems in terms of basic structures, while noting that the developmental issues with which it must deal are closer to those of the Third World. Generally, this is the approach followed in the core volume of the series to which this book belongs.[27] The effect of the Almond and Powell approach is to emphasize both the "penetrative radical authoritarian" character of the system (which it shares with other Communist systems and which distinguishes them from modern democratic systems) and the "authoritarian technocratic mobilizational" developmental strategy (which it shares with countries like North Korea and Cuba and which distinguishes them from most other Third World countries). This classification captures the key variables of political ideology and structure and level of economic development, although it does not fit well with some aspects of the Maoist model.

The Chinese Model. In the absence of consensus on the applicability to China of totalitarian, Communist, or developing country models, most China scholars in practice have treated the Chinese political system as *sui generis.* They have included in their works many references to other bodies of literature, but they have assumed that the system they study is sufficiently distinctive to provide the basis for a separate model. The tendency is a natural one in the China field, encouraged by the sinological tradition to look upon the study of China as a

---

[26]For a sample of this criticism, see Richard Sandbrook, "The 'Crisis' in Political Development Theory," *Journal of Development Studies,* vol. 12, no. 2 (January 1976), pp. 165–85; and Dean C. Tipps, "Modernization Theory and the Comparative Study of Societies: A Critical Perspective," *Comparative Studies in Society and History,* vol. 15, no. 2 (March 1973), pp. 199–226.

[27]Gabriel A. Almond and G. Bingham Powell, Jr., *Comparative Politics: System, Process, and Policy,* 2nd ed. (Boston: Little, Brown, 1978), esp. pp. 71–76, 381–87.

discipline unto itself. Indeed, there has been some resistance among China scholars to the intrusion of social science or comparative concepts, so much so that others have suggested that some of the problems of the field lie in its lack of receptivity to external conceptual guidance.[28]

However, the most vigorous criticism in the 1970s of Western studies of Chinese politics was that they failed to take the Chinese model seriously, that they had imposed their own ethnocentric assumptions and values on Chinese reality, thereby misunderstanding and misinterpreting the Chinese revolution and the Maoist system emerging from it.[29] What are we to make of these seemingly contradictory points? Have Western scholars assumed the validity and utility of a Chinese model or not?

The first step is to clarify what the model might be. In discussion of contemporary politics, the Chinese model is usually synonomous with the Maoist model, simply because it was the promotion of Maoist policies from the mid-1950s down to 1976 that provided the primary rationale for emphasizing the distinctiveness of the Chinese system. There are problems with this linkage, but for the moment let us concentrate on some general elements in the Maoist model. First, it aims at national independence and self-reliance, veering toward autarky in its avoidance of economic or political dependence on other states. Second, it seeks all-around development, emphasizing the agricultural sector, which is most likely to be left behind in rapid development; it favors decentralization to stimulate local growth and initiative, and to direct transferral of resources (personnel, services, facilities, and funds) from urban to rural areas. Third, it emphasizes mass mobilization and participation as techniques for achieving social, economic, and political goals; the destabilizing effects of mass campaigns

[28]"Symposium on Chinese Studies and the Disciplines," *Journal of Asian Studies*, vol. 23, no. 4 (August 1964), pp. 505–38; Chalmers Johnson, "The Role of Social Science in China Scholarship," *World Politics*, vol. 17, no. 2 (January 1965), pp. 256–71; and Richard W. Wilson, "Chinese Studies in Crisis," *World Politics*, vol. 23, no. 2 (January 1971), pp. 295–317.

[29]For a thorough presentation of this theme, see James Peck, "Revolution Versus Modernization and Revisionism: A Two-Front Struggle," in Victor Nee and Peck, eds., *China's Uninterrupted Revolution from 1840 to the Present* (New York: Pantheon, 1973), pp. 57–217.

on bureaucratic procedures and institutions are regarded as healthy or at least acceptable, as is the downgrading of intellectual and technical skills that accompanies this glorification of mass efforts. Fourth, it insists on continuing the revolution, arguing that repeated and possibly violent struggles are necessary to avoid restoration of capitalism, tendencies toward which can arise even within the Communist party; correct ideology — absolute commitment to the collectivist, egalitarian, participatory society — is the key to revolutionary success, must be practiced in daily life, and must be the primary criterion for evaluating people, their performance, and their social and cultural expression.

This is a crude formalization, but it identifies themes that Western scholars commonly attribute to Maoism. While the list is one of principles or goals, they had sufficient practical impact under Mao's leadership to make them seem a more accurate, generalized description of the system than anything derived from non-Chinese experience. Accordingly, China scholars have in the main accepted them as a starting point for analysis and evaluation of the system.

Why, then, has most China scholarship been criticized for imposing Western biases on Chinese reality? The answer lies mainly in the latent influence and assumptions of the totalitarian-Communist and modernization-development models. The former reveals itself in cynicism about how accurately the Maoist model describes the workings of the Chinese political system. It notes that party dictatorship is still dictatorship, even if clothed in Maoist dress, and that the CCP's coercive and propaganda apparatus is fully capable of producing false impressions of Chinese reality.[30] Some students who may see attractive features in the Maoist ideal and acknowledge its prescriptive role in Chinese society may be encouraged by their assumptions about Communist systems to seek out deviations from it in practice.

The influence of conventional ideas about modernization and development is seen in more direct hostility toward the

[30]Simon Leys, *Chinese Shadows* (New York: Viking, 1977), makes the point aggressively; a more scholarly analysis of how the totalitarian idea (not model) affects Chinese politics is Peter R. Moody, *Opposition and Dissent in Contemporary China* (Stanford: American Institution Press, 1977).

Maoist model as such. This literature tends to associate development with an economic takeoff based on leading sectors;
with urbanization, technological revolution, and the emergence of highly trained elites; with greater structural specialization and differentiation, an inevitable bureaucratization;
and with rational, pragmatic, or nonideological modes of planning and decision making. Granted that these propositions
oversimplify the theories, it seems fair to say that the literature
has a bias toward economism, technology, institutionalization,
and rational planning that conflicts with the Maoist view on
many points. Those in sympathy with this literature are likely
to see the Maoist approach as at best ill advised and at worst
irrational or positively destructive of China's developmental
potential. In this view, the problem with Maoism is precisely
the fact that the Chinese *do* practice it; it is accepted as real but
evaluated negatively. By implication, the Chinese will someday
come to their senses and reject it as a false doctrine of development; some suggest they have been doing so since 1976.

The point of this discussion is that acceptance of the Maoist
model as a framework for analysis of Chinese politics has been
qualified and equivocal due to competing assumptions about
what the Chinese reality is and about what is good for China.
There is, of course, another approach, which is to argue that
the Maoist model is a close approximation of reality, that its
effectiveness is apparent and well established in China, and
that it is a viable model of development that might well be
adopted elsewhere. This has been the official Chinese position
for much of the post-1949 period and informs much of the
radical criticism directed at mainstream China scholarship.
There are problems with this position, too. One is that the
Maoist model as it is usually interpreted — the Cultural Revolution years being the key illustration of its content — has not
dominated the entire post-1949 period; in other words, it is
not the same as a Chinese model that would account for those
periods (the early 1950s, the early 1960s, and the post-1976
years) when Maoism was not in command. Another is that its
effectiveness is not beyond dispute within Chinese politics,
where there has been persistent opposition to it and some
evidence of negative evaluation of it consequences. Finally, it
is not certain that Maoism deserves to be elevated to the status

of a model, when it may simply be a set of policies that was particularly attractive to Mao's generation of elites and particularly suitable for China at a special stage of its development; in this perspective, Maoism is no more a Chinese model than, say, the New Deal was an American model. These are all issues for later discussion, introduced here to suggest possible reasons for refraining from an uncritical acceptance of the Maoist model as the best or only guide for the study of Chinese politics.

DIVERSITY AND CHANGE IN CHINESE POLITICS

It is not surprising that none of these perspectives has established its dominance in the study of Chinese politics. As generalized abstractions from reality, models cannot match the specifics of every case they may claim to represent. Their value lies not in literal conformity but in what they emphasize, or suggest, about primary elements and relationships, and in this sense all the models discussed have something to offer as alternative images of the Chinese system. Nonetheless, disarray on this question underscores the high degree of diversity and change that has characterized post-1949 China. A central theme of this book is that the Chinese political system has been fluid and unstable, not in the sense of weakness or vulnerability to collapse, but in its receptivity to institutional change, policy experimentation, and mass campaigns that transform elite conflicts into societal struggles of uncertain consequences. The resulting system resists placement in a single mold.

Change over time is the most obvious problem in trying to classify the Chinese system. The early revolutionary years gave way to a Soviet-style period in 1953–1957, followed by prolonged ascendancy of the Maoist approach and then a retreat from it after 1976. A sense of constant, progressive change, of movement to new stages, pervades the process. It is a dialectical process in which contradictions coexist in each stage and in which new stages contain elements of these earlier conflicts.[31]

[31]The most thorough analysis of the dialectical quality of contemporary Chinese society is Franz Schurmann, *Ideology and Organization in Communist China,* 2nd ed. enl. (Berkeley: University of California Press, 1968).

There is also a cyclical or wave-like process within these larger stages. One theory argues that a recurring cycle can be seen in which "ideological" goals based on normative appeals give way to "order" goals based on coercion and then to "economic" goals emphasizing remuneration — the whole cycle completing itself within a few years.[32] The observer may see Maoism in the first phase, totalitarianism in the second, and revisionism or economism in the third. For example, one can find several briefer periods within the long Maoist ascendancy of 1958–1976 when apparently non-Maoist tendencies were in operation. The problem for the analyst who wants to generalize is clear: how does one distinguish primary and secondary tendencies in this context?

Regional or spatial diversity is another important feature of the Chinese system. Historically, the "little traditions" of localities reflected intricate linguistic, cultural, and social divisions within imperial society. These divisions have not disappeared — although they are greatly reduced — and new ones have arisen because of the uneven spread of modernization. Many Chinese provinces are as large and populous as European countries, forming important units that can and do act differently within the political process. There are major differences between urban and rural areas that manifest themselves in politics. The Great Leap Forward and Cultural Revolution, for example, took different forms in the city and in the countryside. CCP policies, both before and after 1949, have varied with the landscape on which they have operated; whatever the official policy, local diversity produces different results in its implementation or degree of success.[33]

It is not clear how much of China's political instability is due to these environmental factors — the complexity and unevenness of its socioeconomic development, the size and diversity of the country–and how much to the style of its leaders. The

[32]G. William Skinner and Edwin A. Winckler, "Compliance Succession in Rural Communist China: A Cyclical Theory," in Amitai Etzioni, ed., *Complex Organizations: A Sociological Reader* (New York: Holt, Rinehart and Winston, 1969), pp. 410–38.

[33]See John W. Lewis, "The Study of Chinese Political Culture," *World Politics*, vol. 18, no. 3 (April 1966), pp. 503–24, and "Political Aspects of Mobility in China's Urban Development," *The American Political Science Review*, vol. 60, no. 4 (December 1966), pp. 899–912.

latter is important, however, and is yet another legacy of the revolutionary era. Mao and his associates dominated PRC politics for over twenty-five years, prolonging the influence of their revolutionary commitments and experience. This influence included a pronounced ambivalence about institutionalization — recognition of its necessity for reconstruction and development coupled with fear of its capture by conservative, bureaucratic tendencies. Mao's generation was well aware of China's powerful statist tradition and how it used political institutions to impose Confucian orthodoxy on imperial society. Mao himself was particularly concerned that revolutionary transformation be secure before the process of institutionalization became irreversible.

Mao's death in 1976 ushered in a new period, one that is proclaimed as such by his successors and that is rapidly putting the Maoist era in different perspective. The new stage may bring more stability and institutional permanence. But most of the material with which the student of Chinese politics must deal derives from the Maoist era and bears the imprint of the revolution in all the ways noted in the preceding discussion.

CHAPTER II

The Origins of the Communist Political System

THE PEOPLE'S REPUBLIC OF CHINA, officially proclaimed on October 1, 1949, is still a relatively new political system. Its primary origins lie not in the remote past but in a more recent history in which many of today's political elites were participants. The most direct influences on Chinese Communism — the revolutionary setting, Soviet Communism, and the CCP's own pre-1949 history — are largely twentieth-century phenomena. However, China's premodern political tradition is also directly relevant on this point. Not all agree that the People's Republic is a "nation imprisoned by her history,"[1] but few deny that its origins encompass more than the twentieth-century upheavals that brought Communism to power. Since all societies are in some measure a product of their past, a pertinent question is whether the Chinese political tradition exerts an unusual influence on the present. There is good reason to believe that it does, despite the difficulty of offering comparative judgments on such a question.

The longevity and supreme Sinocentrism of the traditional political system are the primary sources of its impact on the present. No system that prevailed for so long and with such a high degree of autonomy could fail to extend its influence beyond its formal institutional life. Even if new institutions could escape the old patterns, traditional values and behavior would endure for an indefinite period of time. The Sinocentric

[1]John K. Fairbank, *China: The People's Middle Kingdom and the U.S.A.* (Cambridge, Mass.: Belknap Press, 1967), pp. 3–4 passim.

28

belief that the best possible society was immanent in Chinese experience, that foreign ways might be absorbed but must never replace the essence of Chinese culture, naturally reinforced the longevity of the traditional order.

Extraordinary concern for the study and writing of their own history is perhaps the most tangible evidence of how the Chinese have perpetuated the influence of their past. In imperial times, the study of history was not only a scholarly enterprise to record and impart information; it was also a means of moral and political instruction, providing statesmen with material to guide and legitimize their political actions. The inclusion of classics of history among the standard texts covered in the examinations (through which officials were chosen and degrees awarded) ensured a common body of historical knowledge among scholars and bureaucrats.[2] Moreover, the tendency to cast political discourse in terms of historical events and personalities did not die with the end of the imperial system in 1911. Despite marked differences in vocabulary and interpretation required by a Marxist approach, the Chinese Communists remain highly sensitive to the political uses and implications of Chinese history and have continued "to find legitimization in China's past for the domestic and external developments of her most recent present."[3] Historical "knowledge," admittedly subject to varying interpretations, was and remains part of the basic framework of Chinese political perception.

The actual closeness in time of the traditional order reinforces this deliberate retention of national historical experience. The imperial system ended only in 1911 with the collapse of the Qing (Ch'ing or Manchu) dynasty. Of the ninety-seven regular members of the Eighth Central Committee of the CCP, elected in 1956–1958, all but one were born by

[2] See W. G. Beasley and E. G. Pulleyblank, eds., *Historians of China and Japan* (London: Oxford University Press, 1961), pp. 1–9, and Wm. Theodore de Bary et al., comps., *Sources of Chinese Tradition* (New York: Columbia University Press, 1960), pp. 266–67. An illuminating account of the importance attached to historical studies is found in Harold L. Kahn, "The Education of a Prince: The Emperor Learns His Roles," Albert Feuerwerker et al., eds., *Approaches to Modern Chinese History* (Berkeley: University of California Press, 1967), pp. 25–29, 34–36.

[3] Harold Kahn and Albert Feuerwerker, "The Ideology of Scholarship: China's New Historiography," in Feuerwerker, ed., *History in Communist China* (Cambridge, Mass.: M.I.T. Press, 1968), pp. 1–13; the quotation is from p. 13.

1912;[4] some of the most senior Communists, including Mao
Zedong, actually served in the military forces that were mobilized against the Manchu government in 1911–1912. For these
men, knowledge of the imperial political system included personal memory as well as historical study. Since certain aspects
of the traditional social order necessarily survived the fall of
the Qing, personal knowledge of it is still held by a significant
proportion of the Chinese population or is in any case no more
than a generation removed. One might still argue that China
is no closer to its traditional past than any number of other
non-Western developing countries. That is not quite true,
however, since the traditional order for most of these countries was overlaid by a colonial regime that brought significant
political alterations. Very few non-Western political elites of
the twentieth century have experienced such an intense confrontation with their own tradition.

Finally, we must put to rest the notion that the influence of
the past is measured only by the continuation or replication of
older patterns. Too often the question of contemporary China's relationship to its political tradition centers only on the
extent to which aspects of the former perpetuate or resemble
those of the latter. In fact, the influence of historical patterns
appears in reactions to them, and even rejection of them, as
well as in their continuation. For example, the Communists'
hostility toward the bureaucratic style must be understood in
the context of the Chinese bureaucratic tradition; the revolt in
recent decades of many Chinese intellectuals against the style
and substance of their culture is meaningless if considered
outside that cultural tradition. These and many other examples show that deviations from the past may nonetheless be in
part produced by it and thus represent a link rather than a
rupture with Chinese history.

In considering the origins of the present political system it
is not possible to describe adequately the historical background and developments that led to its establishment.
Instead, four major sources of influence on Chinese Communism will be discussed, not in an attempt to do them historical
justice but rather to isolate certain factors that have particular

---

[4]Chao Kuo-chün, "Leadership in the Chinese Communist Party," *The Annals
of the American Academy of Political and Social Science*, vol. 321 (January 1959), pp.
44–46.

importance for the present. The four sources are the Chinese political tradition, the revolutionary setting, Soviet Communism, and the CCP's pre-1949 history. Needless to say, the origins of the Communist system do not fall neatly into these four categories. The most salient characteristics of contemporary Chinese politics are those that derive from more than one source or have been reinforced by a variety of experiences.

THE CHINESE POLITICAL TRADITION

Few terms of social analysis are more arbitrary or loaded than the word *traditional.* The usage here refers primarily to China of the late Qing period, roughly the nineteenth century. In fact, the imperial system at this time was not unchanged from earlier periods. It was certainly not representative of the best of traditional China, since a process of dynastic decline was evident throughout the nineteenth century. One could argue, in short, that late Qing China was no longer traditional. On the other hand, some elements characteristic of this period survived well into the twentieth century, suggesting that *traditional* should not refer exclusively to the era of imperial rule. Moreover, the Chinese political tradition actually contained a variety of traditions; any attempt to discuss it as a unitary phenomenon inevitably slights some of its regional and temporal variations in favor of others. Acknowledgment of these qualifications is sufficient, since discussion here will be at a very general level. We wish only to identify major characteristics of the Qing political system that have an unmistakable connection with both earlier and later periods and hence are central in the Chinese political tradition. They are not necessarily permanent or immutable, but they have in fact shown great endurance.[5]

[5]Secondary sources on the Chinese tradition are too voluminous to cite here. For a few general discussions that are particularly useful for relating Chinese political tradition to the present, see John K. Fairbank, *The United States and China,* rev. and enl. ed. (Cambridge, Mass.: Harvard University Press, 1958), pp. 28–67, 87–105; C. P. Fitzgerald, *The Birth of Communist China* (Baltimore: Penguin, 1964), pp. 15–42; Ho Ping-ti, "Salient Aspects of China's Heritage," in Ho Ping-ti and Tang Tsou, eds., *China in Crisis,* vol. 1 (Chicago: University of Chicago Press, 1968), pp. 1–37; and Franz Michael, "State and Society in Nineteenth-Century China," in Albert Feuerwerker, ed., *Modern China* (Englewood Cliffs, N.J.: Prentice-Hall, 1964), pp. 57–69.

Elitism and Hierarchy in Political Authority. The imperial political system was fundamentally elitist in its structuring of political authority. The distinction between ruler and subject, official and citizen, was sharp in both theory and practice. The theory held that certain men were entitled by their virtue, acquired through education, to wield political authority; those lacking virtue were correctly assigned to the status of subjects. In practice, a two-class polity of elites and masses resulted. The elite included officials of the imperial bureaucracy and the degree-holding scholars or "gentry" from whose ranks officials were chosen. They were identifiable not only by office and degree but also by special forms of address, garments, insignia, and legal privilege.[6] Educational accomplishment, measured by degrees attained in the various levels of official examinations, was the primary means of entrance into the elite, although degrees could also be acquired through purchase or recommendation. The elite-commoner boundary was blurred at the local level by wealth, since large landowners and rich merchants had obvious resources for political influence. However, the fact that wealth permitted a person to purchase a degree or to make the necessary investment in education, or was acquired because of degree-holding relatives, meant that elite status remained intimately associated with holding of degree. The number of gentry (referring to degree-holding scholars and officials) increased greatly during the nineteenth century but remained very small relative to the population. Even in the latter part of the century, the gentry and their families constituted less than 2 percent of the population.[7] Broadening the definition of *gentry* to include wealthy families without degree-holding members would raise the absolute number significantly but still include only a few percent of the total population.

This sharp distinction between a small elite entitled to authority and the mass population not so entitled was a basic characteristic of traditional Chinese politics. Supplementing it was a hierarchical structure of authority throughout society

---

[6]Chung-li Chang, *The Chinese Gentry: Studies in Their Role in Nineteenth-Century Chinese Society* (Seattle: University of Washington Press, 1955), pp. 32–43 passim.

[7]Ibid., pp. 137–41.

that created an intricate network of superior-inferior relationships. In general societal terms, the authority structure interacted with other political and economic considerations to produce a relatively complex system of social stratification.[8] Of particular interest here is the way in which it cemented the elite-commoner distinction and ordered political relationships within each of these two general groupings.

Within the political elite the emperor stood alone at the top of the hierarchy, holding absolute power over all his officials and subjects. Although the actual exercise of imperial power might vary with the ability and personality of the sovereign and his ministers, his real and symbolic status as the ultimate locus of political authority was unchallenged.[9] The bureaucracy was divided by ranks and grades, fixing each official's position in a hierarchy descending from the emperor. Beneath the officials came degree holders not selected for official position, also ranked according to the kind of degree held.

Ordinary subjects, who constituted most of the population, did not fall into the bureaucratic or degree rankings. But where this explicitly political hierarchy left off, a highly complex structuring of social relationships took over, having profound implications for the political system. Norms governing kinship relations and obligations set the basic pattern of authority.[10] In simplest terms, authority within a family or larger kinship group was held by the eldest male within generational lines; the older generation held sway over younger ones, and elder males were superior to females and younger males of the same generation. In large lineages containing numerous families and several generations, the resulting relationships became incredibly complicated. The point, however, is that the system did locate ultimate authority in a single person within a kinship group and placed all those beneath him in a hierarchy that called for obedience to those above and expectations of deference from those below. Politically, of course, the family or lineage head was subordinate to the hierarchy

[8]See Ho Ping-ti, *The Ladder of Success in Imperial China* (New York: Columbia University Press, 1962), chap. 1.

[9]Ho Ping-ti, "Salient Aspects of China's Heritage," op. cit., pp. 16–25.

[10]For a brief but stimulating discussion, see Maurice Freedman, "The Family in China, Past and Present," in Feuerwerker, ed., *Modern China,* op. cit., pp. 27–40.

extending downward from the emperor, thereby bringing those beneath him into an ordered relationship with political authority.

The authority structure in traditional China was neither absolute nor perfect. It was not absolute because it left open some relationships of equality (between nonrelated friends or persons holding the same status, for example) and could not always prevent noncompliance with the norms. It was not perfect because it contained conflicting obligations, by far the most important of which was that conflict between political loyalty to the imperial system and familial obligations. What did one do when official and parental desires were in conflict, or when an official's obligations to kinsmen challenged his duty to the emperor? In theory, imperial absolutism gave a clear political answer, but the norms of familial obligations were strong enough to prevent a final resolution. In practice, then, political authority tried to minimize the conflict by avoiding it. Whenever possible, familial obligations were legitimized and made part of imperial edict; for example, officials were granted leave for observance of mourning rites; and heavy penalties were enacted for crimes against kinsmen. The bureaucracy rotated its officials regularly and assigned them away from their native places to avoid conflict of interests. Perhaps most important, officials tried to co-opt local elites so that directives came to the population through the medium of, rather than in competition with, the local authority structure.

This use of the local structure necessarily diluted the political system's direct impact on the population. Political authority was extremely remote from the ordinary subject; its effects were felt largely through a person's immediate superiors, in whose status nonpolitical determinants were paramount. Nonetheless, the *pattern* of hierarchical authority was dominant at both elite and popular levels; any kind of social action, whether perceived as political or not, had to take place within its framework. As a result, the rupture of authority that came with the collapse of the old political system had a traumatic effect on all social relations, and attempts by the Chinese to reconstruct their political system usually have employed elitist and hierarchical authority structures.[11]

The CCP, too, has held an elitist conception of political leadership, and it established, after 1949, a highly structured and authoritarian system. However, authoritarianism in post-1949 China has been in persistent contradiction with populist themes that have challenged and modified its impact. Although Maoist populism is largely a product of the revolutionary period, it also draws on traditional reaction against political authority which, by virtue of its pervasiveness and oppressiveness, created a popular tendency to romanticize the act of rebellion against it.

Autonomy of the Political System. The authority structure of traditional China gave the political system supreme power, since it placed the emperor and his bureaucracy at the apex of the hierarchy. Equally significant was the political system's autonomy or relative independence from external influence or restraint. Theoretically the imperial system had an organic relationship with Chinese society; supposedly modeled on the family, it was to serve society by maintaining order, performing religious functions, and preserving the virtues of the past. Nor was it isolated from its environment, since its national and international responsibilities required a wide range of actions and contacts. Nonetheless, there developed over time a set of institutions and attitudes that made the system incapable of recognizing any legitimate external influence on its actions. It was in a very real sense a law unto itself, self-perpetuating and self-regulating, entering into its relationships with domestic and foreign entities only on an assumption of its own recognized superiority. There were, to be sure, violations of its autonomy through domestic resistance and foreign penetration. The Qing government itself was headed by a foreign imperial line imposed by the seventeenth-century Manchu

[11]See Lucian Pye, *The Spirit of Chinese Politics: A Psychocultural Study of the Authority Crisis in Political Development* (Cambridge, Mass.: M.I.T. Press, 1968), for an extended, provocative discussion of the problem of political authority in modern China.

conquest of China. Accommodation with outside forces was
still the exception rather than the rule for a government that
guarded so jealously both the symbols and reality of its autonomy.

One important aspect of the system's self-governing status
was its handling of political recruitment and advancement.
The imperial bureaucracy set the standards by which political
elites were recruited, managed the examinations and dispensation of office that formalized elite status, and decided internally on matters of assignment and promotion. Individuals
could prepare the way for a political career by acquisition of
knowledge or wealth, but formal certification came only from
the government. Once in office, a man had no recognized
constituency that might dilute his service to the emperor.
There was no concept of political representation, although a
quota system in the examinations encouraged a certain distribution of degree holders among the provinces.

Just as it denied external claims to influence or membership
within it, the regime acknowledged no legal or institutional
limitations on its actions. Particular interests had no right to
be heard or protected, no "constitutional" guarantees against
the exercise of imperial power. The government could initiate,
manage, regulate, adjudicate, and repress as it saw fit. Elites
did admit a moral obligation to provide just and responsive
government, but its enforcement depended on the political
recruitment process, which allegedly chose only men of superior virtue, or on the bureaucracy's own mechanisms of internal control and supervision; that is, it was an obligation
enforceable only by elite self-regulation. In short, the traditional political system was relatively free to accumulate and
exercise total power.[12]

Since the present Communist system also maintains a high
degree of autonomy in its relations with society, it will be
useful for comparative purposes to mention briefly some qualifications on this point. In fact, the government of imperial
China did not make the fullest possible use of its potential
power. Subject to important conditions, it allowed some local

[12]The most thorough and theoretical development of this point is Karl
Wittfogel, *Oriental Despotism: A Comparative Study of Total Power* (New Haven,
Conn.: Yale University Press, 1957), esp. chap. 4.

politics in which it did not insist on direct control, and it tolerated some penetration of particular interests into the bureaucratic process. As we noted earlier, official authority did not bear directly on the population but was brought to it through local intermediaries — the gentry and other lower-ranking authority figures. The institutional basis of this situation was the limited extent of the imperial administrative system, which stopped at the *zhou* (*chou,* department) or *xian* (*hsien,* district or county) level.[13] Each of these lowest units — of which there were in late Qing times approximately fifteen hundred with an average population exceeding two hundred thousand — was the responsibility of a single official known as the magistrate. Although the magistrate had a staff of assistants, the enormity of his job required him to seek formal and informal assistance from prominent local personages and organizations. In effect, he governed his district largely by supervising the actions of the local power structure, intervening with whatever measures seemed appropriate (from informal advice up to and including military force) to maintain order and secure compliance with imperial orders.

The resulting relationship is difficult to categorize. It most assuredly did not produce village democracy, since the local power structure was governed by rigid norms of authority and status. It was not truly administrative decentralization, although the magistrate did have considerable power in a unit of significant size, because all local power was conditional on higher approval; neither the magistrate's authority nor that of lesser figures could stand for a moment against the absolute authority of the center. Nor was it really local autonomy, since the government insisted on its right to intervene at any time and for any reason in local affairs. It was an operating arrangement, undertaken largely for reasons of administrative efficiency and conservatism, in which local authorities were encouraged to control their own areas provided they did so effectively and without violation of imperial requirements.

[13]The following discussion draws mainly on T'ung-tsu Ch'ü, *Local Government in China Under the Ch'ing* (Cambridge, Mass.: Harvard University Press, 1962); Kung-chuan Hsiao, *Rural China: Imperial Control in the Nineteenth Century* (Seattle: University of Washington Press, 1960); and John R. Watt, *The District Magistrate in Late Imperial China* (New York: Columbia University Press, 1972).

The gentry and other wealthy individuals, large lineages, merchant and craft guilds, and even secret societies could thus exercise great power over their subordinates and members and possibly some influence with the magistrate. They could do this, however, only as long as the magistrate viewed the results as beneficial and, above all, as long as their power did not become competitive with that of the magistrate. Administrative efficiency always yielded before the requirements of imperial control and security.

The penetration of particular interests into the official bureaucracy is probably less significant. To a large extent, we are simply noting and indeed repeating a fairly obvious point. The ideal of government by a disinterested, educated elite, chosen through examinations without reference to class or wealth had a profound practical impact on traditional China. Yet it was never a complete description of reality. Wealth did play a role, since officials as well as official status could be bought. Particularistic obligations and loyalties, especially to close family members but also to those of the same clan, locality, or school, could subvert an official's impartiality. The system tolerated these discrepancies within bounds because it had little choice; it was, after all, staffed with men who held values that could support such discrepancies. However, in acknowledging that private or particular interests could find their way into official politics, we should also note how the autonomy of the political system affected their expression.

In the first place, the system was emphatically hostile to the expression of such interests. Toleration was not to imply legal or moral acceptance, and pronounced partisan activity carried the risk of repression and severe punishment. The result was a tendency to keep interest politics out of government, or else to submerge it deeply in the bureaucratic framework. At the local level, individuals and organizations might compete with each other and seek the favor of the magistrate, but heavy pressure on or within the government invited repression. Officials also had their opinions and interests which they sought to advance, but again, efforts to organize large numbers in a noticeable party or to appeal for support from groups outside the bureaucracy risked the charge of "factionalism."[14] Hence, minor issues were contained at the local, largely nonofficial level, while major issues were expressed in a bureaucratic framework that abhorred organized political competition.

We may refer to the resulting form of competition as *bureaucratic politics*. The first condition of bureaucratic politics is that the protagonists must themselves be officials, the more highly placed the better, who reject or conceal any large-scale organizational backing, although they may claim to speak in general terms of popular support for their proposals. Interests lacking influential official spokesmen are in effect denied expression except at the lowest level. Secondly, political struggle itself is carried on by maneuvering within the bureaucratic hierarchy, in which questions of rank and personal influence become all-important. The objective is not to gain support from the largest number of colleagues — which may help but which runs the risk of punishment for factionalism — but rather to get a favorable decision from the authoritative office for the case in question. Secrecy and gossip, friendships and enmities, decisions expressed in changes of personnel, and small coalitions competing for the favor of superiors are, then, the stuff of bureaucratic politics.

The relevance of these points for an understanding of the Communist system is unmistakable. Like their imperial predecessors, the Communist elites have followed their own standards in recruitment and policy, rejecting claims to representation or recognition of partial interests within the government. Competing political organizations or factions, at any level, are anathema to them, and bureaucratic politics have been the prevailing mode of competition. The Communist system has gone much further, however, in extending its authority directly to the mass level, thereby reducing sharply

[14]For illustrative accounts of how imperial absolutism condemned and repressed "factionalism" without necessarily eliminating it, see W. T. de Bary, "Chinese Despotism and the Confucian Ideal: A Seventeenth-Century View," in John K. Fairbank, ed., *Chinese Thought and Institutions* (Chicago: University of Chicago Press, 1957), pp. 163–203; and David S. Nivison, "Ho-Shen and His Accusers: Ideology and Political Behavior in the Eighteenth Century," in Nivison and Arthur F. Wright, eds., *Confucianism in Action* (Stanford, Cal.: Stanford University Press, 1959), pp. 209–43.

even that limited "local autonomy" allowed under the Manchus. At the same time, by enlarging the size and responsibilities of the bureaucracy and by encouraging mass political mobilization, it has made more difficult the task of controlling its officials and maintaining its autonomy in the face of societal pressures and demands.

Ideology as an Integrative Force. The Chinese tradition contained from ancient times a number of philosophical-religious schools of thought. Confucianism, Taoism, legalism, and Buddhism all left their mark, albeit unevenly, on Chinese culture and society. It was Confucianism, however, that became the official ideology of the imperial system. Based on a written and widely studied body of ideas, it was defined as the supreme standard of morality and thus profoundly influenced behavior in all social relationships. The Confucian ethic was exceptionally significant for the political system, since it was the standard by which qualifications for elite status were judged and by which the behavior of officials was controlled. Officials were appointed mainly on the basis of superior performance in examinations that tested their knowledge of the Confucian classics. Study of the classics and mastery of the Confucian style of thought and expression were normally essential to appointment. Although some might gain office without it, internalization of the ethic was crucial for continued service and promotion.

The legitimacy of political authority was said to rest on observance of this moral doctrine, not on wealth, status, power, or representation of interests. Confucian ideology thus became an integrative force that justified political rule, defined the purposes of the state, provided the common values of the elite, and harmonized diverse interests in society. To the extent that it was propagated and accepted, it would bring society and officialdom together in common loyalty to rightful imperial authority.

The insistence that political authority was morally derived and was represented by guardians of moral doctrine was basic to the operation of the imperial system. Given the absence of institutional checks on government power, what was to prevent the abuse of power and to guarantee that the government would truly serve society? Confucian ideology provided the answer: good men, not institutional restraints, are the guarantee of good government. This is not to say that rules and regulations were lacking, since the traditional system had highly formalized standards of status and procedure. However, formal regulations were devices for ordering bureaucratic procedures and clarifying imperial wishes; they supported the system's operation but did not in themselves determine the *quality* of rule. To ensure justice and wisdom in political decisions, the Chinese tradition relied on the personal quality of the office holder rather than on regulations or institutional structure.

No Chinese statesman, ancient or modern, assumed that all men were equal in virtue or that officials would invariably follow the doctrine correctly. Quite the contrary, the Confucian ethic held that men developed different levels of virtue and that the ruler's task was to see that the truly virtuous were the ones who governed.[15] It was perfectly appropriate, then, for the highest authorities to test and supervise their subordinates continuously; to expect continued study and self-cultivation; to reprimand the deviants and laggards; and to force "correct" decisions on those who failed to see the light. Since the ideological rectitude that legitimized authority was a product of learning, not "given" by class or wealth, the system placed great emphasis on education and indoctrination. Instilling or restoring virtue in the minds of men was the road to a good society.

The extent to which this fundamental principle was realized in the practice of traditional politics is questionable, but belief in its validity and the attempt to implement it through the examination system and other institutions made it basic in Chinese political attitudes. The indispensability of official ideology, carefully defined and studied, remains central to Communist views of government, although the substance of contemporary ideology differs significantly from that of the past. Indeed, the CCP has gone far beyond imperial elites in exploiting the integrative benefits of ideology.

In imperial times, the Confucian ethic exerted its greatest

[15]See Kahn, "The Education of a Prince," op. cit. pp. 40–41.

influence on the elites themselves, whose study of it made them well aware of their role in the political system. Commoners, however, were poorly integrated into the traditional polity, which was remote and authoritarian. Aware of popular indifference and resentment, Qing authorities tried to indoctrinate the population in what they regarded as the virtues of worthy subjects — filial piety, respect for elders and superiors, peaceful and industrious conduct, and observance of the law. Through lectures, ceremonies, and schools that extolled the tenets of imperial Confucianism, they hoped to bring the masses into their ideological orbit, to instill positive loyalty and obedience to imperial rule.[16] Neither the effort nor the result was impressive, however. The Chinese countryside remained an "ideological vacuum" in which most inhabitants were "neither positively loyal to the existing regime nor opposed to it" but were simply concerned with the problems of their own daily lives.[17] The Communists, on the other hand, have been relentless in their ideological indoctrination of the common people as well as the elite. While acceptance of the substance of Communist ideology appears to be uneven, its vigorous propagation has brought most Chinese into a new consciousness of their membership in the political system.

THE REVOLUTIONARY SETTING

The Communist system has emerged directly from a revolutionary period that was not of its making. The onset of the Chinese revolution antedated the formation of the CCP. It had been in progress for decades before the party became a major force in Chinese politics and began to shape its direction. Any analysis of contemporary politics must emphasize the fact that Communist China is a product of the Chinese revolution, not its creator.

The CCP's emergence in the midst of an ongoing revolutionary process brought both assets and liabilities. On the negative side, fragmentation of the political order made it difficult to seize national power at one stroke and even more difficult to consolidate rapidly a new regime. The times prohibited an easy transfer of power, as by a palace coup, requir-

[16]Hsiao, op. cit., chap. 6.
[17]Ibid., pp. 253–54.

ing instead a prolonged struggle to create power as well as to seize it. The ongoing revolution also meant that the Communist elites could not define the issues wholly as they chose; powerful movements were already in existence, and to some extent the Communists, like their competitors, had to sink or swim with the tide.

On balance, however, and with the advantage of hindsight, the revolutionary setting of modern China was plainly an asset to the Communist cause. The basic condition of this period was a near total collapse of the traditional order. Actually, the imperial system demonstrated remarkable endurance. Already declining in the early nineteenth century, the Manchu dynasty suffered heavily from accelerated Western penetration after 1840 and from the Taiping Rebellion of 1850–1864. Its apparently imminent demise was forestalled, however, by a partial revival in the decade following the rebellion, when a few energetic officials tried to refurbish the old system and gained a measure of Western cooperation for their efforts.[18] Decline soon resumed, with new Western pressures for privileges and concessions, joined now by the first thrusts of Japanese imperialism and the stirrings of more radical reformers at home. The last few years of the century were disastrous. A humiliating military defeat by Japan in 1894–1895, vast new leases and cessions to the Western powers in 1897–1899, and foreign suppression of the Boxer Rebellion in 1900, followed by the exaction of yet more indemnities and privileges, left the central government economically, politically, and morally bankrupt. Still it held on, embarking at last on a series of reforms that suggested China might yet enter the modern world through the medium of a revived constitutional monarchy. But the reforms accelerated the rate of change and increased demands on the imperial government. In 1911, a number of provinces rebelled under the banner of republicanism; in 1912, the last Qing monarch yielded to the establishment of a new Republic of China.[19]

[18]See Mary C. Wright, *The Last Stand of Chinese Conservatism: The T'ung-Chih Restoration, 1862–1874* (Stanford, Cal.: Stanford University Press, 1957).

[19]For a penetrating survey and analysis of this early period of the Chinese revolution, see Mary Clabaugh Wright, "Introduction: The Rising Tide of Change," in Wright, ed., *China in Revolution: The First Phase, 1900–1913* (New Haven, Conn.: Yale University Press, 1968), pp. 1–63.

It soon became clear that there was no viable replacement for the Manchu government. Unlike Japan, where nineteenth-century political elites had forged a compromise between innovative policies and traditional political symbols, China had rejected the old political order without anything approaching consensus on a new one. The prolonged life of the imperial system had permitted the national crisis to deepen immeasurably even while it restrained and fragmented the counterelites who promoted new approaches. The Revolution of 1911 left as its legacy a thoroughly discredited political tradition that offered no guidelines for a successor and a political vacuum that encouraged further national disintegration. Nominal national leadership was up for grabs, accessible to any group that could muster more force than its opponents. But real power and authority required elites who offered a credible response to the national crisis. In a situation that demanded new leaders and policies, the Chinese Communists' credentials were as good as their competitors and ultimately better. Organized well after the Qing collapse and totally immersed in the revolutionary setting, the CCP necessarily oriented itself toward the major problems of the times. In the process, it became an agent of the Chinese revolution as well as its future master. It is essential, therefore, to look briefly at three themes that have dominated the revolution from its inception down to and including the present.

National Independence. Nationalism was the "moving force" of the Chinese revolution,[20] a unifying theme that brought diverse objectives together in the concept of national regeneration. Perhaps its clearest manifestation was a desire for national independence from foreign influence and control. No other issue was so easy to define in terms of concrete targets and abstract objectives: struggle against foreign opponents to regain national independence and equality. From 1900 to about 1925, virtually all political movements that generated significant popular support — the anti-Manchu struggles, the

---

[20]Ibid., pp. 3–4. See also Michael Gasster, *Chinese Intellectuals and the Revolution of 1911: The Birth of Modern Chinese Radicalism* (Seattle: University of Washington Press, 1969).

frequent boycotts of foreign goods and enterprises, the great strikes and demonstrations of May Fourth (1919) and May Thirtieth (1925) — appealed directly to resentment of the foreign role in Chinese affairs. National independence remained a prominent issue in the Nationalist Revolution of 1926–1928 and in the early years of the KMT government, and with the Japanese invasion of 1937 it again became the paramount national objective. Although China largely regained its independent status in the postwar years, its conflicts with the United States and the Soviet Union have continued the legacy of earlier anti-imperialist struggles.

China was never a full-fledged colony, retaining throughout its modern history formal diplomatic recognition as an independent state. As noted earlier, this fact sets Chinese experience apart from that of most non-Western countries. Both Chinese and foreigners recognized, however, that Chinese "independence" was only nominal. Sun Yat-sen, leader of the early Chinese nationalist movement, called his country a "hypo-colony," by which he meant that China was in fact a colony of many countries rather than of one particular power.[21] Mao Zedong and others used the term "semi-colony" to describe China's condition, with the qualification that outright occupation by foreign powers (as Japanese control of Manchuria after 1931) had transformed certain sections into full colonial status.[22] Whatever the proper term might be, by the early decades of the twentieth century, China had unquestionably lost a large measure of its independence and sovereignty.[23]

By the 1920s the territorial sway of the old Chinese empire was significantly reduced. A number of tributary states that had formerly recognized some degree of political dependence

[21]Sun Yat-sen, *San Min Chu I,* trans. Frank W. Price (Shanghai: Commercial Press, 1928), p. 39 passim.

[22]*Selected Works of Mao Tse-tung* (Peking: Foreign Languages Press, 1965), vol. 2, pp. 309–14.

[23]Details on the various treaties and arrangements through which foreign powers advanced their interests in China are recorded in most standard texts on modern Chinese history. See, for example, John K. Fairbank, Edwin O. Reischauer, and Albert M. Craig, *East Asia: The Modern Transformation* (Boston: Houghton Mifflin, 1965), pp. 144–54, 166–73, 338–48, 365–78, 382–84, 403–4, 468–83, 674–76, 688–91.

on China (Burma, Vietnam, Korea, and Outer Mongolia) were lost. Outright cessions gave the island of Hong Kong to the British, Macao to the Portuguese, Taiwan and the Ryukyus to Japan, and vast areas on the northern and western frontiers to Russia; Tibet [Xizang] was drawn away from Chinese influence; Manchuria was soon to become a victim of Japanese conquest. Within China, some foreign powers claimed large spheres of influence in which they held special economic and military rights. Scattered along the coast and inland waters in cities opened for trade were numerous concessions, or leases to the powers, which the concessionaires administered as their own territory. In these areas, foreigners were guaranteed the right to live, trade, manufacture, and hold land — rights protected by the principle of extraterritoriality that made foreign residents subject to their own rather than Chinese legal jurisdiction. Christian missionaries had unrestricted rights to propagate their faith anywhere in China. Commercial privileges, particularly a fixed limit on the Chinese tariff schedule, gave foreign businessmen important advantages.

The treaty system that established these conditions was of fundamental importance. Needless to say, the Chinese government entered into these treaties under duress, but once sanctified by treaty the various privileges could be altered only by the consent of all parties. More importantly, the beneficiaries could, and did, invoke principles of legality and national honor to enforce them. Especially after the Boxer settlement of 1901, the foreign powers maintained military forces in China to defend their citizens and interests. Their instruments of defense were not limited to military force, however. Foreigners controlled collections of Chinese customs and the salt tax, the most stable sources of central revenue, and provided key staff in the postal, telegraph, and railroad systems. Their role in governmental operations helped ensure that China would meet its treaty obligations, including payments on a staggering foreign debt built up through frequent loans and indemnities.

A few major points follow from this all-too-sketchy outline. From 1900 to 1928, the central government of China was too weak and dependent on the foreign powers to take actions against these other nations. The new KMT government established in Nanjing (Nanking) in 1928 was stronger, and more vigorous in seeking equalization of its status, but it fell far short of the goal of national independence; the Japanese advance was soon to put more Chinese territory than ever under foreign control. In addition to subverting the government's authority, foreign influence was prominent in the major cities and in the more modernized sectors of the Chinese economy. Imperialism never had a direct impact on all or even most areas of Chinese life, but its effects were highly visible and tangible to urbanized laborers, intellectuals, and businessmen who were influential in defining national political issues. Whether it really damaged the handicrafts and land system of the traditional economy and retarded modern economic development remains open to question.[24] What is not in dispute is that most politically conscious Chinese believed that foreign economic activities had a negative effect on Chinese development, and that virtually all Chinese who were exposed to the foreign presence resented its forced and privileged penetration of their country. The leaders of the CCP absorbed the resulting anti-imperialist attitudes, used them in their rise to power, and have continued to nourish them since 1949.

National Unification. A second theme of the Chinese revolution has been national unification under a single, central political authority. In a limited sense, this goal was as obvious and noncontroversial as the drive for independence. The problem was simply a division of power among several competing groups; the solution was for one group to attain sufficient power to establish a durable central government and to subdue its rivals. This simplified view was an understandable response to the domestic political situation that emerged in the wake of the Revolution of 1911. The basic condition of the times was *warlordism,* a term that refers most precisely to the years between 1916 and 1928 when control of the central government in Peking [Beijing] shifted frequently from one military leader to another, but which in a broader sense may

---

[24]See Albert Feuerwerker, *The Chinese Economy, 1912–1949* (Ann Arbor: University of Michigan, Center for Chinese Studies, 1968), esp. pp. 10–19, 63–75; Chi-ming Hou, *Foreign Investment and Economic Development in China, 1840–1937* (Cambridge, Mass.: Harvard University Press, 1965), pp. 211–22, and the sources cited in note 33 of this chapter.

refer to the chronic political and military disunity that prevailed in China from before 1911 down to 1949.

A warlord was a military leader "who established and maintained control over territory by the use of his personal army";[25] that is, he had a territorial base over which he exercised political and military control by virtue of an army loyal to him rather than to some higher leader of government. Warlordism developed when the central government lost its ability to control regional military leaders, leaving a field of warlords who fought among themselves for regional and national supremacy. The seeds of warlordism lay in the regional armies recruited to subdue the Taiping Rebellion. The declining Manchu government never fully regained control over these forces, which grew in numbers and strength. When the last Qing emperor abdicated in 1912, leadership of the new "republican" government passed quickly to Yuan Shikai (Yüan Shih-k'ai), who commanded the loyalty of China's most powerful army and thereby maintained a semblance of unified national control until his death in 1916. Yüan's death opened the gates for the heyday of warlordism, in which no single warlord ever controlled more than a few provinces or was able to maintain an official government in Peking for more than a brief period. The victory of Chiang Kai-shek's Nationalist forces in 1928 brought a significant change, since the KMT represented a much more broadly based movement with genuine programs for national administration and development. The Nationalist movement, however, had won a military victory by striking alliances with some of the warlords, not by eliminating them. As a result, only a few provinces in the Yangtze [Changjiang] valley of central China were solidly under Chiang's control. In fact, his government faced virtually continual rebellion or threat of rebellion from the residual warlords down to the time of the Japanese invasion. It faced as well an armed Communist movement which, though militarily weak and quite different in character from the warlord armies, magnified the extent of national disunity.[26]

The evils of warlordism need little elaboration. The exis-

[25]James E. Sheridan, *Chinese Warlord: The Career of Feng Yü-hsiang* (Stanford, Cal.: Stanford University Press, 1966), p. 16.
[26]Ibid., pp. 1–6.

tence of multiple and shifting centers of power made a travesty of attempts at national government. Taxes multiplied endlessly at the local level to finance the warlords, while the central government was politically and financially impoverished. Foreign powers capitalized on this weakness, trading diplomatic recognition for economic opportunities and supporting those warlords who would favor them or oppose their rivals. Wars and troop movements exacted an enormous cost in lives, military expenditures, looting, and property destruction. [27] For any concerned Chinese, the consequences were simply intolerable, appearing all the more shameful in view of China's tradition of civilian rule under an all-powerful central government. Hence the desire for unification at all costs, with an understanding that military power was absolutely essential to the process. The Chinese revolution would not be complete until one government ruled all of China, having eliminated all possible military resistance.[28]

But forceful establishment of a secure central government could only be a first step toward genuine national unification. Unity and security were essential, but so were governmental effectiveness and legitimacy; although warlordism highlighted the former needs, it also exposed the latter. The point is that military unification alone could not replace the imperial political system, which had combined with its monopoly of force an effective administration operative through the bureaucratic-scholarly-familial hierarchies and a legitimate political authority based on imperial Confucianism. The traditional administrative mechanism and its legitimating ideology fell with Manchu reforms, the Revolution of 1911, and subsequent changes in Chinese society and ideas. The reunification of China thus required nothing less than a new polity that could meet the demands of a modern nation-state. In administrative terms, it required a new system of political recruitment and of handling an expanded range of governmental activities at all levels, down to and including the village. In ideological terms, it called for a new legitimating doctrine that would not only

[27]Ibid., pp. 20–30.
[28]C. Martin Wilbur, "Military Separatism and the Process of Reunification under the Nationalist Regime," in Ho and Tsou, eds., op. cit., pp. 203–4.

justify the exercise of political authority but also seek the allegiance of ordinary citizens and integrate them in the political system. The real problem, then, was disintegration rather than simple disunity; the solution was reintegration on new terms of which the traditional political order had never conceived.[29]

In this broader sense, the reunification (i.e., reintegration) of China actually began with those late nineteenth-century reformers who called for a modernized political structure that would base itself on and claim the support of the Chinese people. Implementation of these proposals began with Manchu reforms that antedated the Revolution of 1911. It was not until the 1920s, however, that the political vehicle for forging a new polity emerged in the mass-based political party. Although never successful at either unification or integration, the KMT government spread new political concepts, institutions, and procedures that clearly foreshadowed much of what was to come under CCP rule. Today the Chinese Communists' understanding of the real dimensions of national unification, their profound commitment to it, and their relative success in attaining it draw heavily on these earlier efforts and experiences.

Socioeconomic Change.   Generalizations about socioeconomic change in a revolutionary era — its causes, extent, and political implications — are always inadequate. No discussion of the Chinese revolution is complete, however, without some reference to this subject. Perhaps the most important point to emphasize is that social and economic conditions in modern China were *potentially* the source of a massive revolution. It was not inevitable that they would *cause* one, or that they would provide the dominant basis of any revolutionary mobilization that might occur; it was inevitable that they would inject the question of radical social and economic change into the revolution that did occur. The potential explosiveness of Chinese society stemmed from a gross discrepancy between perceived possibilities and current reality. On the one hand, foreign penetration and imperial collapse had already initiated some

[29]See "Comments by Wang Gungwu," ibid., pp. 264–70; and Tang Tsou, "Revolution, Reintegration and Crisis in Communist China: A Framework for Analysis," ibid., pp. 277–81.

change in values and social structure, particularly in the cities and among the upper classes. These changes stimulated demands for an accelerated transformation that would legitimize the new values and classes, eliminate China's economic and social "backwardness," and propel China into full equality — in every sense — with the Western powers. On the other hand, prevailing conditions stood in stark contrast and even opposition to these desires; imperialism, warlordism, the persistence of traditional values among most of the population, and widespread poverty and illiteracy seemed to defy the realization of rapid change. For proponents of socioeconomic reform, this gulf between ambition and reality heightened the attractiveness of revolutionary formulae for attaining it. And although the gulf was an immediate obstacle to revolutionary mobilization of the masses, it also created enormous potential support for any movement that could transmit to the common people an image of how their lives could be improved.

National economic development was a prime concern for all Chinese who hoped for national regeneration, since their economy was so weak and backward relative to that of Japan and the Western powers. Contrary to some impressions, the pre-Communist economy was neither incapable of change nor stagnant in the decades preceding 1949. Historically, China had known periods of great wealth and economic change, although dynastic decline and traditional values had inhibited diffusion of the industrial revolution to China in the modern era. Still, industrialization and modern commercialization did come to China well before the Communist Revolution, particularly after 1895. Industrial growth between 1912 and 1949 averaged over 5 percent annually, and was especially impressive in the relatively favorable periods of 1912–1920 and 1931–1936; the gross national product was also growing, although not as rapidly as modern industry.[30]

Despite this beginning, however, the Chinese economy in 1949 was still "near the bottom of the world development scale," with a per-capita GNP of about fifty dollars.[31] Growth

---

[30]See the discussion in Alexander Eckstein, "The Economic Heritage," in Eckstein, Walter Galenson, and Ta-chung Liu, eds., *Economic Trends in Communist China* (Chicago: Aldine, 1968), pp. 64–67.

[31]Ibid., p. 79.

in the modern sectors of the economy, particularly industry, had relatively little impact on the national economic situation simply because they started at such a low level and remained very modest contributors to the national product. The economy was still basically preindustrial and agrarian, and the all-important agricultural sector was characterized by low labor productivity, technological stagnation, and great population pressure on the cultivable land. In short, economic development before 1949 was weak and uneven, being confined mainly to Manchuria and the treaty ports where foreign capital played an important though declining role.[32] Key developmental issues, such as the role of state planning and entrepreneurship, geographic diversification, and agricultural transformation, remained unresolved. The beginnings of economic modernization had underscored the need for a program of national economic development, but its implementation was one of the least advanced of revolutionary objectives.

The human consequences of modern China's economic situation were severe. China's great population explosion came in the eighteenth century, when the population grew from about 150 million to over 300 million and began to strain existing economic resources. Population growth then slowed but did not stop, reaching about 430 million in 1850 and, according to the first Communist census, 583 million in 1953. In the absence of major increases in cultivable land or change in agricultural technology, there developed from the mid-nineteenth century on a basic condition of overpopulation and mass poverty manifested in chronic misery, famine, rebellion, and population movements.[33] In the early decades of the twentieth century, warlordism and civil war compounded the problems of rural life that left much of the population at a level

[32]Ibid., pp. 59–61, 66, 74–80.

[33]Ping-ti Ho, *Studies on the Population of China, 1368–1953* (Cambridge: Harvard University Press, 1959), pp. 270–78. The increasing impoverishment thesis, like that of imperialism's impact (see note 24 of this chapter), remains the subject of lively debate. Studies suggesting that the Chinese economy held its own against both imperialism and population growth include Ramon H. Myers, *The Chinese Peasant Economy: Agricultural Development in Hopei and Shantung, 1890–1949* (Cambridge: Harvard University Press, 1970), and Dwight H. Perkins, *Agricultural Development in China, 1368–1968* (Chicago: Aldine, 1969).

of marginal existence.[34] No single factor explains the depths and complexity of this economic malaise. High rates of tenancy and the presence of a few large landowners were obvious sources of peasant dissatisfaction and obvious targets for reformers and revolutionaries, although neither was a condition typical of all China. High rents and taxes, usurious credit practices, small and fragmented farms, traditional farming methods, low productivity per man, illiteracy, and external disturbances and exactions all contributed to perpetuating the poverty and vulnerability to ruin of most of the rural population. Life in the cities, where a small industrial proletariat was growing, afforded better opportunities for some but scarcely better conditions in general. Low wages, long hours, unsafe working conditions, inadequate housing, and large pools of unemployed or irregular workers were the rule in China's emerging factory cities.[35]

If these economic conditions had existed in a stable social and political setting, their revolutionary potentiality might never have been realized. Such stability was lacking, however, for the collapse of the traditional order had already set in motion far-reaching social changes. Basic in this changing social setting was the discrediting of the old elite. The abolition of the examination system in 1905, followed by the end of imperial rule, destroyed the bureaucratic stronghold of the

---

That finding is reviewed critically in Cheryl Payer, "Harvard on China II: Logic, Evidence and Ideology," *Bulletin of Concerned Asian Scholars,* vol 6, no. 2 (April–August 1974), pp. 62–68, while the larger effects of imperialism are debated by Andrew Nathan and Joseph Esherick in ibid. vol. 4, no. 4 (December 1972), pp. 2–16. Recent essays exploring these questions in greater depth are found in Dwight H. Perkins, ed., *China's Modern Economy in Historical Perspective* (Stanford: Stanford University Press, 1975). For a summary of different views on the economy of modern China, see "Symposium on China's Economic History," *Modern China,* vol. 4, no. 3 (July 1978). Despite all this controversy about the source and precise extent of economic problems in modern China, there is general agreement that the problems were severe and required a new developmental effort to resolve.

[34]For surveys of agricultural and living conditions in this period, see John Lossing Buck, *Land Utilization in China* (New York: Paragon Reprint Corporation, 1964); and R. H. Tawney, *Land and Labour in China* (London: George Allen and Unwin, 1932), pp. 23–108.

[35]See Tawney, op. cit., pp. 121–28, 140–54.

scholar-gentry class, opening the ranks of political elitehood to new claimants and eroding gentry power and status at the local level.[36] As the old criteria of legitimate authority declined, leaving crude military and financial power to fill the vacuum, certain groups experienced significant upward mobility; military leaders and the new Chinese bourgeosie were perhaps the best examples of those groups that were acquiring new power and status. But social change encompassed far more than a partial replacement of the old elite by warlords and chambers of commerce. The penetration of Western values that both hastened and fed upon the rejection of tradition pointed toward a sweeping liberation of Chinese society from the restraints of the past. Exemplified by the intellectual ferment of the May Fourth Movement of 1919, this trend promoted the study of "science and democracy," the emancipation of women from their servile status within the family, and the elevation of youth to more independent and responsible roles in society.[37] The vision of new freedoms and opportunities for previously subordinate groups was spreading, supported now by at least a few concrete examples of the vision's attainability.

The actual extent of social "liberation" was sharply limited, of course. Poverty, illiteracy, and traditional isolation from politics made it difficult to persuade the common people that significant changes in their circumstances were possible. Nonetheless, by the 1920s the banner of socioeconomic reform had passed from scattered intellectuals to organized political parties with increasing evidence that it could be a basis for popular mobilization. Ultimately, the Nationalist Revolution of 1928 remained oriented toward the proven appeals of national independence and unification, but for at least a brief period in 1925–1927 its radical wing (then including the Chinese Communists) was able to organize a worker-peasant

[36]For discussion of the "erosion" of local leadership in modern China, see Hsiao-tung Fei, *China's Gentry: Essays in Rural-Urban Relations,* rev. and ed. by Margaret Park Redfield (Chicago: University of Chicago Press, 1953).

[37]On the May Fourth Movement, see Chow Tse-tsung, *The May Fourth Movement: Intellectual Revolution in Modern China* (Cambridge, Mass.: Harvard University Press, 1960). The emergence of new groups and transformation of old ones is analyzed in Wright, "Introduction: The Rising Tide of Change," op. cit., pp. 32–44.

movement that brought class struggle within Chinese society to the fore. From this point on, fundamental social and economic reform was an unavoidable issue in Chinese politics. It was also the most painful and divisive of the three main revolutionary themes. The KMT after 1928 did more to advance it than any previous government, but persistently gave it lower priority than independence and unification on its own terms. The CCP, on the other hand, perceived social and economic change as an integral part of its program, as inseparable from its nationalist objectives, and was more successful in tapping this vein of potential popular support.

To summarize this discussion, the revolutionary setting of modern China concentrated political energies on the attainment of national independence, national unification and integration, and socioeconomic reform. The Chinese Communist movement, existing wholly within the revolutionary period, necessarily absorbed and responded to these goals. Ultimately, it developed a fuller and more convincing response to them than its great competitor, the KMT. The Chinese Nationalists placed unification first, thereby compromising the struggle for resistance to Japan and postponing a concentrated assault on China's social and economic problems; ironically, the strategy heightened national disunity and weakened the KMT's claim to leadership of the revolution. As an illegal opposition party not bearing responsibility for national government, the CCP could talk in terms of programs rather than priorities and could practice some of these programs in a smaller, more manageable setting. Its victory over the KMT was won by force of arms, but only after it had built up an image of real dedication to the paramount national concerns. Once in power, the CCP demonstrated that its credentials for revolutionary leadership were sound by restoring China to greater independence and unity than at any time in the preceding century and by vigorously promoting its social and economic transformation.

Nonetheless, the Communists' ability to come to grips with these problems was heavily dependent on the efforts of earlier actors in the revolution. The popularization of the drive for national independence was largely the work of the KMT and its forerunners, not the CCP. It was the Nanjing government that secured the first real rollback in Western privileges and began to enter into relations with foreign powers on an equal basis, so that China in 1945 — still under KMT rule — had largely regained its formal diplomatic equality. Although the KMT never truly unified the country, it was the Nationalists — and even some of the warlords — who established the first modern governmental structures based on experiments begun in the last years of the imperial system. The CCP was to extend governmental authority to the people in an unprecedented way, but the crucial first steps of replacing traditional institutions and introducing new ones were taken by its predecessors. Change in the marriage and family system was well advanced by 1949, with KMT legislation in this area bearing strong similarities to later Communist enactments. The Nationalists did much to spread, although little to implement, the idea of agrarian reform. Educational reform began in earnest as early as the last decade of the Qing, producing by 1949 the modern intellectuals, the educational buildings and facilities, and the increased literacy so crucial to many CCP programs. In these and many other spheres, Chinese Communism must be seen as continuing and benefiting from a revolutionary process that it did not initiate or define.

SOVIET COMMUNISM

The role of Soviet Communisim in the Chinese Communist Revolution is one of the most controversial issues in the study of this subject. No simple answer explains adequately the historical relationship between the Russian and Chinese "comrades" or Soviet Communism's influence on the political system developed in China after 1949.[38] It is undeniable, however, that the Soviet Union has had a powerful influence on Chinese Communist politics for half a century. To put this role in preliminary perspective, it is useful to distinguish between Russian control and influence within the Chinese Communist movement.

Soviet Control, 1921–1934. For more than a decade, from the founding of the CCP in July 1921 (the date of the party's First

[38]A useful survey is O. Edmund Clubb, *China and Russia; The "Great Game"* (New York: Columbia University Press, 1971).

Congress) to the early 1930s the Soviet Communist party controlled the official line and leadership of the CCP. Through the medium of Russian advisers and Comintern agents in China, backed by the threat of withdrawing assistance and Comintern recognition, Soviet elites formulated the CCP's major policy statements and chose its highest officials. This control began to slip following the 1927 rupture of the first KMT-CCP alliance. In the aftermath of Chiang Kai-shek's purge of Communist elements within the Nationalist movement, the CCP was too fragmented and the political situation too uncertain for directives from Moscow to determine all operations in China. Nonetheless, Soviet leaders continued to define the CCP general line and pass judgment on Chinese conformance with it. In a key test in late 1930 and early 1931, the Comintern reasserted its control by purging the Li Lisan leadership of the CCP, replacing it with the "returned students" (or "twenty-eight Bolsheviks") faction, a group trained in Moscow and loyal to its authority. Through this group, which dominated the CCP Central Committee until 1934, the Comintern maintained its hold over the Chinese Communist leadership.[39]

The practical consequences of formal Comintern control over the CCP Central Committee in the 1927–1934 period remain in dispute. For a variety of reasons, this control was certainly less meaningful than in the years between 1921 and 1927. Soviet leadership in the later years was increasingly more concerned with European affairs and less obsessed with the domestic political implications of its China policy. The anti-Communist stance of the new KMT government in Nanjing made communications and the support of the CCP more difficult. Most serious of all were de facto political and geographic divisions within the Chinese Communist movement. The events of 1927 shattered its strength in the cities. In the revival that slowly followed, the bulk of CCP activity shifted to the countryside, to the scattered rural "soviets" of South-Central China where Communist guerrillas were struggling to establish territorial bases and a Red Army. The leaders of these rural soviets acknowledged the formal authority of the Central Committee and the Comintern line, but demands of

[39]On this point and the following summary, see ibid., and the sources cited in notes 10–12 of Chapter I, this book.

survival and the autonomy derived from geographic isolation and armed support encouraged them to differ at times with orders from the Party Center. The foremost political representative of the rural areas was Mao Zedong, whose views were in conflict with both the Li Lisan and "returned students" factions; his differences with the latter group led him into rivalry with them for leadership of the party. The resulting competition limited the Comintern's ability to stay in command of the situation in China. Recognizing that the rural soviets and their armed forces had become the real strength of the Communist movement, the Comintern offered doctrinal pronouncements that legitimized their existence and most of their activities. At the same time, once the loyal "returned students" were installed at the party center, the Comintern could ill afford to compromise their formal authority over the Maoist faction. Hence the Comintern favored the "returned students" in their struggle with Mao; yet in doing so it weakened its claim to guide the main force of the revolution.

In the latter part of 1934, KMT military pressure compelled the Communist to evacuate their principal stronghold in southern Jiangsi (Kiangsi) province and embarked on the Long March that was to relocate their major forces in the northwestern province of Shaanxi (Shensi). Early in the course of this march, at the Zunyi (Tsunyi) Conference in January 1935, Mao Zedong successfully challenged the "returned students" faction and became the leading figure within the CCP.[40] Moscow was not thereafter to wield a controlling hand in Chinese Communist affairs. The question of Soviet direction of CCP policy was to arise on several later occasions, most critically CCP acceptance of the Comintern United Front policy in 1935, the CCP decision to work for Chiang Kai-shek's release following his kidnapping in the Sian [Xian] Incident of December 1936, and Chinese entrance into the Korean War in October–November 1950. In each of these cases, however, current evidence suggests that the CCP acted in line with Moscow's wishes not because of Russian orders but rather because Chinese leaders came independently to the conclu-

[40]For details, see "Resolutions of the Tsunyi Conference," trans. with a commentary by Jerome Ch'en, *China Quarterly,* no. 40 (Oct.–Dec. 1969), pp. 1–38.

sion that their own interests were served best by the action in question.[41] In short, Mao's rise marked the end of CCP submission to the dictates of Soviet Communism.

The important point in this brief discussion is that the Soviet Union lost its power to control and discipline Chinese Communist leaders long before they came to power. Even before 1935, men such as Mao had, at least temporarily, acquired opportunities to experiment with their own responses to the Chinese revolution. After 1935, the CCP embarked on yet another period of growth and expansion. This time, however, control of the movement was in Chinese hands, so that decisions concerning both the revolutionary movement and the political system to emerge from it were made by the Chinese Communists themselves.

Soviet Influence. Soviet influence — as distinguished from control — is much more difficult to analyze. Although initially linked with Comintern control, the influence of Soviet Communism became an integral part of Chinese Communism and was to remain long after Moscow's capacity to direct CCP affairs had passed. Even in the initial contacts, at the time of the founding of the CCP, there were subtle differences in the ways that various elements of Marxism-Leninism penetrated Chinese politics.[42] Some elements carried a distinctly positive attraction; the Chinese intellectuals who were to lead the CCP in its early years committed themselves to Marxism-Leninism largely on the basis of those aspects of it that fit their own understanding of China's needs or reinforced currents already

[41]On CCP response to the 1935 United Front and the 1936 Sian Incident, see Lyman P. Van Slyke, *Enemies and Friends: The United Front in Chinese Communist History* (Stanford, Cal.: Stanford University Press, 1967), chaps. 4 and 5. On the Chinese decision to enter the Korean War, see Allen S. Whiting, *China Crosses the Yalu: The Decision to Enter the Korean War* (New York: Macmillan, 1967), pp. 27–30, 152–60.

[42]The discussion here focuses on the development of Marxism-Leninism in China after the Bolshevik Revolution in Russia. Marx and Marxism were known to a few Chinese intellectuals before 1917 but failed to attract much attention until that date. The most attractive brand of European radicalism to the Chinese before 1917 was anarchism rather than Marxism. See Martin Bernal, "The Triumph of Anarchism over Marxism, 1906–7," in Wright, ed., op. cit., pp. 97–142; and Maurice Meisner, *Li Ta-chao and the Origins of Chinese Marxism* (Cambridge, Mass.: Harvard University Press, 1967), pp. 52–57.

flowing in the Chinese intellectual stream. Other elements followed as a consequence of this general and in some ways superficial commitment to Marxism-Leninism; they were not necessarily forced on the Chinese, but they nonetheless injected some novel or unsolicited influences into the Chinese revolution.

From party beginnings to the present, CCP leaders have differed in their interpretation of the Marxist-Leninist message and how to apply it in China. At the most general level, one can distinguish between men like Chen Duxiu (Ch'en Tu-hsiu) and Liu Shaoqi (Liu Shao-ch'i) who tended toward a more "orthodox" or "scientific" use of the doctrine, and those like Li Dazhao (Li Ta-chao) and Mao Zedong, who displayed more "voluntaristic" and "nationalistic" tendencies.[43] But during the critical founding years of the party, most soon-to-be Communists in China shared a revolutionary commitment that overshadowed their theoretical commitment to Marxism-Leninism;[44] that is, they identified more with the Bolshevik Revolution's general message of radical change than with the specifics of its ideology. Anti-imperialism was perhaps the strongest element in this message, not so much through the subtleties of Leninist theories as through the basic insistence that foreign oppression must and would be overthrown. The primary catalyst in the growth of Marxist adherents and left-wing activity in China was the May Fourth Incident of 1919, an incident that symbolized upheaval in diverse areas of Chinese life but was in its political focus an ardently nationalistic, anti-imperialist event. The publicity and definition that May Fourth gave to demands for national independence transformed Marxism-Leninism from an esoteric foreign doctrine to an immediately relevant explanation of a crucial fact of Chinese political life.[45]

The May Fourth Movement, in its broadest sense, also pointed toward another profound attraction in Marxism-Leninism — its claim to science, modernity, and progressive

[43]See "Comments by Michel Oksenberg," in Ho and Tsou, eds., op. cit., pp. 488–90.

[44]See Meisner, op. cit., pp. 56–57; and Stuart R. Schram, *The Political Thought of Mao Ts-tung,* rev. and enl. ed. (New York: Praeger, 1969), pp. 29–32.

[45]Meisner, op. cit., pp. 95–104.

change. At its most fundamental level, May Fourth represented a growing intellectual revolt against the Chinese tradition, a revolt that was divided in its objectives but was clearly set against China's past. Some Chinese who were determined to promote a revolutionary transformation that would propel their country into the modern era on a basis of full equality with the West were to find inspiration and guidance in Marxism-Leninism. The doctrine not only asserted the inevitability of progressive change that would alter China's inferior international status, but it did so with a claim to science and modernity that had previously seemed to be a monopoly of Western capitalism. Particularly important was the Leninist notion that a small group of intellectual elites could, by organized intervention in the historical process, accelerate and guide the promised revolutionary transformation; to Chinese intellectuals aware of their society's inertia and their own traditional role of political leadership, this idea held a special appeal. To be sure, the early Chinese Communists were not uniformly receptive to these various appeals. Perhaps Mao Zedong alone held a kind of "natural Leninism" that made him uniquely responsive to both the revolutionary and organizational themes.[46] But the ideas noted here were central in Chinese intellectual discourse during and after the May Fourth Movement, and they clearly facilitated a growing interest in and commitment to Marxism-Leninism.[47]

Supplementing Chinese responsiveness to these broad revolutionary appeals was the concrete existence and example of a new Bolshevik government in Russia. As suggested earlier, it was the combination of the October Revolution in Russia and the May Fourth Movement in China that opened the way for Chinese acceptance of Marxism-Leninism. The importance of the Russian example bears special emphasis. Like China, Russia was economically backward relative to the leading Western nations and was faced with the task of providing

[46]The phrase is Stuart Schram's from *The Political Thought of Mao Tse-tung,* op. cit., pp. 35, 55. See also Benjamin I. Schwartz, *Chinese Communism and the Rise of Mao* (Cambridge, Mass.: Harvard University Press, 1958), p. 35.

[47]For general discussions of this point, see Chow, op. cit., passim, esp. pp. 1–15, 358–68; D. W. Y. Kwok, *Scientism in Chinese Thought, 1900–1950* (New Haven, Conn.: Yale University Press, 1965), pp. 11–20, 59–77, 162–71; and Schwartz, op. cit., pp. 7–27.

political alternatives to a discredited imperial system. The success and survival of the Bolshevik movement offered empirical proof that there was a new alternative to both Western capitalism and imperial decadence. Soviet Russia was not so much a model in these formative years of Chinese Communism as it was a symbol and example of how a new system dedicated to revolutionary change could emerge from the ruins of an old imperial order, despite the opposition of the leading Western powers.

Important though this example was to the radical intellectuals of China, it was by no means the only concrete result of the October Revolution. In July 1919, soon after the May Fourth Incident, the Soviet government issued the Karakhan Declaration in which it announced its intention to abrogate all "unequal treaties" between Russia and China and to give up all special Russian interests and privileges in China. Although never wholly implemented, the proposal created a highly favorable response and much interest in the new Russian regime from many Chinese.[48] The possibilities of substantive Soviet support were not lost on Chinese revolutionaries, who became increasingly responsive to contacts with Russian representatives. Within a few years, Comintern agents had brought about the organization of the CCP and the Soviet government had entered into an agreement with Sun Yat-sen's KMT government in Canton [Guangzhou] that was to provide it with Soviet advisers and military assistance. The details of these activities, which were also to produce the first KMT-CCP United Front of 1923-1927, need not concern us here.[49] The point is that Soviet Russia was a source of organizational and military aid to Chinese Communists and Nationalists alike, at a time when both were in need of support and not likely to secure it from any other source. As in the realm of ideas, Soviet Communism had something to offer that was seen as supporting and reinforcing, not altering, the shape of the Chinese revolution.

The Chinese Communists, however, could not escape additional consequences of their acceptance of Marxism-Leninism. Although their acceptance derived from a significant correspondence of ideas and interests, they soon discovered that it

[48]Chow, op. cit., pp. 209–214.
[49]See the sources cited in note 54 of this chapter.

led as well to an acceptance of Soviet ideological and organizational discipline. There was no realistic alternative at that point in history. Moscow *was* the authoritative center of the movement they had joined. For the Chinese comrades, the strategy of their revolution was not what they found in the Marxist historical tradition but rather the Soviet Communist party's interpretation of it. Most of them were in any case poorly prepared to resist Russian authority even had they wished to challenge political reality. Their knowledge of Marxism-Leninsim was in fact weak, so that they relied heavily on Comintern advisers, directives and materials from Moscow, and study in the Soviet Union for a theoretical grasp of the doctrine they espoused.[50] Necessarily, then, the establishment of the CCP and its formal affiliation (in 1922) with the Comintern brought many new influences of Soviet Communism into the pattern of Chinese politics.

The Soviet Model. Most fundamentally, the CCP came to accept the Soviet Union as a model and the Soviet Communist party as the most advanced and authoritative among all Communist parties. Even after 1935, when Russian elites had lost their earlier control over Chinese Communism, the CCP continued to acknowledge the primacy of Soviet experience and standing. While insisting that their movement was independent and must "sinify" Marxism-Leninism for application in the Chinese context, CCP leaders avoided open disagreement with Soviet positions and paid ample deference to the Soviet Union as the model socialist state.[51] Ultimately, of course, the

[50]The relative weakness of doctrinal study among Chinese party members, to which I allude frequently, was not overcome until after 1935. It was only during the Yanan (Yenan) Period (1937–1945) of Chinese Communism that CCP leaders found time for serious doctrinal study and writing and that the party set up its own system of schools for party cadres. Even then, standard Soviet study materials occupied a prominent place in the curriculum. See Compton's comments in *Mao's China: Party Reform Documents, 1942–44,* trans. and introduction by Boyd Compton (Seattle: University of Washington Press, 1952), pp. x–xi, xxx–xxxi, xxix–xlv.

[51]The careful balancing of these two themes is evident in the writings of Mao Zedong. See Stuart Schram's comments and the selection of Mao's statements on the subject in Schram, *The Political Thought of Mao Tse-tung,* op. cit., pp. 415–39. Schram also notes (p. 115n) that one of the editorial principles governing the 1951 publication of Mao's *Selected Works* was the deletion of earlier formulations that might be offensive to the Soviet Union.

Sino-Soviet conflict led to China's rejection of the USSR's primacy within the socialist camp; yet the CCP delayed open delineation of the differences between the two parties. The differences began, according to the Chinese, with Khrushchev's criticism of Stalin at the Soviet Twentieth Party Congress in Februrary 1956, but they did not launch direct public attacks on the Soviet leadership until 1963; as late as February 1963, the Chinese claimed, they were deliberately refraining from a full accounting of the conflict.[52] In November 1957, nearly two years after the identified origins of the conflict, Mao was referring to the Soviet Union as an "outstanding example" and the "head" of the socialist camp.[53]

Were this deference entirely a matter of ritual or protocol — which in part it certainly was — its impact on the Chinese Communist system might have been negligible. In fact, however, it was also a reflection of the genuine importance to China of the Soviet model. The influence of this model has been particularly prominent in the organization of the CCP and its conception of its political role. China has had only two significant mass-based political parties, the KMT and the CCP, and both owe their basic organizational structure to Russian advisers who guided their development during the 1920s.[54] The guidelines came from the Soviet Communist party—a hierarchical, disciplined organization based on the principle of democratic centralism that concentrated organizational authority in a small elite at the top. The CCP acquired with this Leninist structure the idea of party dictatorship, the notion that the revolutionary party must ultimately assume dictatorial political power in the name of the proletariat, even though cooperation with other political parties and classes might be

[52] *The Origin and Development of the Differences Between the Leadership of the CPSU and Ourselves,* by the Editorial Departments of *People's Daily* and *Red Flag* (Peking: Foreign Languages Press, 1963), esp. pp. 4–11.

[53] Schram, *The Political Thought of Mao Tse-tung,* op. cit., pp. 435–36.

[54] For discussion and documentation of the Soviet-sponsored organizational development that occurred in both parties, see C. Martin Wilbur and Julie Lien-ying How, eds., *Documents on Communism, Nationalism and Soviet Advisers in China, 1918–1927* (New York: Columbia University Press, 1956), pp. 79–205. Comintern recognition of the Chinese parties' organizational weaknesses in 1921–1922, before Soviet advisers assumed a prominent role in China, is described in Allen S. Whiting, *Soviet Policies in China, 1917–1924* (New York: Columbia University Press, 1954), pp. 87–91.

necessary at earlier stages of the revolution. While the KMT formally retained Sun Yat-sen's goal of constitutional government that would limit its monopoly of power, in practice it too clung to a system of single-party rule. Both party organization and party system in modern China reveal, therefore, the force of Bolshevik organizational patterns.

Moreover, Soviet influence on the institutions of Communist China went far beyond the organization of the CCP itself. It appeared as well in the state structure and administrative practices that emerged after 1949, in the "transmission belt" structure and function of non-Party organizations (primarily those for youth, workers, and women), and in the intimate guiding relationship established by the CCP over all other institutions. This is not to say that the institutionalization of CCP leadership in China has been a direct or permanent copy of Russian experience;[55] it is simply to point out that organizational patterns evolved in Soviet Russia have been the primary model for those constructed by the CCP.

Ideological Influences. Soviet Communism's impact on CCP ideology is far more difficult to assess. On the one hand, the basic ideology is Western in origin and was transmitted to China largely via Soviet Russia. The early leaders of the CCP came independently to a revolutionary commitment that made Marxist-Leninist themes of social transformation and anti-imperialism attractive; but they also accepted, with varying degrees of enthusiasm, Russian authority to interpret the doctrine and prescribe its operative implications. Reluctance to challenge this authority endured into the late 1950's and placed limits on the way in which the Chinese were to formulate their own views. On the other hand, the CCP experienced a degree of physical separation from Moscow and a duration of revolutionary practice before coming to power that permitted it to test, absorb, and in some cases "sinify" the doctrine. Through this process, the doctrine acquired an indigenous

---

[55]For example, the 1954 Constitution of the People's Republic of China contained a number of institutional provisions differing from those in the Soviet Union. See the analysis in Franklin W. Houn, "Communist China's New Constitution," *The Western Political Quarterly,* vol. 8, no. 2 (June 1955), pp. 199–233; and H. Arthur Steiner, "Constitutionalism in Communist China," *American Political Science Review,* vol. 49, no. 1 (March 1955), pp. 1–21.

character, so that its acceptance derived from application to and modification within the Chinese political context, not simply from Russian authority. It is an oversimplification, then, to conclude that Maoisim is *either* a creative, indigenous product *or* only an application to China of a foreign doctrine.[56] It is a blending of both; it is foreign in its origins but has over time been handled by the Chinese with sufficient independence to make it their own.

This view permits us to acknowledge that Soviet Communism did introduce significant new concepts into Chinese politics, without our assuming that all of them were to be observed rigidly or permanently by the Chinese Communists. Some of the areas in which the CCP's historical experience led it to its own particular emphasis and constructions will be discussed in the next section, after referring briefly here to a few of the most influential ideas that came with the acceptance of Marxism-Leninism. Foremost among the latter are the concepts of class struggle, class analysis, and the leading role of the proletariat. Although some of the early Chinese Communists, such as Li Dazhao, were quite receptive to the idea of class struggle, the centrality of class conflict in Marxist analysis was generally a notion foreign to the Chinese comrades that simply had to be learned.[57] Part of the difficulty lay in a political tradition that had emphasized social harmony and restrained social conflict.[58] But even those Chinese whose revolutionary sentiments had led them from images of "harmony" to those of "struggle" found a strict socioeconomic definition of social groups and conflicts unfamiliar. Particularly troublesome was the exalted political role attributed to the urban working class, a class of very small proportions in early modern China. In time, the Chinese Communists became accustomed to analyzing both national and international politics in terms of strug-

[56]By *Maoism* or *Maoist* I mean the ideas revealed in Mao Zedong's writings and revolutionary policies but do not necessarily imply that they constitute a new and distinct theoretical development of Marxism-Leninism. That issue requires for clarification the depth of analysis employed in the sources cited in footnotes 10–12 of Chapter I, this book.

[57]See Meisner, op. cit., pp. 140–46, showing that even Li Dazhao's enthusiasm for class struggle fell significantly short of a truly Marxist class analysis.

[58]See Arthur F. Wright, "Struggle vs. Harmony: Symbols of Competing Values in Modern China," *World Politics,* vol. 6, no. 1 (Oct. 1953), pp. 31–44.

gles and alliances between different classes. They accepted, too, the formal acknowledgment of proletarian leadership in the revolution, and after 1949, they were to grant industrial workers special economic and political privileges. Class analysis is now a fundamental element in Chinese political thinking, although it has clashed frequently with desires for national unity and with the realities of Chinese social structure.

The millennial Marxist vision of a classless society, populated by a new socialist man and based on collective ownership and organization, has also had a profound impact on Chinese Communism. Utopian views of man and society were by no means foreign to China, but this particular utopia contained some novel implications. What Marxism-Leninism foretold was a new society that would be both universal and modern; that is, it would ultimately emerge all over the world and would be based on a postindustrial economy.[59] The doctrine thus broadened the revolutionary struggle to include not only China but all other societies as well; its acceptance encouraged the Chinese to see their revolution as part of a world revolution, to see that the ultimate resolution of class struggle would be on an international rather than simply Chinese dimension. The universalism transmitted by Soviet Communism has never overshadowed Chinese nationalism, but it has given to the present Chinese political system a sense of intimate, reciprocal involvement in the international system that was not characteristic of China in the past.

The Marxist vision also led the CCP to adopt more specific guidelines for the reconstruction of China that were not necessarily called for by national traditions or conditions. It is in this area that the Soviet model has been of immense importance. Marxism-Leninism did not foretell the exact nature of the future society; it simply stated that any given society would move through a socialist stage to the communist ideal, with the new forms revealed only after the revolution. Once the first socialist society had emerged in Russia, however, the requirements of the "socialist road" became concrete. If China were to follow this road, how could it stray from the path already mapped by the Soviet Union, which was acknowledged to be

[59]Cf. Franz Schurmann, *Ideology and Organization in Communist China,* 2nd ed. enl. (Berkeley: University of California Press, 1968), pp. 40–42.

the most advanced socialist country? The Soviet model was crucial to CCP elites, not because the Russians could force them to follow it, but rather because the Soviet Union seemed to provide the only example of how to move toward their ultimate objectives. When the CCP came to power, it simply assumed that socialist construction required such policies as rapid industrialization, centralized economic planning and administration, and the collectivization of agriculture. It decided, in short, to follow the Soviet model, despite the fact that China's economic conditions were quite different from those in Russia following the October Revolution.[60]

In the early years of the People's Republic, therefore, Soviet influence was very prominent. Efforts to implement general features of the Soviet developmental model supplemented the strictures on doctrine and organization absorbed in earlier years. Russian advisers, assistance, plans, blueprints, and texts came in. But present in the system, too, and ultimately more powerful, were the influences of the CCP's own past. The way in which the Chinese Communists had blended the lessons of both Soviet Communism and their own unique national experience led to modification and then rejection of the Soviet model.[61] Since the middle 1950s, Soviet influence in China has receded to a more subtle role reflecting its subordination to the national experience of Chinese Communism.

CCP HISTORY

The historical experience of the CCP is the last topic to be discussed in this survey of the origins of the Chinese political system. As with the previous topics, discussion will be selective, seeking only to identify major trends that have had a pronounced impact on later political patterns and attitudes. After a brief review of key periods in party development,[62]

---

[60]See Schram, *The Political Thought of Mao Tse-tung*, op. cit., pp. 75–76.

[61]See Schurmann, op. cit., esp. pp. 13–15, 33–45, 239–42.

[62]For surveys of pre-1949 CCP history, see Jerome Ch'en, *Mao and the Chinese Revolution* (London: Oxford University Press, 1965); Jacques Guillermaz, *A History of the Chinese Communist Party, 1921–1949* (New York: Random House, 1972); James Pinckney Harrison, *The Long March to Power* (New York: Praeger, 1972); and Richard C. Thornton, *China, The Struggle for Power, 1917–1972* (Bloomington: Indiana University Press, 1973). Many key documents of the 1921–1949 period are translated and analyzed in Conrad Brandt, Benjamin Schwartz, and John K. Fairbank, *A Documentary History of Chinese Communism* (Cambridge, Mass.: Harvard University Press, 1952).

which will be useful for future reference, we will examine some of the elements of CCP political style that grew out of its revolutionary struggles between 1921 and 1949.

The First United Front, 1923–1927. Soon after its First Congress in 1921, the CCP entered into an alliance with the KMT to hasten the conclusion of the "national revolution" against imperialism and the northern warlords. This decision, which was imposed on the CCP by the Comintern against the wishes of some Chinese comrades, led to a United Front in which Communists joined the KMT as individuals and accepted its formal leadership of the alliance while retaining membership in a separate Communist party. The United Front was in effect from 1923 through the summer of 1927, when the KMT expelled the Communists and broke off its contacts with Soviet advisers.[63]

During this period of cooperation with the KMT and heavy-handed direction from Moscow, the CCP began to transform itself from a tiny group of Marxist (or pseudo-Marxist) intellectuals into a mass-based revolutionary organization. Most of its growth and organizational success among workers and peasants came after the May Thirtieth Movement of 1925, which launched a wave of strikes and protests in Chinese cities and set the stage for the KMT's Northern Expedition against the Peking government. Party membership grew from about one thousand in May 1925 to ten thousand at the end of the year, and to nearly fifty-eight thousand by April 1927;[64] trade unions and peasant associations expanded rapidly during the same period, with Communists playing a major role in their growth and activities. Despite Comintern efforts to restrain the most radical tendencies of this upsurge, conservative leaders of the KMT became increasingly concerned about the direction of the alliance. A reaction began with Chiang Kai-shek's assault on the Communists in Shanghai in April 1927, and by the summer of that year the KMT had embarked on a thorough supression of the CCP and its organizational bases. The period ended with a shattering defeat for the United Front

[63]See Conrad Brandt, *Stalin's Failure in China, 1924–27* (Cambridge, Mass.: Harvard University Press, 1958).
[64]Ch'en, op. cit., pp. 100, 116.

policy and a near-catastrophic destruction of Communist supporters.

The Soviet Period, 1928–1934. The rupture of the first United Front left the CCP a fragmented, outlaw party. Its Central Committee continued to operate underground in the cities trying to rebuild the proletarian base, but KMT power easily contained these efforts. The real focus of the movement shifted to the countryside, where small Communist forces survived by virtue of armed support and mobile tactics in relatively isolated areas. Gradually these forces grew and acquired loose territorial bases referred to as soviets. In November 1931 the CCP established the Chinese Soviet Republic, which nominally brought together a number of soviet areas scattered about Central-South China, although one was located in the northwestern province of Shaanxi.[65] The stronghold of the Soviet Republic was the Central Soviet District, consisting of a large block of *xian* in Jiangxi province, where the capital was located and where Mao Zedong was a leading political figure. The fortunes and territories of the CCP shifted frequently during the soviet period. At one point in 1933, party membership had risen to a new high of three hundred thousand.[66] But increasing military pressure from the KMT took its toll. In late 1933, Chiang Kai-shek launched the fifth in a series of campaigns against the Jiangxi Soviet, and by the latter part of 1934 this campaign had forced the Communists to abandon their stronghold and set out on the Long March to Shaanxi.

Although the soviet period culminated in military defeat, it brought major changes to the Communist Revolution. It resolved a bitter intra-party struggle between urban and rural orientations in favor of the latter. After the establishment of the Soviet Republic in 1931, central party organs began to move from Shanghai to Jiangxi, tacitly acknowledging that the CCP's center of gravity was in the countryside. This shift was formalized in early 1935 when Mao Zedong, the foremost proponent of the rural revolutionary strategy, became party leader. Second, the period marked the origins and develop-

[65]Ibid., pp. 153–54, 165–66, 171–72.
[66]John Wilson Lewis, *Leadership in Communist China* (Ithaca, N.Y.: Cornell University Press, 1963), p. 110.

ment of the Chinese Red Army, which was henceforth to be the bulwark of the CCP in its struggle for survival and power. Indeed, the movement became nearly inseparable from its military arm, with territorial influence being chiefly a function of Red Army strength and effectiveness. Virtually all CCP members acquired military experience, while the Red Army itself was thoroughly penetrated by party organization and controls.[67] Finally, these years witnessed the crystallization of Mao's military strategy, in which major emphasis was placed on guerrilla-type units operating from a territorial base area with extensive popular support,[68] and the beginnings of CCP governmental experience. In the Jiangxi Soviet, the Communists had their first opportunities to establish governmental organs and to experiment with various economic and social policies, particularly land policy. These efforts met with mixed results, but the experience gained had considerable influence on later patterns of CCP rule.[69]

The Second United Front, 1935–1945. While the Chinese Communists were on the Long March to Shaanxi, which their first units reached in October 1935 in greatly weakened condition, a second United Front with the KMT was taking shape as a response to growing Japanese pressures on China. Although the CCP had urged resistance to Japan for many years, it was only after 1935 that this slogan acquired concrete political significance. The Comintern's 1935 call for an international united front against fascism, the increasing threat of renewed Japanese advances, and the CCP's removal to an area closer to the North China trouble spots, all made KMT-CCP cooperation a possibility. The path to a new alliance was not easy,

[67]On the origins and early years of the Red Army, see Samuel B. Griffith, II, *The Chinese People's Liberation Army* (New York: McGraw-Hill, 1967), pp. 1–46.

[68]A convenient collection of Mao's military writings is *Selected Military Writings of Mao Tse-tung* (Peking: Foreign Languages Press, 1963). The major works in question date mainly from 1936–1938, when Mao had time to reflect and write on his Jiangxi experiences.

[69]See Ilpyong J. Kim, "Mass Mobilization Policies and Techniques Developed in the Period of the Chinese Soviet Republic," in A. Doak Barnett, ed., *Chinese Communist Politics in Action* (Seattle: University of Washington Press, 1969), pp. 78–98; and James R. Townsend, *Political Participation in Communist China* (Berkeley: University of California Press, 1967), pp. 43–51.

given profound suspicion and hostility on both sides, but after the Sian Incident of December 1936 the groundwork had been laid. With the beginning of full-scale war between China and Japan after July 7, 1937, the second United Front became a reality.[70]

This alliance was significantly different from the first, however, being essentially an armed truce in the interests of anti-Japanese unity. The KMT gave up its campaigns to crush the Communists, while the CCP abolished the Soviet Republic and agreed to regard its areas and armies as formally subordinate to the national government. In fact there was little cooperation between the two parties; there was a loosely observed understanding that the two parties would not go to war and that Communist-controlled territories and forces would retain de facto independence. The CCP used the security thus gained to expand its influence at the expense of both Nationalist and Japanese authorities. In January 1937, Mao's forces occupied the town of Yanan in northern Shaanxi, which was to become the center of a new stable base area known as the Shaanxi (Shaan-Gan-Ning) Border Region. Throughout the Anti-Japanese War, Yanan was not only the capital of Shaan-Gan-Ning, but also the de facto capital of a growing number of other border regions and anti-Japanese bases that accepted Communist leadership. By 1945, according to Communist sources, there were nineteen such areas, most of them in North China but some in the lower Yangtze region and South China as well; the CCP had grown to 1,210,000 members, had armies totaling 910,000 men, and governed areas with a population of 95,500,000.[71] Since CCP strength at the end of the Long March was only a fraction of its Jiangxi peak, the Yanan period was one of truly impressive Communist growth and expansion.

The second United Front was a decisive period in the evolution of Chinese Communism. The remarkable increase in CCP strength that occured between 1937 and 1945 transformed the terms of Chinese politics. Communist forces entered the postwar period still inferior to the Nationalists in numbers and armaments but, for the first time, as genuine competitors for

[70]Van Slyke, op. cit., pp. 48–93.
[71]Townsend, op. cit., p. 52.

national political power. Supporting this growth of raw power was a consolidation of party leadership, in both personnel and techniques, that reflected the maturation of the CCP as an organization. Mao Zedong's rise to leadership in 1935 had not eliminated all his competitors, but in Yanan he discredited or drove out of the party any who might contest his dominance. Through the *zheng-feng* (*cheng-feng*, rectification) campaign of 1942–1944[72] and the decisions of the party's Seventh National Congress in April–June 1945,[73] Mao established his "thought" as the CCP's guide for the application of Marxism-Leninism to China. With the relatively stable political conditions that prevailed in Shaan-Gan-Ning (although not necessarily in other Communist bases), this consolidation of Mao's political and doctrinal authority was translated directly into practice; Maoist methods for educating and disciplining party members, controlling bureaucracy, leading and working with the masses, organizing the economy, and many other tasks were applied systematically and formalized as integral parts of the CCP's political style.[74]

Another development of the 1935–1945 years was the nationalization of the CCP's appeal. During the soviet period, the CCP had retained a basic class orientation, demonstrated in the Central Committee's attempts to build a proletarian party and in the Soviet Republic's land policy which was at times harsh and confiscatory toward the wealthier rural classes. After the emergence of the United Front, the CCP moved toward more moderate economic policies that would permit multiclass support. The focus of the movement became national struggle rather than class struggle, a shift reflected in

[72]For documentation of this campaign, see *Mao's China: Party Reform Documents, 1942–44*, op. cit.

[73]The revised Party Constitution adopted at the Seventh Congress included a specific reference to Mao's thought as the guiding principle of party work. See Brandt, Schwartz, and Fairbank, op. cit., pp. 419, 422. Shortly before the Congress opened, the Central Committee also adopted a "Resolution on Certain Questions in the History of Our Party," which affirmed the rectitude of Mao's political career and scored his various opponents for their errors and deviations. The text is in *Selected Works of Mao Tse-tung* (Peking: Foreign Languages Press, 1965), vol 3, pp. 177–225.

[74]For analysis of major CCP policies in Shaan-Gan-Ning, emphasizing their centrality in the post-1949 Communist system, see Mark Selden, *The Yenan Way in Revolutionary China* (Cambridge, Mass.: Harvard University Press, 1971).

doctrinal statements about the character of the Chinese revolution and in the ardently nationalistic propaganda of the period. The real significance of the second United Front was not, then, meaningful cooperation with the KMT, which was never realized, but rather its impact on the Communist revolution. The United Front was a statment of Communist revolutionary strategy, a strategy that saw the road to power as built on the broadest possible national base rather than on narrow or rigid class lines. It was a strategy of "uniting with all who can be united," and to give meaning to it, the CCP adopted not only nationalistic propaganda but also an operational style that attracted positive support from a broad multi-class base. Superficially, the United Front appeared to suggest cooperation between two parties, each representing a different class base; in fact, the CCP used it to establish itself as the leader of a truly national movement.[75]

The Civil War, 1946–1949. For a brief period after the Japanese surrender in August 1945, the two major contenders for power negotiated, with American mediation, for a peaceful solution to their conflict. The American role was compromised from the first, however, by its past and continuing support for the Nationalist government; while the profound suspicion and hostility between the KMT and CCP made workable agreements unlikely. By 1946, a civil war had begun, raising to an unprecedented military scale the struggle that these two parties had waged for twenty-five years. The Nationalist armies were superior on paper and scored some initial successes, but the Communists soon made evident their superiority in the field. The tide had turned by 1948, and within a year the Nationalist forces were defeated. The KMT retreated to the island of Taiwan and the CCP established its new government on the mainland.

For the CCP, the civil war was yet another military struggle for survival, a campaign fought on a larger scale than ever before but still a continuation of the reliance on armed force that had marked party history since the late 1920s. It was a continuation, too, of the effort to build and lead a national

[75]Van Slyke, op. cit., pp. 99–116.

movement. Of course, the shift from a Japanese foe to a Chinese foe required some sharpening of distinctions among opposing political forces in China. The CCP responded with a more radical land program that drove the rural elite into the ranks of the "enemy"; many Chinese officials and bourgeoisie whose anti-Japanese credentials had been acceptable to the Communists were now on the other side. But despite the inevitable rise of class conflict, actual and impending, the CCP stuck to its themes of a national movement with a multiclass base. The leadership was "proletarian" — that is, the CCP — but the Communists insisted that it was a movement that all Chinese save a few reactionaries and traitors could join.

The pattern of party history, sketched so crudely in these pages, will be a frequent source of reference in later chapters. Additional details will be brought out at times to illuminate specific aspects of post-1949 politics. It is important, however, to emphasize a few salient features of CCP historical experience that shaped the Maoist approach to PRC development. Although they appear less influential since Mao's death, they remain an important part of the CCP's political tradition.

Mobilization and Struggle. The CCP came to power with the conviction that mobilization and struggle are the essence of politics. Until the very end of the revolutionary period, it was a threatened minority movement beset by hostile military forces and a social environment frequently unsympathetic to or uncomprehending of its cause. Nearly every task seemed linked to survival and hence demanded maximum effort and sacrifice, both collectively and individually. Military-type virtues — enthusiam, heroism, sacrifice, and collective effort — acquired great value. Passivity smacked of opposition and was all the more troublesome because it was so natural a response in the traditional political culture of the Chinese peasant.[76] When victory finally came, it was a product in part of successful political mobilization growing out of a wartime struggle for national survival. To the CCP elite, therefore, politics was not simply a matter of peaceful political competition or manage-

[76]See Richard H. Solomon, "On Activism and Activists: Maoist Conceptions of Motivation and Political Role Linking State and Society," *China Quarterly*, no. 39 (July–Sept. 1969), esp. pp. 76–79.

ment of material resources — concentration on either of
which would have yielded the advantage to better-endowed
opponents — but an effort to mobilize and activate human
resources in a crisis situation.

The Mass Line. Closely related to these themes is the party's
"mass line," a fundamental CCP principle that has its origins
in the circumstances faced on the road to power.[77] The mass
line is perhaps the most complicated and pervasive concept in
CCP doctrine. In one dimension it is a method of leadership
that stems from the party's reliance on popular assistance in
its revolutionary base areas. It is a recognition of the fact that
the movement could not be sustained by party members alone
but depended also on the intelligence, food supplies, new
recruits, and even performance of administrative duties that
the non-party masses could provide. Leadership remained a
party prerogative, but leadership could not be effective or
achieve permanent results without mass support.

In a second dimension, the mass line has a control function
with respect to bureaucrats and intellectuals. The Chinese
Communists have been highly sensitive to the bureaucratic-
intellectual tradition in which they have operated, to the excesses and abuses of offical power. Their hostility toward the
traditional offical as representative of a feudalistic and oppressive culture was joined by an innate suspicion of the modern
bureaucrat as well, for the latter represented the growth of
urban and Western influences in China and was all too likely
to be ideologically sympathetic toward the KMT or foreign
powers. The bureaucrat as stereotype, then, was corrupt, aloof
from the masses, self-seeking, politically opportunistic, and
intellectually elitist; it was a stereotype, unfortunately, for
which many real examples could be found. The mass line
evolved in part as a response to these concerns and as an
antidote to the abuse of bureaucratic power within Communist-controlled organizations. By insisting that officials have
contact with the masses, the CCP hoped to uncover abuses and
foster a new type of bureaucrat; by entrusting many adminis-

---

[77]The best description of the empirical conditions fostering the mass line
is in Selden, op. cit. For more general discussion, see Lewis, op. cit., pp. 70–
100; and Townsend, op. cit., pp. 46–64, 72–74.

trative duties to popular groups, it hoped to reduce or dilute the bureaucratic structure as such. Despite the inevitable growth of bureaucracy after 1949, the Maoist tradition within the party has never given up the mass line as a means of controlling the behavior of bureaucrats and intellectuals.

Finally, the mass line is an expression of populism, of identification with and commitment to the welfare of the people. While populist values have been in clear conflict at times with the drive for national economic construction and consolidation of Communist power, they nonetheless have real roots in CCP history. The Chinese Communists spent most of their years before coming into power in intimate association with the peasantry. Although they retained their sense of the harsh realities and priorities of their revolution, they did experience firsthand the conditions of Chinese life that generated so much of the revolutionary impulse in that society. The party unavoidably grew away from this experience after 1949, but mass line exhortations to "eat, live, work, and consult with the masses" remain partly as a symbol of past experience but also as ongoing reminders not to lose touch with the popular needs that are said to legitimize the revolution.

This last dimension of the mass line is directly relevant to Mao Zedong's "rural orientation" referred to earlier. In the soviet period, Mao was the main spokesman for a rural-based revolution, one that could survive and grow in the countryside with the capture of cities postponed until they were surrounded by the rural bases. This was essentially a matter of strategy, advanced in opposition to the party center, which insisted that a socialist revolution called for early conquest of urbanized areas, if not literal emergence from them. But there was more to the rural orientation than questions of tactics and strategy, for Mao recognized early that revolution in an overwhelmingly agrarian society required a revolution in the countryside. The villages were not simply a staging area for proletarian revolution; they were the stronghold of the old society and a primary arena in which revolutionary change must occur.[78] In other words, the mass line necessarily carried

[78]Mao's classic statement on these themes is his 1927 "Report on an Investigation of the Peasant Movement in Hunan," trans. in Brandt, Schwartz, and Fairbank, op. cit., pp. 81–89.

with it a strong orientation toward the peasants, simply because the Chinese Communists could not talk about their popular base or obligations without talking about the peasantry.
In this light, Maoist emphasis on the countryside is not necessarily favoritism for the village over the city. It is rather an
expression of realism: China cannot change in a meaningful
sense unless there is change in the rural areas where the vast
majority of the people live.

Self-Reliance. The idea of self-reliance is a third element of
the Maoist political style that draws strength from historical
experience. The conditions encouraging it were the relative
geographic, economic, and political isolation of Communist
base areas from 1927 on. These areas were generally shut off
from significant contacts with the outside and even with each
other by military and economic blockades; moreover, they
were relatively backward in themselves, being poorly served by
surface and wire communications. Each base area was largely
on its own, depending for survival on its own military and
economic self-sufficiency.

The principle of self-reliance has both national and international implications. On the national scale, it has fostered in
Chinese Communism a preference for local units that are relatively self-sufficient and hold considerable responsibility for
the maximum development of their own resources with a mini-
mum of external assistance. It is a preference for a system with
decentralized features, although decentralization is in some
ways a misleading word, since the party places even greater
emphasis on maintaining the primacy of central authority.
What self-reliance really suggests is a system in which local
units are clearly subject to central control and discipline but
in practice meet their obligations on their own without requiring much central interference or assistance. Whatever the institutional complications might be, however, there is no doubt
that the CCP attaches great value to the development of self-
reliant individuals and units.

Mao was equally firm about the importance of self-reliance
in international affairs. He saw CCP victory in China as due to
its own efforts and resources; foreign assistance, as during the
first United Front, was actually counterproductive. Chinese

views on this question clearly draw on Mao's interpretation of national as well as party experience. They remain sensitive to the way in which a foreign presence may lead to foreign interference and control; they are sensitive, too, to their country's limited capacity for providing material assistance to other countries. Although they welcome international support and will offer it themsleves to other countries and movements with which they sympathize, they still insist that each must rely essentially on its own resources to accomplish its goals.

Education and Will. The most difficult doctrinal problem the Chinese Communists have faced as Marxist-Leninists has been how to create a socialist revolution and build a socialist society in an agrarian country so close to its feudal past. How could this cause succeed in the absence of a proletarian class base? Their answer is that proletarian ideology can be created by education rather than by objective economic conditions. The question emerged in full force after 1927, when the CCP was forced to seek survival in a distinctly nonproletarian setting. Mao responded by building a Red Army, composed of peasants, former bandits, Nationalist soldiers, and other motley elements whose ideological commitment was to be instilled by education. Subsequently, the party applied the same principle to its new peasant and intellectual recruits, to its base-area populations, and ultimately to the Chinese people as a whole.

The Maoists never assumed that the educational road to ideological purity would be easy, and they warned repeatedly (the Cultural Revolution being the best example) that powerful nonproletarian influences in their society can corrupt even those who seem to have been converted. This did not lead them to despair of the possibilities of socialist education, however. Rather, it prompted them to devise techniques of education, indoctrination, and rectification that might be sufficient to overcome these obstacles and threats. The techniques referred to — mass propaganda media, political study, guided small-group discussions, constant criticism and self-criticism — appeared in the soviet period and matured in Yanan. They remain the CCP's basic hope for producing a new socialist society in China in advance of widespread industrialization.

But education is a slow process, and what is instilled by one kind of education can presumably be undone by another. How could education alone, with its time-consuming and academic features, be a workable tool for revolution? Granted it might substitute for class experience, but would it accelerate significantly the revolutionary process? For Mao Zedong, at least, there was another necessary ingredient: human will. Recall here the earlier discussion of mobilization and struggle, the insistence that revolution requires active human effort. For Mao, human will and effort can be the decisive factor in any given situation; they should be guided by ideological understanding, but it is the initial human will to act that is crucial and permits the educational process to work through the testing and application of ideas in practice. The entire history of the CCP, with its struggle and ultimate victory under extremely adverse conditions, reinforced the strength of this conviction.

CONCLUSION

This chapter has emphasized the influence of China's past, the way in which the political tradition, the revolutionary setting, Soviet Communism, and the CCP's own history helped shape the post-1949 system. Perhaps the clearest legacy from the past is the continuing tension between authoritarianism and populism — between tendencies to concentrate power in a small elite with a statist, bureaucratic approach to government and inclinations to distribute throughout society the material, psychic, and political rewards of the revolution. Authoritarianism comes directly from the imperial tradition, reinforced by the crisis of revolution that demanded even stronger and more concentrated authority to cope with domestic crisis and foreign penetration. Soviet Communism and decades of civil war hardened CCP attitudes toward political competition and nourished the CCP's insistence on party dictatorship.

Populism, too, has its roots in the old order, which set peasants apart from the Confucian elite, isolated them from government, and supported a long tradition of popular rebellion. Inherited resentment of elite oppression joined with the new ideology of class conflict and working class leadership, and with the rural-based revolutionary strategy to produce a movement strongly oriented toward mass mobilization and participation. Both authoritarianism and the reaction against it are part of the PRC's inheritance.

The origins of the PRC reveal its link with the past, but linkage is not identity. The Chinese political system of the 1980s promises to be very different from that of the 1960s, despite claims to kinship with Maoism, just as the Maoism of the 1960s had evolved from its Yanan parentage. The contrast between Communist and imperial systems is even stronger, of course. The imperial state was relatively passive, acting largely to maintain the status quo and to restore balance in the wake of human or natural disruptions; aloof and complacent, it kept affairs of state to itself and hoped that society and the external world would do much the same with their concerns. The new state aggressively pursues social change, reaching out to regulate an immense sphere of human activity. It assumes conflict in society, intervenes to control that conflict and demands that citizens lend active support to its interventions. It recognizes the international forces that bear on the nation's destiny and is increasingly involved in efforts to shape them to its own advantage. Whatever the links with the political tradition, the revolution has brought fundamental changes in the content and assumptions of Chinese politics.

CHAPTER III

The Political Framework: Institutions and Policies

THE FRAMEWORK OF CHINESE POLITICS has been in flux since 1949, with repeated upheavals, shifts, and experiments in both institutions and basic policy lines. One can see throughout the influence of certain patterns and issues — some inherited from the revolutionary era, others arising in the course of socialist construction — but their context has changed with each new set of movements and reforms. It is important to emphasize this dynamic, evolving aspect of political structure, partly because it is essential for understanding PRC political history and partly because it reflects the fluid character of Chinese politics in the Maoist era. This chapter provides a general survey of post-1949 institutions and policies, thereby describing the framework within which the political process takes place and introducing issues that will receive closer analysis in subsequent chapters.

POLITICAL INSTITUTIONS

PRC political institutions include three major organizational hierarchies — state, party, and army — plus a variety of mass organizations that provide additional links between these hierarchies and the citizenry. All have changed frequently since 1949, internally and in their relationship to each other, making it difficult to generalize about their roles. Broadly speaking, the CCP provides overall political and ideological leadership, the state attends to formal administration, the army is responsible for national security and military affairs, and the mass organizations mobilize the population. But even this broadest and most superficial of generalizations is invalid for the Cultural Revolution and accurate only with qualifications for some other periods. The Maoist era was one in which "politics took command" of structure, sacrificing institutional stability to the demands of political struggle and change. Nonetheless, the most important units must be identified to make sense of the qualitative changes that deservedly command more attention.

State. The PRC's initial state structure, from 1949 to 1954, was a temporary administrative system that relied heavily on regional military units to oversee reconstruction and early reforms; the Chinese People's Political Consultative Conference (CPPCC), a holdover from the pre-1949 United Front, served as the nominal national representative authority. A state constitution was adopted in 1954, establishing a centralized government to administer the transition to socialism. Soon, however, the Great Leap Forward (1957–1960) brought important changes, as decentralization and CCP assertiveness weakened central state organs, while the introduction of people's communes in 1958 created new patterns of local administration. The Cultural Revolution (1966–1969) further unsettled the 1954 system and, in effect, abolished the existing constitution. State structure remained in limbo, with no formal guidelines in effect, until a second constitution was adopted in 1975. The 1975 constitution incorporated many Cultural Revolution principles, significantly altering the previous structure. However, in March 1978 another new constitution was adopted which was somewhat closer to the 1954 model. The discussion that follows describes the 1978 constitution (see Chart I).

According to the constitution, the National People's Congress (NPC) is the "highest organ of state power." It is a large (3,459 deputies for the March 1978 session), representative body, consisting of deputies elected by provincial-level congresses and army units. It has a term of five years and is to meet once a year. However, the constitution allows NPC meetings to be advanced or postponed, the latter happening frequently; there was no meeting of the NPC between February 1965 and

CHART I. *State Structure of the PRC, 1978 Constitution*

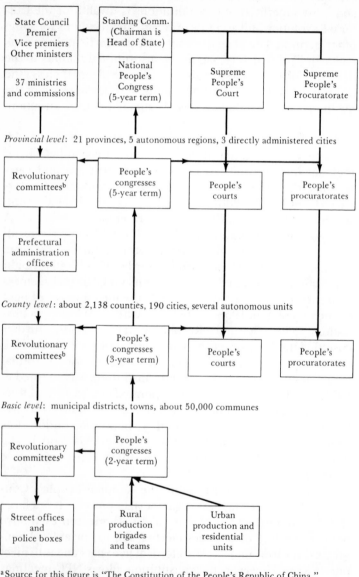

Provincial level: 21 provinces, 5 autonomous regions, 3 directly administered cities

County level: about 2,138 counties, 190 cities, several autonomous units

Basic level: municipal districts, towns, about 50,000 communes

[a] Source for this figure is "The Constitution of the People's Republic of China," adopted March 5, 1978, by the First Session of the Fifth National People's Congress, text in *Peking Review* (no. 11, March 11, 1978), pp. 5-14.

[b] Name changed to "people's governments" in June 1979.

January 1975, for example. In any case, NPC meetings are short and ceremonial, hearing and then ratifying major reports and documents presented to them. The NPC symbolizes the regime's legitimacy and popular base, publicizes major events in the life of the nation, and honors the politically favored deputies elected to it, but the congress is not in practice a "highest organ" of political power. That power resides in the CCP, with the state constitution acknowledging party leadership over the state.

The NPC's extensive formal powers of legislation, amendment, and so forth are exercised in fact by its Standing Committee, a much smaller permanent body which nonetheless remains essentially a clearing house for the ratification and issuance of state decisions. The Chairman of the Standing Committee serves as the PRC's ceremonial head of state. The 1954 constitution had a Chairman of the PRC government as a whole, a position held by Mao (1954–1959) and then by Liu Shaoqi (1959–1966), both men using it as part of their power base. Both constitutions instituted after the Cultural Revolution have omitted it, presumably to avoid any possible challenge to the Chairmanship of the CCP.

The State Council is the chief administrative organ of government. It includes the Premier—Zhou Enlai (Chou En-lai) from 1954–76, Hua Guofeng (Hua Kuo-feng) since 1976—several vice premiers, and the ministers who head the ministries and commissions of the central government. The State Council consists almost entirely of high-ranking party members. As translator of party decisions into state decrees, with administrative control over governmental actions at all levels, it is the true center of state power.

The constitution entrusts exercise of judicial authority to a Supreme People's Court at the central level and to unspecified local and special people's courts. All courts are formally responsible to the congresses (or the NPC Standing Committee in the case of the Supreme People's Court) at their respective levels; however the constitution also provides that higher-level courts supervise the work of lower levels. A distinctive feature of Chinese courts is the selection of mass representatives, known as "assessors," who participate in judicial hearings and decisions. The procuratorates, also formally responsible to congresses at each level, are supervisory, investigative, and prosecutory bodies. These organs were an important part of the legal system of the 1950s but not mentioned in the 1975 constitution. Their restoration in 1978, with expanded sections on the court system as well, coincides with the renewed interest in "socialist legality" that has marked the post-Mao period. Even so, the actual operation of the PRC's formal legal organs is rather obscure and they appear to be firmly controlled by the political-administrative hierarchy.

Local state structure consists of three formal governmental levels — provincial, county, and basic — plus a variety of units between and beneath them. Provincial-level units include twenty-one regular provinces, five "autonomous regions," and three large cities (Peking, Shanghai and Tianjin (Tientsin) plus their surrounding areas (see Appendix A). These units, all of which are directly under the central government administration, contain more than 2,300 county-level governments, most of which carry the name of county *(xian);* however, the county level also includes close to 200 municipalities plus some autonomous *xian* and prefectures. Subdivisions of county-level units form the basic level of the structure; these include about 50,000 rural people's communes, districts within cities, and towns. Before the communes were established in 1958, the basic-level rural unit was the *xiang* (township). Many other terms for minority areas and special administrative units have been used over the years since 1949.[1] However, the 1978 constitution simplifies the terminology, referring only to those units mentioned here and to the prefecture (a special administrative office of provincial governments). The word *autonomous* designates a unit heavily populated by non-Chinese minorities, holding constitutional rights to preserve certain aspects of minority culture and to address the special needs of its peoples. They remain fully subject to higher-level administrative control, however.[2]

Each local government unit has two main organs: a repre-

---

[1] For a detailed discussion of pre-Cultural Revolution administrative divisions, see A. Doak Barnett, *Cadres, Bureaucracy and Political Power in Communist China* (New York: Columbia University Press, 1967), pp. 107–20, 313–24.

[2] For thorough analysis of minority regions and policy, see June Teufel Dreyer, *China's Forty Millions* (Cambridge: Harvard University Press, 1976).

sentative body known as the people's congress and an administrative body known as the revolutionary committee; the
administrative organs were called people's councils under the
1954 constitution but were replaced by revolutionary committees during the Cultural Revolution. Local people's congresses, like the NPC at the national level, meet briefly and
irregularly and have little real power. It is the revolutionary
committees, like their central counterpart State Council, that
manage governmental affairs at their respective levels. They
are elected by their congresses, but that election, as well as all
their actions, are subject to approval by higher levels and
ultimately by the State Council. The decentralization promoted by the Maoist approach from about 1957 on is a conditional grant of powers to lower levels that does not alter the
constitutional authority of the central government over the
entire administrative structure.

From the citizen's point of view, the most important units
are those beneath the basic level of government. These include production brigades and production teams in the rural
communes; and urban districts, residential units, factories,
schools, and so forth in the cities. All of these are political as
well as production and/or residential units. They elect deputies to basic-level congresses — the only direct elections in
which all citizens participate, since deputies to higher congresses are chosen by congresses of the next lower level. (Both
direct and indirect elections in China generally consist of approval of a slate of candidates worked out in preelection consultation under party leadership.) They are also units which
have some kind of organization for management of their internal affairs and give citizens opportunities for participation in
discussion of matters relating to daily work and living conditions. Moreover, the citizen is most likely to encounter the
government directly in the administrative offices and police
stations established by basic-level governments within these
units.[3]

[3]Citizen participation in basic-level government, its subordinate units, and
in mass organizations, is analyzed in James R. Townsend, *Political Participation
in Communist China* (Berkeley: University of California Press, 1967), pp. 103–
73. Reforms in 1979 extended direct election to the county level and changed
the name "revolutionary committees" to "people's governments."

Party. The CCP constitution adopted at the Eleventh Party Congress in August 1977 sets forth a pattern of organization roughly parallel to that of the state (see Chart II). The positioning of some form of party organization alongside most state organs strengthens CCP leadership of the political system by encouraging institutional supervision and the assignment of many party members to overlapping roles in both hierarchies. Whatever formal powers a state organ holds, it is the party organ at the corresponding level that is the politically authoritative voice. The party constitution stipulates that all state organs, army units, and other organizations must accept the absolute leadership of the party.

The 1977 party constitution, like its state counterpart, defines the representative congresses or general members' meetings as the "leading bodies" at their respective levels. However, as in the state system, the committees elected by these congresses — or the standing committees and secretaries elected by the full committees — exercise congressional powers and become the de facto seat of party power at their respective levels. The constitution states that the National Party Congress shall be convened every five years and that it may be convened early or postponed. This is a realistic provision, historically speaking, since party congresses have been rare and irregular; the Seventh Party Congress met in 1945, the Eighth in 1956, the Ninth in 1969, the Tenth in 1973, and the Eleventh in 1977. Despite their infrequency, meetings of a National Party Congress are important events. Each of the last five has produced a new constitution and elected a new and significantly altered Central Committee.

The Central Committee (CC) acts for the Congress and is the most important representative body in the PRC. It is identified by the number of the congress that elected it, with its full meetings known as "plenums." Thus, the first full meeting of the CC elected by the Eleventh Congress was the First Plenum of the Eleventh CC. Plenums meet irregularly, perhaps once a year on the average, although up to four years have elapsed between some plenums. However, because most CC members are high-ranking officials who hold important positions in Peking or the provincial capitals, many partial or informal meeting

CHART II. *CCP Structure, 1977 Constitution*

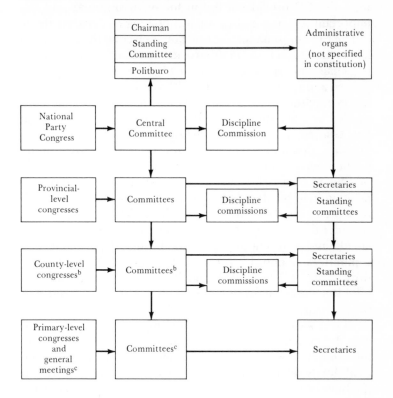

[a]County-level organizations include congresses and committees at the regimental level and above in the PLA.

[b]Primary-level organizations include branches, general branches, or committees set up in factories, mines, communes, offices, schools, shops, neighborhoods, PLA companies, and other such units.

Source: This chart is based on the Constitution adopted by the Eleventh National Congress of the CCP on August 18, 1977, text in *Peking Review*, no. 36 (September 2, 1977), pp. 16–22.

of CC members occur.[4] Through plenums and other meetings, the CC provides a forum for discussing and ratifying important policies, if not actually initiating or deciding them.

The CC's most important function is electing the party's top leadership, namely the Politburo, its Standing Committee, and the chairman and vice chairman of the CC. The Politburo elected at the First Plenum of the Eleventh CC in August 1977 had twenty-three regular and three alternate members and was headed by a Standing Committee of five members (Chairman Hua Guofeng plus the 4 vice chairmen). The Politburo and its Standing Committee exercise all functions and powers of the CC between plenums and constitute the supreme political elite of China. They are headed, of course, by the chairman, a position held by Mao Zedong from the 1930s until his death in September·1976, when he was succeeded by Hua.

Under the 1956 constitution, a body known as the Secretariat administered central party work through departments and committees responsible for particular lines of state and party work. The 1973 and 1977 constitutions, influenced by Cultural Revolution attacks on bureaucracy, omitted reference to the Secretariat. The latter states only that: "Party committees at all levels should set up their working bodies in accordance with the principles of close ties with the masses and of structural simplicity and efficiency." Despite this virtual silence, the CCP clearly retains its powerful central bureaucracy. Through this bureaucracy, the Politburo supervises execution of day-to-day party work, from the provincial level down to the primary party units that are established in each and every unit of Chinese society.[5]

[4]An extremely useful guide to, and analysis of, such meetings is Kenneth Lieberthal, *A Research Guide to Central Party and Government Meetings in China, 1949–1975* (White Plains, N.Y.: International Arts and Sciences Press, 1976).

[5]A CIA reference aid (CR 77–13125, September 1977) lists the following agencies under CC/Politburo direction: General Office (presumably responsible for central coordination); Organization Department (for personnel administration); United Front Work Department; Propaganda Department; International Liaison Department (for relations with other communist parties); Military Commission; Party School; Bureau for Translating Works of Marx, Engels, Lenin, Stalin, and Mao; New China News Agency; Broadcasting Affairs Administrative Bureau; *Red Flag* [*Hongqi* (*Hung Ch'i*)]; *People's Daily* [*Renmin Ribao* (*Jen-min Jih-pao*)]; *Peking Daily*] [*Beijing Ribao* (*Pei-ching Jih-pao*)]; *Kwangming Daily* [*Guangming Ribao* (*Kuang-ming Jih-pao*)]. *Red Flag* is the CC's theoretical journal, *People's Daily* its offical newspaper. *Peking Daily* and *Kwangming Daily* are two other leading national newspapers.

The "organizational principle" of the entire party structure, according to the 1977 constitution and its predecessors, is "democratic centralism." Democracy requires that all "leading bodies" be elected by their members or congresses, report to those members and congresses, and listen to their opinions and criticisms. Centralism requires "unified discipline" within the whole party. "The individual is subordinate to the organization, the minority is subordinate to the majority, the lower level is subordinate to the higher level, and the entire party is subordinate to the Central Committee." Centralism is also evident in the provision that congresses are convened by their committees and that the convening of all local congresses and committees must be approved by higher party organizations.

The 1977 constitution contains strong language on the necessity of maintaining party discipline, and its supporting documents were full of criticism of factional activities. The most concrete constitutional sign of this urge to eradicate the factionalism that engulfed the CCP during and after the Cultural Revolution is the establishment of "commissions for inspecting discipline" at the county and all higher levels of party organization. The commissions are to strengthen education about discipline, check on its observance, and struggle against violations of it. Formal election is by party committees at the level in question, but one may assume that the commissions will be an integral and potent part of the centralized administrative organs of the CCP. They appear to be similar to the Control Commissions authorized by the 1956 constitution but eliminated from the 1969 and 1973 constitutions; if so, they represent another sign of the partial return since 1976 to the administrative system of the 1950s.

Army. The People's Liberation Army (PLA) is the third major arm of national political structure in China. From its founding in the late 1920s until 1949, PLA organization was virtually inseparable from party organization and held major governmental responsibilities in the areas under CCP control. Since 1949, the PLA has continued to perform a variety of nonmilitary functions, including party recruitment and training, economic construction, and education. During the early reconstruction years (1949–1954) and the Cultural Revolution it also assumed important administrative powers. Moreover, the salience of internal and external security issues in Chinese politics has placed the PLA, willingly or unwillingly, close to the center of many national policy debates. Its support for a particular policy has been decisive at times, as in 1967 when it resisted further radicalization of the Cultural Revolution or in 1976 when it supported Hua Guofeng's move against the Gang of Four.

The PLA includes all of China's military forces. Its exact size is unknown but probably approaches 4 million; one recent estimate is 3.7 million, with over 3 million in ground forces and the remainder divided among the other service arms — air force, navy, armor, artillery, second artillery (strategic missiles), engineers, railway engineers, and telecommunications.[6] In other words, the PLA is largely a ground army, divided between main force units and regional forces (see Chart III). The main forces, with about two-thirds of total PLA strength, are under direct central command and include most of the other service arm units; they are responsible for the PLA's national defense and strategic missions. The regional forces are controlled through the eleven military regions (subdivided into twenty-eight military districts);[7] they are responsible for internal and border security, for the provision of garrisons for local defense and a reserve pool for training, and for recruitment into the main forces. Regional forces also provide PLA direction of the militia and the Production and Construction Corps, the latter being paramilitary units engaged in both border defense and large-scale economic activities in key frontier regions.

The militia includes three organizational levels.[8] The armed militia (about seven to nine million) have the most advanced

[6]Harvey W. Nelson, *The Chinese Military System: An Organizational Study of the Chinese People's Liberation Army* (Boulder: Westview Press, 1977), pp. 1–2, 227–28. Nelson offers an excellent general analysis of the PLA; see also Jencks cited in Chart III.

[7]The 11 military regions in the mid-1970s were Shenyang, Beijing (Peking), Jinan (Tsinan), Nanjing, Wuhan, Fuzhou (Fuchou), Guangzhou (Canton), Kunming, Chengdu (Ch'engtu), Lanzhou (Lanchou) and Xinjiang (Sinkiang). There were 13 military regions until about 1969, but the Inner Mongolia [Nei Monggul] and Tibet regions were then absorbed into adjoining regions. The military districts were based on the 26 provinces and autonomous regions, two of which were subdivided to create the total of 28 districts.

[8]Nelson, op. cit., pp. 22–23.

CHART III. *Military Structure*

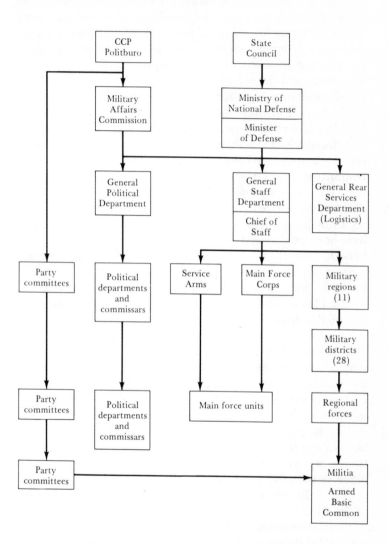

Source: Adapted from Harlan Jencks, "The Politics of Chinese Military Development, 1945–1977" (Ph.D. diss., University of Washington, 1978), chap. VI.

arms and training, the most regular local defense duties, and
are the most ready to supplement the PLA in time of need. The
basic militia (fifteen to twenty million) have received some
military training but are not armed and not engaged in regular
duties. The common militia may number one hundred million
or more but are a very irregular and poorly trained force. The
PLA and local party committees have shared control of the
militia, and there have been frequent shifts and controversy in
the balancing of this control over the years since 1949. The
PLA has tended to favor a compact and highly trained militia
integrated with the military structure; whereas party committees have supported the idea of a larger mass militia more
responsive to political controls. PLA fears of the politicized
mass militia were confirmed in the early 1970s when the Gang
of Four (the four leading "radicals" purged by Hua in October
1976) began to develop new urban armed militia that could
have been used — and apparently almost *were* used in September–October 1976 — for armed support of one party faction
against another. The purge of the radicals was probably followed by strengthed PLA control over milita units.

The PLA is subordinate administratively to the Ministry of
National Defense within the State Council and is headed by the
Minister of Defense. However, the 1978 state constitution asserts that the PLA (including field armies, regional forces, and
milita) is led by the CCP and that the Chairman of the CC is
the commander of the armed forces. Party leadership of the
PLA rests mainly on two structures: the Military Affairs Commission of the CC and the system of political departments
within the PLA. The Military Affairs Commission has always
been one of the most important of the party's central administrative organs; like other such organs, it is not mentioned by
name in the 1977 party constitution, but it has held general
responsibility for setting military policy throughout the history
of the PRC.

Political departments are a regular part of each PLA unit's
general headquarters down to the division level and are represented by a political office in the regiment and political officers
at battalion, company, and platoon levels. Thus a political
commissar (or political officer at lower levels) works alongside
the commanding officer of every army headquarters or unit,

with responsibility for implementing CCP policies and carrying out educational programs among the troops. Political departments and their commissars are not subordinate to the military commanders in their units, but rather to the CCP organizational network. Their chain of command within the army ascends through higher political departments to the General Political Department and the Military Affairs Commission. At the same time, each is responsible to the unit's CCP committee, which provides further political leadership to the party members who constitute a high proportion of PLA personnel. The party committee will normally include the three key figures in a PLA unit — military commander, political commissar, and party secretary; in many cases, one man fills more than one of these roles.

The central PLA command includes the General Political Department supervising the hierarchy of political departments and commissars; the General Rear Services Department which is responsible for logistical support; and the General Staff Department, headed by the chief of staff, which controls the main force and regional units. The chief of staff has been one of the most vulnerable positions in top-level PRC leadership, with at least eight changes in the post since 1949; in contrast, only two men have held the party chairmanship (Mao and Hua) or the premiership (Zhou and Hua). The chief of staff appears to experience in acute form the general PLA problem of answering to both military-administrative and political demands. At the same time, there is no clear or simple division between political and military lines within the PLA. All high PLA commanders are party members, most older party leaders have had military experience, and the close association between the CCP and the PLA has been in place for decades. Although the PLA has distinct military interests that conflict at times with other priorities, its close integration with the party prohibits generalizations about sharp divisions between the organizations. Both politicization and military professionalism are part of PLA experience; neither theme alone explains its complex and influential role in PRC politics.

Mass Organizations. Chinese political structure also includes many mass organizations that mobilize ordinary citizens and that supplement and support the three dominant institutions of party, state, and army. In general, mass organizations are national in scale and have a hierarchy of units extending downward from the central level to a mass membership defined by a common social or economic characteristic, for example, youth, students, women, workers, or other occupational groups. These organizations play a key role in implementing the party's mass line of "coming from the masses and going to the masses." They provide a sounding board for popular opinions, channel representatives into state and party structure, and mobilize support for CCP policies from different segments of the population. In some cases, they perform administrative and service functions for the groups they represent.

The most important mass organization before the Cultural Revolution was the Communist Youth League (CYL). During the 1950s and early 1960s, the CYL was responsible for leadership over all youth activities and other youth organizations, was a major source of new recruits for the CCP, and generally assisted in the basic-level implementation of all party policies. Other important mass organizations in the period before the Cultural Revolution included the Young Pioneers, for children aged nine to fifteen (seven to fifteen since 1965); the All-China Women's Federation; the All-China Federation of Trade Unions; and a variety of associations for specialized occupational and professional groups. Closely related were the "democratic parties," a collective designation for eight minor political parties that cooperated with the Communist-led United Front of the late 1940s and continued to operate after 1949, in a sharply limited status, by virtue of their acceptance of CCP leadership.

All of these mass organizations were suspended during the Cultural Revolution. They were replaced by Red Guards (mainly student organizations) and "revolutionary rebels" (mainly organizations of workers and peasants), which were localized popular organizations that played a vigorous, militant, and sometimes independent role in the course of the Cultural Revolution. Despite their prominence in the early stages of that movement, their evident strength in the major cities, and their close ties with some Maoist leaders, Red

Guards and "rebels" never established themselves as national organizations and were disbanded in the later stages of the Cultural Revolution.

The mass organizations began to revive after 1969. By the early 1970s, the CYL, Women's Federation, Trade Union Federation, and Young Pioneers were reorganizing, as were some of the professional associations. Rebuilding was slow, however, suggesting that these organizational forms remained controversial. Following the fall of the Gang, which was blamed for "wreaking havoc" on mass organizations, reactivation accelerated, and national congresses of the CYL, Women's Federation, and Trade Union Federation were planned for late 1978.[9] The professional associations became prominent again and even the "democratic parties" — which had been portrayed in the Cultural Revolution as strongholds for China's "bourgeois intellectuals" — received some mention.[10] The revival of these organizations is one of the clearest signs that the post-Mao leadership favors a more highly institutionalized structure than that associated with the Cultural Revolution decade.

This brief review of political structure has identified the PRC's principal institutions and major changes in them since 1949. A survey of post-1949 periods, campaigns and policies puts structural change in a fuller context and shows how revolutionary politics have resisted tendencies toward institutionalization. From 1949 through 1976, debate among Chinese elites centered on the direction, timing, and pace of change, with campaigns and development policies the main reference points. Maoist insistence on "continuing the revolution" was sometimes actively hostile toward institutionalization; a more conservative position sometimes argued that the time for institutionalization had arrived but stopped short of defending the

[9]See "Mass Organizations Reactivated," *Peking Review*, no. 20 (May 19, 1978), pp. 10–13; *Peking Review* is cited hereafter as *PR*.

[10]In a December 1977 speech to the Standing Committee of the CPPCC — the united front organization that disappeared during the Cultural Revolution — Ye Jianying (Yeh Chien-ying) noted the CCP's desire "to exist side by side with the democratic parties for a long time to come, exercise mutual supervision and bring their initiative into play to serve socialism;" the phrasing is similar to party statements of the 1950s. See *PR*, no. 1 (January 6, 1978), p. 14.

sanctity of institutions as such. It has only been since Mao's death in 1976 that Chinese leaders have been more openly supportive of institutionalization. The survey that follows is, therefore, much closer to the real framework and substance of Chinese politics that any description of institutions is.[11]

RECONSTRUCTION, 1949–1952

The CCP came to power in 1949 with good reason for confidence. The Red Army had inflicted a decisive military defeat on the Nationalist forces, producing for the first time in decades a Chinese government that did not face the threat of large-scale armed opposition within its mainland territory. The party was disciplined and experienced by its long years of struggle, including considerable practice in administration of large areas of rural China. Its political authority was solid for a new revolutionary regime, partly due to positive support generated by its nationalist and reformist programs — particularly among youth and intellectuals and within the areas in which it had operated — and partly due to its demonstrated military and political effectiveness which brought widespread acceptance, if not support, from a population very weary of strife and uncertainty. These conditions stimulated high hopes for the rapid emergence of a China, in which the citizen might find increased opportunity as well as national respect. For a variety of reasons, however, the new system was to take shape more slowly and with much more turmoil than these factors would suggest.

The Sino-Japanese War, the civil war, Russian confiscation of industrial equipment in Manchuria, and the collapse of KMT governmental authority had left a shattered and inflation-ridden economy. For the first few years, therefore, the Communists concentrated on restoring plants, production, and transportation facilities and on bringing inflation and governmental revenues under control. By the end of 1952, eco-

---

[11]This survey focuses on national policies, excluding discussion of their different timing and impact in localities. In fact, the "view from the center" seldom represents reality for all China at a given time. An excellent study of local implementation and modification of central policies is Ezra Vogel, *Canton Under Communism: Programs and Politics in a Provincial Capital,* 1949–1968 (Cambridge, Mass.: Harvard University Press, 1969).

nomic reconstruction was basically completed, with production levels restored in the main to peak prewar levels.[12] While it was in progress, however, the CCP had little choice but to postpone its plans for the socialization of the economy.

A second major problem was that the CCP was simply not prepared in 1949 to establish direct control throughout the political system. Although its national leadership was visible and unquestioned, it did not possess the resources to staff all posts necessary for carrying out its objectives. Extensive experience in rural administration, much of it under wartime conditions, was inadequate training for the varied and complicated tasks faced in reconstruction of the entire country; many party members were illiterate and unaccustomed to urban life, let alone its administration. Yet even if the quality of party membership had been better suited to its new responsibilities, its numbers were insufficient. KMT resistance had collapsed so quickly from late 1948 on that Communist forces had acquired large areas that were politically unassimilated. Despite rapid recruitment, the CCP could not consolidate its political control immediately. To deal with this situation, it adopted a dual strategy of institutional temporizing and popular mobilization.

In the realm of governmental institutions, the new leaders accepted temporary solutions, permitting many existing arrangements and officials to stand, albeit without any guarantee of permanence. Thus, the central government functioned under the nominal authority of the CPPCC, with many nonparty members within the United Front assigned to high positions. Six large administrative regions were established for the country, each coinciding with a military region so that the pattern of military conquest flowed naturally into a decentralized system of regional governments based on a combination of civil and military authority. At lower levels many former officials remained in office with local party organs playing a relatively discreet role. In short, the CCP simply postponed the creation

---

[12]See the discussion in W. W. Rostow, *The Prospects for Communist China* (New York: Wiley and the Technology Press, 1954), pp. 237–54.

of a permanent governmental structure until its political control was consolidated. It used the interim period to build up its organizational strength, while at the same time trying to weed out unreliable officials and party members. Much of this basic political work was accomplished in the 1949–1952 period, although the new state structure was not established until 1954.

Political Mobilization. While economic reconstruction and political consolidation delayed establishment of a socialist system, encouraging many nonparty intellectuals, businessmen, overseas Chinese, and former officials to commit themselves to the People's Republic, there was no delay in efforts to mobilize the population. During the earlier course of the revolution under both Communist and non-Communist leadership, many groups in Chinese society had experienced political mobilization, a term which denotes the process by which resources — in this case, human resources — are made available for use by political authorities. Yet this mobilization had been partial and sporadic in terms of Chinese society as a whole and was based on a level of socioeconomic development that made it difficult to sustain. The population in 1949 was overwhelmingly rural, illiterate, and poorly served by modern transportation and communications. Traditional avoidance of external concerns and demands remained strong in the villages. In areas under their control, the Communists had proven their ability to combat these difficulties by promoting their programs through intensive face-to-face contact, but prior to 1949 only a minority of the population was so affected. Identification with the nationalist mobilization against Japan had given the CCP substantial legitimacy beyond its own areas, which assisted greatly the establishment of its authority, but there was no guarantee that popular energies could be similarly employed in socialist construction. Accordingly, the new leaders decided that a thoroughgoing mobilization to support political consolidation and preliminary social reforms must precede institutionalization of the new system.

The primary vehicle for this task was a series of mass movements, each aimed at the twin goals of attacking a particular political or social issue and mobilizing popular resources under CCP leadership. The land reform movement, begun earlier in "liberated" areas but carried out throughout China in 1950–1952, established peasants' associations to redistribute the land and to smash the power and status of the landlord class. A campaign for "implementation of the marriage law" began in 1950, aiming at reform of the traditional marriage system and the prevailing inequality of women in all spheres of social life. "Resist America-Aid Korea," a movement in progress throughout the Korean War of 1950–1953, worked to support the Chinese war effort and arouse anti-American sentiments. In 1951 the CCP carried out a "suppression of counterrevolutionaries" campaign to eradicate remnants of armed resistance and other enemies of the regime. A "three anti" movement (against "corruption, waste, and bureaucracy" in government offices) in the winter of 1951–1952 reviewed and disciplined officials, both party and nonparty, who failed to meet CCP standards. A subsequent "five anti" movement (against businessmen allegedly engaged in "bribery, tax evasion, theft of state property, cheating on government contracts, and stealing state economic secrets") drastically reduced the economic resources and political status of the urban middle class. In the "thought reform of intellectuals" campaign, all higher intellectuals underwent challenge, criticism, and self-examination in which their basic beliefs were tested for loyalty to the new order.

These campaigns followed in rapid succession, involving almost every citizen in some way. None of the specific issues was permanently resolved (each campaign was to be renewed or modified in later ones), and the impact on the people was mixed. For some, the movements brought upward mobility and a new sense of involvement in political action; for others, they brought personal losses, uncertainty, and fear, for there were excesses and an element of calculated and spontaneous terror, particularly in the movements for land reform and suppression of counterrevolutionaries. These early mass movements nonetheless contributed heavily to Communist political consolidation through the expansion of mass organizations, the establishment of propaganda networks, the recruitment of new activists and party members, the elimination of opponents, and the initiation of new social relationships. Later events cast doubt on the thoroughness of the mobilization achieved, but in this area, too, the CCP achieved something of fundamental importance by surpassing previous levels of mobilization and redirecting it from predominantly nationalist goals to those of radical social and economic change. From the CCP's point of view, the way was prepared for socialist construction.[13]

THE FIRST FIVE-YEAR PLAN, 1953–1957

The First Five-Year Plan (FFYP), officially in effect from 1953 through 1957, was not made public until 1955 and was to undergo a profound reappraisal before its conclusion. Despite this evidence of irresoluteness, which is vital to an appreciation of later events, it is important to emphasize that the FFYP years constitute a distinctive phase in the history of the People's Republic. Generally the middle 1950s was a period of rapid economic development along the lines of the Soviet model, accompanied by a trend toward moderation and institutionalization in political life relative to the reconstruction era.

The FFYP's concentration on industrial development, especially heavy industry, was its most pronounced characteristic.[14] To achieve the control of economic resources necessary for massive industrial investment, the leaders moved quickly to establish centralized and planned direction of the entire economy. Private industrial and commercial operations were eliminated, except for the smallest entrepreneurs, by transforming them into cooperatives or joint state-private enterprises in which state control was paramount and by setting up state enterprises in key sectors. Rationing and quotas for state purchase and supply of major agricultural products controlled

[13]A useful collection of articles dealing with most topics covered in this section is A. Doak Barnett, *Communist China: The Early Years, 1949–55* (New York: Praeger, 1964).

[14]For an official description of the Plan, and its first published exposition, see Li Fuchun (Li Fu-ch'un), "Report on the First Five-Year Plan" (July 5–6, 1955), in Harvard University, Center for International Affairs and East Asian Research Center, *Communist China, 1955–1959: Policy Documents with Analysis* (Cambridge, Mass.: Harvard University Press, 1965), pp. 42–91; this documentary collection is cited hereafter as *Communist China, 1955–1959.*

consumption and guaranteed extraction of resources from the agricultural sector to support state investment. The CCP also had plans for agricultural collectivization, which moved slowly from 1952 to 1955. From late 1955 on, however, following an important statement by Mao in July of that year,[15] the pace of collectivization accelerated. By the end of 1956 virtually all agricultural households were in collectives, and the socialization of the economy was essentially complete (see Table I). The economic results of FFYP efforts, which were assisted by Soviet aid in the most critical construction projects, were impressive. Estimates of average annual growth in the national product for 1952–1957 range from a low of 5.6 percent to a high official Communist report of 9 percent; even the lower estimates place China high in international rankings of economic growth for this period.[16] The weak point in the Plan was agriculture, where production increases were probably only slightly ahead of population growth.[17] Since agriculture was a major drag on average growth rates, industrial gains were obviously much greater than suggested by the above figures.

A number of significant political and social trends accompanied rapid industrialization. The state apparatus established in 1954 assumed direction of the economy and developed as a highly centralized and bureaucratized structure; the central economic and planning ministries became particularly powerful organs in the new system. The party and Youth League were recruiting heavily to meet demands for more officials and cadres. Urban population and the industrial labor force grew rapidly, as did the number of students (particularly those training in scientific and technical fields) in educational institutions. Expansion and improvements were also notable in transportation, communications, publications, and public

[15]Mao, Zedong, "The Question of Agricultural Cooperation" (July 31, 1955), in *Communist China, 1955–1959*, pp. 94–105.

[16]For citation and discussion of various estimates of growth, see Ta-chung Liu, "Economic Development of the Chinese Mainland, 1949–1965," in Ping-ti Ho and Tang Tsou, eds., *China in Crisis*, vol. 1 (Chicago: University of Chicago Press, 1968), esp. pp. 617, 625–27.

[17]Choh-Ming Li, *Economic Development of Communist China: An Appraisal of the First Five Years of Industrialization* (Berkeley: University of California Press, 1959), pp. 71–74.

health and sanitation. The FFYP was, in brief, a period of real modernization.[18]

With increasing emphasis on economic growth and material progress, some of the political tensions of the early years began to recede. Mass campaigns became more oriented toward increasing production. Revived drives against counterrevolutionaries and "bourgeois" intellectuals in 1955 were reminders of the CCP's determination to suppress political opposition, but by 1956 a climate of relative liberalization was apparent in a more open communications policy that permitted some questioning of party behavior and orthodoxies. In foreign policy, following the Korean Armistice of 1953, the People's Republic adopted a "peaceful coexistence" stance that led to expanded diplomatic contacts and negotiations with non-Communist countries.

"Liberalization" and the Debate of 1956–1957. "Liberalization" culminated in the "hundred flowers" campaign of May–June 1957, a brief outburst of criticism, largely by intellectuals, that led to a political reaction and ultimately to a rejection of much that was implicit in the FFYP approach to China's development.[19] Far more was at issue in both the cultivation and later weeding of these "flowers" than the limited question of tolerating intellectual dissent. What was involved was a serious debate about how China was and should be developing. The debate was carried on mainly in 1956–1957, but some of its issues had been signaled earlier, and most were to remain as increasingly bitter points of conflict from 1959 down to the Cultural Revolution. The debate centered on CCP dissatisfaction with, or uneasiness about, the emerging results of the FFYP; hence it is easiest to discuss within that context. Rather than trying to specify individual or factional positions within

[18]For figures on the trends referred to here, see Nai-Ruenn Chen, *Chinese Economic Statistics* (Chicago: Aldine, 1967); and *Ten Great Years: Statistics of the Economic and Cultural Achievements of the People's Republic of China* (Peking: Foreign Languages Press, 1960).

[19]For documentation and analysis of the "hundred flowers" period, see Roderick MacFarquhar, *The Hundred Flowers Campaign and the Chinese Intellectuals* (New York: Praeger, 1960) and *The Origins of the Cultural Revolution, 1: Contradictions Among the People, 1956–1957* (New York: Columbia University Press, 1974).

the leadership, generalized conservative and radical responses to the FFYP will be noted to suggest the boundaries of the debate.[20]

A salient issue was the proper balancing of agricultural and industrial development and how to attain it. CCP elites were united in insisting that industrialization must proceed; yet they also acknowledged that the development of agriculture and light industry was relatively weak and must be strengthened to ensure adequate resources for investment in heavy industry. The growth of urbanized populations and consumer demands heightened their fears of shortages in agricultural and consumer products. Accordingly, they approved modest increases over FFYP targets for state investment in agriculture and light industry, but the conservatives were unwilling to go much beyond that. They were pessimistic about the results of rural collectivization in both production and peasant response; they preferred to go slowly, to avoid upsetting the agricultural scene, and to let industrialization lead the peasants gradually into a more collectivized economy. Radical opinion favored a more forward policy, pushing ahead with collectivization and relying on the forces generated by it to bring about rapid social and economic change in the countryside. The struggle between these positions, beginning with Mao's promotion of accelerated collectivization in late 1955, led to several fluctuations in agricultural policy during 1955–1957.

A second acknowledged defect of the FFYP was its encour-

[20]Intraparty conflict is treated at greater length in Chapter VI, this book. The "conservative" and "radical" labels are admittedly vague but seem preferable to alternatives (Liuists and Maoists, pragmatists and idealists, revisionists and revolutionaries) that imply a degree of personal or ideological cleavage not clearly evident at the time. The 1956–1957 debate was not one in which rigid, unchanging positions were taken; differences were real, but compromises, shifts of circumstance, and a strong desire to maintain unity blurred their lines. Most of the key documents relevant to the discussion in the text are available in *Communist China, 1955–1959* and *Eighth National Congress of the Communist Party of China,* vols. 1–2 (Peking: Foreign Languages Press, 1956). One important document not so included is Mao Zedong, "On the Ten Great Relationships" (April 1956), translated in Jerome Ch'en, ed., *Mao* (Englewood Cliffs, N.J.: Prentice-Hall, 1969), pp. 65–85. For detailed analysis of policy shifts in this period, see Parris H. Chang, *Power and Policy in China* (University Park: Pennsylvania State Press, 1975); and Franz Schurmann, *Ideology and Organization in Communist China,* 2nd ed. enl. (Berkeley: University of California Press, 1968).

agement of excessive centralization and bureaucratization, leading to general agreement that the central ministries should transfer some powers to lower units and that criticism of bureaucratic behavior was in order. The radicals had in mind actual simplification and staff reductions in the bureaucracy — in 1956 Mao proposed a two-thirds cut in party and governmental organs[21] — and the general principle of expanding committee or popular supervision over leading cadres. This position had considerable support, since state ministerial power was a growing challenge to party authority and a symbol of Soviet influence. In one of its earliest retreats from Soviet-style arrangements, the CCP had already rejected the "one-man management" system in enterprises in favor of greater control by party committees; by the Eighth Congress in September 1956, the idea of strengthening leadership by party committees in all lines of work was established policy.[22] However, conservatives had little enthusiasm for any general dilution of the authority structure, nor were they ready to renounce the value of bureaucratic and technical specialization. It remained to be seen how far the radicals could go in pushing the mass line (not simply strengthened party committees) as a counterweight to bureaucratism.

Finally, the FFYP period raised fundamental questions about the CCP's relations with other groups in Chinese society — questions underscored by the sobering impact of Khrushchev's denunciation of Stalin in early 1956 and subsequent upheavals in Poland and Hungary. Here, too, there was at least a partial consensus within the CCP elite that political consolidation and the establishment of a socialist economic system had basically unified China, so that the danger of counterrevolution was no longer great and the party could be less authoritarian in its relations with nonparty elements. These were the convictions that encouraged the liberalization of 1956–1957, but the leaders were by no means of one mind concerning their implications. A more conservative viewpoint saw economic and political consolidation as marking the end of the revolutionary period; henceforth, the CCP could exercise leadership through its new institutions rather than

[21]Mao Zedong, "On the Ten Great Relationships," in Jerome Ch'en, op. cit., p. 77.
[22]Schurmann, op. cit., pp. 263–87.

through mass movements, now typed as necessary in their time but prone to error, excess, and inefficiency. In place of continued political mobilization and struggle, this viewpoint suggested codification of laws, stricter observance of institutional procedures, and the granting of some material concessions to the people, particularly to intellectuals and technicians whose skills were necessary but still underutilized. Essentially, the conservatives leaned toward placating or co-opting nonparty groups without emphasizing or expanding their political role. Mao's famous speech, "On the Correct Handling of Contradictions Among the People," was the best expression of a more radical position.[23] Its central thesis was that "nonantagonistic" contradictions exist even in socialist society and must be debated openly to achieve resolution. While affirming basic party leadership and rectitude, Mao assigned nonparty groups a crucial, dialectical role in the political process in which their participation not only would transform themselves but also would prod the socialist system to strengthen itself. It was this push from Mao, against the reservations of some of his colleagues, that enabled liberalization to become briefly the "hundred flowers."

The CCP soon found the criticism by intellectuals too severe and the dangers of its spreading too great to permit the "hundred flowers" experiment to continue. Critics were silenced and in some cases punished, while the party moved to resolve its debate by establishing a new approach. The result was the Great Leap Forward, which began to take shape in late 1957 and was to dominate Chinese politics for the next three years.

THE GREAT LEAP FORWARD, 1957–1960

The Great Leap Forward was not a concrete plan with consistent guidelines or objectives, but rather a set of policies held together by a political mood or frame of mind. (The beginning of the Leap coincided roughly with the Second Five-Year Plan for 1958–1962, but that Plan soon fell by the wayside). This

---

[23]Text in *Communist China, 1955–1959,* pp. 273–94. The original speech, given at an enlarged meeting of the Supreme State Conference on February 27, 1957, was never made public. The offical version ultimately released in June 1957, after the "hundred flowers" outburst had been cut off, contained admitted alterations.

mood was expressed in highly rhetorical terms full of over-powering claims and exhortations. The rhetoric implied that all of China was moving together, whereas in fact there were numerous variations or deviations of time and place. It implied unified and permanent commitment, but Leap policies were not fully formed until the fall of 1958 and were undergoing partial revision almost immediately, indicating that commitment to the movement was not as firm as claimed. In other words, there was a good deal of uncertainty about the Leap's objectives, peformance, and even duration; yet its impact on Chinese politics was immense.

Great Leap Themes. Four interlocking themes that permeated the rhetoric of the Great Leap Forward convey a general impression of the movement's quality.[24] One was a fervent optimism that proclaimed China's ability to accomplish monumental tasks in a short period of time and insisted that earlier problems had been identified and corrected. Another was the glorification of the mass line principle that human effort and will are the decisive factors and hence that popular mobilization is an effective method for resolving problems in all spheres of action. This elevation of the mass line placed a great emphasis on the quantity of manpower mobilized, extolled the virtues of sacrifice and manual labor, and devalued the specialized skills and professional knowledge of the intellectual elite. One specific result was the practice of *xiafang* (hsia fang) ("downward transfer"), in which office workers and intellectuals were sent down to lower levels to engage in more menial lines of work.

A third theme was "politics takes command," asserting that correct political consciousness is the best and indeed the only proper base for social action. This principle demanded the widest possible propagation of official ideology in an effort to ensure that mass mobilization be motivated and guided by political considerations. It also had great implications for the

[24]The best expression of the Great Leap approach, displaying all of the themes mentioned here, is Liu Shaoqi, "Report on the Work of the Central Committee of the Communist Party of China to the Second Session of the Eighth National Congress" (May 5, 1958), text, under a different title, in *Communist China, 1955–1959*, pp. 416–38.

CCP, which as the sole judge of political rectitude was the only organization capable of defining which politics were to be in command. The result was a sharp increase in the power of party committees as they moved to implement central policies.

Finally, the Great Leap rested on the belief that simultaneous advances in all economic, political, and cultural spheres were possible and on the refusal to admit that there were insurmountable limitations or mutually exclusive possibilities in development. The idea of an all-around advance was expressed in what was perhaps the most representative slogan of the period: "Build socialism by exerting our utmost efforts and pressing ahead consistently to achieve greater, faster, better, and more economical results." As the slogan and Liu Shaoqi's discussion of it suggest,[25] the Great Leap philosophy insisted that speed could be combined with efficiency, quantity with quality, and agricultural and local development with industrial and national development. The key to such development was to be a loosening of institutional restraints — to be implemented through decentralization and mass movements — that would encourage each social unit to develop its own capacities to the fullest extent.

Emergence and Origins. The apparent unanimity with which these themes were articulated from late 1957 on obscures the Leap's gradual and controversial emergence. Many of its features actually appeared in late 1955 and early 1956, following Mao's July 1955 speech on agricultural collectivization. In his report to the second session of the Eighth Party Congress in May 1958, Liu referred to this earlier "leap" of 1955–1956 as setting the proper pattern for China's socialist development.[26] Mao's conservative opposition persisted, however, halting the 1955–1956 "leap" and bringing on the 1956–1957 debate. Even after the "antirightist" campaign in summer 1957 had silenced the "hundred flowers" critics, conservative economic policies were still in evidence. The critical decisions that initiated the Great Leap Forward came only at the Central Com-

[25]Ibid., pp. 424–32.
[26]Ibid., pp. 424–27.

mittee's Third Plenum in September–October 1957.[27] Two actions of this plenum are of particular note. One was a decision to expand the antirightist struggle — until that point largely concerned with the "hundred flowers" experience — into a thorough, nationwide rectification campaign that would provide socialist education for the masses of workers and peasants and eradicate "rightist" and various erroneous tendencies within the party and other elite groups.[28] The other action of the plenum was approval of a program of decentralization in which control over many enterprises and financial resources would be transferred from the central ministries to provincial authorities. These decisions provided the basis for a general intensification of ideological indoctrination, for purging or eclipsing "conservative" party officials, and for raising the authority of party committees (particularly at the provincial level) at the expense of central state organs.

During the winter of 1957–1958 a massive labor mobilization was undertaken in the countryside for work on irrigation and flood control projects. The expanded scale of rural organization provided incentive for merging some existing cooperatives into large units. With the spring planting of 1958, the mobilization extended to agricultural production itself, stressing a variety of labor-intensive techniques. The nonagricultural population was also pressed into productive service by organizing units for labor in the countryside, in street factories, or in various sideline and spare-time enterprises. This massive outpouring of human effort, which was essentially an effort to raise production dramatically without major reallocation of capital resources, stimulated optimistic economic forecasts that steadily raised output targets. The first experimental rural people's communes appeared in the summer of 1958, carrying further the merging of rural organization into larger units that had begun in the winter; in August the Central Committee formally approved them and called for their nationwide establishment.[29] Within a few weeks communes had

[27]See the discussion in Schurmann, op. cit., pp. 195–210.

[28]See Deng Xiaoping (Teng Hsiao-p'ing), "Report on the Rectification Campaign" (September 23, 1957), in *Communist China, 1955–1959*, pp. 341–63.

[29]"Resolution of the Central Committee of the Chinese Communist Party on the Establishment of People's Communes in the Rural Areas" (Aug. 29, 1958), in *Communist China, 1955–1959*, pp. 454–56.

become the primary production and administrative units for the rural population, essentially completing the framework of the Great Leap Forward.

How can one explain the CCP's adoption of the Great Leap approach when it was contrary to many more conservative tendencies in the party and was to lead to such damaging results? The decisive factor was probably the authority and persuasive powers of Mao Zedong, who initiated Leap policies and campaigned vigorously for their realization.[30] The Leap's tortuous emergence — the debate of 1956–1957 was followed by purges of many provincial-level leaders in the 1957–1958 rectification campaign[31] — and early modification indicate that the CCP elite was never wholeheartedly committed to it. Rather, opposition was silenced or shelved in a decision to let Mao have his way with a maximum display of support and unity, but many people concealed reservations. The question remains, however, as to why Mao's arguments were sufficiently persuasive to carry the day, even if only temporarily.

It must be emphasized that the Great Leap Forward had a powerful and understandable attraction for the Chinese Communists. The CCP's commitment to social change, a restoration of Chinese power, and surpassing the West was firm. Its leaders were cool toward compromises that might slow the rate of advance, particularly in pursuit of their industrial goals. The idea that backward sectors must speed up rather than force advanced sectors to slow down was an attractive one. Mao was perhaps uniquely aggressive in his determination to advance, accepting greater sacrifices and risks than many of his colleagues, but his demand that the revolution must push forward had great appeal. The Leap was also close to Chinese Communist historical experience in many of its specific features. Its reliance on struggle and sacrifice, direct party leadership of mass movements, and local initiative rather than bureaucratic controls was consistent with CCP response to challenges faced on the road to power. The 1956–1957 debate, despite its controversies, had revealed a general preference for decentralization, intensified party leadership, and

---

[30]Liu Shaoqi, op. cit., repeatedly attributed the Leap's slogans and general definition to Mao.

[31]See Frederick C. Teiwes, "The Purge of Provincial Leaders 1957–1958," *China Quarterly*, no. 27 (July–Sept. 1966), pp. 14–32.

greater stimulation of agricultural development without sacrificing industrialization. The Leap had sturdy roots, therefore, in both historical experience and recent policy positions.

The sharpest area of conflict between Maoist and conservative positions was the question of institutionalization and liberalization, and here the "hundred flowers" campaign
provided an answer. Mao had argued that nonparty groups
must be brought into the political process to expose both their
own and CCP shortcomings. When they finally responded for
a few short weeks in May–June 1957, they soon crossed the
limits of what party leaders regarded as tolerable opposition.
In response, and with Mao's support,[32] the CCP moved to a
tough political line that rejected any significant criticism of its
leadership. Liberalization was discredited and so too were the
intellectuals and professionals who had suggested that their
kind of work required greater freedom from political controls
— a suggestion now branded as simply a cover for antiparty
politics. The experience was equally damaging for the proponents of institutionalization, for it indicated that the establishment of socialist institutions had not completed the socialist
revolution. Mao might have been wrong about the beneficial
effects of "blooming and contending," but he was right about
the perseverance of "contradictions" in a socialist society. If
the new state system had not eliminated bourgeois politics,
what grounds were there for placing one's faith in institution-
alizing and regularizing its procedures? The consensus after
the "hundred flowers" experience was that efforts must turn
to the creation of socialist man and that the revolution must
continue without interruption. Thus, the representative organs of state as well as its central ministries lost favor, while
reliance on intensive party-led campaigns for political education rose to the fore.[33]

Our discussion to this point has outlined some of the reasons for the CCP's late 1957 shift from the Soviet-style FFYP

[32]Among Mao's additions to the published June version of his February
1957 speech on contradictions were six criteria for judging whether words and
actions were "right"; the criteria specified as "right" only those words and
actions that consolidated or strengthened socialist transformation, the people's democratic dictatorship, democratic centralism, and party leadership.
Communist China, 1955–1959, pp. 274, 290.

[33]See the discussion in Townsend, op. cit., pp. 92–99, 142–44, 185–88.

to a developmental approach more consonant with Chinese experience and conditions. The Great Leap Forward, although controversial, was neither novel nor divorced from Chinese political and economic reality. What was so striking and ultimately damaging about it was not its rationale but the fanaticism with which it was pursued, and for an appreciation of that we must look more closly at the optimistic mood which nurtured it. While a high degree of optimism seems to be inherent in Maoism, there were a number of "objective" considerations in 1957–1958 that encouraged the CCP elite to believe that conditions were favorable for a new spurt of development.[34] Domestically, the economy was on the upswing after a disappointing lag in 1956–1957, and the antirightist and rectification campaigns seemed to have consolidated the party's leadership; the 1958 harvest was to be excellent, the early signs of which prompted the progressive raising of economic targets that took place in that year. In the troubled field of Communist bloc relations, where "dark clouds" were acknowledged in 1956, the defeat of counterrevolution in Poland and Hungary, the consolidation of Khrushchev's power in the Soviet Union, and the management of a compromise statement at the Moscow Conference of Communist parties in November 1957 all contributed to a belief that the solidarity and strength of the camp was growing. Perhaps most significant of all was the Chinese belief that the cold war balance of power had shifted to its side, expressed in Mao's statement that "the east wind prevails over the west wind." The Soviet Union's growing technological prowess, revealed most dramatically in the October 1957 *Sputnik* launching, and a moderate recession in the West were other primary elements in this favorable estimate of the international situation. It is easy in retrospect to note how fragile these trends were, but they nontheless led CCP leaders to act with a confidence bordering on recklessness.

Communes and Economic Crisis. Some of the consequences of the Great Leap approach — its constant meetings and indoc-

---

[34]All the following points are expressed in Liu Shaoqi, op. cit; and Zhou Enlai, "The Present International Situation and China's Foreign Policy" (Feb. 10, 1958), in *Communist China, 1955–1959*, pp. 401–10.

trination to stimulate maximum efforts — are implicit in what has been said, but there are others that demand special attention. The people's communes, for example, had a profound impact on rural society. Decentralization of powers from central to provincial authorities was a key policy of the Leap, but in the countryside the communes represented a policy of centralization. That is, the communes concentrated economic and political powers in a basic-level unit significantly larger than any that preceded it. Actually, this "centralization" had been in progress for many years. Before communization, the basic rural administrative unit was the *xiang,* of which there were about 220,000 in 1952–1955; but a policy of amalgamation after 1955 increased their size so that by the summer of 1958 there were only some 80,000 *xiang.* The basic agricultural production unit was orginally the peasant household, numbering over 100 million in the early 1950s, but collectivization gave the Agricultural Producers' Cooperative (APC) primary responsibility for managing and distributing the agricultural product; there were about 750,000 APCs in 1958, most of them based on natural villages. After communization, both administrative and production responsibilities were combined in the management committees of some 25,000 communes. This concentration of power in a larger and unfamiliar political-economic unit caused great disruption and uncertainty, due to boundary changes, shifts of personnel, and conflict with established production and marketing relationships.[35]

The impact of the communes went far beyond disruption of institutional patterns, however. As seen by the leadership, they were to be large, self-sufficient communities that would lead their members rapidly toward modernization and a communistic way of life. They were to establish their own factories, schools, nurseries, mess halls, and militia units to provide for maximal development and deployment of manpower under collective management. Most "private plots," the small lots of

[35]For a detailed analysis, see Roy Hofheinz, "Rural Administration in Communist China," *China Quarterly,* no. 11 (July–Sept. 1962), pp. 140–59; G. William Skinner, "Marketing and Social Structure in Rural China," part 3, *The Journal of Asian Studies,* vol. 24, no. 3 (May 1965), pp. 363–99; and Kenneth R. Walker, *Planning in Chinese Agriculture: Socialization and the Private Sector, 1956–1962* (Chicago: Aldine, 1965), esp. pp. 3–19.

land retained for individual household use in the APCs, were absorbed into collective production, and there were experiments with a "free supply" system of payment according to need rather than according to work. The impact of the communes on existing economic and social structure clearly had great modernizing potential, but the changes were far too abrupt for easy management or acceptance.

In the economic realm, the Leap had some positive accomplishments but ended in a severe crisis in 1959–1961. There was a bumper harvest in 1958, a great surge in rural construction, and some initial gain in industrial output; encouragement of rural industry accelerated the transmission of technical skills and equipment to the countryside. Yet overall the Leap was an economic failure, particularly in relation to its high hopes.[36] Bad weather had an adverse effect on the 1959 harvest, but the all-around deterioration that followed reflected basic faults in the approach itself. Agricultural decline continued in 1960, leading to shortages of investment funds and raw materials that forced a slowdown in industry. Food shortages lowered both physical and psychological work capacity, reinforcing downward production trends. Personnel transfers at the basic level brought inexperienced men to new posts and disrupted the cohesion of work groups. Disregard of specialists led to errors in attempted technological innovations. Ideological indoctrination produced diminishing returns as it cut into the scant leisure time of an overworked labor force. Planning and accurate statistical reporting languished and overly ambitious or enthusiastic cadres pushed the commune policy to radical extremes; although the central authorities explicitly approved neither of these trends, they were the natural results of the prevailing political mood. The deepening rift with the Soviet Union and the departure of Soviet technicians in 1960 added to the bleakness of the picture.

The severity of the 1959–1961 economic crisis had major political consequences. The resentments of an overworked and hungry population began to turn against the party cadres who were so totally identified with implementation of the Leap

[36]For a summary of economic problems in this period, see Alexander Eckstein, "On the Economic Crisis in Communist China," *Foreign Affairs,* vol. 42, no. 4 (July 1964), pp. 655–68.

policy. Apathy, disobedience, and even instances of insurrection spread in rural areas. The position of basic-level cadres was particularly acute, for they were caught in the middle between popular discontent and directives from higher levels. Their response ranged from illicit concessions to the people to excessive "commandism" and brutality, or simply to an abdication of offical responsibility and integrity. In short, the crisis involved political authority as well as the economy.[37] Inevitably it produced great tension within the political elite, which faced the task of changing a policy to which it had, at least publicly, committed itself so heavily. The change took place in a period of retrenchment, but it also raised many new and old controversies about the wisdom of the Great Leap Forward.

RETRENCHMENT AND RECOVERY, 1961–1965

The years from 1961 to 1965 form a less distinct period than those discussed previously. What cohesion they have stems largely from an economic retrenchment policy that emerged in 1961 and continued in force through 1965. Many of its basic features remained even through the Cultural Revolution. On the political side, however, there was a significant break in this period, coming at the Tenth Plenum of the Central Committee in September 1962. Before that date, a climate of political retrenchment, moderation, and uncertainty prevailed; following it a complex struggle between mobilization and institutionalization took place, leading into the open conflict of the Cultural Revolution.

The preceding discussion has indicated the conditions that made some kind of retreat from the Great Leap virtually inescapable. Indeed, the first signs of retreat came as early as December 1958 at the Central Committee's Sixth Plenum,[38] which noted that full Communism was still a long way off, that

[37]The best evidence of these difficulties is found in *Gungzuo Tong xun* (*Kung-tso T'ung hsün*), ("Bulletin of Activities"), a secret journal of the PLA General Political Department of which twenty-nine numbers for the January–August 1961 period are available. They are translated in J. Chester Cheng, ed., *The Politics of the Chinese Red Army* (Stanford, Cal.: Hoover Institution, 1966). For a brief analysis of their contents that is particularly relevant to points discussed here, see John Wilson Lewis, "China's Secret Military Papers: 'Continuities' and 'Revelations'," *China Quarterly*, no. 18 (April–June 1964), pp. 68–78.

[38]For documentation, see *Communist China, 1955–1959*, pp. 483–503.

the "free supply" system should be limited, that commune members must be guaranteed adequate hours for rest, and that tighter planning and organization was necessary. It was this meeting that announced Mao's decision to retire from the chairmanship of the government, a move which may or may not have been forced upon him but which certainly was recognized by senior elites as reducing his political responsibilities. Leap policies came under direct attack at the Eighth Plenum in July–August 1959, with Defense Minister and Politburo member Peng Dehuai (P'eng Teh-huai) serving as spokesman for the critics. The Plenum dismissed Peng from his position in the Defense Ministry (but not from the Politburo), launched an intensive campaign against "right opportunism" and "conservatism," and reasserted the rectitude of the communes and the Great Leap Forward. This was done, however, only by a great investment of Mao's personal prestige, indicating that support for the Leap was wavering.[39] During 1959 and 1960, the communes were quietly modified to lessen their disruptive impact.

Retrenchment Policies. Economic retrenchment became official at the Ninth Plenum in January 1961, which tacitly — although never explicitly — conceded that Leap policies had brought errors and considerable opposition. A new slogan of "taking agriculture as the foundation of the national economy" revealed that the leadership was at last prepared to reduce capital construction in industry to alleviate the agricultural crisis. The Plenum also called for better economic planning and coordination, more production of consumer goods, and more quality and diversity in industrial output.[40] During the next two years many concrete aspects of economic retrenchment became clear. The heyday of party committee control ended with some central ministries and the managerial specialists at the enterprise level regaining considerable influence.[41] The

[39]The official published documents of the Eighth Plenum are in *Communist China, 1955–1959,* pp. 533–40. Much additional documentation on the Peng affair became available during the Cultural Revolution and has been translated in *The Case of P'eng Teh-huai* (Hong Kong: Union Research Institute, 1968), esp. pp. 1–47.

[40]See the documents and commentary in *China Quarterly,* no. 6 (April–June 1961), pp. 183–90.

[41]Schurmann, op. cit., pp. 177–78, 218–19, 297–98.

private plots were returned to individual use, and "rural trade fairs" or free markets were permitted in the countryside to stimulate exchange and distribution of the agricultural product.[42]

Perhaps the greatest changes came in the structure of the communes, however (see Table I). During consolidation in the winter of 1958–1959, the 25,000 communes had settled into a relatively uniform pattern of "three level management." Each commune was divided into production brigades generally equivalent to the village-based advanced APCs existing before communization, and each brigade was divided into production teams of twenty to forty households each. Initially, the commune-level government had controlled production and distribution within the commune, but during 1959 these critical powers had passed to the brigade level. Then, during retrenchment, controls shifted downward again to the production team, which acquired virtual independence in managing its own agricultural production and distribution although it still had to fill certain output and labor quotas to higher levels. In the same period, many communes were subdivided so that the total number increased from 25,000 to about 75,000 — that is, almost the same number of rural administrative units as existed in 1958 before communization. With the average commune now comparable in size to its administrative predecessor (the *xiang*), the brigade essentially a continuation of the village APC, and the team (with primary production responsibilities) a familiar grouping of households by work or residential patterns, the commune system lost its most radical structural characteristics.[43]

The continuing shortage since 1958 of reliable data on the Chinese economy makes estimates of the success of economic retrenchment difficult. Recovery did take place from about 1962 on, so that 1957 output levels were surpassed by 1965.

---

[42]On the importance of these apparently minor concessions to peasant "capitalism," see Walker, op. cit., pp. 86–92 and passim.

[43]This is not to say, however, that the commune system became only a new name for old patterns. The communes retained administrative powers over large-scale operations, were not identical in every case to the units that preceded them, and preserved a framework facilitating future shifts in both administrative and productive relations. See Skinner, op. cit., esp. pp. 395–99.

As in earlier years, gains in industry were stronger than in agriculture, which remained the critical economic problem area.[44] The retention of the major retrenchment policies through the 1970s indicates at least minimal satisfaction of the elite with their results.

Retrenchment initially penetrated politics as well as economics. During most of 1961–1962 there was a noticeable slackening of ideological indoctrination and mass movements coupled with an inward-looking party rectification campaign. The primacy of politics receded as agricultural, industrial, and educational units were encouraged to devote more time to their nonpolitical functions. For nonparty intellectuals there was a revived "blooming and contending" that encouraged resumption of academic research and debate, although not the outspoken political criticism of 1957. Party officials were not so restrained, however, and some of them began to publicize views that were critical of the Leap, Peng Dehuai's dismissal, Mao's policy leadership, and even Mao's abilities and personality.[45] Much of this criticism came in subtle form through the medium of drama and literary essays, but Maoists later charged that in 1962, Peng actively sought reinstatement and vindication with the support of Liu Shaoqi by circulating a lengthy defense of his position among party leaders.[46]

New Political Offensive. The Tenth Plenum in September 1962 marked the end of political retrenchment and the beginning of a new political offensive. Although its official communiqué referred only briefly to the existence of "opportunist" and "revisionist" elements within the CCP,[47] subsequent developments made clear that the Plenum had launched a new effort to counter the anti-Maoist tendency of 1961–1962. The next three years brought a number of campaigns aimed at stimulating

[44]For a sampling of estimates for 1957–1965 and the difficulties and controversy that surround them, see Ta-chung Liu, op. cit., pp. 631–50, and the "comments," ibid., pp. 650–90.

[45]Merle Goldman, "The Unique 'Blooming and Contending' of 1961–62," *China Quarterly,* no. 37 (January–March 1969), pp. 54–83.

[46]"From the Defeat of Peng Teh-huai to the Bankruptcy of China's Khrushchev," *Hongqi* editorial, no. 13 (Aug. 17, 1967), in PR, no. 34 (Aug. 18, 1967), pp. 18–20, 35.

[47]Text in PR, no. 39 (Sept. 28, 1962). pp. 5–8.

TABLE I. *Development of Collectivized Agriculture*

	Household	Small village or village section (usually 20–40 households)	Large village or village cluster (usually 100–300 households)	Rural marketing area
1949–1952	Land reform ends large holdings and tenancy, destroys old rural power structure	...	...	...
1952–1955	...	Mutual aid teams of 4–10 households lead into lower agricultural producers' cooperatives, which become BAU.[a]	...	...
1955–1957	Households retain small private plots.	Early coops become production teams within higher coops.	Higher agricultural producers' cooperatives emerge, become BAU, full collectivization begins.	...
1958–1959	Private plots absorbed by communes.	Become production teams within communes.	Become production brigades within commune.	People's Communes formed and become BAU; early total of 25,000 large-scale communes, many exceeding marketing area in extent.

Experimentation with highly collectivized communities; large-scale rural labor mobilization for water conservancy and other construction projects.

1960–1962	Private plots returned to households.	Production team becomes BAU.		Communes reduced in size to total of 75,000, probably based on marketing areas.
	"Agriculture as Foundation" policy adopted; increased emphasis on rural mechanization, agricultural technology, use of chemical fertilizers.			
1963–1978	Private plots retained despite some "radical" pressure to return them to collective.	Most production teams remain BAU, despite some pressure to move to higher level.	A few production brigades serve as BAU.	Communes grow slowly in size, due to population increase and some unit combinations, with total of 50,000 in mid-1970s. Most remain coterminous with marketing areas, which are also expanding due to modernization of countryside.
	"Agriculture as Foundation" policy continued, with increasing modernization and diversification of rural economy; great emphasis on developing small-scale rural industry and social services after Cultural Revolution			

a BAU (Basic Accounting Unit): The unit that is responsible for making work assignments, organizing agricultural production, and collecting and distributing the agricultural product; it handles its own accounting and is responsible for its own profits and losses; hence, it is an important indicator of the level of collectivization. Originally the household, it moved to the cooperatives, briefly up to the commune in 1958–1959, and then back to the production team.

class struggle and ideological education in the name of Maoist orthodoxy. Two of the most important of these were the Socialist Education Movement and the drive for "cultivation of revolutionary successors." The former was actually a series of campaigns that sought to remedy persistent defects in lower-level cadre work by intraparty rectification combined with mass criticism and education; it insisted on continuing class struggle to defeat bourgeois and revisionist influences both within and outside the CCP.[48] The latter addressed itself to young people who were in line for political leadership but who lacked the actual revolutionary experience of their seniors; they were to immerse themselves in physical labor, ideological study, and class struggle to acquire the experience and attitudes necessary to "carry the revolution through to the end."[49]

These movements, combined with the polemics of the now open Sino-Soviet conflict and a number of related campaigns, fostered an intense political rhetoric reminiscent of the Great Leap Forward. In fact, political tension seemed in some ways higher than in 1957–1960, since struggle was said to be against class enemies and anti-Maoist ideology, whereas the Leap had fought mainly against nature and institutional limitations on productive capacities. Yet somehow the 1962–1965 rhetoric was not translated fully into practice. The socialist education movement dragged on indecisively, and the peasant associations that were to be revived to help implement it never acquired much prominence. "Experts" and youth participated in campaigns to "revolutionize" themselves, but in a regularized way that permitted continuation of their professional work or study. "Revolution," in short, was becoming an institution of the regime, a routinized procedure for education and training that would support rather than alter the system. In that ten-

---

[48]For analysis and documentation, see Richard Baum and Frederick C. Teiwes, *Ssu-Ch'ing: The Socialist Education Movement of 1962–1966* (Berkeley: University of California, Center for Chinese Studies, 1968). A valuable collection of primary data on cadre problems in this period in a Fujian county is C. S. Chen, ed., *Rural People's Communes in Lien-Chiang,* trans. Charles Price Ridley (Stanford, Cal.: Hoover Institution, 1969).

[49]See *Training Successors for the Revolution Is the Party's Strategic Task* (Peking: Foreign Languages Press, 1965); and Hu Yao-pang, *Revolutionize Our Youth!* (Peking: Foreign Languages Press, 1964).

dency lay some of the basic controversies that brought on the Cultural Revolution. Before moving on to that topic, however, we should look briefly at one structure in which the Maoist revival did have a dramatic impact — the PLA.

As noted earlier, military organization was very prominent during the reconstruction period. Following the end of the Korean War and the establishment of the new state system, the PLA's political power declined. Its budget and size were reduced, and it began to assume a more standardized professional role. However, Lin Biao's replacement of Peng as defense minister in 1959 initiated a process of politicization that was to make the PLA Mao's ultimate power base in the Cultural Revolution.[50] Mao's determination to maintain a politicized army is understandable given the CCP's historically intimate identification with its military arm, and his reliance on military models for political action was demonstrated in the Great Leap's heavy use of military metaphors.[51] Still, the forcefulness of the PLA's rise was surprising particularly in view of the resistance Mao's ideas were meeting elsewhere. Under Lin's direction, the PLA's General Political Department and party organization within the army were greatly strengthened, while the study of Mao's thought was promoted vigorously. By 1963–1964, as these efforts bore fruit, the PLA and individual soldier-heroes became the foremost Maoist models for emulation by the rest of society. The army's political department system began to spread to party and government structures with new political departments appearing under the Central Committee and most of the economic ministries. Army cadres were prominent in the staffing and organizing of these new organs. On the eve of the Cultural Revolution, the PLA was publicly identified as the most successful organizational practitioner of Maoism, and it had acquired, through the preferential placement of demobilized soldiers as well as the new political departments, a network of political influence throughout the system.

[50]See Chalmers Johnson, "Lin Piao's Army and its Role in Chinese Society," *Current Scene,* vol. 4, nos. 13–14 (July 1 and 15, 1966); and Ralph L. Powell, "The Increasing Power of Lin Piao and the Party-Soldiers 1959–1966," *China Quarterly,* no. 34 (April–June 1968), pp. 38–65.

[51]See T. A. Hsia, *Metaphor, Myth, Ritual and the People's Commune* (Berkley: University of California, Center for Chinese Studies, 1961).

THE CULTURAL REVOLUTION, 1966–1969

The Great Proletarian Cultural Revolution was probably the most significant period in post-1949 Chinese politics. It shed more light on basic issues and conflicts within the Communist system than any previous period and added new dimensions to external impressions about the characteristics of that system. Precisely because of its importance, it will be a subject for analysis in several other chapters. Our purpose here is to present only an introductory description of its nature, development, and results.[52]

Dual Character of the Cultural Revolution. There is no simple answer to what the Cultural Revolution was, but much of its significance and complexity is explained by its dual character. In the first sense, it was a national political movement organized and directed by a group of political elites under the leadership of Mao to rectify the CCP in accordance with Maoist policies. As a rectification campaign the Cultural Revolution sought to test the quality of all officials, particularly those at high levels, reforming or purging those who were not following Mao's prescriptions for Chinese society. The Maoists regularly described the Cultural Revolution as an organized political campaign with centrally defined leadership, guidelines, and stages, although they did not define it exclusively in

[52]The volume of documentation and analysis on the Cultural Revolution deserves an extended bibliographical essay, but space permits only a few suggestions here. A convenient collection of documents is *CCP Documents of the Great Proletarian Cultural Revolution, 1966–1967* (Hong Kong: Union Research Institute, 1968); cited hereafter as *CCP Documents.* A vivid firsthand report is David Milton and Nancy Dall Milton, *The Wind Will Not Subside: Years in Revolutionary China: 1964–1969* (New York: Pantheon Books, 1976). Recent scholarly monographs focusing on the period include Byung-joon Ahn, *Chinese Politics and the Cultural Revolution* (Seattle: University of Washington Press, 1976); Lowell Dittmer, *Liu Shao-ch'i and the Chinese Cultural Revolution* (Berkeley: University of California Press, 1974); and Hong Yung Lee, *The Politics of the Chinese Cultural Revolution* (Berkeley: University of California Press, 1978). For general histories of the CCP and PRC that set the campaign in its broader context, see Jacques Guillermaz, *The Chinese Communist Party in Power, 1949–1976* (Boulder: Westview Press, 1976); and Maurice Meisner, *Mao's China: A History of the People's Republic* (New York: Free Press, 1977). The emergence of "two-line" struggle in the retrenchment period, leading into the Cultural Revolution, is set forth in Richard Baum, *Prelude to Revolution: Mao, the Party and the Peasant Question, 1962–66* (New York: Columbia University Press, 1975).

these terms and did not in fact maintain central control throughout its course. The Cultural Revolution was, therefore, comparable to other political movements in the history of the CCP and was directly related to some of them, particularly the rectification of 1957–1958, the drive against "right opportunism" [Peng Dehuai] of 1959, and the socialist education movement. It stands apart from other campaigns, however, because of its duration and impact (although land reform was a competitor on this score) and because the central leadership was so deeply divided by it.

In the second sense, *cultural revolution* refers to a distinctively active period in an ongoing process of change in the thought and behavior of the Chinese people. The cultural revolution as a process of social change involves all Chinese (not just the CCP), has been promoted by many Chinese elites (not just the Maoists or even the Communists), and had its beginning long ago (not just in 1965–1966). The phrase *cultural revolution* is an old one in Communist terminology and has clear links with non-Communist cultural reform efforts such as the May Fourth and "new culture" movements of the 1910s. Thus the cultural revolution as a broad movement antedates the Cultural Revolution and is continuing even though the latter is over.

How was the Great Proletarian Cultural Revolution related to this broader cultural revolution? The movement was directly concerned with the content of art, literature, and drama, insisting that cultural expression celebrate the nationalistic and proletarian values of socialist society, be hostile toward class and foreign enemies, and reject the values of traditional China. It is no accident that the Cultural Revolution began with attacks on writers and party officials responsible for controlling cultural expression. The movement also emphasized from the first a thorough reform of the educational system to make it more accessible to ordinary workers and peasants and to place it wholly in the service of Maoist-defined national goals.[53] Finally, the Cultural Revolution had to do with culture

[53]Educational reform was signaled by Mao's directive of May 7, 1966. The "May Seventh Directive" was not published, but later references and quotations revealed its main content. For a collection of documents on educational reform, see American Consulate General, Hong Kong, *Current Background*, no. 846 (Feb. 8, 1968).

in its broadest sense, with what we might call the Chinese life-style. It inveighed against the "four olds" (old ideas, culture, customs, and habits), "selfish" orientations toward consumption and material gain, personal ties that interfered with political obligations, bureaucratic and elitist behavior, and the special honor and status accorded purely intellectual pursuits; and it upheld a self-sacrificing, collectivist, politically activist, and populist ideal. The Cultural Revolution's concern with cultural expression, transmission, and behavioral manifestations was manifestly political, but that is precisely the point: it was a rectification campaign that sought simultaneously to accelerate the politicization of Chinese culture.

It was the interaction of political rectification and cultural change that gave the Cultural Revolution so complex and even contradictory a character. From the Maoist point of view, political leadership had to be rectified to ensure that cultural revolutionization would continue, and the cultural revolution had to be intensified to assist rectification; both elite direction and mass spontaneity were necessary and presumably complementary. In practice, the tension between order and mobilization, between authority and spontaneity, became severe. In the later phases of the movement a tendency to restore order and limit mobilization prevailed. However, the fact remains that both meanings of *cultural revolution* were parts of the movement and had a significant influence on the policies emerging from it.

Stages: Mobilization, Red Guards, Power Seizures, and Consolidation. Periodization of the Cultural Revolution is an arbitrary business, but it is necessary to place its major shifts in order. The first phase of mobilization lasted from the fall of 1965 through July 1966. In this period, the central leadership engaged in a largely hidden struggle over how to respond to Mao's call (at a September 1965 meeting of the Central Committee) for a major assault on revisionist influences. Open criticism was directed at a small number of intellectuals and party propagandists who had published anti-Maoist pieces in 1961–1962, but the top antagonists were not initially identified. Much of this inner struggle centered around the work of a Central Committee Cultural Revolution Group set up to direct the campaign. The conflict exploded in May–June 1966 when the Central Committee repudiated its first Cultural Revolution Group (subsequently establishing a more radical one), purged several high-ranking leaders, and reconstituted the Peking Municipal Party Committee.[54] The most prominent victim was Peng Zhen (P'eng Chen) — mayor of Peking, first secretary of the Peking Party Committee, and a member of the Politburo and the first Cultural Revolution Group — who was identified as the main culprit in the Cultural Revolution Group and the patron of revisionist intellectuals in Peking. During June and July, the Cultural Revolution broadened into an open mass movement to uncover all "bourgeois authorities," particularly in educational and propagandist institutions. However, many party leaders continued to restrain its most radical tendencies.

A second stage of public attack, dominated by Red Guard activities, lasted from August through November. It was initiated at the Eleventh Plenum (August 1–12, 1966), which adopted a crucial "Sixteen Point Decision" on the Cultural Revolution marking the ascendancy of Maoist forces at the party center.[55] This decision aimed the movement at "persons in authority who are taking the capitalist road" — gradually revealed to be Liu Shaoqi, Deng Xiaoping, and a host of other senior elites — and named the mass movement, especially "large numbers of revolutionary young people" (the Red Guards), as the main force for carrying it out. With this official sanction, facilitated by an earlier closure of the schools, Red Guard organizations mushroomed, bringing millions of young

[54]See, in particular, the "May Sixteenth Circular" of the Central Committee, text in *CCP Documents,* pp. 20–28.

[55]Text in *CCP Documents,* pp. 42–54. Use of the word *Maoist* throughout this discussion seems necessary for simple reference to the promoters of the Cultural Revolution as distinguished from those who resisted or tried to defuse it in some way. It does not imply they all held precisely the same views or supported the movement for the same reasons. In fact, there was great controversy about who was really a "Maoist" and who was not, and many participants were doubtlessly surprised by the labels ulimately attached to them. Nor is it certain that the Maoists, even in this qualified sense, had a genuine majority on the Central Committee at the Eleventh Plenum, due to the presence of nonmembers and the possibility of intimidation at that meeting. From August 1966 on, Maoists controlled communications issued in the name of the Central Committee, but the course of the Cultural Revolution suggests that they did not have a formal majority on the Committee until after the purges of 1966.

people into the streets to demonstrate support for Chairman Mao, to denounce and terrorize those said to be his opponents, and to destroy various symbols of bourgeois or reactionary culture. However, while their actions revealed near fanatical devotion to Mao, they could not drive his opponents from office. Red Guards began to differ on who was truly Maoist or revisionist, splitting into competitive and even hostile organizations — a development naturally encouraged by party officials who were under attack. By late 1966 the Maoist leaders were preparing a new offensive in which a literal "seizure of power" by "revolutionary rebels" would take place in all party, state, and economic organizations.

The seizure of power stage, which lasted from December 1966 through September 1968, markedly escalated the Cultural Revolution by extending it into the countryside, economic enterprises, and government and party offices. The new "revolutionary rebel" groups were drawn largely from the working population and hence were significantly broader mass organizations than were the student-based Red Guards. The very idea of a power seizure from below was a direct assault on local party authority and organization. Understandably, the first efforts to seize power produced immediate confusion and violence, as local "rebels" struggled with officials and each other for control of offices and communications centers. Localized civil disorders, occasionally becoming armed conflict between rival mass organizations, continued for roughly the next two years, although their intensity fluctuated constantly depending on time and place. The Maoists in Peking must have accepted this upheaval as necessary and to some extent desirable, but they acted quickly to place limits upon it. Most important, they issued instructions in January 1967 that the PLA was to intervene with any force necessary on the side of the "leftists" and that it was to assume control of key communications, transportation and other facilities.[56] In effect, China came under a kind of martial law in which the PLA became the de facto administrative authority and arbiter of local disputes; local CCP organization simply ceased to function, and even central party organs went into partial eclipse. Moreover, the

[56]See the directives in *CCP Documents,* pp. 186, 195–97, 200–1, 208, 211–13.

tactic of power seizure by mass organizations soon was modified by an endorsement of "revolutionary committees" based on a "three-way alliance" as the appropriate organs for replacing the old state and party committees.[57] The "three-way alliance" meant that revolutionary committees were to be composed of "leaders of revolutionary mass organizations, PLA representatives, and revolutionary leading cadres." In practice, this permitted many former cadres to remain in office, significantly reduced the influence of mass organizations on the committees, and gave the PLA a decisive voice in negotiating the establishment and membership of the committees.

The twenty-one months required to set up revolutionary committees in all provincial-level units were full of conflict and policy shifts, but when the last was formed in September 1968 it was clear that a trend toward restoration of order and authority was under way. Army commanders and former cadres held most leading positions on the new committees, mass organizations were being broken up and repressed, and students were under orders to go back to school or to work in the countryside. Party organization was still a shambles, however, and the provincial revolutionary committees had barely begun to straighten out the reorganization of power in their subordinate units. Accordingly, a fourth and final stage of consolidation ensued in which the leadership claimed overall victory in the Cultural Revolution but acknowledged that substantial tasks of party building and general economic and political stabilization remained.[58] Although the Twelfth Plenum in October 1968 had claimed that "ample conditions had been prepared" for a Ninth Party Congress, that Congress — marking the conclusion of the Cultural Revolution as a rectification campaign — did not meet until April 1969.

REFORM AND CONTINUED CONFLICT, 1969–1976

The Ninth Party Congress formally committed the CCP to reform the Chinese system in accordance with Mao's prescriptions. For a variety of reasons, however, the effort fell short of

[57]"On the Revolutionary 'Three-in-One' Combination," *Hongqi* editorial, no. 5 (March 30, 1967), *PR* no. 12 (March 17, 1967), pp. 14–16.

[58]See "Communiqué of the Enlarged 12th Plenary Session," *PR*, supplement to no. 44 (November 1, 1968).

the ideals articulated early in the Cultural Revolution. For one thing, the post-1969 leadership was not united in its interpretation of the Cultural Revolution's legacy and soon succumbed to renewed factional conflict. Second, the institutional uncertainty and disarray produced by the campaign complicated efforts to advance new policies. Finally, the PRC now faced new issues — most importantly, Mao's approaching death and how to deal with the Soviet threat — that would transform the stakes and substance of Chinese politics. As a result, the practice of Maoism in 1969–1976 was different from the rhetoric of 1965–1967. Nonetheless, reforms after the Cultural Revolution had a great impact on Chinese society and came to represent — both in China and abroad — at least a modified application of the Maoist model. We will note some of the most important reforms and then review the problems that altered or obstructed their progress.[59]

One striking feature of the immediate post-1969 period was an effort to maintain the spirit of the Cultural Revolution by infusing public life with its symbolism. Mao's personal authority continued to serve as the legitimator of policy, and Maoist themes — self-reliance, mass line, continuing the revolution, the primacy of politics — permeated all areas of Chinese life. Official statements held that the Cultural Revolution was still in progress, that Chinese society was still engaged in a fierce struggle between the Maoist and revisionist lines that would require militant action, as well as more cultural revolutions, against those who would compromise the goals of the revolution. This radical rhetoric discouraged specification of national policies and plans, encouraging instead an experimental approach that permitted much local diversity and aimed more at reform of thought and behavior than at attainment of quantifiable targets.

More concretely, the idea of continuing the revolution was translated into measures designed to foster a more egalitarian

[59]For detailed analysis of this period, see Jurgen Domes, *China After the Cultural Revolution* (Berkeley: University of California Press, 1977). A substantial collection of key documents for 1973–1978, illustrating conflicting programs within the CCP leadership before 1976 and the post-1976 polemics against the Gang, is Raymond Lotta, ed., *And Mao Makes Five: Mao Tsetung's Last Great Battle* (Chicago: Banner Press, 1978); the editor's introduction argues that the Gang of Four were the real Maoists and that their purge represented a right-wing coup against the true Chinese Left.

society by shifting resources and status to less privileged sectors of Chinese society — that is, from elites to masses and from city to countryside. Bureaucratic organizations were simplified, their personnel reduced. All cadres spent several months in May Seven Cadre Schools, where they engaged in a mixture of manual labor and ideological study. Technical and professional specialists were urged to "integrate with the masses" and renounce their "bourgeois" dreams of individual recognition and advancement. There were reports of salary reductions at the upper end of the pay scales, coupled with pressure on all citizens to abjure privileged life styles. Revolutionary committees, which had become the administrative organs of government, were extended into other units, thereby providing some mass representation in the management of factories, enterprises, schools, and other institutions.

Maoist reforms had their greatest impact in the realm of education, culture, and public health. As schools reopened after the closures of the late 1960s, several changes became evident (see Chapter V for fuller discussion). Primary school attendance swelled, becoming nearly universal as resources were concentrated on this effort; middle school (secondary level) enrollment also grew rapidly, but university enrollment remained far below the pre-1966 years. Courses of study were shortened; grades, examinations, and theoretical study were played down; political education, applied and practical studies, and experience in manual labor held priority. Virtually all middle school students received rural work assignments on graduation. Cultural policy promoted simple revolutionary themes in a populist style, limiting cultural expression to a few officially approved forms while criticizing anything smacking of "feudal" or "bourgeois" influences; foreign influences were also objects of suspicion. In public health, as in education, there was a major effort to serve rural areas. Large numbers of doctors and medical teams moved to the countryside. The general thrust of reforms was to provide minimal health care for the population as a whole rather than specialized care for the few who had access to advanced medical centers in the cities. Medical training emphasized training of generalists and armies of paramedics (the "barefoot doctors") who could extend simple treatment or referral services into the villages.

Despite the Cultural Revolution's attacks on Liu Shaoqi's

"revisionist" economic policies, the broad outlines of the economic policies of the early 1960s remained in place. "Agriculture as the foundation," the three-level commune system with the production team as the basic accounting unit, and household retention of private plots all persisted, although there was some discussion of reviving more collectivist measures. The Cultural Revolution spirit did, however, encourage an "antieconomist" stance that was critical of emphasis on material incentives or production goals. Local initiative, development of rural, small-scale industry, and worker participation in management received greater attention than in the past.

These reforms had heavy rhetorical support and considerable impact, but they soon ran into difficulties. Sino-Soviet border clashes in 1969 and the beginning of American retreat from Vietnam led to the limited Sino-American rapprochement signaled in the Shanghai Communiqué of February 1972. The PRC began to reorient its foreign relations toward greater contact with capitalist countries to build a united front against the USSR; the Soviet threat also raised serious questions about China's economic and technical development that put Cultural Revolution assumptions about the primacy of politics in a different light (see Chapters IV and VII for further discussion). Moreover, Mao's failing health and declining role in governmental affairs compelled other leaders to face the political and strategic implications of the post-Mao era, even though they were reluctant to depart from the leader's prescriptions while he was alive.

Institutional uncertainties also obstructed the reforms. State and party organs were slow to recover from the shattering events of 1966–1969. Many experienced cadres were purged or away from their original work assignments. The 1954 state constitution was discredited, but a new one was not adopted until January 1975. The CCP was taking in many new members even though the fate of old cadres was not yet clear. The role of mass organizations and the PLA was in flux, the former beginning to revive and the latter retreating from its political prominence of the late 1960s. The resolution of these institutional issues was in itself a matter of dispute, but as long as they remained unresolved, they weakened administrative effectiveness.

Most importantly, these problems combined with the residue of Cultural Revolution factionalism to produce serious splits within the leadership (see Chapter VI for further discussion of elite conflicts). The initial post-1969 leadership was a coalition of three groupings: the most ardent Maoists or "radicals" who drew strength from their close association with the Chairman and their manipulation of his directives — Jiang Qing (Chiang Ch'ing), Mao's wife, was the key figure in this group; the military elite who, though not united, benefited from Defense Minister Lin Biao's designation as second-in-command and Mao's chosen successor; the veteran administrators, led by Zhou Enlai, who represented what was left of the "moderate" position in Chinese politics.

This coalition proved unstable. A major rupture occurred in 1971 with the purge of Lin Biao for allegedly plotting a coup against Mao.[60] Lin's downfall — apparently due mainly to his ambitious drive for power but also involving more obscure differences with Mao, particularly on policies toward the Soviet Union and the United States — was accompanied by the purge of several other high-ranking military leaders and was followed by a reduction of PLA influence, leaving the "radicals" and "moderates" in uneasy balance. The former tried to protect the more radical version of Cultural Revolution reforms, whereas the latter tried to moderate their effects and concentrate more on economic development. There was backsliding on some of the reforms as Zhou Enlai sponsored the restoration of many old cadres who had been purged in the Cultural Revolution. The most prominent example was the return of Deng Xiaoping, who had been linked to Liu Shaoqi as a leading "capitalist-roader" in the Cultural Revolution but who had, by 1975, moved into virtual leadership of the government as Zhou's health failed. The 1972–1976 period, then, was marked by increasing tension within the leadership, with discordant interpretations of key campaigns (particularly the "criticize Lin Biao and Confucius" movement),[61] by increasing

---

[60]For documentation and analysis, see Michael Y. M. Kau, ed., *The Lin Piao Affair: Power Politics and Military Coup* (White Plains, New York: International Arts and Sciences Press, 1975).

[61]Merle Goldman, "China's Anti-Confucian Campaign, 1973–74," *China Quarterly*, no. 63 (September 1975), pp. 435–62.

labor disputes and social unrest, and by a pronounced economic slowdown in 1974–1976. When Zhou Enlai died in January 1976, the "radicals" — apparently with Mao's support —
engineered Deng's second purge, the premiership going to a
relative newcomer, Hua Guofeng. However, Deng's removal
exacerbated the conflict, providing further unrest manifested
in an unruly demonstration in Tiananmen square in Peking in
April 1976. Mao's death on September 9, 1976, removed the
last barrier to an open confrontation.

THE POST-MAO PERIOD, 1976–1978

In early October 1976, Hua Guofeng arrested the Gang of
Four — the epithet chosen for the four leading radicals (Jiang
Qing, Yao Wenyuan, Zhang Chunqiao (Chang Ch'un-ch'iao)
and Wang Hongwen) — and unleashed a vitriolic campaign
against them for distorting Mao's directives, sabotaging the
government and economy with their factional activity, and
generally following a "rightist" line under the guise of "radicalism." Hua became Chairman of the CCP and of the CC's
Military Affairs Commission, while continuing to hold the
premiership. For the next several months, the new leadership
concentrated on consolidating its position and charging the
Gang with responsibility for nearly all of China's problems
over the preceding decade. This was done in the name of Mao,
who was said to have picked Hua as successor and to have
recognized the Gang's disruptive and deviant character well
before his death. Hua and his colleagues clearly wanted to
retain Maoist legitimacy and avoid explicit departures from
the Maoist legacy. At the same time, criticism of the Gang
inevitably suggested criticism of the Cultural Revolution and
pointed toward changes in Cultural Revolution policies.

These changes began to take concrete form after the Eleventh National Congress of the CCP in August 1977, which
produced the new party constitution discussed earlier and
confirmed Hua's leading position. Equally important was the
reinstatement of Deng Xiaoping (as CCP vice chairman and
later vice premier of the government), who quickly became a
spokesperson for new policies. In March 1978, the Fifth NPC,
with its adoption of a new state constitution, gave further
impetus to the emergence of a new line. These two meetings,

plus a number of national conferences on particular policy areas, produced evidence of significant modifications in Cultural Revolution policies.[62]

Basic to the policies enunciated in 1977–1978 was the assertion that China had entered a "new period" of socialist development. In his report to the Eleventh Party Congress, Hua announced that the Cultural Revolution was over, and his report to the Fifth NPC some seven months later was largely devoted to expounding the general tasks of the new period to come. With this shift, criticism of the Gang began to give way to a more positive focus on the tasks ahead. The effect was to reduce substantially the salience of Cultural Revolution themes. As noted in the earlier discussion of political institutions, a new emphasis on order, discipline, socialist legality, and organizational regularity appeared, coupled with sharp attacks on the disruptions and factionalism of the preceding period. Aware of the possible charge that this was a repudiation of Maoism, the new leaders turned to some of Mao's writings previous to the Cultural Revolution for justification of their actions. They also suggested that Mao's directives, while correct in their original context, were not necessarily valid in a literal sense under different circumstances.[63] This subtle

[62]See *PR*, nos. 35 and 36 (August 26, September 2, 1977) for documentation on the Eleventh Party Congress; and *PR*, nos. 10 and 11 (March 10, 17, 1978), for documentation on the Fifth NPC. Major policy statements at conferences include Deng Xiaoping's speeches at the National Science Conference, *PR*, no. 12 (March 24, 1978), pp. 9–18; and at the National Education Conference, *PR*, no. 18 (May 5, 1978), pp. 6–12; and Hua Guofeng's speech at the National Finance and Trade Conference, *PR*, no. 30 (July 28, 1978), pp. 6–15. For analyses of events leading to the Gang's fall, the purge itself, and initial post-Mao policies, see Jürgen Domes, "The 'Gang of Four' — and Hua Kuo-feng: Analysis of Political Events in 1975–76," *China Quarterly*, no. 71 (September 1977), pp. 473–97; Tang Tsou, "Mao Tse-tung Thought, the Last Struggle for Succession, and the Post-Mao Era," Ibid, pp. 498–527; Harry Harding, Jr., "China After Mao," *Problems of Communism*, vol. 26, no. 2 (March–April 1977), pp. 1–18; and Kenneth Lieberthal, "The Politics of Modernization in the PRC," Ibid, vol. 27, no. 3 (May–June 1978), pp. 1–17. For a strong argument that the Gang represented Maoism, and that post-1976 events constitute a revisionist betrayal of the Cultural Revolution, see Charles Bettelheim, "The Great Leap Backward," *Monthly Review*, vol. 30, no. 3 (July–August 1978), pp. 37–130.

[63]Joint editorial of *People's Daily*, *Red Flag* and *Liberation Army Daily* on the first anniversary of Mao's death, text in *PR*, nos. 37, 38 (September 13, 1977), pp. 21–23.

playing down of the late chairman's thought was matched by a distinct elevation of Zhou Enlai's status, thereby diluting further the preeminence of Mao's position. In all of these ways, Hua's administration began to free itself from the restraints of Cultural Revolution symbolism without repudiating Maoism as such.

The major theme for the new period was the "four modernizations" — that is, to attain the all-around modernization of agriculture, industry, national defense, and science and technology by the end of the century, thereby placing the Chinese economy in the front ranks of the world and approaching or overtaking the most developed capitalist countries in agricultural and industrial output. A Ten-Year Plan for 1976–1985 adopted equally ambitious short-run goals of 4–5 percent annual increases in agricultural output and over 10 percent annual increases in industrial output. This explicit commitment to a monumental modernization and economic development program — its origins attributed to Zhou Enlai's proposals at previous NPC meetings — went hand in hand with open criticism of China's "backwardness" and 1974–1976 economic problems. Although spokespersons routinely attributed the ills of the previous decade to the Gang's influence, they acknowledged that future development called for far more than removal of the troublemakers. Measures cited to stimulate economic development included tighter factory discipline, more scientific and rational management practices, increased foreign trade and technology imports (with promotion of tourism to help pay the price), and judicious use of material incentives and other rewards for individual achievement.

The most striking changes were in education, science, and technology. Deng Xiaoping went so far as to say that the key to the four modernizations was the modernization of science and technology[64] — an opinion fundamentally at odds with the Cultural Revolution version of Maoism. Large increases in college enrolments were planned, with greater reliance on examinations, grades, and other academic criteria for admission and promotion. Advanced studies and theoretical research came back into favor, with teachers and researchers

[64]Deng's speech at the National Science Conference, op. cit., p. 10.

promised higher status, more individual recognition, and better working conditions. Schools were urged to identify the best students early — particularly in scientific and technical fields — and to accelerate their progress; elite schools for the gifted were approved. A kind of "hundred flowers" spirit developed in intellectual and cultural life as new academic debates opened up, foreign contacts increased (including plans to send large numbers of Chinese students to the United States), and greater diversity became apparent in forms of cultural expression.

This sketch suggests that a significant modification of developmental strategy was underway by 1978, involving a repudiation of many Cultural Revolution policies. Indeed, in late 1978 Deng lent his support to an overall condemnation of the Cultural Revolution that came very close to a repudiation of Maoism as well; Hua held back, indicating the controversiality of how to handle Mao's legacy. In the long run, however, the issue of Maoism may become less salient or even irrelevant. The point of the "new period" argument is that China must adopt new policies, must respond to and master the demands of modernization, if it is to become a leading world power. We will give more consideration to the rationale and implications of that argument, and how it relates to the Maoist model, in later chapters.

CHAPTER IV

The Communist System: Change and Ideology

COMMUNIST SYSTEMS raise major conceptual problems in the study of comparative politics. We touched lightly on this in Chapter I, particularly in reference to the inadequacies of the totalitarian model, and now we must explore it more carefully in generalizing about the Chinese system. What makes conceptualization difficult, as one student of comparative communism has pointed out, is that Communist systems tend to be identified in general typologies as stable and institutionalized, whereas studies of specific Communist systems reveal acute problems in coping with change and institutionalization.[1] Indeed, tension between stability and change seems to be inherent in such systems, which seek to stabilize and concentrate power in the political system in order to transform the social system. In practice, the political system cannot alter society significantly without serious repercussions.[2] As demonstrated in the preceding chapter, China is a prime example of the way in which efforts to transform society threaten the stability of the regime promoting that transformation.

Change is a two-dimensional problem in classifying the Chinese system. There is initially the question of how much the system has changed in terms of its own internal characteristics.

[1]Chalmers Johnson, "Comparing Communist Nations," in Chalmers Johnson, ed., *Change in Communist Systems* (Stanford, Cal.: Stanford University Press, 1970), pp. 1–3 passim.
[2]Richard Lowenthal, "Development vs. Utopia in Communist Policy," in Johnson, ed., ibid., p. 33.

Has it retained its basic character, has it moved from one kind of system to another, or has it been so fluid and unstable that it defies classification? The other dimension is the comparative one. Regardless of how stable or unstable the Chinese system has been, is it appropriately grouped with certain other systems? More concretely, in terms of the framework that guides this study,[3] does the Chinese system belong with other Communist systems in Almond and Powell's classification, or does it belong in a subtype of that category or perhaps in a distinct category of its own?

These are not easy questions to answer. The discussion that follows concentrates on the first question about internal change but also tries to respond to the comparative dimension. The answers given are tentative and, as in most such efforts, somewhat arbitrary. The purpose is not to persuade the reader that they are the only correct answers but to bring out some of the issues involved in a full and accurate response.

The analysis assumes that it is most useful to classify the PRC as a Communist political system, that is, a socialist system under the rule of a single party that proclaims adherence to Marxism-Leninism. Since this is a very loose categorization, the first task is to take note of patterns of change in post-1949 China that might challenge or refine it. The analysis addresses both cyclical change—movement through different but recurring styles of action—and long-term secular change in which the system has evolved new characteristics. The discussion of change concludes with an effort to periodize the development of the Chinese political system, focusing on three different phases in its evolution. We shift then to a discussion of ideology, emphasizing its importance as an element of identity and continuity in the Chinese Communist system, but also noting how it has contributed to the fluidity and conflict that make generalizations about the system so difficult. The chapter concludes with some summary observations on the problem of classification.

Since this chapter dwells heavily on elements of internal change and deviation from more generalized models, it is

[3]See Gabriel A. Almond and G. Bingham Powell, Jr., *Comparative Politics: System, Process, and Policy,* 2nd ed. (Boston: Little, Brown, 1978), and Chapter I of this book.

worth stressing here that the People's Republic has been and remains a Communist system. Its elite ideology commits it to rapid modernization in pursuit of an envisioned classless society throughout the world, which is seen as requiring a socialist economy, a party dictatorship, creation of a new socialist man, and long-term struggle with capitalist systems.[4] From this elite ideological political culture the system derives additional characteristics: a differentiated political structure largely controlled by governmental elites, a mixed subject-participant political culture among ordinary citizens, and a high degree of penetration and mobilization of society to bring about its socialist transformation. These are valid as generalizations about the Chinese system, even though they must be qualified in more detailed analysis. Moreover, the salience of change and instability in post-1949 China does not mean that the Communist government is weak or vulnerable to an overthrow or transformation leading to a non-Communist system. The PRC has not faced, and probably will not face in the foreseeable future, a serious threat to its survival.

The possibility of counterrevolution by non-Communist Chinese elites has been virtually nil since the reconstruction period. The only likely source of such a movement is the Nationalist government on Taiwan, which does not have the power to carry it to a successful conclusion. The bid of the democratic parties for more political influence in 1957 was no threat at all, even though it was treated as such by the CCP. Foreign intervention or assistance would, of course, significantly alter the picture. Yet despite the CCP's sensitivity to this possibility, neither the United States nor the Soviet Union seems likely to embark on a serious effort to force a change in the present system. The risks are enormous in view of China's developing nuclear capacities, and it is doubtful if a foreign-sponsored effort could succeed politically even if it held military superiority.

[4]See Lowenthal, op. cit., pp. 39–54; and Benjamin I. Schwartz, *Communism and China: Ideology in Flux* (Cambridge, Mass.: Harvard University Press, 1968), esp. pp. 23–26. For Chinese statements on the requirements of a Communist system, see the pamphlets by the editorial departments of *Renmin Ribao* and *Hongqi*, *Is Yugoslavia a Socialist Country?* (Peking: Foreign Languages Press, 1963) and *On Khrushchev's Phoney Communism and Its Historical Lessons for the World* (Peking: Foreign Language Press, 1964).

The most plausible threats to the Communist system's survival come from within, and here two possibilities suggest themselves. One is that the present regime might disintegrate, fractured by internal rivalries or disasters that would leave behind something like the warlord era following the fall of the Qing dynasty. A precedent for this possibility is already before us in the Cultural Revolution, which some observers saw as a typically Chinese dynastic disintegration.[5] The threat of disintegration and civil war was sufficient to bring the CCP back from the precipice, however, and in retrospect it seems that the danger of collapse was not so great as the events of 1966–1968 suggested. The combination of Mao's authority at the center and the power of the People's liberation Army in the provinces placed limits, although not without difficulty, on the spread and duration of local conflicts.

A second possible form of transformation from within is the one cited by the Maoists during the Cultural Revolution; that is, a "capitalist restoration" in which a group of "authorities taking the capitalist road" convert the party into a "revisionist" instrument to dismantle the socialist system. It was Mao's contention, of course, that this had happened already in Yugoslavia and the Soviet Union and that it would have happened in China save for the Cultural Revolution. Given the subsequent purges of Lin Biao and the Gang, it appears that transformation from within, by high-level CCP elites, is the most likely possibility for a fundamental change in the Communist system. A case could be made that Lin's attempted coup — assuming that was indeed his intent — would have constituted such a change. It is less certain that the Mao-Liu and Hua-Gang conflicts posed choices between a Communist and non-Communist system. The argument here is that they demonstrated different variants of the system, rather than non-Communist alternatives to it, although we will note some of the arguments to the contrary. Whatever position one takes on this question, there is no doubt that elite conflicts with the CCP have signaled acute problems of institutionalization and sharp controversies over the proper path of Chinese socialist

[5]For example, see L. La Dany, "Mao's China: The Decline of a Dynasty," *Foreign Affairs,* vol. 45, no. 4 (July 1967), pp. 610–33.

development. A closer look at patterns of change in the post-1949 system is in order.

CYCLICAL CHANGE

Cyclical change refers to regularized movement from one condition to another, each representing a recurrence of some previous condition. The movement may be frequent and even extreme, but the larger pattern has a static quality owing to its repetition of previous phases. In simplest form this type of change may be oscillation between two poles, or it may involve progression through a more complicated cycle of multiple stages. Description of cycles in social history necessarily simplifies or distorts reality; there is always some evolutionary change in human affairs so that no cycle is exactly like its predecessors. It is analytically useful, however, for identifying patterns of change, their limits or boundaries, and the ways in which they do or do not replicate previous conditions.

Mobilization-Consolidation. In the case of post-1949 Chinese politics, analyses of cyclical change tend to focus on oscillation between two opposed styles or policy positions—commonly identified as a Maoist or radical position on the left and a bureaucratic or moderate position on the right—and their alternate manifestation in periods of campaign mobilization and consolidation. The Maoist position initiates the cycle, with a mobilization based on ideological goals and typically relying on mass movements; the bureaucratic position, typically oriented toward economic goals and relying on more institutionalized procedures, come to the fore to consolidate campaign results. One can fit much of PRC history into this mold, showing a rough alternation between left and right leadership tendencies and between mobilization and consolidation phases, and suggesting an initial way of understanding variation in CCP rule.

Recurring mass campaigns have been a distinctive feature of the Chinese system.[6] Despite their bewildering diversity (in

[6] See Gordon Bennett, *Yundong: Mass Campaigns in Chinese Communist Leadership* (Berkeley: University of California, Center for Chinese Studies, 1976); and Charles P. Cell, *Revolution at Work: Mobilization Campaigns in China* (New York: Academic Press, 1977).

scope, duration, goals, and intensity), they tend to progress through mobilization and consolidation phases; the former defining, testing, and attacking campaign goals; the latter assessing, correcting, and consolidating their results. The also tend to give Chinese political life a pulsating quality of advance and retreat, of political intensification and relaxation. The tone of politics in a particular locality or policy sector depends heavily on whether or not a campaign affecting that unit or sector is in progress and, if so, what phase it is in.

It is tempting to extend campaign characteristics to larger cycles in the Chinese political process. The most explicit and provocative effort has described a six-phase cycle in rural policy, with eight cycles initiated between 1949 and 1965.[7] It is also possible to distinguish some generalized mobilization and consolidation periods in national politics; the former dominated by major national campaigns; the latter sorting out and modifying the results. Mobilization periods occurred, for example, in 1949–1952 (land reform and other early campaigns), in 1955–1956 (accelerated collectivization), 1957–58 (the Leap and communes), and in 1965–1967 (the early Cultural Revolution); each was followed by a consolidating relaxation and/or modification of campaign goals and policies. One can see "radical" initiatives in the mobilizations, "moderate" guidance in the consolidations.

The student of Chinese politics must be sensitive to the campaign syndrome and its relationship to the tone of national politics, but must not push this type of generalization too far. Campaigns have been too numerous and diverse to yield a single, consistent pattern in the system as a whole. The larger national cycles seem most valid for the 1950s and possibly the early 1960s, when relative consensus among elites permitted this policy alternation. It is much harder to sort out mobilization and consolidation phases from the early 1960s on as radical and moderate positions hardened into more open and constant conflict; rather than alternation, one tends to see confused competition in which rival elites turned campaigns

[7]G. William Skinner and Edwin A. Winckler, "Compliance Succession in Rural Communist China: A Cyclical Theory," in Amitai Etzioni, ed., *Complex Organizations: A Sociological Reader,* 2nd ed. (New York: Holt, Rinehart and Winston, 1969), pp. 410-38.

on each other in a way that destroyed any sense of cyclical progression. These conflicts also brought out details, or alleged details, of earlier ones, thereby revealing some of the inadequacies of simplified cyclical models for Chinese politics. With these cautions—which reflect the unavoidable tension between a search for generalizations and the uniqueness and complexity of historical events[8] — let us look briefly at two other areas in which campaign mobilizations have had significant impact.

Institutional Instability. The political structure of the PRC has experienced periods of both institutionalization and institutional instability, with the most intense national campaigns the primary source of instability. The distinction here is not simply institutional growth versus institutional destruction; obviously, some parts of the political structure have been more durable than others, so that the changes referred to have never been total reverses. Rather, it is one between development of institutions along prescribed or established lines in certain periods and open-ended experimentation with institutional forms in others. In periods of institutionalization, the elements and interrelationships of the structure have been fixed so that its development has followed predictable patterns; in periods of institutional fluidity, existing forms have been challenged or new ones introduced so that the outcome has been in doubt.

The years between 1949 and 1953 constituted a period of institutional fluidity, since many institutional arrangements were temporary and a great deal of experimentation was taking place. By the end of 1953, the basic outlines of socialist political and economic structure had been established, bring-

[8]For an interesting debate on cyclical analysis, bringing out both its empirical weaknesses and its utility for certain analytic purposes, see Andrew J. Nathan, "Policy Oscillations in the People's Republic of China: A Critique," *China Quarterly,* no. 68 (December 1976), pp. 720–33; and Edwin A. Winckler, "Policy Oscillations in the People's Republic of China: A Reply," Ibid., pp. 734–50. For further analysis, focusing more sharply on alternation between charismatic (Maoist) and bureaucratic leadership styles, see Paul Hiniker and Jolanta Perlstein, "Alternation of Charismatic and Bureaucratic Styles of Leadership in Postrevolutionary China," *Comparative Political Studies,* vol. 10, no. 4 (January 1978), pp. 529–54.

ing on a period of institutionalization, generally coinciding with the First Five-Year Plan and formalized by the 1954 constitution. There were continued institutional changes during these years, particularly the speedup of collectivization in 1955, but they were essentially changes in the pace or timing of existing plans. The Eighth Party Congress in 1956 was still dominated by a tendency toward institutionalization. The Great Leap Forward was a period of pronounced institutional fluidity characterized by general rejection of the Soviet model and experimentation with the new forms and relationships (described in Chapter III). Institutionalization resumed in 1960, building on a combination of pre-Leap patterns of organization and some of the policies initiated in the Leap — for example, commune nomenclature and framework, verbal commitment to class struggle and "revolutionary" transformation, and repoliticization of the PLA. This period continued until 1965, when the Cultural Revolution shattered the prevailing pattern of institutional development and opened up the system to major structural innovations. The period after the Ninth Congress established prescriptive guidelines for renewed institutionalization on Maoist terms, but in this case intensifying elite controversy over Cultural Revolution reforms paralyzed the process. After 1976, the post-Mao leadership explicitly encouraged an institutionalization that bore many similarities, in both tone and structural content, to the mid-1950s institutionalization that accompanied the FFYP and the adoption of the 1954 state constitution.

Variations in Popular Political Life. Popular political life is another area in which campaigns have encouraged major variations. One of the most important is the distinction between periods of *antagonistic* and *nonantagonistic* struggle. The former directs movements against groups or personalities said to be hostile toward the socialist system, that is, "enemies of the people." Frequently occurring in mobilization phases, it produces great political tension owing to the severe consequences — public denunciation and sanctions — that attend identification as an "enemy." Examples include mobilizations against landlords and counterrevolutionaries in 1950–1951, against "rightists" in the summer of 1957, against "capitalist-

roaders" in 1965–1967, and against the Gang and their supporters in 1976–1977.

"Nonantagonistic" struggle is more likely to occur between
campaigns or in consolidation phases, when coexistence
among different classes in socialist society is being emphasized. It criticizes errors and deviations, but the object is education and reform rather than punishment or explusion from
the ranks of the people. Examples include investigation of land
reform results in 1951, the early "hundred flowers" criticism
in 1957 (before the CCP initiated antagonistic struggle against
the critics), and criticism during 1961–1962 of cadre behavior
during the Great Leap. In both the Cultural Revolution and
the campaign against the Gang, antagonistic struggle eventually focused on a few key enemies, promising reintegration for
other targets who reformed. Alternation between these different forms of struggle is neither neat or predictable, but it is an
important campaign-related feature of Chinese politics.

Mobilization and consolidation has also produced variations
in the degree of party control over popular political action.
The mass line leads the CCP to mix its concern for organizational control with calls for mass spontaneity and initiative. As
a result, mobilization phases have sometimes produced cases
in which local initiative has carried the movement beyond its
central guidelines, whereas consolidation phases have been
vulnerable to popular reactions exceeding the leadership's
view of appropriate rectification of mistakes.

The reconstruction years and the Cultural Revolution stand
out as periods in which the looseness of controls relative to the
intensity of the campaign permitted considerable spontaneous
mass activity. In some cases, the actions in question — primarily by peasants' associations in land reform, by Red Guards or
rebels in the Cultural Revolution — had official approval but
not direct leadership. In other cases, they moved in a "basically correct" direction against the center's targets but did so
with excessive violence or zeal; or, alternatively, they got completely out of hand and became a vehicle for localized interests
hostile to central objectives. The early part of the Great Leap
was another period of considerable latitutde in local implementation of central directives. Here initiative led not so much
to excessive or unauthorized political struggle as to overly

ambitious efforts by local cadres to realize the Leap's more radical features. The peasants did not generally encourage this "spontaneity" (although some apparently pushed for the "free supply" system), but they were inevitably caught up in it through the countless mass political meetings and discussions that the movement required.

While spontaneity in mobilization phases has tended toward unwanted violence and radicalism, in consolidation phases it has sometimes appeared in reaction or even rebellion against party authority. For example, most of the criticism by intellectuals during the "hundred flowers" campaign was within the guidelines of the CCP's call for rectification, but some of it did attack the party's leadership as such. More important, student critics engaged in physical assaults on cadres and efforts to organize interuniversity exchanges of experiences and ideas. Peasant and worker unrest during the same period was relatively high, with many reports of peasant withdrawals from cooperatives.[9] The occurrence of localized uprisings in 1960–1961 was noted in the previous chapter, and the land reform-collectivization years were punctuated by recurring peasant and local cadre reaction against the Communist agricultural program whenever the pace of mobilization relaxed.[10]

Once again, the point is not to argue that there is a clear correlation between campaign phases and popular political spontaneity; both variables are too complex for that. For example, there was a good deal of spontaneous or deviant activity throughout 1974–1978 — factory disruptions, dissident wall posters, the Tiananmen Incident of April 1976, and some remarkably open articles in the cultural "thaw" of 1977–

[9]Roderick MacFarquhar, *The Hundred Flowers Campaign and the Chinese Intellectuals* (New York: Praeger, 1960), pp. 130–73, 231–47.

[10]See the following articles by Thomas P. Bernstein: "Leadership and Mass Mobilisation in the Soviet and Chinese Collectivisation Campaigns of 1920–30 and 1955–56: A Comparison," *China Quarterly,* no. 31 (July–Sept. 1967), pp. 1–47; "Problems of Village Leadership After Land Reform," *China Quarterly,* no. 36. (Oct.–Dec. 1968), pp. 1–22; and "Cadre and Peasant Behavior Under Conditions of Insecurity and Deprivation: The Grain Supply Crisis of the Spring of 1955," in A. Doak Barnett, ed., *Chinese Communist Politics in Action* (Seattle: University of Washington Press, 1969), pp. 365–99. Bernstein's analysis of land reform and collectivization provides an excellent illustration of the complex alternation between mobilization and consolidation, and antagonistic and nonantagonistic struggle, in Chinese politics.

1978 that was not linked clearly to particular phases of a campaign cycle. What is significant here is that popular political action has repeatedly exceeded officially prescribed limits on both ends of the political spectrum, suggesting that such swings are not aberrations but a regular part of the political process. Its limitations notwithstanding, cyclical analysis makes an important contribution in reminding us that there is no single version of "normal" politics in China.

SECULAR CHANGE

Cyclical interpretations of Chinese politics founder on the reality of secular change. That is, even if there is a tendency to follow an oscillating pattern of mobilization and consolidation, long-term evolutionary change alters the issues and context so that earlier patterns cannot be repeated. This section identifies three particularly important areas of secular change — socioeconomic change, changes in political culture and participation, and changes in political leadership. The discussion will be quite general, drawing on the survey material introduced in Chapter III and anticipating some points to be developed more fully later in the text.

Socioeconomic Change. Socioeconomic change in post-1949 China has altered significantly the social basis of Chinese politics, creating new sources of influence and conflict within the system. The question here is not whether Communist efforts at economic development have been uniformly successful, or whether Chinese social structure has undergone a total transformation since 1949. The regime's developmental record is strong, revealing an overall pattern of economic growth and social change that nonetheless leaves China a largely agrarian society in the early stages of industrialization. Precise calculations of the rate and extent of change are in dispute due to the inadequacy or unreliability of available data. What is not in dispute, however, is that Chinese society has experienced fundamental changes that have altered the relative weights of various political actors and issues. These changes have come about largely as a result of rapid modernization and socialization of the system, either accelerated or initiated following the Communist victory in 1949.

One of the most pronounced changes has been the elimination or political neutralization of some social strata and the expansion of others. The landlords, merchants, and industrialists who held substantial political influence before 1949 have disappeared; while the ranks of industrial workers, state employees, and intellectuals (including middle school graduates as well as more highly trained technical and professional personnel) have increased sharply. The urban population of China also has grown rapidly although remaining a small proportion of the total. Significant changes also have affected the numerically dominant rural population, for collectivization transformed the peasant from tenant or owner-cultivator to an agricultural worker whose labor and rewards are largely determined by a local collective organization that is incorporated into the national economic and administrative system.

By 1957 all of these changes were highly visible (and in the case of rural collectivization and destruction of the old economic elite, essentially completed). They have continued since the late 1950s, although in a less pronounced and dramatic way than in the first decade of Communist rule. In fact, a fundamental alteration in the relationship between Chinese government and society occurred between 1949 and the late 1950s, centering on an unprecedented expansion of governmental resources, personnel, operations, claims, and power. This alteration did not take place at one stroke in 1949–1950 with the shift from Nationalist to Communist political leadership; rather, it came about as a consequence of that shift and the program of industrialization and socialism promoted by the new national leadership. It was only after the completion of the First Five-Year Plan that the new relationship of government to society was really established. The old indicators of economic and social status — wealth, land ownership, education, age, sex, and kinship ties — had declined rapidly as sources of political power, although they certainly continued to have some political relevance particularly at the basic level. Indeed, the scope of governmental programs and demands was such that the citizen's economic and social status had become largely a function of governmental policy or of an explicitly political definition of favored and disfavored classes. Political power in the new relationship fell exclusively to manifestly political roles; that is, to authoritative positions in the party, state, or army hierarchies, recruitment to which was controlled by CCP policies. As of 1957 it appeared that the physical location of governmental power and of those most likely to gain access to it increasingly was located in the cities in the complex of government offices, state economic enterprises, and educational facilities that seemed to be the vanguard of China's socialist future.

The new development thrust that began in the late 1950s modified the initial trend in one important respect — it limited urban growth while promoting rural economic and social development. The urban-rural gap remained, with the best facilities and higher-income groups (high-level cadres, professionals and technicians, and skilled workers) still concentrated in the cities, but rural areas experienced considerable agricultural modernization and growth of educational, health and communications facilities. By the late 1970s, the socioeconomic revolution had penetrated deeply into the countryside, distributing its gains much more broadly throughout Chinese society.

In other respects, however, the main trends established in the 1950s continued. Industrialization continued to progress faster than agricultural growth, with the Chinese economy interacting more with the world economy and moving into high-technology areas. New industrial centers emerged, hastening national economic integration. Increased manufacturing potential and modest gains in per-capita income brought growing consumer demands. As foreshadowed by the 1950s, the government's scope of responsibility expanded, its tasks becoming more complex and controversial. The revolution's leveling tendencies — supported by Maoist egalitarianism — reduced the sharpest social cleavages of the past, but abundant conflicts over development and distribution of the social product remained. These conflicts were now injected into the government, which became the arena for the resolution of almost all competing interests.

Just as Chinese society of the late 1950s was different from that of 1949, so was society of the late 1970s different from that of the late 1950s. The period of Maoist ascendancy, spanning the Great Leap and the Cultural Revolution, had brought substantial changes to the countryside, while trying to forestall institutionalization of a new urban-bureaucratic elite. At the same time, continued economic growth and development produced at least partly contrary pressures for a new wave of modernization that would rely on social forces held in check during the Maoist era.

Political Culture and Participation. The CCP's socialization and mobilization efforts have changed the mix of Chinese political culture, raising the general level of political awareness and increasing the proportion of politically involved citizens. The substance and degree of this change is controversial, since much of the evidence that relates to it is indirect or ambiguous. The proposition rests, however, on some solid foundations. One is that the CCP has unfolded a political education movement of great magnitude, backed by an organizational and communications network surpassing anything known in China's past. Another is that the CCP has mobilized the population for direct participation in political campaigns and basic-level affairs; heavy party controls raise questions about the meaning of this participation, but it surely contributes to popular politicization. Finally, formal education has spread, with primary education becoming nearly universal and secondary education now available to nearly 40 percent of primary graduates; increasing political skills, literacy, and knowledge accompany this trend.

Equally significant is the expansion and diffusion throughout Chinese society of those who constitute China's political elite and subelite; that is, people who have received a relatively intense kind of political education and, as either cause or effect, have assumed distinctive political roles. We should note here an important aspect of China's political heritage: although traditional Chinese political culture was dominated by feelings of powerlessness and isolation with respect to political authority, there was always in Chinese society a small elite of scholar-officials marked by a highly developed sense of political obligation and participation. What the Chinese Communists have done is to reinforce this sense of elite political responsibility (although altering the determinants of elitehood), while greatly expanding the numbers of those who qualify for it. The size of the CCP — the simplest indicator of political elitehood in contemporary China — gives one measure of this expansion. Combining party membership with Youth League membership produces a figure roughly representative of a distinctive political stratum from which most in-office elites are chosen. This figure — about 83 million in 1978[11] — may be contrasted with the 1–2 million gentry who were the actual and potential political elite of late Qing China.

The significance in this comparison is not simply the difference in absolute numbers but the fact that the pool of potential political elites in comtemporary China is so readily expandable. Since political elite or subelite status depends initially on the acquisition of political education or experience to which exposure is almost automatic for all younger generations, or even more simply on what higher elites perceive to be distinctive political consciousness, the pool of potential political recruits is truly enormous — in sharp contrast to the pool in imperial China that was normally limited to those who engaged in exacting and lifelong scholarly study. Although for many of the CCP old guard the necessary credentials came through a lifetime of revolutionary activity, since 1949 they have been attainable in rather ordinary ways. For example, any Chinese who has served in the PLA or received a middle school or higher education — unless he has some specific political mark against him — is really part of the subelite, simply because he has received a level of political education and training in other skills that sets him apart from the rest of the population. After three decades of Communist rule, this pool is so numerous and so widely diffused throughout Chinese society that higher in-office elites can no longer assume that only a small, easily identifiable stratum is politically relevant. Between official and what may still be a politically unsophisticated mass of citizens, there is now a broad intermediate stratum, relatively youthful, that is a political force of some importance.

The expansion of political education, activity, and potential elitehood among the Chinese population does not necessarily

[11]The Eleventh Party Congress in 1977 reported over 35 million party members. CYL membership in 1978 was 48 million; see *PR* no. 20 (May 19, 1978), p. 10.

produce a uniform political culture. There is ample evidence — particularly in the Cultural Revolution and the turmoil of 1974–1978 — that mobilization of the Chinese citizenry has led to sharp conflicts at the popular level; in some cases these conflicts mirror elite differences, in others they reveal more distinctly local or popular issues. What the expansion signifies is, first, that the body of citizens mobilized for politics since 1949 now dwarfs the old revolutionary cadre; second, that the intermediate political stratum is very diverse in its social background and interests. The result is to inject into the system new influences that necessarily alter perceptions of the key issues in Chinese politics.

Political Leadership. The structure of political leadership has also evolved since 1949, going through three major stages. The first stage lasted roughly from 1949 to 1959 and was dominated by the emergence of the CCP as the supreme commander of all organized social activity in China. The pattern of change displayed itself in two interlocking processes. One was a general growth and/or strengthening of political organization — party, state, army, and mass organizations. The other was the increasing dominance of the party alone over the others. Initially in 1949 the new regime's organizational power rested heavily on the PLA and a variety of rather loosely constructed local groups (the peasants' associations, for example). From the early 1950s, tasks of national, regional, and local government increasingly were brought under the umbrella of the new state structure. While the PLA underwent modernization and mass organizations continued to grow in membership and organizational sophistication, their political roles receded relative to that of the state. Meanwhile, the CCP and the Communist Youth League recruited at a rapid rate, consolidating the party's position throughout the political structure. With the weakening of central state organs and advancement of the "politics takes command" slogan in 1957, the CCP's preeminence in the system was clear. Whatever its shortcomings, the implementation of the Great Leap Forward was dramatic evidence of the party's decisive leadership and control over an organizational network that permeated all levels of Chinese society.

The second stage from 1959 through the Cultural Revolution presents a different picture, however. Organizational growth slowed or even stagnated as the leadership became embroiled in increasingly bitter debates over policy and its own proper composition and style. The earlier emphasis on building the socialist political and economic structure gave way to a much more pronounced concern about the fundamentals of Communist ideology at home and abroad. The party's capacity to manipulate the system declined as a result of economic crisis, lowered prestige, and internal divisions. State organs, managerial personnel, and above all the PLA began to reassert their political roles. Before the Cultural Revolution, these trends did not seem to presage major change in the political system. They represented significant cracks in the structure of CCP control, suggesting it was not as total as the Great Leap period had indicated, but they did not point clearly to any particular alternative. It was only in the Cultural Revolution that the party organization and leadership inherited from the 1950s was literally dismantled and reconstructed, that the PLA assumed de facto administrative power over much of China, and that Mao Zedong established his personal leadership and ideology as the sole source of political authority.

The Maoist ascendancy reached its peak in the late 1960s and then gradually faded. Although the elevation of party leader above party organization held on until Mao's death, as did Cultural Revolution rhetoric and many of the policies established under his personal authority, an institutional revival was evident by the early 1970s. CCP growth resumed, mass organizations revived, and the national bureaucracies were again becoming more prominent. This trend accelerated after Mao's death, leading into a third stage of renewed organizational dominance.

The discussion in Chapter III noted the current stage's major departures from its predecessor; we need not review them. An interesting and less obvious question is how the third stage differs from the first. A cyclical perspective might suggest that the post-Mao stage shares with the mid-1950s an emphasis on institutionalization, consolidation, bureaucratic controls, and party organizational authority. Yet political leadership in these two stages is different. The earlier CCP was oriented toward the Soviet model; the current one formally accepts the Maoist model, even as it modifies it, and continues to look at the Soviet Union as a negative example. The earlier CCP was still a relatively tightly knit organization, with a large corps of members who shared a common revolutionary experience; now the CCP is many times larger, and quite different in its social composition and experience. Moreover, aside from change in the leading organization itself, the national and international political and economic context underwent a fundamental transformation over these two decades, so that the current leadership necessarily brings a different perspective to bear on the problems it faces.

Periodization of the Communist System. This discussion indicates that change in the post-1949 system has been frequent and complex, but it also suggests two major turning points that divide PRC history into three major periods. The turning points are the Great Leap Forward and the death of Mao; the periods are 1949–1957, 1958–1976 and the post-Mao period. Neither the turning points nor the periods are clear-cut. There is room for argument on any effort to characterize PRC history in this way, with the analysis here providing more than a little fuel for such controversy. Nonetheless, there are constellations of policies and characteristics that support this periodization as a way of generalizing about the system's evolution.

The first years (1949–1957) of the PRC were a transitional period in several senses. In CCP perspective, they involved the "transition to socialism," essentially the socialization of the economy (completed by 1956 with the "high tide" of agricultural collectivization) and the consolidation of CCP rule (decisively demonstrated in 1957 by the defeat of nonparty criticism and initiation of the Leap). In developmental perspective, the period transformed China from a disorganized and fragmented society into one in which state-sponsored organization was in place for nearly all political, economic, social, and cultural affairs. This inclusive pattern of organizational memberships and controls marked a decisive mobilization of the Chinese population as a whole. In ideological terms, 1949–1957 was a transition from dependence on the

Soviet Union — the "lean to one side" policy of 1949 and commitment to the Soviet model in the FFYP — to definition of an independent Chinese socialism in the Leap and the Sino-Soviet conflict. Within the period, of course, Soviet-style heavy industrialization, with all its concomitants, was a dominant influence. The primary accomplishment of the transitional period was the construction of the Communist system, with a far-reaching organization of society and mobilization of resources for socialist construction.

The Maoist period (1958–1976) began with the Great Leap, which introduced themes that were to dominate Chinese politics for nearly two decades: the rise of Mao's personal authority; the split with the USSR and establishment of an independent line in domestic and foreign affairs; an emphasis on deeper penetration and broader distribution of revolutionary ideology and social services throughout society, especially in rural areas; and an effort to avoid institutionalization of control by a new bureaucratic elite that might compromise the preceding goals. It reached a peak in the Cultural Revolution, which advanced all these themes so vigorously that it came to epitomize the Maoist model. It came to an end with Mao's death, although more than the leader's passing marked its conclusion; accomplishment of some of its goals and modification of others also delineate its end. The period's general characteristics are clear from previous discussion, but there are three points that deserve emphasis.

The first of these is that Maoist self-reliance, in the sense of independence from the Soviet Union, was only part of the period's international dimension. Inasmuch as Mao remained committed to China's overall development and emergence as a world power, the consequences of the Sino-Soviet conflict pushed the PRC toward expanded economic and diplomatic contacts with other countries to replace the economic and security ties that the USSR had provided in the transitional period. Hence, the Maoist period coupled self-reliance with a general trend, evident from the early 1960s on (albeit interrupted in the peak years of the Cultural Revolution), toward greater and more diversified contacts with the global community, and particularly with capitalist countries.

Second, the Maoist system's penetrative and distributive

thrust went significantly beyond the transitional period's organization and mobilization of the country. The latter was essentially an organizational effort, one that established the institutions of a socialist economy, of party government, and of mass organization. The Maoist objective was to deepen the organizational revolution so that it penetrated to the level of individual thought and action, aiming directly at the creation of "socialist man;" and to distribute the impact of socialist institutions beyond the leading urban-industrial sector into the countryside, thereby extending to the village level not only collectivized production but also the supporting services (education, health care, communications facilities, agricultural technology) that would make peasants full participants in China's modernization.

The third point, closely related, was the Maoist insistence that ideological transformation, not institutionalization, was the guarantor of continuing the revolution. The transitional period had assumed that ideological transformation would follow from party leadership and socialist institutions — the more rapid the institutional consolidation of the system, the sooner the emergence of socialist man. With the example of Soviet and Chinese revisionism in mind, revealing "capitalist" tendencies *within the proletarian vanguard itself,* Mao argued that ideological transformation of leaders and masses alike was essential if socialist institutions were to remain socialist; institutionalization in advance of victory on the ideological front was an invitation to the consolidation of elitist, bureaucratic rule that would ultimately degenerate into capitalism.

The new period that Mao's successors hail may be labeled a modernization period, following the key slogan of attaining the "four modernizations" by the end of the century. It shares certain institutional forms and biases with the transitional period, certain international and distributive policies with the Maoist period, but it appears to merit its official designation as a new period. It assumes that the goals of its predecessors have essentially been accomplished, that the institutional and ideological foundations of Chinese socialism have been laid, and that the task of the next two decades is to proceed rapidly, on these foundations, with economic development and technological modernization. If there is a new model here, to replace the Soviet model of the 1950s and the Maoist model of the 1960s and 1970s, it appears to be a technocratic model that sees the increasing application of science and technology as the driving force of the PRC's next developmental push. The period is too fresh, however, for confident projections of its shape or prospects.

How do patterns of cyclical change relate to this periodization, which rests on and emphasizes secular change in PRC history? The cyclical perspective reminds us that the periods are not sharply delineated, that their characteristics are not exclusively the property of a single period. Separation between periods is blurred by the fact that each is largely a response to its predecessor and hence continues some of the earlier debates and features. The turning points, in other words, are arbitrary designations of a longer evolutionary flow of events. Indeed, one could borrow from cyclical analysis to portray the periods (adding one earlier period) as dialectical alternations of mobilization and consolidation: there is a first revolutionary mobilization that begins with KMT–CCP civil war in 1946 and terminates with completion of land reform in 1952; the FFYP is a consolidation period; the Maoist period is a prolonged second mobilization, synthesizing elements of the first two periods; the modernization period brings renewed consolidation, now synthesizing the second and third periods.

Cyclical analysis also calls our attention to contrary impulses within each period. The transitional period contained forerunners of the Maoist period in the peasants' associations, in the "little leap" of 1955–1956, and in a broad debate, beginning as early as 1954, on the wisdom of following the Soviet model. The Maoist period contained at least two more conservative interludes in the retrenchment of the early 1960s and, more erratically, in mixed retreats from the Cultural Revolution peak. The modernization period began with "struggle" against the Gang before yielding to a consolidation focus after the Eleventh Party Congress of August 1977. It is probably safe to predict that the current period will display "radical" features at times, even if it holds in the main to the course attributed to it here. There has been a "right" and a "left," with individuals scattered between the poles, on nearly all important issues in post-1949 politics. The policy stance of right and left changes as the issues change. At the same time, because they are Chinese, and because they are politicians, the representatives of right and left will continue to define their positions with reference to the precedents of the Chinese past, keeping alive a sense of recurring conflicts and of known alternatives to the dominant policies of the moment.

IDEOLOGY AS A SOURCE OF IDENTITY AND CONFLICT

The importance of ideology has been implicit throughout the preceding discussion. Despite all the shifts and conflicts that have marked the history of the PRC, its leadership has remained committed to fundamental principles that have lent identity and continuity to the political system and maintained certain similarities with other Communist systems. Richard Lowenthal argues that it is ideology that differentiates Communist systems from other revolutionary nationalist movements that also seek "politically forced development." The primary characteristics of Communist systems, according to Lowenthal, stem from a drive for rapid development — the "politically forced development" that links them to other revolutionary nationalist movements in underdeveloped countries — plus a commitment to attain a classless society on a world scale.[12]

As noted at the outset of this chapter, the more concrete consequences of this ideological commitment are the following: the economic strategy of development is socialism, requiring nationalization and collectivization of the economy; the political vehicle of development is "proletarian dictatorship," requiring a virtual monopolization of state power by the ruling Communist party; the ultimate objective of development is a classless Communist society, requiring the creation of a new "socialist man" through continued class struggle and repeated efforts to establish a uniform collectivist consciousness in place of competing individual or group interests; the world context of development is seen as an unremitting struggle between capitalist and socialist systems, requiring constant preparation for and participation in opposition to capitalism.

[12]Lowenthal, op. cit., pp. 34–50.

No significant group of Chinese leaders has renounced its belief in the necessity for modernization via the socialist economy, maintenance of party dictatorship, creation of a new socialist man, and global opposition to capitalism. Charges of "revisionism," "anarchism," "betrayal," and deviations of "left" and "right" are evidence of both the seriousness and the substantive direction of political conflicts in China. They are evidence, too, that all participants recognize adherence to the ideology as the primary legitimator of political leadership. However, they cannot be taken at face value as proof of rejection of ideological fundamentals. On that point, the record suggests that all factions within the post-1949 political elite have claimed adherence to the beliefs cited above.[13]

We must emphasize, however, that these commitments establish only the most basic structure and goals of the system. Although sufficient to distinguish the Communist system from other types for purposes of general classification, they are by no means definitive in all matters of doctrine and policy, leaving many points of access for variation and controversy. The commitment to modernization and socialization of the economy does not resolve questions about the rate and timing of economic advance, the balance among sectors, and the permissible extent of minor deviations from the socialist principle; the exercise of proletarian dictatorship through the Communist party does not specify a single model of party composition, procedures, and style; the attempt to create a classless society based on the new socialist man — the most distinctive and idealistic of Communist goals — does not reveal how this effort will relate to the work assignments and differentiation implied by demands for rapid economic development and maintenance of party dictatorship; global opposition to capitalism and imperialism leaves open the degree to which considerations of national interest, security, and resources will govern foreign commitments. Moreover, institutional and policy formulations inevitably reflect the social, political, economic, cultural, and geographic conditions of the society in question and the changes that occur in these conditions over time. In short, ideology establishes long-range

[13]Some objections to this interpretation are cited later in this chapter.

goals and a rough systemic framework for achieving them but does not provide solutions to all the crucial policy choices that Communist elites face. At the same time, it requires that all decisions be justified in terms of its basic tenets, to retain the legitimacy and identity of the system.

For the Chinese Communists, therefore, Marxism–Leninism–Maoism has been a source of both unity and conflict. It has distinguished them from their competitors, imbued them with conviction and purpose, and given them a common world view and set of goals. Yet it could not dictate agreement on all issues, and its centrality in the system has ensured that political disagreements would provoke controversy and shifts in the ideological realm. As a result, Chinese Communist ideology, like other aspects of the system, has been in flux. The following discussion will attempt to illustrate how ideology has defined some basic characteristics of the system without fixing them in a rigid or unchanging mold.

Breadth and Fluidity of Boundaries. First, ideology has a pronounced impact on the general configuration of political activity within the system. The insistence on party leadership normally restricts debate and decision on major political issues to a narrow segment of society, essentially the highest levels of CCP organization. The structure for implementation of these decisions, on the other hand, is broad and diverse. The socialization of the economy requires a large state bureaucracy to manage the myriad responsibilities assigned to the public realm. It is supplemented by a network of communications media and mass organizations that function primarily to mobilize support for the decisions of the leadership, an effort reinforced periodically by mass movements that push the network's activity to even higher levels. However, this structure is by no means limited to support for policy decisions, since it is actively engaged in political socialization of the population and the recruitment of citizens to political roles. The effort to transform the political consciousness of the citizenry en route to a classless society requires intensive political education and the creation of abundant opportunities for participation in the political system.

This description is too loose to tell us much about how the

system works or compares to others, but it leads to an initial characterization of its boundaries as extremely broad. The combination of commitments to all-around modernization at a rapid rate and to the universal transformation of social consciousness extends the political system's concerns to every individual and every kind of social action. The age, sex, occupation, residence, or group identity of individuals are essentially irrelevant here, as is the question of whether the activity involves individual, familial, economic, or cultural pursuits; all fall potentially within the boundaries of the political system. It may never push out to these maximal boundaries, due to leadership priorities and resource limitations, but it does approach them. Its organizational capabilities are immense, permitting regular politicization of a wide range of social action and selective incorporation of additional areas.

These broad boundaries are also very fluid, since the definition of what is political and how it should be handled is not fixed but is left largely to the judgment of the leadership. In periods of consolidation, the boundaries may contract. They expand when the leadership mobilizes a new push for economic or social advance, bringing into fuller play the permanent political structure, which includes study groups, mass meetings, demonstrations, and various citizens' committees and organizations, and possibly activating intermittent structures such as mass trials, struggle meetings, and other more violent forms of direct popular action. None of these popular activities, including the intermittent ones and those that may exceed or contravene elite expectations, should be regarded as aberrations; they are part of the political system, whether representing a sanctioned exercise of political authority or an unsanctioned expression of popular mood. It is the nature of the system, in extending its boundaries so broadly, to permit considerable fluidity in its operation. It could not be otherwise for a regime aiming at the total transformation of such a large, diverse, and complex society.

Unity Through Struggle. Second, ideology has given structure to the party's intense concern for unity and integration within the political system, which has found expression in a drive for unanimous commitment to the ideology itself. That is, CCP elites have responded to disintegrative tendencies in their society by seeking ideological conformity, evidenced in the gradual advancement of the thought of Mao Zedong as the single source of political authority and legitimacy. It is this effort to integrate society on an ideological base that most clearly reveals ideology as a contributor to both unity and conflict within the system.[14] The Chinese Communists have shared their concern for national unity with all modern Chinese political elites, of course, but they have pursued it with exceptional vigor because of their insistence on unopposed party leadership over a supreme effort at a complete transformation of society. The problem for the CCP — or any other Chinese elites, for that matter — was simply that China was not easily unified. There was no basis in 1949 for a classless or conflict-free society. Instead, there were gross discrepancies in the distribution of wealth and power, great differences between regions and between urban and rural areas, and great gaps in the physical foundations (such as communications and transportation facilities) of national integration. Moreover, any serious program of national economic development would necessarily strain existing resources and increase the potential for conflict.

How, under such circumstances, was unity to be defined and achieved? The essential Maoist response has been to define the Chinese political system as a coalition of basically compatible groups unified by a broad collective interest and arrayed against a small number of clear and irreconcilable enemies. "Who are our enemies? Who are our friends? This is a question of first importance for the revolution. . . . To ensure that we will definitely achieve success in our revolution and will not lead the masses astray, we must pay attention to uniting with our real friends in order to attack our real enemies."[15] Throughout the history of the Chinese Communist movement

[14]For a thorough analysis of this point, see Tang Tsou, "Revolution, Reintegration and Crisis in Communist China: A Framework for Analysis," in Ping-ti Ho and Tang Tsou, eds., *China in Crisis,* vol. 1 (Chicago: University of Chicago Press, 1968), pp. 227–347.

[15]Mao Zedong, "Analysis of the Classes in Chinese Society," March 1926, in *Selected Works of Mao Zedong* (Peking: Foreign Languages Press, 1965), vol. 1, p. 13.

runs this attempt to identify the "people" (all those with whom the CCP can unite) and the "enemies" (who are the targets of the people's struggle) in such a way as to maximize the coalition without compromising revolutionary objectives.

Since the anti-Japanese war, when the CCP first began to lead a broad-based mass movement, three variant formulations of the coalition have been offered. During the Yanan period, the response was a relatively easy and nationalistic one. The "people" were essentially all Chinese, the "enemies" the Japanese and a few Chinese traitors. Class issues were not forgotten but were made secondary to the national issue, which permitted a highly inclusive definition of which Chinese could be part of the United Front. During the Civil War of 1946–1949 and the early years of the People's Republic, Mao advanced a class-based definition that excluded some Chinese who might earlier have belonged to the anti-Japanese people. "Who are the people? At the present stage in China, they are the working class, the peasantry, the urban petty bourgeoisie and the national bourgeoisie. . . . They enforce their dictatorship over the running dogs of imperialism — the landlord class and bureaucrat-bourgeoisie, as well as the representatives of those classes, the Kuomintang rectionaries and their accomplices."[16] This definition reduced the scope of the people and authorized sharp internal conflict within Chinese society, but it still portrayed a high degree of national unity. The Korean War, the program of national reconstruction, and the relative smallness and distinctness of the enemy classes permitted retention of much of the nationalistic flavor of the wartime period. Moreover, the enemies were presumably doomed as class components, although not necessarily as individuals, within mainland society — the landlords and bureaucrat-bourgeoisie by land reform and socialism, the KMT forces by suppression of counterrevolutionaries. In effect, the definition forecast rapid progress toward total national unity simply by elimination of the enemy. By 1956–57, party elites were proclaiming unprecedented national unity, the effective defeat

[16]"On the People's Democratic Dictatorship," June 30, 1949, in ibid., vol. 4, pp. 417–18.

of the classes specified above, and the secure establishment of a socialist system.[17]

However, it was precisely at this juncture that Mao offered a third definition of the people, shifting the operative distinction from class status to ideological commitment. The shift was explained most forthrightly in the published version (June 1957) of Mao's February 1957 speech, "On the Correct Handling of Contradictions Among the People." Mao opened by asserting that "never has our country been as united as it is today" — recording his recognition, too, of progress toward eradication of class enemies. His real message in this regard was to observe that the people change in composition from one historical period to another. Noting the meaning of the term in the two earlier periods, as described above, he then said: "At this stage of building socialism, all classes, strata, and social groups which approve, support, and work for the cause of socialist construction belong to the category of the people, while those social forces and groups which resist the socialist revolution, and are hostile to and try to wreck socialist construction, are enemies of the people."[18] Since this formulation, Chinese politics has been oriented heavily toward continued class struggle, but the cutting edge of the definition has been ideological commitment as evidenced in attitudes and behavior rather than actual class background or circumstances. The people have been those supporting socialism and the party (during the Cultural Revolution usually interpreted to mean support for Mao and his thought); the enemies those said to oppose correct ideology. This is not to say actual class background is politically irrelevant. Attacks on old enemy classes, and tension between children of "good" and "bad" family background, were prominent features of the Red Guard movement in the early Cultural Revolution, and the Gang continued to press against certain privileged or "bad" strata

[17]One of the major pieces of Maoist evidence about Liu Shaoqi's "revisionism" is his articulation of these points in his "Political Report" to the Eighth Party Congress in September 1956; text in Harvard University, Center for International Affairs and East Asian Research Center, *Communist China, 1955–1959: Policy Documents with Analysis* (Cambridge, Mass.: Harvard University Press, 1965), pp. 164–203.

[18]Ibid., pp. 275–94; the quotations are from pp. 275–76.

until the Gang's downfall in 1976.[19] Nonetheless, the Cultural Revolution radicals also blurred the meaning of objective class background by identifying all opposed to their version of Maoism as bourgeois elements. In the main, the Maoist period brought heightened insistence on ideological education and a tendency to interpret all political conflict as ideological conflict, with enemy-class character attributed to those said to deviate from Maoist ideology.

From one perspective, this ideological distinction between people and enemies has symbolized a high degree of national unity, because it has excluded relatively few Chinese from the ranks. The largest categories of enemies were those of the early years — the landlords, bureaucrat-bourgeoisie, and counterrevolutionaries. While there was much abuse of decisions concerning who belonged in these categories, the fact remains that they were relatively distinct and declining groups whose exclusion did not seriously compromise the scope of the national coalition. Further, as the distinction shifted to more ideological grounds, it became theoretically possible for almost anyone to join the people provided that evidence of ideological commitment were forthcoming. In practice, then, the distinction has allowed for a very high proportion of Chinese — invariably said to be over 90 percent — to qualify as among the people; whereas the actual enemies made the target of political activity have been limited to a few percent of the population.[20] The division of Chinese society into two hostile

[19]For analysis of CCP class concepts and their role in post-1949 political struggles, see Richard Kraus, "Class Conflict and the Vocabulary of Social Analysis in China," *China Quarterly,* no. 69 (March 1977), pp. 54–74; Hong Yung Lee, *The Politics of the Chinese Cultural Revolution: A Case Study* (Berkeley: University of California Press, 1978); and Gordon White, *The Politics of Class and Class Origin: The Case of the Cultural Revolution* (Canberra: Contemporary China Centre, Australian National University, 1976).

[20]The assignment of an undesirable political label is a formal act in China; those so labeled are usually given a specific designation which can be removed only by an appeal to the authorities. In the elections of 1953–1954 and 1956, the number deprived of political rights ranged from 1.52 percent to 0.62 percent of the total population, or less than 3 percent of the voting-age population. See James R. Townsend, *Political Participation in Communist China* (Berkeley: University of California Press, 1967), p. 118. A more thorough analysis of this subject estimates that before the Cultural Revolution at most 3–4 percent of the population carried adverse political labels; see Gordon A. Bennett, "Political Labels and Popular Tension," *Current Scene,* vol. 7, no. 4 (Feb. 26, 1969), p. 2.

camps, precisely for purposes of political struggle, has not debarred the overwhelming majority from inclusion in a national coalition assumed to be unified in their long-term interests.

Obviously, however, there is a very forced and insecure quality to the constantly professed unity of the people, for it relies heavily on the threat of expulsion from community ranks of anyone in a clearly oppositional role. The unity of the system is maintained, in the last resort, by withdrawing membership from those said to violate it. Those branded as enemies lose their right to participate in the political community, to express and defend their position. In other words, they are not allowed to damage the unity of the people either conceptually or politically. The fact that relatively few actually receive enemy status is scarcely reassuring, since virtually everyone is vulnerable to exclusion regardless of previous political status. The purges of Liu Shaoqi, Lin Biao, the Gang, and other high-level cadres are dramatic evidence of the uncertainties produced by this ideological definition of the political community. The Cultural Revolution demonstrated as well the potential for indictment of much larger groups, although many branded as enemies by the radicals were later rehabilitated, especially after 1976. The Gang's fall in its turn brought extensive purges and public indictments of the cadres associated with them. It is here that the disintegrative effect of the ideology, which contributed so much to the reunification of China and the integration of its revolutionary elite, becomes evident. Marxism–Leninism welded the CCP together and guided a program of national development that could enlist the support or acquiescence of most Chinese. However, the post-1957 shift that led to the establishment of Maoism as the only standard for legitimate participation in the system forced numerous elites who would not agree into ideologically prescribed roles of opposition. The ideology itself became controversial, and a process of distintegration set in, culminating in a forced reconstruction of unity by a major purge of dissidents from the ranks of the people.

It must be emphasized that the Maoist view does not deny the existence or legitimacy of all conflict among the people. Mao was highly sensitive to the fact that actual social conditions in China produce divergent political styles and interests, a topic that he analyzed in his speech on "contradictions." Simply put, Mao distinguished between "antagonistic" and "nonantagonistic" contradictions. The former are those between the people and their enemies, to be resolved by the exercise against the enemies of dictatorship, compulsion, and denial of political rights. The latter are among the people, to be resolved by democratic methods of persuasion and education.[21] Nonantagonistic contradictions exist for various reasons—misconceptions, inadequate education, human mistakes and frailties, the continuing influence of feudal and bourgeois ideas, incomplete or improper development of socialist institutions, the possibility of choice or variation in policy decisions, and so forth. Yet Mao insisted that they are reconcilable rather than permanent and destructive, because they rest on the basic unity of the people and identity of their long-term collective interests; they can and must be handled openly through discussion, education, and persuasion. Maoist doctrine thus leaves some room for serious political debate and an immense space for popular political education and expression of views. The limiting factor is the boundary line between people and enemies, the refusal to tolerate fundamental opposition to the ideology or political leadership. While the boundary does not exclude political debate and conflict as a matter of course, its delineation in particular circumstances is arbitrary. Debate on important issues becomes a hazardous undertaking, left largely to those elites who feel they have some influence over where the boundary will be drawn; and, as the Cultural Revolution era shows, even they can misjudge the crucial outcome.

If political conflict within the system is tentatively legitimized but made hazardous by the possibility of being defined as antagonistic, what form does its expression take? The taking of positions on controversial issues of doctrine or policy is confined essentially to high-level elites, joined infrequently by elements of the more politically conscious citizenry. Such issue-oriented conflict is typically carried on in a semisecret

[21]Mao Zedong, "On the Correct Handling of Contradictions Among the People," op. cit., esp. pp. 275–81. See also Mao Zedong, "On the Ten Great Relationships," in Jerome Ch'en, ed. *Mao* (Englewood Cliffs, N.J.: Prentice-Hall, 1969), pp. 65–85.

style in which the positions and personalities in opposition are not made explicit. Yet the infrequent occasions in which debate opens up and broader segments of the population join in are extremely significant. The most prominent examples of open-ended public debate and criticism have been the "hundred flowers" period of 1957 and the early Cultural Revolution; the 1974–1976 years also included important displays of diverging mass political sentiments, especially in the Tiananmen Incident. It is instructive to note that periods of relatively intense popular political activity have coincided with serious intraparty debate over basic developmental choices. Despite the generally controlled character of popular politics in the PRC, "crisis periods" seem to create expanded opportunities for mass participation.[22]

The Clash of Political Cultures. For most citizens, political participation seldom has such direct relevance to major doctrine or policy issues. Instead, it involves opportunities for discussion of how to implement higher-level policies or guidelines in basic-level units and for engagement in the clash of political cultures that permeates the Chinese system and is another of its most striking features. The clash of political cultures is virtually constant and universal, bringing citizens into a struggle to overcome disfavored attitudes and orientations toward politics and to replace them with the political culture prescribed as appropriate for the new socialist society.

Every political system contains divergent political cultures. What is distinctive about China is, first, the gap between the dominant political culture inherited from the old society and the ideologically prescribed political culture the elites wish to establish in the new society; and, second, the intensity of efforts to bridge this gap by making individual attitudes and orientations a subject for public examination, struggle, and reform. The citizen's participation in this process means measurement of his own and others' thought and actions against

[22]For a discussion of "crisis periods," in which great pressures for change and adaptation in a political system produce heightened levels of system activity and significant developmental choices, see Gabriel A. Almond, "Political Development: Analytical and Normative Perspectives," *Comparative Political Studies*, vol. 1, no. 4 (January, 1969), pp. 454–57.

the official standard, to expose and correct departures from it. The process has little to do with high-level policy debate or decision making, but it is unquestionably political and may involve intense individual and group conflict. As the citizen engages in the clash of political cultures, he necessarily becomes a participant — even if a reluctant one — in the transformation of Chinese society.

Although the pattern of political culture in China is highly complex, it is possible to identify the major poles around which struggle takes place. One of these is the "subject-partici-pant" political culture of the masses, who identify with the political system and are responsive to its effects on them but who recognize the limits and hazards of active participation in it. This orientation serves simultaneously as a basic support of the system and as a primary target of CCP efforts at attitudinal transformation. In reality it is extremely diffuse, spreading out over a range of attitudes. Remnants of an older parochial culture that sees political authority as an external force to be avoided or placated must persist although now it is surely diminished in importance. At the other end of the continuum and growing in importance are more activist orientations that approach the political culture prescribed by the elite.

The ideological political culture of the CCP is the protago-nist of attitudinal conflict in China. It dominates politcal insti-tutions and communications media, provides the vocabulary through which all political activity is described, and represents the official standard for the resolution of divergent political orientations. It thereby creates an impression that it is very widespread, an impression the leadership encourages even while insisting that the struggle must continue unabated. In fact, the Cultural Revolution demonstrated that the official ideological political culture was itself fragmented, with little evidence that the announced end of the campaign in 1977 had resolved the problem. Again, the range of orientations is great, but for purposes of generalization it is useful to distin-guish between Maoist and bureaucratic political cultures as two main variants within the elite, representing the attitudinal base for the two main lines in intraparty struggle. So important is this difference that it has assumed greater salience than the clash between CCP values and those of the surrounding society. After the lessons of the Great Leap and Sino-Soviet split, Mao came to see the most serious clash of political cultures within the current and future political elite, not between the party as such and old social forces. The Gang continued to push this view, particularly in their arguments that bourgeoisie were lodged within the party. The Gang's purge reduced the emphasis on dangers of bourgeois influences within the party, but the salience over the past twenty years — and indeed throughout China's revolutionary era — of conflict over the cultural dimensions of politics suggests that it will remain central in Chinese politics for some time to come.

CLASSIFYING THE CHINESE SYSTEM

This chapter began with the assertion that the PRC is a Communist system, thereby accepting the label most commonly applied by foreign observers who see the ruling party and its ideology as dominating, if not wholly determining, the character of the political system. The label also reflects the self-definition of Chinese elites, who consistently proclaim their commitment to a socialist system based on Marxism–Leninism–Mao Zedong thought. The discussion then noted some of the post-1949 changes that challenge the appropriateness of any single classification for a system that has experienced such profound shifts. Particular attention was given to cyclical change and secular evolution, and to the emergence of elite conflicts that produced charges that one faction or another had tried to overthrow the socialist system. The conclusion drawn from this discussion is that the PRC can usefully be classified as a Communist (socialist) system, but that some further specification is necessary to accommodate the most important shifts occurring since 1949. We have suggested a periodization that divides the post-1949 system into three subtypes corresponding to important developmental stages. The first is the transition period of 1949–1957, one that concentrated on the construction of socialist economic and political institutions and took the Soviet model as its guide. The second is the Maoist period of 1958–1976, marked by efforts to deepen the revolution, distribute its benefits more broadly throughout society, and sharpen ideological struggle even at the cost of institutional upheaval; the articulation of a Maoist model guided these efforts and also legitimized the PRC's transition from dependence on the Soviet model to independent status as a global actor. The third is the post-1976 modernization period that emphasizes accelerated economic development along lines of a modified Maoist model, one that appears to have a distinct technocratic quality.

The identification of three different periods and models in the post-1949 evolution of the Chinese Communist system recognizes important changes within the system but stops short of arguing that it has changed from one type to another. The relationships between the periods, their elements of change and continuity, will emerge more clearly in the remaining chapters that probe Chinese political processes in more detail. However, there is no point in evading the fact that the approach suggested here conflicts with other perpectives and does not resolve the classification issue. To begin with, it does not match the Almond and Powell classification (see Chapter I, p. 21) of China as a "penetrative-radicial-authoritarian" system pursuing an "authoritarian-technocratic-mobilizational" strategy. The PRC seems to have exhibited these characteristics sequentially, and in different mixes, rather than as a single package. The transition period concentrated on mobilization of national resources and the building of a new authority structure, transforming China from a premobilized society into one ready for a more ambitious development effort; the Maoist period emphasized radical penetrative and distributive policies while balancing authoritarian structures with egalitarian, populist tendencies; the modernization period seems more authoritarian and technocratic in development strategy and probably less radical in its short-run social goals than its predecessor. The Almond and Powell classification is a suggestive characterization of Third World Communist systems but an imperfect fit with any one of China's development periods; it seems to fit the Chinese system best only in the most recent post-1976 period.

A second problem concerns the looseness of boundaries implied by viewing all post-1949 changes as "within the Communist system." Is this an abdication of judgment, a definition so broad that everything is included and all distinctions are lost? Our image of the Communist system is admittedly broad, but it is not without boundaries and certainly not without distinctions about political differences. For example, we may think of Chinese politics as including several positions on a left–right spectrum, using key individuals or groups to illustrate them: Zhou Enlai is a center figure, Mao is center-left, the Gang of Four is left and some Red Guard groups of 1967–68 are ultra-left; moving to the other side, the Hua-Deng post-1976 leadership is a center-right coalition, the capitalist tendencies of the early 1960s are right, and the bourgeois intellectual demands of 1957 are ultraright. Such pigeonholing is open to endless qualifications and disputation. Perhaps the greatest problem is that individuals have changed their positions on the spectrum from one period to another. Mao was further to the left in 1965–1967, probably close to the center at other times; Liu Shaoqi was on the right in the early 1960s although he had earlier been further left; Lin Biao was a leader of the Cultural Revolution left only to mount a coup attempt that probably deserves a rightist label. Another source of confusion is disputed classification of purged opponents. Lin Biao was called both a leftist and a rightist when he was purged. Hua initially labeled the Gang "sham leftists" (real rightists), but by 1979, presumably on Deng's authority, they became "ultra-leftists."

The point here is not to resolve such details but simply to illustrate the breadth of the Chinese political spectrum and the problem of deciding where its real boundaries lie. Our approach is to accept broad boundaries, so that only the most extreme Red Guards and the bourgeois intellectuals are clearly outside the system; the former veered close to anarchism in their assault on party centralism, the latter had hopes for a legitimate political opposition; neither position had any place in a Communist system. The left and right are included, however, as the marginal extremities of the Chinese Communist political spectrum, as positions that have been occupied by important party elites and that shade off into the central mainstream, so that it is difficult to exclude them without excluding a healthy proportion of post-1949 political action.

The victors in CCP intraparty struggles have been less tolerant of deviations, of course, and have had no qualms about denouncing defeated rivals as outside the system. If one wishes to accept this more politicized view, then the boundaries can be narrowed and the center pushed left or right to accommodate the position one wants to accord legitimacy.

The important points to glean from this exercise in relativism are these. First, despite all the shifts and conflicts, there has been a relatively broad central mainstream — from center-left to center-right — in post-1949 politics, one that has carried most policies and actors along with it while casting aside those who lost the current. Second, the mainstream itself has altered course from time to time, so that positions on either bank were alternately caught up or left stranded. As it veered left in the early Cultural Revolution, Liu Shaoqi and Deng Xiaoping were stranded; as it veered right after 1976, Deng was freed and the Gang was left stranded. Where one marks the boundaries of the mainstream depends on whether one charts its course over time — which is the perspective adopted here — or fixes its banks at a particular stage.

A third and closely related problem is how to deal with the substance of the charges that some Chinese leaders have violated the requirements of a Communist system. For those making such charges, the preceding discussion is a gloss that evades the real issue of correct and incorrect applications of the ideology. Of the many instances of such charges in post-1949 politics, four are of particular importance and interest: (1) the Maoist charge that Liu Shaoqi and others had forsaken socialism and were embarked in the early 1960s on a road leading to capitalist restoration; (2) the Soviet argument that the Cultural Revolution represented an antiparty movement smacking of idealism, petty bourgeois nationalism, and Trotskyism; (3) the assault by Hua Guofeng and his colleagues on the Gang of Four for a subjective distortion of historical materialism, leading the rightist (later called ultra-leftist) sabotage of the socialist economy and party discipline; (4) the counterattack in defense of the Gang that charges the Hua-Deng leadership with betraying Maoism, class struggle, and Third World revolution while following revisionist policies

and forging an alliance with the capitalist world.[23] The positions represented in these polemics are too complicated to
analyse here, but the fact that each claims adherence to Marxism–Leninism indicates the difficulty of deciding when a nominally socialist system has lost its claim to purity.

Three observations may serve as a partial response to the
question of the PRC's credentials as a Communist system.
First, to repeat an earlier point, none of the major groupings
in Chinese politics has abandoned its formal commitment to
the four principles of a socialist economy, party dictatorship,
creation of socialist man, and long-term struggle with capitalism. Second, each of the groups identified in the charges noted
above has made compromises in practice with some of these
principles. In other words, there is some evidence to support
the accusations that those indicted have, to some degree,
moved in the directions indicated. One can argue that the
degree was not so great as the polemics maintain, but there
can be no doubt that variations in the practice of Chinese
socialism have stretched older ideological categories.

Third, there is a particularly serious question about the
extent to which the PRC remains committed to global opposition to capitalism. Chinese leaders of all persuasions have
affirmed this commitment, with the recent growth of contacts
between the PRC and capitalist countries explained as a tactical united front against Soviet "hegemonism" that does not
alter China's long-term struggle for the international victory

[23]For a sampling of analyses and/or documentation on each of these posi-
tions, see the following: (1) Charges against Liu, and their documentation, are
thoroughly analyzed in Lowell Dittmer, *Liu Shao-ch'i and the Chinese Cultural
Revolution* (Berkeley: University of California Press, 1974); (2) see Wang Ming,
China: Cultural Revolution or Counter-Revolutionary Coup? (Moscow: Novosti
Press, 1969), B. Zanegin, et al., *Developments in China* (Moscow: Progress Pub-
lishers, 1968); and the articles translated in *Chinese Law and Government,* vol.
I, no. 3 (Fall 1968), pp. 3–62; (3) see Hua Guofeng's "Political Report" to the
Eleventh CCP Congress in *PR,* no. 35 (August 26, 1977), pp. 23–57, and the
CCP CC Document *Zhong fa* (*Chung-fa*) 24 of December 10, 1976, in *Classified
Chinese Communist Documents: A Selection* (Taipei: Institute of International Rela-
tions, 1978), pp. 83–104; (4) see Charles Bettelheim, "The Great Leap Backward," *Monthly Review,* vol. 30, no. 3 (July–August 1978), pp. 37–130, and the
analysis and documents in Raymond Lotta, ed., *And Mao Makes 5: Mao Tsetung's
Last Great Battle* (Chicago: Banner Press, 1978), which also includes some
documents relevant to (3).

of socialism over capitalism.[24] Nonetheless, by 1978 the PRC was moving rapidly toward stronger economic, political and cultural ties with capitalist countries and was most hostile in its foreign relations toward the USSR and Vietnam. The origins of this situation reside in the Sino-Soviet conflict, which made rivalry between the two largest socialist states and alterations in their relations with world capitalism a fact of international life. In an era of national Communism and nuclear armaments, the security needs of socialist states have made unqualified opposition to external capitalism an untenable position. The principle remains an article of faith, but its practice is so attenuated by global realities that it no longer serves as a consistent guide to the definition of a Communist system.[25]

[24]For two recent affirmations, from different Chinese factions, see Hua's "Political Report," op. cit., esp. pp. 39–43, and Qiao Guanhua's (Ch'iao Kuan-hua) speech of May 20, 1975, in *Classified Chinese Communist Documents: A Selection,* pp. 546–71; Qiao was foreign minister at the time but later dismissed for complicity with the Gang. This is not to deny that there are important differences of emphasis in the way Hua and the "radicals" elaborated on the united front strategy; see the items cited under (4), note 23.

[25]For an early exposition of this theme, see the collection of essays by Richard Lowenthal, *World Communism: The Disintegration of a Secular Faith* (New York: Oxford University Press, 1964).

CHAPTER V

Political Socialization and Communications

THE DESIRE OF CHINESE ELITES to create a new socialist society gives them an intense concern for the processes of political socialization and communications. They cannot accept socialization as a given process that simply maintains existing attitudes and orientations but they insist that the process itself must change in order to facilitate transformation of popular social consciousness. By the same token, they see the establishment of new patterns in the structure and content of socialization and communications as essential to the attainment of the desired political culture. In the absence of adequate data on popular attitudes, assertions about contemporary Chinese political culture are highly speculative. We can inform our speculation, however, by studying the relationship between Maoism and the inherited political culture, initial CCP efforts to structure agents of socialization, the Cultural Revolution's impact on socialization, and the post-1976 modification of Cultural Revolution reforms.

MAOISM AND THE INHERITED POLITICAL CULTURE

A useful way of introducing post-1949 socialization and communications processes is to draw a broad contrast between Maoist and traditional political cultures. Neither of these categories is precise or even demonstrably "real." The Maoist political culture is essentially an ideal prescription that has guided CCP socialization efforts for most of PRC history;

177

it has not been unchallenged even as an ideal, however, and actual practice has fallen short of its standards. Traditional political culture is an equally loose category that conceals major differences and discontinuities in patterns of political attitudes existing in China before 1949. Nonetheless, the contrast identifies key themes that have exerted great influence on CCP socialization debates and policies and that establish a framework for evaluating the direction of change in Chinese political culture.[1]

Collectivism. The Maoist prescription calls for a redefinition of the social units to which primary loyalties are due and from which authority flows. In traditional China, this dominant social institution was typically a kinship unit: individuals geared their actions to its maintenance and prosperity and accepted the authority of its leaders over a wide range of their social behavior. The family or clan, however, was only the most

[1]The following discussion attempts to synthesize a complex subject, on which a substantial scholarly literature has emerged. The work most directly relevant to the question addressed here is Richard H. Solomon, *Mao's Revolution and the Chinese Political Culture* (Berkeley: University of California Press, 1971). Reviews challenging Solomon's assertions about traditional and/or Maoist culture include Pi-chao Chen, "In Search of Chinese National Character Via Child-Training," *World Politics,* vol. 25, no. 4 (July 1973), pp. 608–35; and those by Thomas Metzger and F. W. Mote in *Journal of Asian Studies,* vol. 32, no. 1 (November 1972) pp. 101–120. Continuities between Confucian and Chinese Marxist assumptions about human nature and the proper functions of government are emphasized in Donald J. Munro, *The Concept of Man in Contemporary China* (Ann Arbor: University of Michigan Press, 1977). The initial impact of the Communist revolution on Chinese social institutions is analyzed in a two-volume study by C. K. Yang, *Chinese Communist Society: The Family and the Village* (Cambridge: M.I.T. Press, 1968); a short essay on this topic is Francis L. K. Hsu, "Chinese Kinship and Chinese Behavior," in Ping-ti Ho and Tang Tsou, eds., *China in Crisis,* vol. 1 (Chicago: University of Chicago Press, 1968), pp. 579–608. The most important recent work on Chinese society, emphasizing the tenacity of some traditional social patterns, is William L. Parish and Martin King Whyte, *Village and Family in Contemporary China* (Chicago: University of Chicago Press, 1978). Other useful studies of Chinese political socialization processes include William Kessen, ed., *Childhood in China* (New Haven: Yale University Press, 1975); David M. Raddock, *Political Behavior of Adolescents in China* (Tucson, University of Arizona Press, 1977); Amy Auerbacher Wilson, et at., eds., *Deviance and Social Control in Chinese Society* (New York: Praeger, 1977); and Martin King Whyte, *Small Groups and Political Rituals in China* (Berkeley: University of California Press, 1974). See also Richard W. Wilson, *Learning To Be Chinese: The Political Socialization of Children in Taiwan* (Cambridge: M.I.T. Press. 1970).

obvious beneficiary of a particularism that favored exclusive and personal relationships over inclusive and public ones. In other words, individuals saw their loyalties and responsibilities largely in terms of their own particular experience, creating a web of obligations that would protect and benefit the "insiders" (those who shared a particular experience or relationship) at the expense of "outsiders." Although kinship claims were normally most formidable in this network, it supported as well the claims of native village or locality, common school or work associations, and so forth, against the claims of external social groupings. Particularism restricted "individualism" as well as larger community interests, but it tended to place "selfish" interests — in the sense of those identified with one's limited personal associations — above those of the public realm. Local organizations could not easily ignore or flout the dictates of political authority, since imperial power was ultimately supreme in both theory and practice; but they were the operative authority in most cases, and their hold over individuals was strong enough to offer real competition to the demands of the political system.

In the Maoist ethic, collectivism replaces particularism as the determinant of both loyalty and authority. Political authority, at whatever level, is superior to the claims of constituent elements within the community: loyalties belong to the collective regardless of personal associations and ties. As slogans like "serve the people" and "fight self" suggest, this principle requires dedication to the public cause and a conscious suppression of inclinations to place selfish concerns above those of the collective. The shift here is partly one of degree, since in traditional China, too, the individual was expected to subordinate his interests to those of a larger group. The difference is that the Maoist collective is a wider and more inclusive one. For example, the locality, which in imperial times was a relatively large and inclusive group as seen from individual perspective, is in the Maoist view one of the lowest collectives in an ever-widening sphere of political community that blends into the national political system and even an international political movement. The shift is also qualitative, however, in its insistence that political authority is supreme in all areas of life and that the individual's obligation extends to all members of his community, not just to those with whom he has a personalized or particular relationship.

Struggle and Activism. The traditional orientation emphasized the maintenance of harmony in social relations. People were to be orderly and peaceful, avoiding or suppressing displays of antagonism. Reality fell short of this ideal, of course, as the system had its share of rebellions and individual hostilities; the insistence on suppression of conflict may, in fact, have encouraged violent and disorderly action when the restraining norms were broken.[2] The tendency to restrain conflict was nonetheless powerful and was made relatively effective by insistence on submission to authority and an acceptance of "face-saving" or compromise solutions to disputes. The political realm was recognized as particularly susceptible to conflict and, the values of its scholar-elites notwithstanding, quite capable of harsh and arbitrary action — hence the common image of the tiger of government. Both prudence and social norms therefore dictated great caution in dealing with conflict, which easily led the common man with his relative political ignorance and powerlessness to political passivity or avoidance of political issues. Maoist doctrine portrays society as permeated with class struggle both as a consequence of exploitation and a condition of social progress. Citizens are expected to participate actively and voluntarily in this struggle, sharpening its features and challenging openly those whose positions or actions stand in the way of the socialist path. Commitment to political activism and struggle is to replace old inclinations toward passivity and harmony.[3]

Self-Reliance. Traditional authoritarianism and the strictures against challenging its harmonious ordering of society led to a heavy dependence on those holding positions of authority.

[2]See Richard H. Solomon, "Mao's Effort to Reintegrate the Chinese Polity: Problems of Authority and Conflict in Chinese Social Processes," in A. Doak Barnett, ed., *Chinese Communist Politics in Action* (Seattle: University of Washington Press, 1969), pp. 271–361.

[3]See Richard H. Solomon, "On Activism and Activists: Maoist Conceptions of Motivation and Political Role Linking State to Society," in *China Quarterly,* no. 39 (July–Sept. 1969), pp. 76–114; and Arthur F. Wright, "Struggle vs. Harmony: Symbols of Competing Values in Modern China," *World Politics,* vol. 6, no. 1 (October, 1953), pp. 31–44.

Paternalistic protection from superiors was the primary guarantee of security and gain. Pursuit of goals without elite approval risked failure as well as possible displeasure from those whose blessings counted most. Supplementing dependency on human authority, diverse practices of religion and superstition existed through which most Chinese sought protection and signs of good or bad fortune from suprahuman forces. If all protection failed, a sense of fatalism could cushion the blow — although again we should note that rebellion was a periodic response to adversity and oppression. Self-reliance is the Maoist principle opposed to this dependency orientation. It insists that human efforts can overcome all obstacles, and it urges the people to employ their own initiative and capacities to accomplish the tasks that face them. Dependence on religion, superstition, and higher authorities is discouraged, as is resignation to one's fate. The proper outlook, in the new culture, is that individuals need not and should not expect paternalistic protection and assistance from any source, including the government.

Egalitarianism and Populism. Hierarchical relationships were viewed as natural and necessary in the ordering of traditional Chinese society. The principles governing social hierarchy were complex, involving mixed considerations of age, generation, kinship, sex, wealth, scholarly attainment, and official status. Nonetheless, individuals knew who their superiors and subordinates were in various settings, so that a demarcation of authority and status was clear in most social relationships. Persons in higher roles in the hierarchy expected deference from those in lower ones and were characterized not simply by authority but by privilege and symbolic superiority relative to those beneath them. The Maoist view of social stratification is much more egalitarian. Although recognizing the existence of classes, the inevitability of some division of labor in society, and above all the necessity of maintaining political authority, it is hostile toward the elaboration and reinforcement of hierarchy. It seeks to minimize material and psychological inequalities generally and to eradicate what it regards as irrational subordination, such as that of younger generations and women. In the inescapable political and administrative hierarchy, it is hostile toward privileges, symbols, and economic differences that set elites apart as a special group and give them an aura of superiority extending beyond their specific political roles.

The Maoist orientation is similar to the traditional one in assigning elites a role as model for the most valued life-style, but the style itself differs greatly in the two cases. The ideal life style in traditional society was that of the scholar-official elite, whereas in the Maoist ethic it is that of the common man. The former placed the burden of attainment on the people, allowing elites to perpetuate their way of life; the latter places a distinct burden of change on elites who are expected to model a style of life traditionally considered beneath them. In more specific terms, traditional culture valued intellectual attainment and pursuits, bureaucratic or managerial roles, mental labor, and the contemplative life; the Maoist ethic values practical work, participation in the "front line" of production, manual labor, and the active, physical life. Although not overtly materialistic, the former encouraged material gain to support pursuit of elite status and some conspicuous consumption to demonstrate its attainment; the latter encourages self-denial, savings, and frugality, making a virtue of what was and remains an economic necessity for most of the people.[4]

This outline greatly simplifies the traditional–Maoist comparison and says little about actual political orientations in contemporary China. Neither model has been so pure and static in its application, and neither represents adequately the complex mix of attitudes that now prevails in Chinese political culture. Yet despite its limitations, the outline does suggest why political socialization has such a prominent place in Chinese politics. At issue here is not simply the transferral of allegiance to a new regime but the creation of a new political community in which all individuals will transform their images of public life and their roles within it. The Maoist prescriptions indicate the general direction of desired change and the magnitude of the task. They also help explain why the CCP has tried to expand the scope of socialization — to include adults

[4]For stimulating discussion of Maoist populism, see Maurice Meisner, "Leninism and Maoism: Some Populist Perspectives in Marxism-Leninism in China," *China Quarterly,* no. 45 (January–March 1971), pp. 2–36.

as well as children, elites as well as masses — and to establish political control over all socializing agents.

Realization of a Maoist political community may be remote and possibly utopian, but there are some conditions that favor the struggle to attain it. With its relatively homogeneous cultural tradition and common written language, China does not face severe ethnic or cultural cleavages. The national minorities constitute only about 6 percent of the population and live largely in frontier and mountainous areas. They figure prominently in questions of national security and integration but have little effect on policies relating to political socialization.[5] Cultural variations among the Han Chinese are probably a greater problem. For example, the adoption of Mandarin as the official language in non-Mandarin speaking areas, particularly the provinces of southeastern China, has created tensions between local and outside cadres and special complications in education and communications. Variations in lineage organization with their impact on land ownership patterns have led to different timing and results in land reform and collectivization.[6] On balance, however, the Chinese sense of cultural unity and identity overshadows these local variations and tends to support the acceptance of a new political culture that places such emphasis on national uniformity. The Chinese government traditionally has played a direct role in setting the moral and cultural tone of society. The principles advanced now are new, but the nationwide articulation of an official doctrine by representatives of the political system is not.

Moreover, changes already under way in Chinese society have blurred the confrontation between traditional and Maoist political cultures. The demise of state Confucianism, the imperial bureaucracy, and the examination system early in this century removed the political system's institutionalized support of the old culture. Political upheaval, economic change, the growth of modern schools, and the emergence or importation

[5]For a general survey of ethnic and cultural patterns in China, see Hu Chang-tu et al., *China: Its People, Its Society, Its Culture* (New Haven, Conn.: Human Relations Area File Press, 1960), esp. pp. 64–139.

[6]Guangdong (Kwangtung) province is an excellent example on both points; see Ezra F. Vogel, *Canton Under Communism: Programs and Politics in a Provincial Capital, 1949–1968* (Cambridge, Mass.: Harvard University Press, 1969), esp. chaps. 2, 3, and 5.

of new ideas encouraged social ferment and mobility. A "family revolution" began to disrupt the old society's dominant socializing agent.[7] To some extent the political orientations encouraged by the unfolding revolution were supportive or anticipatory of those demanded by the CCP. The mobilization of mass support for transcendental causes such as national unity and independence, the practice of KMT one-party rule with its intolerance of political opposition, and a growing conviction that China needed a new dispensation of political authority were preparing the way for reception of the Communist political style. As one scholar has suggested, the Chinese people in 1949 were in a sense ready for the CCP's demand for political commitment, if only to resolve the terrible divisions and uncertainties of preceding decades.[8] The old orientations had not disappeared, of course, but the institutions that had maintained them were in flux, and there was at least some receptivity to the official political culture of the new government.

Finally, we should take note of the manifest political resources of the CCP. Backed by substantial experience in mass political mobilization, widespread acceptance of its legitimacy, a dedicated cadre of party members and supporters, and demonstrated military superiority, the Communist government was able to establish a network of political organization unparalleled in Chinese history. With these resources vigorously brought into play, the prospects for inducing significant changes in Chinese political culture were at least credible, although not guaranteed.

When one turns to more specific problems, however, the difficulty of implanting a Maoist socialization process in China becomes apparent. Powerful influences external to the Communist system were present in 1949 and were inevitably to continue in force for some time to come. The CCP clearly benefits, in its desire to remold political attitudes, from the relative youth of the population. Over 53 percent of the popu-

[7]Marion J. Levy, Jr., *The Family Revolution in Modern China* (Cambridge, Mass.: Harvard University Press, 1949).

[8]Lucian W. Pye, "Mass Participation in China: Its Limitations and the Continuity of Culture," in John M. H. Lindbeck, ed., *China: Management of a Revolutionary Society* (Seattle: University of Washington Press, 1971), pp. 15–19.

lation was under twenty-five in 1953, a figure estimated to have risen to about 57–59 percent by 1965.[9] To put it in a different perspective, approximately 40 percent of the population in 1963 was fourteen or under, born since 1949; by 1985, those born since 1949 will be approaching 75 percent of the population.[10] In other words, the age structure of the population creates good opportunities for influencing the socialization experience. Yet in 1949 this was a future-oriented advantage that did little to resolve the immediate problem, which was that virtually the entire adult population had received primary socialization and education in a non-Communist setting. There was nothing the CCP could do to alter the fact that the parents, teachers, and workers of the first decade would reflect a pre-Communist socialization process, necessarily transmitted to some degree to the next generation. Moreover, even the most rigid control of the social environment could not exclude some extrasystemic influences. For example, KMT and American propaganda directed at the mainland, the passage of Chinese back and forth from the mainland (especially through Hong Kong), and the presence of foreign travelers and residents in China all ensured some external inputs of information. Most significant during the 1950s were Chinese contacts with other Communist countries, especially the Soviet Union. Hundreds of Russian teachers and thousands of Russian experts served in China in this period, while some sixty thousand Chinese had studied in the Soviet Union by the early 1960s.[11] As the Maoists put it, the influence of feudalistic, capitalist, and revisionist ideas remains long after the establishment of the socialist system.

Deficiencies in the tools of socialization were another formidable problem, given the 1949 level of economic and technical development. Schools, teachers, and books were in short supply for an effort aiming at universal education. CCP political

[9]John S. Aird, "Population Growth and Distribution in Mainland China," in Joint Economic Committee, Congress of the United States. *An Economic Profile of Mainland China,* vol. 2 (Washington, D.C.: Government Printing Office, 1967), pp. 364–65.

[10]Ibid.

[11]R. F. Price. *Education in Communist China* (New York: Praeger, 1970), pp. 101–4.

biases aggravated these shortages through destruction of library resources judged politically faulty and through suspicion of existing mass communications media. The rate of illiteracy — exactly unknown but estimated as high as 85–90 percent of the population in the early years[12] — was an obvious liability, as were the differences in spoken languages in different parts of the country. Socialization takes place regardless of such deficiencies, of course, but the point is that it was not easy for the CCP to transfer the burden of political socialization to those public institutions where its control was most secure.

Underlying all of these problems is the fact that the structure of human relationships does not necessarily govern their content.[13] The resources of the CCP came to bear most forcefully and effectively on social structure, changing the institutions of Chinese society and their relationship to each other. There is no need to review here the specific changes in question, the most relevant of which will be discussed in subsequent sections. Generally, the CCP has changed the structure of political socialization by reducing the role of kinship organization and by expanding greatly the scope of public, politically dominated mechanisms of socialization. However, this cannot guarantee that the content of attitudes associated with declining institutions will disappear or that the content of those associated with new relationships will follow the expected pattern. The CCP itself is a case in point. A new institution in Chinese society, carefully structured to embody the political orientations desired by its leaders, the party nonetheless failed to live up to Mao's expectations. If the "vanguard" of the revolution could not rid itself of the influences of the past, how effective has been the reform of less politicized institutions? The Cultural Revolution is, of course, the crucial episode for an analysis of this question. We will return to it after discussion of the agents of socialization including the family, the educational system, the communications network, and political and social experience.

[12]Ibid., p. 202.
[13]Hsü, op. cit., pp. 581–83 passim.

AGENTS OF SOCIALIZATION

The Family. The Chinese Communists have looked on traditional kinship organization — including both the nuclear family (parents and children) and the larger lineages or clans that
were so influential in parts of China — as a citadel of oppression, reactionary values, and potential opposition to socialism.
Accordingly they have tried to carry out a reform of the family
system that has produced much tension and resistance along
the way. This confrontation between state and family has led
some observers to conclude that the CCP wishes to destroy the
Chinese family. In fact, official policy has been complicated,
flexible, and even ambivalent. Some features of the old system
were initially marked for destruction: the organizational power
of the lineage; traditional marriage practices, which symboli-
cally and in practice helped perpetuate the subordination of
women and youth to family elders; and those values articulated
in both state Confucianism and popular religion that made
kinship obligations paramount within the sphere of social relationships. However, aside from destruction of lineage organizations that extended their influence over several families
and even whole villages, Communist policy with respect to
basic kinship structure has not been particularly radical. The
typical family unit is the nuclear family, or the stem family,
including one or more grandparents — a unit which was in fact
common in pre-Communist China and which is close to the
pattern prevailing in industrialized Western societies. Although the destruction of traditional characteristics deserves
emphasis, so does the effort to establish what may legitimately
be called a modern family system.[14]

With reference to political socialization, the basic intent of
Communist policy has been to transfer major responsibility to
the public realm and to secure compliance within the family to
norms established by political authority. Since the public institutions of socialization are discussed below, we focus here on
efforts to shape and define the family's role in the new society.

---

[14]Maurice Freedman, "The Family Under Chinese Communism," *Political
Quarterly,* vol. 35, no. 3 (July–Sept. 1964), pp. 342–50.

Broadly speaking, there have been five stages in the post-1949 development of CCP attitudes toward the family.

The first stage, from 1949 to the Great Leap Forward, was one of attempted neutralization of the family's traditional power by explicit attacks on familial authority. The most important step was adoption of the "marriage law" in 1950, followed over the next few years by a campaign to propagate and enforce its provisions. Basic provisions of the law included the following: the establishment of marriage as a civil act entered into only upon "complete willingness" of both parties and registered by government authority; the prohibition of "polygamy, concubinage, child betrothal, interference with the remarriage of widows, and the exaction of money or gifts in connection with marriage"; the establishment of full legal equality of both sexes in home and social matters; the granting of divorce on both parties' consent, or on one party's demand if backed by legal approval.[15] The marriage law also offered legal protection for children against abuse by their parents, a principle given teeth by the marked rise of young activists to positions of political responsibility. The assault on subordination of youth to elders was publicized dramatically in frequent denunciations by youth of alleged political crimes of their elders, including close relatives.[16] The confiscation and redistribution of lineage lands and holdings, coupled with the establishment of new organs of local government, eroded the power of extended kinship organizations.[17] These efforts were by no means completely successful or even uniformly implemented. The marriage law campaign created such instability that it was somewhat relaxed after 1953. On the other hand, the direction of CCP law, policy, and propaganda was unmistakable. The influence of the old kinship system might continue informally but only in a context of legal restrictions and political intimidation.

[15]See Yang, op. cit., "The Chinese Family in the Communist Revolution," chaps. 2–4; the marriage law appears as an appendix on pp. 221–26. It should be noted that the marriage law was fully in line with the "family revolution" in progress for several decades, and similar to the Nationalist reforms of the early 1930s; however, the Communists enforced their law much more vigorously than did their predecessors.

[16]Ibid., chap. 5.

[17]Ibid., chap. II.

The first wave of family reform receded during the institutionalization of the middle 1950s, but the Great Leap brought a second one that threatened briefly the structure of the nuclear family itself. Although a radical restructuring of the family was not a primary goal of the Leap, the mobilization of 1958 was a serious challenge to the single-family home. Expansion of the labor force took many women out of the home, while some work projects required splitting of families, residential change, or overnights away from the family; communal mess halls were to provide meals, permitting confiscation of many home utensils; communal nurseries and old-age homes were to care for the very young and very old. Yet the commune experiment did not contine along these lines. The most radical features of communal living were never established uniformly and were moderated during the winter of 1958–1959. When the dust had settled, the family unit remained intact although surely somewhat shaken by the experience.

With the post-Leap retrenchment came a new official view of the family's role in socialist society. Earlier an object of suspicion to be neutralized or even sacrificed in the course of revolution, the family was now regarded as a possible ally of the state in socialist construction. One of the best indicators of the new attitude was a relatively sympathetic portrayal in literature of kinship relationships and traditional authority figures such as fathers and "old peasants."[18] From the official point of view, expressed in retrenchment policies and editorial comment as well as in literature, the relaxation of earlier pressures on the family was not an abdication to traditional values as such. It was rather an acknowledgment that social change is a long-term process which can be promoted by models of "correct" behavior within the reformed institutions of the old society. The family and the village could become positive agents of socialization, reinforcing state policy by their encouragement of production skills, hard work, community service, and respect for authority.

However, the CCP's attempt to co-opt the family's socializ-

[18]For documentation and analysis, see Ai-li S. Chin, *Modern Chinese Fiction and Family Relations: Analysis of Kinship, Marriage and the Family in Contemporary Taiwan and Communist Chinese Stories* (Cambridge, Mass.: Center for International Studies, M.I.T., 1966).

ing influence ran a serious risk. How could it be sure that a warmer attitude toward traditional social institutions, even if partially reformed, would not encourage demonstration of old values as well as new? In fact, evidence in the early 1960s revealed the continued existence of kinship influence in local politics, arranged marriages and sale of brides, corruption and personal aggrandizement and other feudalistic practices.[19] This tendency was not condoned by the leadership, nor could it be attributed solely to social policy, since it thrived on the "revisionist" economic reforms of the period. Nonetheless, a certain tolerance of traditional kinship practices was implicit in the effort to capitalize on the family's stabilizing influence.[20]

Attitudes toward the family mirrored the basic dilemma of the 1960s — how to reconcile maintenance of authority and stability with continued revolution — and were, therefore, necessarily involved in the socialist education campaigns and the Cultural Revolution. As might be expected, the early stages of the Cultural Revolution brought sharp attacks on relationships suggestive of traditional prerogatives. Once more, the independence of youth was encouraged, sometimes taking the form of denunciation of parents and elders. The family was not a target of special hostility but neither was it immune from revolutionary struggle; it was to "revolutionize" itself, fearlessly rooting out any evil tendencies that might persist or arise within it.[21]

As the Cultural Revolution receded, however, a fifth stage emerged that revealed a family pattern little changed from the third phase of the early 1960s.[22] The organized power of the lineages was gone, the status of youth and women had risen significantly, and the state or collective had established its formal authority over kinship units. Yet the nuclear or stem family remained the primary residential and child-rearing unit,

---

[19]John Wilson Lewis, "The Leadership Doctrine of the Chinese Communist Party: The Lesson of the People's Commune," *Asian Survey,* vol. 3, no. 10 (October, 1963), pp. 457–64; and C. S. Chen, ed., *Rural People's Communes in Lien-chiang,* trans. Charles Price Ridley (Stanford, Cal.: Hoover Institution, 1969), esp. pp. 44–49.

[20]Chin, op. cit., pp. 79–85.

[21]Tsao Hsin-hua, "Using Materialist Dialectics to Revolutionize the Family," *PR* no. 47 (Nov. 20, 1970), pp. 10–12.

[22]The authoritative study is Parish and Whyte, op. cit.

continued to serve as an important economic unit by pooling its members' incomes and expenditures, provided some education and health care expenses, and took care of most of the aged in Chinese society. Despite progress in the direction indicated by the marriage law reforms, many traditional marriage practices — payment of bride prices, patrilocal residence for newlyweds, and some (less than formerly) parental involvement in mate selection — remained common, tolerated if not approved by cadres. Urban families were closer to the official model than those in rural areas, where one might expect a gradual weakening of traditional customs, but it seemed that the "family revolution" had reached a plateau in which the attainment of many initial reforms had essentially satisfied state demands.

The family's emergence as a cooperating rather than target institution in Communist society is due in part to its residual strength, its capacity to meet human needs that cannot be satisfied elsewhere. Elites have also discovered that extreme disruption of family life, as in the first push toward marriage reform or in 1958, is counterproductive. In other words, there is an economic rationale to the implicit toleration of some traditional practices, a toleration that seems to enhance social stability and economic production, just as retaining family responsibility for certain welfare costs reduces public expenses in these areas. Finally, reforms in other areas (education, collectivization of the economy, and creation of new political organizations) both shape and limit the family's socializing role. As time goes by, parents influenced by other socializing agents are more likely to reflect the official ethic, while institutional changes reduce the family's role relative to public organizations. All of these considerations help to explain why the CCP has compromised some of its revolutionary values, such as the drive for full equality of women in marital practices and roles, in exchange for stabilization of the family's place in the new society.

The Educational System. The system of public education that has emerged in China since 1949 is one of the state's most effective agents for altering Chinese political attitudes. This is not to say that it has created a Maoist political culture among all those exposed to it thus far, or that it can ever be a wholly successful instrument for establishing attitudes favored by future elites. The influence of other socializing forces, conflict among elites over the functions and content of education, and limitations on the capacity of schools to accomplish what is demanded of them all ensure that students will never conform to any single attitudinal pattern. Still, the educational system carries a heavy long-term responsibility for change. Unlike the family, which affects everyone at an impressionable age but is difficult to penetrate, the schools are subject to a high degree of state control. In contrast to the communications network and generalized political experience, which have their greatest impact on adults in rather uneven and unpredictable ways, the schools provide a mechanism for universal, sustained, and structured contact with all school-age citizens.

The educational system includes five major branches: preschool programs, primary schools, middle schools (including junior and senior levels, plus a variety of vocational and technical schools), institutions of higher education, and various part-time and spare-time schools that overlap in level with the more standardized full-time schools. Although the system is a centralized one, governed throughout by regulations and/or control from central ministries that establish national standards for administration and content, it has much variety within it. Particularly at preschool, primary, and part-time and spare-time levels, there are some nongovernmental schools established by local units or volunteers; although subject to governmental approval and regulation, and possibly recipients of subsidies, such schools inject an element of citizen participation into educational operations. Lengths of term and courses of study are not uniform for all schools of the same level, and there have been frequent revisions of central educational policies since 1949. When one adds to this the incompleteness of data on enrollment and other matters, it is clear that generalizations about the system must be very general indeed.[24]

In terms of political socialization, progress toward universal education is the system's most basic objective. To shift the

[24]A very useful overall account, these problems notwithstanding, is Price, op cit.

burden of socialization toward the public realm and to establish widespread mass literacy to facilitate continued political education and involvement, the schools must approach universality of enrollment for school-age population groups. Universal education for the entire population is, of course, a distant goal due to the backlog of uneducated adults and the difficulty (in any society) of matching resources with societal demands. In practice, a high and increasing proportion of enrollment of school-age children surely represents significant progress. However, given the intense concern of Chinese elites for universal attitudinal change, what might bring "significant progress" in the long run has not guaranteed the elite satisfaction — hence the frequency and centrality in Chinese politics of controversy over the educational system.

The primary schools carry the major burden of efforts to achieve universal education and the basic literacy associated with it. Before the Cultural Revolution, the standard primary course was a six-year program beginning at about the age of seven and customarily divided into four-year junior and two-year senior primary schools. Enrollment increased sharply during the 1950s, reaching 86.4 million in 1958 (see Table II) — a figure representing perhaps 80 percent of the primary school-age group (seven to twelve years) of the time. In effective terms, the percentage receiving full primary education was certainly lower than this. Some overage students would be included due to late starts, and enrollment as such was no guarantee of completing the six-year program. In many rural areas, completion of only the junior primary course was apparently the norm. Moreover, 1960 probably marked the high point of attendance in the regular schools (before the Cultural Revolution), at least as a percentage of school-age population, as enrollments slowed or fell in the early 1960s while population continued to grow.[24]

Middle and higher schools also expanded rapidly during the 1950s but remained accessible to a very small number of people. Their basic function was to provide advanced academic,

[24]See the discussion in Leo A. Orleans, "Communist China's Education: Policies, Problems and Prospects," in *An Economic Profile of Mainland China,* vol. 2, pp. 505–12.

TABLE II. *Enrollments and Graduates by Level of School (in Thousands)*

| | Primary schools | | Middle schools | | Universities | |
Year	Enroll-ment	Gradu-ates	Enroll-ment	Gradu-ates	Enroll-ment	Gradu-ates
Peak year prior to 1949	23,683	4,633	1,879	399	155	25
1949	24,391	2,387	1,268	352	117	21
1952	51,100	5,942	3,126	289	191	32
1958	86,400	16,225	9,990	1,504	660	72
1960	. . .	. . .	. . .	. . .	955	135
1965	116,000	. . .	14,418	. . .	674	170

The Cultural Revolution: All schools closed for at least two years, with primary schools the first to reopen, universities the last. The closures produced a notice-able lag in graduates from middle schools and universities. No complete figures on post-Cultural Revolution enrollments are available, but the following esti-mates indicate the main trends. University enrollments for 1978 were expected to increase by nearly 300,000 over 1977 due to the new priorities established in that period.

1967	. . .	. . .	. . .	690	. . .	10
1970	. . .	. . .	. . .	1,266	. . .	40
1975	130,000	. . .	34,000	. . .	400	. . .
1977	150,000	. . .	59,079	. . .	584	. . .

Sources: Figures for the years down to 1958 are from John Phillip Emerson, "Employment in Mainland China," United States Congress, Joint Economic Committee, *An Economic Profile of Mainland China* (Washington: Government Printing Office, 1967), pp. 424–25. The 1960 university enrollment is from Emerson, "Manpower Training and Utilization of Specialized Cadres, 1949–68," in John Lewis, ed., *The City in Communist China* (Stanford, Cal.: Standford University Press, 1971), p. 200. Enrollments for 1965 are from *Peking Review*, no. 5 (Feb. 3, 1978), p. 17. Enrollments for 1975 are from *The United States and China*, A Report to the Senate Foreign Relations Committee and the House International Relations Committee, United States Congress (Washington: Government Printing Office, 1975), p. 21. Graduates for 1960, 1965, 1967, and 1970 are from Leo Orleans, "China's Science and Technology," in United States Congress, Joint Economic Committee, *People's Republic of China: An Economic Assessment* (Washington: Government Printing Office, 1972), pp. 218–19. Enrollments for 1977 are from Suzanne Pepper, "An Interview on Changes in Chinese Education After the 'Gang of Four'," *China Quarterly*, no. 72 (December 1977), pp. 815–16.

vocational, and political training to select students who formed the pool from which China's new elite would be re-cruited. This task rested mainly on the regular middle schools which trained the vast majority of new teachers, technicians and low-level government cadres. Middle school enrollment is difficult to estimate, owing to the variety of schools operating at this level, but regular middle schools probably reached a peak enrollment of about ten million in 1958–60.[25] Thus, only about 10 percent of primary graduates continued on to regular middle school, and most who did so completed only the three-year junior middle school course; about one out of six junior middle school graduates went on to senior middle school[26] Further screening occurred at the college level, which accommodated 955,000 students in regular universities in the peak year of 1960; university enrollments fell significantly thereafter.[27]

In summary, the regular school system greatly expanded educational opportunities during the 1950s but then began to lose its momentum. At its best, it was providing a few years (not necessarily the full six) of primary education for most children, a three-year junior middle school course for a select minority, and higher education (senior middle school and college) for a tiny fraction of the population.

By the late 1950s, some Chinese leaders had developed serious concerns about the emerging system of regular schools, foremost among them the following: primary schools were serving inadequately the rural areas, where most of those children attending school briefly or not at all were located, and were of no help in meeting the needs of illiterate or minimally educated adults; middle schools, located mostly in the cities and offering a full-time study program, were largely the preserve of a new educational elite who were prepared for and could afford this commitment to advanced training; the universities were even more limited in their admissions policy and their academic approach to specialized training. In brief, the system was seen as giving relatively advanced and prolonged education to the few, encouraging in them hopes for a purely official career, while limiting its benefit to rural areas and the working population. Two major lines of reform appeared in response. One was proposed reform of the regular system

[25]Ibid.; and Price, op. cit., p. 128. The continued growth of primary and middle enrollments down to 1965, shown in Table II, probably indicates inclusion of various part-time school enrollments in the totals for that year.
[26]Orleans, op. cit.
[27]Ibid.

itself, with calls for reduction in years of study, less emphasis on specialized academic programs, and the injection of some working or production experience into the regular school schedule.[28] The other was a strenuous effort during the Great Leap Forward to expand spare-time and part-time ("half-work–half study") schools. Such schools had existed in various forms since the early 1950s, but their intensified promotion as an alternative to the regular full-time schools was a distinctive feature of the Great Leap period. Spare-time schools are essentially courses in adult education frequently organized by local production units to provide basic training in literacy, occupational skills, and politics for the working population. Part-time or "half-work–half-study" programs are diverse, operating at many levels under different forms of management and offering different combinations of study and work experience. Aimed mainly at young people, they attempt to offer an educational program nominally approximating that of the regular schools but without separating the student from his or her production responsibilities. The best example is the agricultural middle schools, which flourished in the late 1950s as a response to the regular schools' failure to provide adequate education for rural youth.[29]

These efforts failed to restructure the educational system. The collapse of the Great Leap, the economic crisis and retrenchment policies that followed, and general inertia or resistance of many within the school system forestalled radical departure from established patterns. In theory, the regular schools committed themselves to a more "proletarian" line, giving prominence to politics and the working class in their policies and requiring participation in productive labor of their staff and students; in practice, these measures were routinized to minimize their impact. The spare-time and part-time schools survived, continuing to serve at least some of their intended functions by bringing political and practical educa-

[28]Price, op. cit., p. 33–37.

[29]For details on spare-time and part-time education in the late 1950s and early 1960s, see Robert D. Barendson, *Half-Work Half-Study Schools in Communist China* (Washington, D.C.: U.S. Department of Health, Education and Welfare, Office of Education, 1964), and Paul Harper, *Spare-Time Education for Workers in Communist China* (Washington, D.C.: U.S. Department of Health, Education and Welfare, Office of Education, 1964).

tion to millions excluded from the regular schools, but they remained subordinate to the latter in academic quality and social prestige. A frontal assault on the educational establishment was postponed until the Cultural Revolution.

Despite Maoist rejection of the educational system in the late 1960s, largely on the grounds that it was not performing satisfactorily its political mission, the schools have had a great influence on political socialization in post-1949 China. By any comparative standard, they have been highly politicized in terms of large blocks of time devoted to explicit political education, the injection of political information and desired political attitudes into basic subjects of instruction (most prominently, into the materials used in the standard readers), an effort to permeate the classroom with official views of public and private morality, and the establishment of party supervision and control over the system as a whole. As a result, certain political themes have been a heavy and inescapable part of the school experience. None of them is surprising, given the nature of the system, but the most salient of them should be noted. One is patriotism, the attempt to transmit basic information about China, its accomplishments and resources, and to instill feelings of love, loyalty, and respect for it. Another is support for the Communist political system encouraged through transmission of knowledge about the history and achievements of the CCP and its leaders, particularly Mao Zedong, and the portrayal of the party as the benevolent and righteous leader of the country. Coupled with this is explicit criticism of negative political models, such as the old feudal system, the KMT, American imperialism, and Soviet revisionism. Finally, political education has emphasized strongly the qualities of the model citizen: hard work, sacrifice, and discipline for the sake of society and the collectivity.[30] With half of the population now exposed to some regular education under Communism, and with the variety of irregular education programs that have supplemented the regular schools, we can assume the emergence in China of widespread subject orienta-

---

[30]For a detailed analysis of political socialization in Chinese schools, see Charles Price Ridley, Paul H. B. Godwin, and Dennis J. Doolin, *The Making of a Model Citizen in Communist China* (Stanford, Cal.: Hoover Institution Press, 1971), pp. 3–208; sample selections from primary-school readers are included on pp. 239–404. See also Price, op. cit., passim.

tions — founded on a basic identification with the national political system — coupled with growing enclaves of citizens holding more specialized knowledge about politics and more participant orientations toward their own role in it.

The assertion rests on the simplistic proposition that the political content of Chinese education is sufficiently forceful to have some long-term effect on a population that is increasingly composed of citizens who have partaken of it. There are, of course many other influences that resist and even oppose the pressures of the educational system — for example, the enduring dictates of the traditional political culture and the possibility of contradictory socializing experiences elsewhere in comtemporary society. Nor is the educational system itself without its internal conflicts over political socialization — conflicts which compromise its capacity to transmit unequivocally the elements of a Maoist political culture. One of the sharpest conflicts is between obedience to political authority and encouragement of individual activism; the former's subject orientation toward unfailing acceptance of party leadership cannot always be reconciled with the latter's more participant orientation toward individual political initiative and action. Tension is inherent, too, in the juxtaposition of collectivist values emphasizing selfless social service, particularly in rural occupations and areas, with distinct encouragement of achievement orientations that support individual and national advancement.[31] There is even conflict on the fundamental question of how prominently political socialization should figure in the general educational process. At the root of this is the "red-expert" problem: the question of how to balance competing demands for political education in the service of attitudinal change and technical education in the service of economic transformation, as well as how best to manage national development given limited educational resources.[32] As

[31]For a fuller discussion, see Ridley, Godwin, and Doolin, op. cit., pp. 195–208.

[32]See Donald J. Munro, "Egalitarian Ideal and Education Fact in Communist China," in John M. H. Lindbeck, ed., *China: Management of a Revolutionary Society* (Seattle: University of Washington Press, 1971), pp. 256–301; and Suzanne Pepper, "Education and Political Development in Communist China," *Studies in Comparative Communism,* vol. 3, nos. 3–4 (July–October 1970), pp. 198–223.

the subsequent discussion will argue, these are conflicts that continue to plague the political socialization process. Yet their very existence and the seriousness with which elites debate them suggest that the new educational system is making its mark on the Chinese political culture.

The Communications Network. Political communications in China as in other societies include an immense variety and volume of messages. Although China may be considered a closed system in which communications patterns and media are tightly restricted by government controls, its tendency to politicize so many areas of human action ensures a heavy flow of communications about politics. Our interest here is primarily in only one sector of this flow — that which flows outward from elites to create citizen support for the system and thereby enters into the socialization process. Other major sectors of political communications, such as the expression of political interests and the demands and exchanges relating to the making and implementation of decisions, will be examined in subsequent chapters.

The public communications network in China is almost exclusively an official (state or party) operation, subject in its content and management to the control of central political authorities. The organization of this official monopoly on public communications is complex. State agencies administer most major media — such as the New China [Xinhua] News Agency, radio and television stations, the film industry, and most publishing enterprises — but the CCP and its supporting mass organizations also publish important newspapers and periodicals. Regardless of the administrative source or level of operation, however, all media are subject to the general controls and policies established by the CCP Central Committee's Propaganda Department. Through its sections for specific communications areas and its authority over propaganda departments within lower-level party organizations, it seeks to ensure that all media follow central party policy in the dissemination of information and ideas through the printed and spoken word.[33]

[33]Alan P. L. Liu, *Communications and National Integration in Communist China,* new enl. ed. (Berkeley: University of California Press, 1975), pp. xvii–xxv, 34–52.

Party supervision of all public communications has been a formal principle of organization reflecting elite intent and authority, but it has not in practice been absolute. The division of operational control among state, party, and mass organization units at various administrative levels has permitted some deviation from the central line. Moreover, the central line as such has been ambiguous or disputed at times, resulting in intended or unintended conflicts between messages put forth by different sources. The Propaganda Department itself was torn apart in the first year of the Cultural Revolution, although some unnamed persons and organization undoubtedly resumed its functions when the CCP began to rebuild in the late 1960s. However, these departures from total control do not alter two generalizations that follow from the attempt to achieve it. One is that virtually all information disseminated through the network is that which central elites or subordinates acting on their perceptions of central intent have approved for public release. The public is told what political elites want it to know; competing or contradictory messages have no organized vehicle for response. The other is that a clear sense of hierarchical authority permeates the system and is in fact essential to its effective operation. Communications from more authoritative sources will overrule those from subordinate ones; contradictions and confusion require direction from above for resolution. In the absence of consistent messages from the highest authorities, lower communications agents and the body politic as a whole tend toward inaction or conflict.

A second characteristic of political communications in China is the governing influence of ideology and its special vocabulary. As Schurmann points out, the "closing" effect of official control over communications is not simply secrecy or censorship — much significant information is transmitted publicly — but rather the requirement that communications be cast in the language of the official ideology. The ideologically specific meaning of concepts and terms becomes a separate language system for public discourse; it provides a unifying bond and mechanism for those who "speak" it, at the same time screening out those who do not or those concepts that have no place in it. As with all languages, employment of it involves not simply the use of certain words but internal-ization of the manner of thinking that makes those words intelligible.[34] As a result, much of what passes through the communications system is aimed in the first instance at elites or subelites who have the capacity to understand it and the responsibility to disseminate it — with appropriate explana-tion and reference to local circumstances — to the general population.

Finally, the style of public communications is distinctly pedagogical. Questions are posed, arguments listed, and con-clusions drawn; reason and persuasion attempt to guide the recipient to a specific position; slogans and catchword devices (such as the use of numbered sets of points, commonly identi-fied by numbers only once the points are known) which lend themselves to memorization and repetition abound; good and bad "models" illustrate how policies should be implemented — which experiences should be emulated and which shunned. As the Great Leap slogan put it, "the whole nation is a class-room," and the communications system plays a vital part in the education or reeducation of the nation's population.

Political communications in China vary in their intended audience, the kind of medium employed, and the intensity of the exchange. In terms of the intended audience, we may distinguish among private or secret media, the elite media, and mass media. The private or secret media are those modes of communication limited to a very specific audience and include private letters, telegrams and telephone conversations, and restricted or classified publications or documents. They may have the highest political importance, but their bearing on political socialization is marginal and they are, for obvious, reasons, largely beyond reach of the analyst.[35]

The elite media are public communications that are openly disseminated but have a specialized audience composed

---

[34]Franz Schurmann, *Ideology and Organization in Communist China*, 2nd ed., enl. (Berkeley: University of California Press, 1968), pp. 58–68.

[35]It is worth noting, however, that many secret documents, publications, and exchanges have become available to external analysis through intelligence activities and the Red Guard publications of the Cultural Revolution. Inter-views with emigres, letters from the PRC, and the observations and conversa-tions reported by visitors to the PRC also provide information on nonofficial communications in China.

mainly of the most literate and politically involved citizens. The best examples are the official newspapers and periodicals of the party Central Committee, the People's Liberation Army command, and some other national-scale organizations such as the Youth League. These are the most authoritative publications in China and may in some cases have substantial circulation. However, since their circulation figures represent a national audience and since they maintain a relatively sophisticated level of analysis, their readership is a sharply limited one in terms of the total population. At the apex of this group, and of the entire political communications network, is *Renmin Ribao* (*Jen-min Jih-pao, People's Daily*), the Central Committee's official newspaper. Other prominent include *Hongqi* (*Hung Ch'i, Red Flag*), the Central Committee's theoretical journal; *Jiefangjun Bao* (*Chieh-fang-chün Pao, Liberation Army Daily*), the PLA General Political Department's newspaper; *Zhongguo Qingnian* (*Chung-kuo Ch'ing-nien, Chinese Youth*) and *Zhongguo Qingnian Bao* (*Chung-kuo Ch'ing-nien Pao, Chinese Youth Daily*), the official periodical and newspaper of the Youth League; and a number of nationally distributed specialized journals and newspapers oriented toward cultural and intellectual circles, economic problems, philosophical and historical inquiry, and so forth. Despite their importance, the elite media are still vulnerable to political difficulties. *Renmin Ribao* and *Hongqi* both experienced reorganization and temporary suspension during the Cultural Revolution. *Zhongguo Qingnian, Zhongguo Qingnian Bao* and several other elite publications were suspended from 1966 until the late 1970s.

The mass media are those aimed at the ordinary citizen, radio being the most important among them. Bridging the literacy barrier (although not always linguistic barriers), amenable to extension into remote areas, and capable of immediate and simultaneous transmission of messages to large audiences, radio is government's best instrument for mass communication. The radio network begins with Radio Peking, extends through dozens of provincial and municipal broadcasting stations as well as thousands of local stations, and ends with millions of receiving sets and loudspeakers wired from the local stations. It is the wired stations and loudspeakers that serve the masses best, as they permit broadcasting into mess halls, train stations, schools, factories, meeting houses, and other public places.

Newspapers in the mass media category include local newspapers (normally published by provincial and municipal party committees), rural editions of the local press designed to serve the surrounding countryside, newsletters or papers put out by units, enterprises, and schools for their own clientele, and a variety of ephemeral reading matter suitable for handouts or posting. Among the latter items, the most interesting are the *dazibao* (*ta-tzu-pao,* big character posters), which are handwritten statements of criticism and opinion posted in public places. At times, and especially during the Cultural Revolution, they have reproduced major documents and news items as well as conveying individual or group opinion. Although the mass-oriented press has sufficient volume and diversity to penetrate most localities, it falls far short of universal contact due to limits on production and distribution, the disinclination of some people to read newspapers, and above all, the still formidable problem of illiteracy in the countryside. The same limitations apply even more strongly to books and periodicals, although a few items — such as *Quotations from Chairman Mao Zedong* and other heavily propagandized stories and articles — have attained a genuine mass readership.

Other mass media include films, live dramatic performances, and television. The Chinese film industry is an active one albeit one which is still developing and peculiarly vulnerable to political shifts. Enough films and facilities have been produced since 1949 to make viewing common in the cities. Rural viewing is less frequent but has been expanded greatly by traveling projection teams and efforts to set up permanent projection facilities in communes. In contrast to newspaper reading, which may be a chore even for the literate, film viewing is easy and entertaining. It has tremendous potential for government communication with the masses, even though most peasants still see only a few films a year. Dramatic performances (plays, opera, ballet, and variety shows) are frequent and popular in the cities, with traveling troupes offering less frequent rural performances. Television use began to expand rapidly in the late 1970s and will no doubt become a prominent feature of Chinese communications in the 1980s.[36]

The preceding discussion has identified some of the audiences and media that are involved in the Chinese communications network but has said nothing about one of its most important and distinctive forms — face-to-face contact in meetings or small-group encounters. Several factors may account for the Chinese emphasis on direct, personal contact in political communications. One is surely the problem of illiteracy, which, as noted, affects the use of formal media as well by elevating radio and film use relative to that of the printed media. Another is China's level of modernization, in which manpower is still abundant relative to technological resources.

The CCP's historical experience of mass mobilization, under circumstances in which face-to-face contact was sometimes the only possible means of communication, also influences its contemporary style. Apart from these societally specific influences, there is the fact that face-to-face contact is a highly effective means of communication in any society.[37] These factors have combined to produce in China a communications system that deemphasizes the use of standard media and favors direct, personalized communications.

The resource that makes this possible is an army of political cadres and activists sufficient in number to penetrate every working and/or residential collectivity in China. In the early years of the PRC, when party and mass organization ranks were thin and the formal communications network was yet to be established, the CCP trained "propagandists" and "reporters" with specific responsibility for carrying government messages to the people. As administrative and political posts were filled, and as the regime gained experience in coordinating mass movements with the growing communications network, these specialists became unnecessary. Responsibility for direct contact with the masses came to rest on members of the local

[36]For a much fuller description and analysis of the media referred to in this section, see Liu, op. cit., pp. xxxiii–liii, 118–167; and Godwin C. Chu, *Popular Media in China: Shaping New Cultural Patterns* (Honolulu: University of Hawaii Press, 1978).

[37]Gabriel A. Almond and G. Bingham Powell, Jr., *Comparative Politics: System, Process, and Policy,* 2nd ed. (Boston: Little, Brown, 1978), pp. 142–143.

subelite: basic-level cadres, designated or "natural" leaders of work or residential groups, party or Youth League members not holding higher cadre posts, persons with middle school or higher education, demobilized soldiers, and others whose personal motivation had led into "activism" without special background or experience. Higher-level cadres supervise their work and, when necessary, supplement it with personal visits. These low-level cadres and activists are expected to grasp political issues revealed in the formal media and call them to popular attention, explaining and persuading as necessary to secure mass support. They may do this through regular discussion and study groups that go over current news and issues, through special meetings called for problems of particular urgency, or simply through the give-and-take of daily conversation. Of course, there is no guarantee that the full potential of this form of communication is realized, due to variations in ability and motivation of the imtermediaries, but the possibility of establishing personal contact with and response from individual citizens is one of the great strengths of the network.

Although it is impossible to say exactly what impact the political communications network has on Chinese political attitudes, a few comments about variations in the intensity of the communications experience may shed some light on this question. First, it is safe to assume that reception of political propaganda is nearly universal and fairly frequent for all Chinese citizens. That is, virtually all are exposed regularly to the messages of at least some of the formal media — primarily press, radio, and films — all of which have a high political content. The cumulative effects of this reception probably have raised the general level of knowledge about political personalities and affairs, created a greater sense of indentification with the national political system, and encouraged among citizens greater receptivity to the demands and values of political elites. However, the degree of attitudinal change as contrasted to a greater awareness of and knowledge about politics may be minimal, simply because ordinary propaganda does not require a response. No matter how frequent and extensive its coverage, media propaganda permits the recipient to remain passive. If passivity is a cover for resistance, then repeated exposure to the message may even have negative effects.

The intensity of communications is heightened considerably by the addition of discussion and study under the guidance of a political cadre or activist. At least three changes occur with this injection of personal contact into the process. First, the group leader's presence permits "translation" of generalized, jargon-ridden messages into everyday language and examples. Second, the peer group setting, in which the citizen joins with relatives, friends, or coworkers, increases pressures for comformity and participation. Finally, the group may be sufficiently small and the cadre sufficiently skilled and aggressive to break the passivity barrier, forcing the citizen to respond and thereby to expose his attitudes to possible change. The range of settings in which such political study and discussion takes place is great. It might be a highly informal one in which the cadre seizes an opportunity, at work or rest, to discuss with one person or more the political implications of recent events or work experience. It might be a more structured setting, such as a regularized meeting for newspaper reading, radio listening, news analysis, or discussion of work tasks. Or it might approximate a true political study group, in which assigned materials are reviewed and each member's views subjected to criticism and self-criticism.

The difficulties that may weaken mass political study and discussion are also numerous. The cadre or activist carries a heavy responsibility for the success of the enterprise. If the leader is poorly informed, unclear about policies, authoritarian, defensive, or vindictive in style, then the quality of group discussion will suffer accordingly. So, too, with the participants themselves, whose level of knowledge and interest will influence the tone of discussion. Political study is definitely not the same thing for all political study groups; one in a school or state office, for example, will differ from one in a commune. Some of what passes for political study or discussion in the countryside is little more than a cadre lecture or briefing, simply because the peasants are too tired, busy, poorly informed, or poorly motivated to make much more of it. Moreover, since group members, including the leader, are so frequently comembers of other natural social groupings, there is a danger that desires for group solidarity will encourage avoidance of conflict or routinization of criticism and self-criticism. Despite these real limitations — examples of "commandism" and "backwardness" in group discussion abound in the Chinese press and in the accounts of people who have been participants — face-to-face political discussion does intensify media impact in a way that guarantees some citizen response.[38]

The most intensive political communications in China occur in "rectification," "struggle," and "thought reform." Here, particular individuals or groups are criticized in a highly structured setting that allows no escape from confrontation with norms prescribed by the elite. Rectification campaigns aim at various levels or sectors of the elite, especially CCP members. Normally they identify certain categories of shortcomings and subject officials to close scrutiny to determine which among them might manifest the deficiencies under attack. Although a few negative "models" might be named at the outset, the political disposition of most members of the target group depends on their response during the course of the campaign. Rectification (that is, acknowledgment of errors and renewed commitment to the "correct" line or standpoint) and not purge is the result for most. Yet some will be found seriously deficient, the consequence being demotion or purge and more hostile struggle. Struggle and thought reform are the extreme form of political education brought to bear on individuals whose political "guilt" is already established, whether through a rectification campaign or through information developed in other ways. The structural and psychological dynamics of struggle and thought reform are too complex for analysis here,[39] but there is little question about their capacity to produce extreme disorientation in the subject although not necessarily a permanent attitudinal change in the desired direction. It must be remembered that relatively few Chinese have been on the receiving end of these techniques — at least since the early postliberation years, when whole social groups such as landlords or intellectuals were designated for struggle and

---

[38]See Whyte, op. cit., for a thorough analysis of political study in small groups, suggesting that it is more effective in downward communications and organizational control than in bringing about genuine attitudinal change.

[39]For a pioneering exploration of this topic, see Robert Jay Lifton, *Thought Reform and the Psychology of Totalism* (New York: Norton, 1961).

reform. Rectification is basically a form of communication and control among the elite. Struggle and thought reform are political and psychological assaults on even more limited numbers, primarily deviant elites and those identified as enemies of the regime.

To summarize, China has acquired the superstructure of a modern communications system and is now developing its infrastructure. Coverage is most complete for the cities and for the more literate and better-educated citizens. Political communications rely heavily on face-to-face contacts that supplement the formal media, particularly by encouraging individual response. The overall impact of communications is greatest for elites, who experience its most intensive forms more frequently and at a higher level of interaction and who are more likely to encounter the full range of media output. In terms of socialization, the system is most effective in expanding knowledge about politics and heightening sensitivity to political issues. Its role in inducing attitudinal change is more questionable, but is has in the political discussion group a mechanism that can penetrate to the level of individual attitudes and has probably encouraged more participant orientations toward politics.

Political and Social Experience. Socialization is not a process that ends with childhood or formal education. It continues throughout life, as the pattern of daily life and perceptions of major events reinforce, challenge, and alter the orientations formed in earlier years.[40] The leaders of post-1949 China have tried to capitalize on this fact, using their power to structure public organization and activity in ways that provide an environment supportive of the political culture they hope to establish. Mao Zedong in particular insisted on the necessity of "combining theory with practice," of providing or even forcing opportunities for the testing and practice of abstract political concepts.[41] From the Maoist perspective it is not enough to study political ideas and principles; they must be applied in

[40]Almond and Powell, op. cit., pp. 79–80.
[41]The theme permeates Mao's writings and political style; for a formalized statement, see "On Practice," *Selected Works of Mao Tse-tung* (Peking: Foreign Languages Press, 1965), vol. 1, pp. 295–309.

social action before they truly become part of one's social being. The CCP's attempt to create political and social experiences that will assist internalization of the desired political culture is most evident in political campaigns and organization at the basic level and in the compulsory dilution of elite status and privilege. We also want to consider briefly the impact of more generalized, unstructured political experiences on the Chinese population.

One of the CCP's most ambitious goals has been to involve every Chinese citizen in regular, organized political activity at the basic level, largely through mass movements, representation in basic-level government, membership in mass organizations, and participation in the management of primary production and residential units.[42] All of these are multifunctional political phenomena. They are structures for the implementation of central policy, for political recruitment and control, and to some extent for local interest articulation and decision making. Their function of socialization is important and at times paramount. The point is simply this: in pre-Communist China, most citizens had no role in political life and were divorced in any positive sense from the processes of formal government; the Communist goal, on the other hand, is to ensure that every citizen begins to experience some political roles by participating in rallies, meetings, discussions, and elections that relate to public affairs. In most cases, real initiative and control in these activities rests with higher authorities, and no doubt some "participants" simply are performing assignments for which they have little understanding or enthusiasm. Yet these are not overriding limitations with reference to socialization. Even if the setting is structured and the conduct of the activity ritualistic, the participant is learning something about the governmental process, the possibilities of political association, and his or her relationship to politics. The act of participation may foster positive awareness of political identity even if its real efficacy is low.

[42]See the outline of major campaigns and basic-level organization in Chapter III, this book. A fuller discussion is found in James R. Townsend, *Political Participation in Communist China* (Berkeley: University of California Press, 1967), chaps. 5–7. See Liu, op. cit., chap. 5, for an analysis of mass movements with particular reference to their role in political communications.

These phenomena are not uniformly effective, however, in providing meaningful political experiences. The system of elections and basic-level congresses flourished briefly in 1954–1957 and had an important symbolic role in affirming the popular base of government, but it was disrupted by the Great Leap and the Cultural Revolution. Local branches of the nationally organized mass organizations, such as the unions and Women's Federation, have offered opportunities for mass involvement in specialized projects (for instance, labor insurance and welfare, child care, mediation of local disputes), although they have been very much a part of the national bureaucratic hierarchy and accordingly were pushed aside during the Cultural Revolution. The socializing impact of the mass campaigns is ambiguous. As the focal point of political life and the vehicle for the most intense political activity, they have done more than any other mechanism to involve the population in the full range of political situations the system offers. They have probably increased the salience of politics for all, generated (at least on occasion) enthusiasm for collective action for many, and led substantial numbers into genuine political activism. Their negative effects also have been great, however, due to their frequently excessive demands and politically threatening nature. Most Chinese have seen their own lives disrupted by one or more of these campaigns or else know of people who have suffered heavily from them.[43] The most constructive settings for political socialization have probably been the production and residential groups that have encouraged considerable popular participation in the manage-

[43]This disruptive potential is illustrated by the increased flow of emigrants from the mainland to Hong Kong that has occurred in the later stages of nearly all major campaigns. The occurrence of some negative socialization experiences does not mean, of course, that campaigns are counterproductive as a whole; for a careful evaluation of campaign accomplishments and short-comings, see Charles P. Cell, *Revolution at Work: Mobilization Campaigns in China* (New York: Academic Press, 1977), pp. 117–69. For direct analysis of campaign socialization processes, see Sidney Greenblatt, "Campaigns and the Manufacture of Deviance in Chinese Society," and Gordon Bennett, "China's Mass Campaigns and Social Control," in Wilson, et al., eds., op. cit., pp. 82–139. For a fascinating case study of one student's movement from early enthusiasm to later disillusionment in the Cultural Revolution, see Gordon A. Bennett and Ronald Montaperto, *Red Guard: The Political Biography of Dai Hsiao-ai* (Garden City: Doubleday, 1971).

ment of their affairs (such as work assignments, public improvement projects, remuneration systems, etc.). While higher-level authority and policy penetrates these groups freely, they have provided the most stable setting for open discussion and action on community problems.

Elites and subelites have participated more heavily than the masses in the activities described thus far and have in addition been the target of several measures designed to force a reduction in their status and privilege. Some of these have been explicitly egalitarian, such as the abolition of rank insignia and titles in the PLA in 1965 and reduction of wage differentials during the Cultural Revolution. By far the most ambitious, however, has been the practice of *xiafang* (assignment to lower levels) and related efforts to give cadres, students, and intellectuals experience in manual labor.[44] Like the mechanisms for mass participation, *xiafang* is a multifunctional policy aimed at reducing bureaucratic staff and transferring underutilized urban resources to the countryside as well as establishing more populist orientations. The socialization function is still important, however, for both the privileged strata directly affected and the masses who observe the results. For those already employed in various bureaucracies, *xiafang* may mean temporary or permanent assignment to a lower level or a system of participation in manual labor at regular intervals. For students, it may mean an initial work assignment in rural or frontier areas (increasingly over the 1960s a permanent assignment) or some formula for interrupting academic study with work experience. Whatever the specifics, the practice seeks to give those holding or aspiring to official positions a taste of what manual labor is like, to overcome any notions in

[44]Theoretical and developmental underpinnings of *xiafang*, and its multifunctional character, are analyzed in Pi-chao Chen, "Overurbanization, Rustication of Urban-educated Youths, and Politics of Rural Transformation," *Comparative Politics,* vol. 4, no. 3 (April 1972). pp. 361–86, and Rensselaer W. Lee, III, "The *Hsia Fang* System: Marxism and Modernisation," *China Quarterly,* no. 28 (October–December 1966), pp. 40–62. A comprehensive study of the transfer of urban youth to the countryside is Thomas P. Bernstein, *Up to the Mountains and Down to the Villages: The Transfer of Youth from Urban to Rural China* (New Haven: Yale University Press, 1977). *Xiafang's* impact on bureaucracy is assessed in Khien Theeravitaya, "The *Hsia-Fang* System: Bureaucracy and Nation-Building in Communist China, 1957–1969," (Ph.D. diss., University of Washington, 1971).

their minds that educational or political credentials exempt them from discomfort and hard work, and to persuade the masses that elites in the new China will not be permitted to isolate themselves from the sometimes harsh realities of the common man's life situation.

Xiafang has encountered resistance not only from elites who have no sympathy for its objectives or believe it a waste of their talents but also from peasants or basic-level cadres who may see it as disruptive and ineffectual or who may feel that those sent down still get the best work available. Breaking down barriers of status cannot be painless in a society where scholars and officials traditionally held such privileged positions and where political authorities today command such power. Any measure designed to counteract the separation of elites and masses would produce resentment and disorientation. What is significant about *xiafang* is that it has been carried out on a very large scale and that it is the regime's most tangible demonstration of the new populist values. Reinforced by other populist influences (in changing styles of speech, dress, and public behavior, for example), it represents a beginning effort to alter one of the world's oldest elitist value systems.

Political attitudes may also reflect life experiences not structured, sanctioned, or anticipated by the government as socializing devices. The most dramatic example is the economic crisis of 1959–1961, due in part to natural disasters, which shook popular confidence in the CCP and encouraged a retreat into traditional political orientations. More generally the alternating pattern of mass movements and the apparently interminable search for new "enemies" and "renegades" may lead to a certain political weariness even among those basically sympathetic with the overall direction of government policies. Perhaps the constant striving for a political ideal that is never reached will ultimately create a counterculture of public accommodation and private cynicism. However, we should not assume that the general pattern of post-1949 events has had a negative impact on the bulk of the population. Despite economic fluctuations and the evident unpredictability of politics, the standard of living and China's international standing have improved. The impressions of foreign visitors in recent years seem to reveal a nation positively proud of its accomplishments and hopeful of its future. Although certain groups may be disillusioned with politics, there is no real challenge to the CCP's legitimacy. Most Chinese have accepted the present government — we cannot answer with confidence the crucial question of how different motivations and degrees of commitment distribute themselves among the population — and as a consequence of their acceptance they have unavoidably participated in the establishment of a collectivized society, the sacrifice of some personal interests in favor of national goals as defined by elites, the effort to elicit political activism at the grass roots, the practice of a populistic social ethic, and all the personal and group struggles generated by these changes.

SOCIALIZATION AND THE CULTURAL REVOLUTION

Agents and processes of political socialization became a prime issue and a target for reform in the Great Proletarian Cultural Revolution. Why were the Maoists so dissatisfied with a system that seemed to penetrate society thoroughly and to show plainly the influence of Mao's hopes for a new Chinese political culture? What were the results of the assault on the established system? What does the Cultural Revolution and its aftermath suggest about long-term patterns of change in Chinese political culture?

The first point to emphasize is that the attack on the socialization process was by no means a total one. Although campaign rhetoric sometimes suggested a cross-the-board failure by the "authorities following the capitalist road" to promote socialist values, the Maoists in practice showed little desire to alter policies and institutions in certain key areas. For example, as noted earlier, the Cultural Revolution brought no concrete change in policy toward the family, indicating that the advance of socialism has so circumscribed the social influence of this institution that it is not now a center of controversy. The disruption of the communications system, which was one of the campaign's most startling features, seems in retrospect to have been a symptom rather than a motivating factor of the conflict; that is, it was due to a struggle to control the communications network rather than to change it. The Maoists recognized early that they could not succeed without control of the public media, which were largely dominated by their opponents in the state and party bureaucracies. The effort to reverse this situation brought purges of party propaganda departments, suspension of key organs like *Renmin Ribao* and *Hongqi,* physical seizures by the PLA and Red Guards of printing and broadcasting facilities, the emergence of a variety of unofficial and unauthorized Red Guard publications, and general decline and confusion in the output of authoritative information.[45] However, once the "capitalist roaders" were purged and some social order restored, the new leadership began to reconstruct a centralized, authoritative communications system. Although the process was a slow one (the volume of publication, for example, remained significantly less than before the Cultural Revolution) the basic structural characteristics of the earlier system reappeared.

Dissatisfaction with the established pattern of political socialization centered, then, on the educational system and the general quality of public life. Although issues of control were present here too — the attacks on schools and mass organizations obviously sought to purge or neutralize officials deemed hostile to the Maoist coalition — the Cultural Revolution represented a profound concern about how the structure of educational and organizational life was shaping Chinese political orientations. Hostility toward the schools rested on the Maoist conviction that the "revisionists" had erected a "two-track system" in which one track of irregular or less prestigious schools provided a token and inadequately supported form of mass education, while another track leading to the best higher schools catered to an academically and career oriented elite. One of the more specific charges against the regular middle schools and colleges, which bore the brunt of criticism, was that they tended to be the preserve of privileged youth due to their tuition fees, adacemic admissions standards, emphasis on grades and examinations for determining advancement, and the continuing influence of bourgeois teachers. Children of workers and peasants found it difficult to acquire the kind of primary education facilitating entrance into this system or, if

[45]See Liu, op. cit., pp. 52–86; and Chang Man, *The People's Daily and the Red Flag Magazine During the Cultural Revolution* (Hong Kong: Union Research Institute, 1969).

admitted, to perform well enough to advance upward on the academic ladder. Children of bourgeois background, the Maoists insisted, were still overrepresented in the school population of the early 1960s. Another charge was that these schools, despite providing routinized political education and labor experience for students, were turning out graduates whose skills and ambitions were largely professional or bureaucratic and hence at odds with the Maoist ethic and the practical work assignments that many would receive.[46] In short, the Maoists perceived the educational system as "cultivating successors" who were to an alarming extent "revolutionary" in neither social background nor outlook.

The concern over the quality of social experience was naturally more diffuse. In simplest terms, the Maoists argued that the "revisionists" were structuring mass participation and organization to serve their own bureaucratic requirements and interests rather than to maximize popular political activity and bring cadres and citizens closer together. Liu Shaoqi served as the scapegoat for and principal example of this tendency. Much of the criticism against him was hyperbolic in tone and divorced from the context of his actions and statements, but there is little doubt that he represented a political style that emphasized the prerogatives of authority and the need for discipline and obedience from the rank and file.[47] Charges that Liu wanted people to serve as "docile tools" and "stainless screws" and that he supported the idea of "joining the party to become an official" convey the spirit of Maoist fears that his administration encouraged a "subject" rather than "participant" political culture for the masses and an elitist orientation within the entrenched bureaucracy. In the socialist education

[46]Marianne Bastid, "Economic Necessity and Political Ideals in Educational Reform During the Cultural Revolution," *China Quarterly*, no. 42 (April–June 1970), pp. 16–22; John Gardner, "Educated Youth and Urban-Rural Inequalities, 1958–66," in John Wilson Lewis, ed., *The City in Communist China* (Stanford, Cal.: Stanford University Press, 1971), pp. 235–86; and Munro, op. cit., pp. 272–83. For an account of pre-Cultural Revolution revisionist influences in China's foremost academic institution, see Victor Nee, with Don Layman, *The Cultural Revolution at Peking University* (New York: Monthly Review Press, 1969), pp. 25–47.

[47]See Lowell Dittmer, *Liu Shao-ch'i and the Chinese Cultural Revolution* (Berkeley: University of California Press, 1974), esp. pp. 214–293.

campaigns and the early stages of the Cultural Revolution, the Liuists apparently tried to limit mass criticism, to direct it away from the real centers of power, and to mobilize the established mass organizations for their own defense rather than in opening up the mass movement. The lessons likely to be gained from political action under these circumstances were of course in conflict with the expressed values of the official propaganda media. From the Maoist perspective, an effort to stimulate mass activity and crack the apparent invulnerability of elites and large-scale organization was necessary to make social practice supportive of the desired values.

The upheavals of 1966–1967 shattered the institutional context of political socialization. Schools closed in the summer of 1966, not to reopen for formal instruction for two or three years. In the interim, educational facilities became staging areas for political debate, organization, and struggle, and in some cases command posts for student combat. Cadres at every level came under mass criticism frequently leading to public humiliation and dismissal. The old mass organizations fell into disarray or inactivity, while new associations of Red Guards and other "rebel" groups sprang into action sometimes forming citywide federations and commanding real power and constituencies at the local level. As the communications system ceased to provide authoritative direction, these groups began to develop their own information, platforms, and publications in the midst of a barrage of competing political messages. This exercise in spontaneous mass action was not, however, to continue for long. Alarmed by the threat of anarchy and civil war, heightened by factionalization within its own ranks, the Maoist coalition began to institutionalize its reforms.

Educational reform was the Cultural Revolution's most concrete contribution to a new socialization process.[48] Authorities embarked on a renewed affort to universalize basic education by expanding primary, middle, and part-time schools. This wider distribution of educational opportunities relied on a

[48]For an excellent analysis of education before and after Mao's death, see Suzanne Pepper, "Education and Revolution: The 'Chinese Model' Revised," *Asian Survey,* vol. 18, no. 9 (September 1978), pp. 847–90.

complicated mix of ingredients: administrative decentralization and transferral of teachers to rural areas; reduction of the number of years of schooling, generally from six to five in primary schools and six to five or four in middle schools (in practice there were many different variations of primary and middle school terms); expansion of class size; and use of non-professional teachers. University enrolments and years of study were sharply reduced, with abolition of or deemphasis on entrance examinations and a requirement that all middle school graduates must complete at least two years of work in the countryside, factories, or armed services before going on to college. A selection pattern that called for recommendation by an applicant's coworkers and close scrutiny of political qualifications tended to restrict youths from "bad" class background, and favor those of working class background, in college admission. At all levels, there was an increase in political education and work experience, a decrease in hours devoted to academic subjects, and a decline of classroom lectures, examinations, and grades relative to collective discussion and evaluation of performance. A striking curricular reform was the focus on practical applications, implemented by bringing workers into the classroom to teach and sending students to factories and fields to receive on-the-spot instruction.

These reforms were experimental in character, linked to a decentralized approach and surrounded with controversy, so that it is difficult to say how thoroughly they were put into practice. They increased primary and secondary enrolments substantially (see Table II) but weakened higher education; they heightened politicization of the schools while downgrading academic orientations; and they encouraged great interaction between schools and society, pushing the former toward a more populist, service-oriented role. Debate and backtracking indicated, however, that there was considerable doubt from the early 1970s on about the experiment's popularity and permanence.

Cadres were a prominent target in reform of social relationships, with initial reductions of staff due to political purges and administrative simplification. Efforts to bridge the elite–mass gap included some narrowing of wage differentials and pressure on cadres and other privileged elements to abjure distinctive titles, dress and life styles. May Seven Cadre Schools (so called from the date of a Mao directive on cadre reeducation) gave nearly all officials a long period of physical labor and ideological study; although nominally voluntary, these schools created a regular pattern for cycling bureaucrats through an experience that stressed the imperative of "serving the people." Other professionals went through somewhat comparable experiences of rural or lower-level work assignments.

For ordinary citizens, the Cultural Revolution also brought significant changes in socializing experiences. One was strengthened popular participation in primary units, especially through the revolutionary committees set up in factories, schools, offices, hospitals, neighborhoods, and so forth. Mass representatives on these committees provided a vehicle for acting on Maoist themes, such as popular supervision and criticism of cadres, that the Cultural Revolution had advanced. The decentralizing tendencies of the campaign also made participation in primary units more significant by giving them a greater role in managing social services and making decisions on production and worker remuneration.

A second shift affecting the general population was a new cultural policy associated with Jiang Qing. The range of cultural expression was curtailed, with a sharp drop in the volume of books and periodicals published relative to the pre-1966 period. Public performances were limited mainly to a few "revolutionary" dramas, presented over and over on stage and in film. Worker-peasant art and creativity was praised, individual virtuosity downplayed, and most traditional and foreign cultural influences viewed with suspicion. Populism, nationalism, and Maoist revolutionary themes pervaded not only culture narrowly defined but also much of the general tone of Chinese public life.

Finally, the Cultural Revolution left a certain combativeness or struggle orientation that had not been so marked before the great campaign. Chapter VI will address this trend more carefully, but it is important to note that the 1969–1976 years included many signs of popular conflicts or tensions, indicating that factionalism developed during the Cultural Revolution was slow to die and that many were still willing to air disagreements publicly. The writing of *dazibao* continued, as did criticism of cadres and reports of unruly meetings or demonstrations. While some of this discontent was directed against the reforms of the Cultural Revolution, its spirit was in line with the campaign slogan "it is right to rebel." Despite all the qualifications in this discussion — and the Cultural Revolution unquestionably produced many of the negative socialization experiences referred to earlier — a general conclusion seems warranted: the Cultural Revolution brought Chinese socialization policies closer to Maoist ideals than ever before.

POST-1976 SOCIALIZATION

The events that followed Mao's death altered the pattern just described. Although it is too soon to assess their permanence, much less to judge their impact, the major changes can be summarized. Let us begin with education, which is the most significant area of change and where, by the fall of 1978, a new policy had taken shape.

At the heart of the new educational policy was a centralizing, regularizing trend aimed at raising academic standards. Primary and secondary terms were standardized at five years each (mainly an affirmation of Cultural Revolution practice, although an extension for some schools that had experimented with even shorter terms), while universities returned to the four-year or five-year programs common before 1966. Time devoted to academic subjects increased, with a corresponding decline in the earlier stress on political study, labor experience, and practical applications. Classroom discipline, respect for teachers and academic grading and examination systems were promoted. Educational authorities reinstituted the policy which had existed before the Cultural Revolution of designating certain schools as key schools, with higher academic standards and an admissions policy that would channel the academically stronger students into them. Tracking within schools emerged, with official endorsement, dividing students into faster and slower classes according to academic performance.

The new policy had its greatest impact on universities, which began to recruit rapidly on the basis of new college entrance examinations given for the first time in December 1977 (producing nearly three hundred thousand new college students in

1978). Relaxation of the requirement for precollege work experience permitted many middle school graduates, apparently 20–30 percent of the new admissions, to enter college directly. Graduate study resumed, with much publicity given to research scholars and the necessity for advanced theoretical research. The new leaders invoked Mao's name in blessing these changes, saying that he had never opposed examinations or academic study as such; the educational policy of the Cultural Revolution was generally linked to the Gang and denounced as sabotaging China's modernization.

Official commentary acknowledged that these changes would favor children from cadre and intellectual families and from urban areas due to their advantages on the examinations determining entrance to key schools, faster classes, and higher-level schools. They acknowledged, too, that elimination of the three great differences — between town and country, worker and peasant, and mental and manual labor — would be delayed as a result.[49] In this compromise on the broadest of Maoist socialization ideals was a fundamental shift of perspective. The defense of the shift argued that the differences cannot be eliminated quickly in any case, that they will disappear only as a result of material changes stemming from modernization, and that the new educational policy will contribute to their ultimate disappearance by hastening modernization; further, since modernization requires advanced science and technology and high performance in all intellectual sectors, those who work in these areas are really "laboring" people, too, working for socialist progress just like workers and peasants. In other words, the egalitarian, classless society of the future can only be a product of material change, not of ideological rhetoric divorced from objective reality, so that the promotion of material change and modernization has first priority in the attainment of communism.

This invocation of the primacy of material factors, with its not-so-subtle repudiation of ideological sloganeering and of emphasis on subjective factors, was related to other changes in socialization practices. One of the most obvious changes was in the broader cultural and intellectual sphere; it experi-

[49]See, for example, *PR*, no. 30 (July 28, 1978), pp. 18–19, 22.

enced a marked opening to less politicized expression, a revival of many long-dormant academic and cultural publications, and some interesting debates on subjects virtually taboo during most of the previous decade. The slogan of "let a hundred flowers bloom" took on new meaning in this atmosphere, which nourished a more open interest in foreign and traditional culture. The announcement of greatly expanded study and research exchanges with foreign countries, although justified mainly in terms of the priority of scientific and technological development, had profound long-term implications for the socialization experiences of Chinese intellectuals.[50]

Finally, the "four modernizations" policy had potentially far-reaching effects on the political and social experience component of Chinese socialization. Emphasis on order and discipline, the abolition of revolutionary committees in primary units (and later, in 1979, in local government units), and the reinvigoration of the old mass organizations all pointed toward more structured and regularized forms of participation. The defense of professional and technical authority (especially in factories and schools) coupled with official praise for individual professional achievement seemed likely to encourage sharper awareness of social stratification. Greater use of material incentives and acknowledgment of consumer demands raised further questions about the possible growth of revisionism and materialism in Chinese society. All these measures were hedged in with mass line affirmations, and in fact there was little evidence to suggest strictly economic differentiation was increasing; the initial wage increases granted in 1977 and the pattern of other material incentives under discussion seemed to favor lower-paid strata or at least to be ambiguous in their effect on income inequalities. Nonetheless, the new policies as a whole had shifted the thrust of socialization practices away from the highly politicized populism of the Cultural Revolution toward themes more supportive of social order

[50]A useful collection of articles and materials on recent cultural trends, and the repudiation of the Gang's cultural policies, is "Culture and the Performing Arts in China," Press Briefing Materials prepared by the China Council of the Asia Society and the Minnesota China Council. (New York: China Council, June 1978).

and discipline, economic performance, and professional-educational advancement and achievement.

We conclude with four observations that summarize, or possibly refine, the preceding discussion. First, there are elements of continuity in PRC socialization policy that counterbalance some of the fluctuations described. In rural China (where over 80 percent of the population resides) family and village life has been relatively stable since the early 1960s, despite some calls during the Cultural Revolution for radicalization of kinship and production units. In terms of socialization, the most important changes have been the gradual development of better rural educational opportunities and communications facilities, deepening the incorporation of rural China into the national educational and communications networks. Post-1976 policies support continued expansion of primary and secondary education and continued efforts to modernize the countryside. They continue to support as well the spare-time, part-time schools that are particularly important in the countryside and are pushing new adult-education programs. Most middle school graduates continue to receive rural work assignments, most cadres and intellectuals still undergo some kind of *xiafang* experience. Work experience and practical training have been reduced but not eliminated in the new school curriculum. In short, official socialization policies have maintained a steady emphasis on the needs of rural areas and their integration with the more modern sectors.

Moreover, despite the post–1976 cultivation of the intellectual elite and a shift of emphasis on the "red-expert" scale, the PRC remains a highly politicized and relatively egalitarian society.[51] Social and economic inequalities existed throughout the Maoist period and may grow in its aftermath. Deviance from official norms was possible before Mao's death and may be more common in the future. Nonetheless, highly politicized official norms still dominate the educational, communications,

[51]Although there is much debate on this question, the "relatively egalitarian" label seems justified; see Martin King Whyte, "Inequality and Stratification in China," *China quarterly,* no. 64 (December 1975), pp. 684–711; Marc Blecher, "Income Distribution in Small Rural Chinese Communities," Ibid., no. 68 (December 1976), pp. 797–816; and Richard Curt Kraus, "The Limits of Maoist Egalitarianism," *Asian Survey,* vol. 16, no. 11 (November 1976), pp. 1081–1096.

and organizational networks, exerting strong pressures toward political sensitivity and conformity. The content of these norms has never been static, with changes particularly evident since Mao's death. But there are also core themes — acceptance of party leadership, service to state and society, the illegitimacy of gross inequalities, and emphasis on collective over individual goals and obligations — which are well entrenched in the official political culture that dominates the socialization process.

Second, the Cultural Revolution and its aftermath suggest that cumulative Maoist socialization efforts have had a significant impact on popular political orientations, in terms of mass identification with the national political system, awareness of political issues, and willingness to participate in the politics of primary units. The strength and spontaneity of Red Guard involvement in the Cultural Revolution, largely in affirmation of Maoist values, was testimony to the impact of Maoist socialization on the younger generation educated since 1949.[52] Whatever the degree or motive of participation in that campaign, it represented an open questioning of or assault on political authorities, an experience not likely to be forgotten by any who experienced it. The simmering basic-level politics that followed over the next decade, with unrest in schools and factories and large-scale demonstrations like the 1976 Tiananmen Incident, indicate active participatory tendencies in Chinese society, tendencies that are not necessarily antiestablishment but which are not necessarily confined either to unquestioning support of political elites. Whether these will endure under a post-Mao leadership that is more hostile toward factionalism and disorder than was Mao remains to be seen, but it is not likely that they will disappear without a trace, without a more direct confrontation between participatory and order themes than has yet taken place.

Third, Chinese socialization processes have produced among the citizenry a mixed subject-participant political culture, meaning that most citizens fill "subject roles" in which they identify with the national political system and are in-

---

[52]Richard W. Wilson and Amy A. Wilson, "The Red Guards and the World Student Movement," *China Quarterly*, no. 42 (April-June 1970), pp. 88–89.

volved in implementation of its policies, and that some fill "participant roles" of attempting to influence policy making.[53] The emergence of this political culture in a society previously characterized by little popular involvement in politics is the most significant product of post-1949 political socialization. Beyond that, it is difficult to specify the dimensions of the mix and in particular to assess the frequency and character of participant orientations. A few added comments are in order, however. One is that the subject-participant mix, whatever its configuration, does not guarantee unanimous support for political elites and their policies; broad citizen identification with the system has not precluded diverse kinds of opposition and dissent, ranging from passive resistance to active criticism.[54] Effective opposition is rare, given elite resources, but the point is that the spread of subject and participant roles does not produce uniformity of attitudes toward different leaders and policies.

Another important point is that participant roles are more common among the urban and better-educated strata, which are the recipients of the most intense forms of political education. The Cultural Revolution was primarily an urban phenomenon,[55] as were most post-1949 episodes of pronounced popular political activism — land reform being a major exception. In assessing the significance of this pattern, we must remember that the spread of education and modernization will increase the proportion of the population exposed to more intense politicization experiences.

Finally, the analysis of popular political roles and attitudes is complicated by the fact that opportunities for participation are concentrated in very small-scale units. For most Chinese, the main arena for political action is a primary unit: production brigade or team, factory or enterprise, office, school, or neighborhood. Participation in the affairs of such units can be highly political and can cement ties to the national political system,

[53]Almond and Powell, op. cit., pp. 112–23.

[54]For analysis of different types and instances of opposition in the PRC and of the limits of such opposition, see Peter R. Moody, *Opposition and Dissent in Contemporary China* (Stanford: Hoover Institution Press, 1977).

[55]Richard Baum, "The Cultural Revolution in the Countryside: Anatomy of a Limited Rebellion," in Thomas W. Robinson, ed., *The Cultural Revolution in China* (Berkeley: University of California Press, 1971, p. 367, passim.

but it is also difficult for the analyst to observe this participation systematically. Moreover, these units are defined by non-political functions and are permeated with highly personalized relationships (kinship, neighbor, peer group, small-group leader or follower, and so forth), making it difficult to say exactly when and how their activities are "political."

Fourth, the "clash of political cultures," that is, the confrontation between different images of what the Chinese political community should be, is unresolved. Specifically, the issue raised by Mao Zedong in the late 1950s, to be debated throughout the Maoist period, was that the primary danger to the revolution lies in revisionism from the top, not resistance from below. The split between the Maoists and their opponents covered a great range of issues, but a central one was the question of whether correct ideology must be implanted in advance of material modernization, to ensure avoidance of revisionism or capitalist restoration in the course of economic development, or whether it can be expected to flow naturally from the development of the socialist economy. The post-Mao leadership has moved toward the second position, without denying the relevance of the Maoist concern, so that the issue remains alive. The short-run question is how permanent the post-1976 policies will be, whether or not there will be a revival of a more fundamentalist Maoist position as represented by the Cultural Revolution. If the Hua-Deng emphasis on economic modernization continues, then the question becomes the long-term cultural or ideological consequences of the economic and technological revolution. In trying to accelerate this revolution, through new domestic policies and foreign involvements, the CCP leadership is entering what for them is uncharted territory. Whether the PRC will be able to modernize without succumbing to the revisionism that Mao feared remains to be seen.

CHAPTER VI

Political Interests, Recruitment, and Conflict

THE CENTRAL PROCESS in every policial system is the conversion of demands representing the interests, goals, and desires of individuals or groups within the society into political decisions which are then applied and adjudicated through governmental structures. This process includes two stages, the first being the *input* stage in which demands are fed into the decision-making structures, the second being the *output* stage of the making and implementation of decisions. Although the real world of politics seldom divides itself so neatly, the distinction is useful for analytical purposes. This chapter explores the input process of demands on the system, while the following chapter examines the output process of transmitting decisions into governmental action.

Almond and Powell divide the processing of demands into "interest articulation" and "interest aggregation."[1] The former refers to the process by which individuals and groups make demands upon the political decision makers, the latter to the conversion of demands into general policy alternatives. In modern democratic societies, these two functions have relatively distinct structural counterparts. Interest articulation typically finds its most effective channels in the communications media and a variety of more or less organized interest groups, while interest aggregation is performed primarily by political

---

[1] Gabriel A. Almond and G. Bingham Powell, Jr., *Comparative Politics: System, Process, and Policy* (Boston: Little, Brown, 1978), chap. VII, VIII.

parties. Analysis of political demands in the Chinese system cannot rely on comparable institutional patterns, but the functional distinction between articulation and aggregation leads to an opening generalization about the handling of conflicting interests in China.

In a directive written for the Central Committee in June 1943, Mao Zedong offered a classic statement of the mass line which still stands as the CCP's core conceptualization of how the political process ought to work:

> In all the practical work of our Party, all correct leadership is necessarily "from the masses, to the masses." This means: take the ideas of the masses (scattered and unsystematic ideas) and concentrate them (through study turn them into concentrated and systematic ideas), then go to the masses and propagate and explain these ideas until the masses embrace them as their own, hold fast to them and translate them into action, and test the correctness of these ideas in such action. Then once again concentrate ideas from the masses and once again go to the masses so that the ideas are persevered in and carried through. And so on, over and over again in an endless spiral, with the ideas becoming more correct, more vital and richer each time.[2]

This statement suggests a number of basic principles that are relevant to the analysis in the next two chapters. Of immediate interest is the implicit distinction between interest articulation and aggregation: the masses articulate (express their "scattered and unsystematic ideas"), the party aggregates (turns them into "concentrated and systematic ideas"). As this core concept developed over the years, the CCP established a set of techniques and institutions designed to operationalize it. Prominent among these are discussion groups, mass movements and meetings, representative bodies, mass organizations, and mass media, all seen in part as structures for encouraging the expression of popular opinions and demands. The structural channels for articulation are, therefore, extensive, and they carry a large volume of popular political debate and discussion. At the same time, they function in a

[2]Mao Zedong, "Some Questions Concerning Methods of Leadership," *Selected Works of Mao Tse-tung* (Peking: Foreign Languages Press, 1965), vol. 3, p. 119.

political context that significantly curtails the scope and effectiveness of the demands they transmit.

One major restriction is that the CCP monopolizes the aggregation function. The party sees expressed interests as "scattered and unsystematic" and intends that they remain so except as they are "concentrated and systematized" by its organization alone into policy alternatives. There are, of course, organizations other than the CCP that have the potential capacity, in terms of their memberships and scale, to aggregate the demands of particular groups in Chinese society. These organizations are not autonomous, however. Their leadership is dominated by party members whose job it is to ensure that the organizations in question do not compete with the CCP in the formulation of policy proposals or advance demands that are in conflict with the CCP's general line. The official monopoly on communications media reinforces this pattern; even if a group wishes to act in a more autonomous way, it cannot make its position known to a larger public except through media that are subject to close party supervision.

Moreover, the distinction between "people" and "enemies," between "nonantagonistic" and "antagonistic" contradictions,[3] has its most forceful practical impact in making vulnerable all expressions of competition in political demands and policy alternatives. Whenever the element of conflict or "contradiction" is introduced, it brings with it the possibility that one side or the other may be cast in an "antagonistic" role, meaning not simply loss of the issue in question but exclusion from the political arena. That this practice has a certain legitimacy in Chinese political culture (in the belief that political roles should normally conform to and support the prescriptions of a single source of authority) does not lessen its restrictive effect on the expression of political demands.

The initial generalization that follows is this: the articulation of popular interests consists, in the main, of fragmented, unsystematic demands that have few resources for effective political organization and communication, or of more organized demands that tend to support known party policy; the effective expression and aggregation of competing demands is largely

[3]See the discussion in Chapter IV, this book.

a function of elites whose position legitimizes their handling of controversial issues and provides some protection against the possibility of exclusion from the political process. Given the fact that effective articulation and aggregation of conflicting interests is normally carried out by elites, this chapter gives particular attention to the recruitment process which determines the composition of political leadership and to major patterns of elite conflict in post-1949 China. However, political conflict exists at all levels of Chinese society and is expressed in certain ways outside elite circles. We turn first, therefore, to a closer consideration of the popular articulation of interests.

POPULAR ARTICULATION OF INTERESTS

Conflict and Stratification in Chinese Society. Despite the prominence in Chinese politics of struggle against "antagonistic" contradictions in which the "enemy's" position is denied any right or means of expression, a wide range of conflict remains "nonantagonistic" and hence entitled to public airing. Nonantagonistic conflict is also seen in terms of "correct" and "incorrect" resolutions, but CCP theory insists that the incorrect position should express itself and be "corrected" by persuasion rather than repression. The best statement of this principle is, of course, Mao's 1957 speech on contradictions. In that speech, Mao also forthrightly identified some of the class or group dimensions of such conflict:

> In the conditions existing in China today what we call contradictions among the people include the following: contradictions within the working class, contradictions within the peasantry, contradictions within the intelligentsia, contradictions between the working class and peasantry, contradictions between the working class and the peasantry on the one hand and the intelligentsia on the other, contradictions between the working class and other sections of the working people on the one hand and the national bourgeoisie on the other, contradictions within the national bourgeoisie, and so forth. Our people's government is a government that truly represents the interests of the people and serves the people, yet certain contradictions do exist between the government and the masses. These include contradic-

tions between the interests of the state, collective interests and individual interests; between democracy and centralism; between those in positions of leadership and the led, and contradictions arising from the bureaucratic practices of certain state functionaries in their relations with the masses.[4]

Omitted from Mao's 1957 speech was a discussion of contradictions within the leadership, but elsewhere he spoke freely of this problem. Thus, in August 1966 at the Eleventh Plenum of the Central Committee, he commented that there were, and always had been, factions within the party.[5] His most thorough and direct analysis of competing demands facing the CCP leadership was an April 1956 document in which he identified ten major problem areas, the resolution of which required choice of a correct balance between opposing interests. The ten problems were the relationship between industry and agriculture and between heavy and light industries; between coastal and inland industries; between economic and defense constructions; between the state and productive units and individual producers; between the center and the regions; between the Han and other nationalities; between the party and others; between revolution and counterrevolution; between right and wrong; between China and other countries.[6] Note that only one of the ten problems involves the category of "counterrevolution" in which, according to Mao, dictatorship should be employed against one side of the relationship.

The CCP's attempt to grapple with the problem of conflict within the accepted classes and structures of socialist society also acknowledges the existence of politically derived stratification. One scholar has reconstructed official statements on stratification before the Cultural Revolution into the following social hierarchy:

[4]Mao Zedong, "On the Correct Handling of Contradictions Among the People," in Harvard University, Center for International Affairs and East Asian Research Center, *Communist China, 1955–1959: Policy Documents with Analysis* (Cambridge, Mass.: Harvard University Press, 1965), p. 276.

[5]"Selections from Chairman Mao," *Translations on Communist China*, no. 90, JPRS-49826 (Feb. 12, 1970), pp. 6–7.

[6]Mao Zedong, "On the Ten Great Relationships," in Jerome Ch'en, ed., *Mao* (Englewood Cliffs, N.J.: Prentice-Hall, 1969). pp. 65–85.

I. The ruling elite or "vanguard"
  A. Party cadres
  B. Party members
  C. Communist Youth League members
  D. Nonparty cadres
II. The working class and its allies ("the people")
  A. Workers
  B. Peasants, with "poor and lower-middle peasants" on a par with workers and distinctly above wealthier peasants
  C. Intellectuals and petty bourgeoisie
  D. National bourgeoisie
III. Declassed "enemies of the people"[7]

In contrast to this image of horizontal divisions, another scholar has conceptualized Chinese society in terms of vertical lines between institutional sectors; that is, party, government, and army rule over five major socioeconomic sectors — industry, agriculture, business, schools, and army — or more simply over two great divisions of cities and villages.[8]

Finally, Mao's increasing concern, from the early 1960s on, about the emergence of new bourgeois elements among the people or even within the party, led him to apply old class labels to groups defined by ideology rather than by social background. The result was great flexibility if not confusion in class analysis, since class references were sometimes to the official labels which all Chinese were assigned in the early 1950s and sometimes to current manifestations of "revolutionary" or "counterrevolutionary" character which might be different from the original class label.[9]

[7]John W. Lewis, "Political Aspects of Mobility in China's Urban Development," *American Political Science Review*, vol. 60, no. 4 (December 1966), pp. 906–7. I have simplified Lewis' description of the hierarchy.

[8]Franz Schurmann, "The Attack of the Cultural Revolution on Ideology and Organization," in Ping-ti Ho and Tang Tsou, eds., *China in Crisis* (Chicago: University of Chicago Press, 1968), vol. 1, pp. 539–40. Cf. Schurmann's earlier and fuller discussion of classes and contradictions in *Ideology and Organization in Communist China*, 2nd ed. enl. (Berkeley: University of California Press, 1968), pp. 73–104, in which he stresses the bifurcation of elites into "red" and "expert" components, and suggests a basically three-class society of political cadres, intellectuals, and masses.

[9]Richard Curt Kraus, "Class Conflict and the Vocabulary of Social Analysis in China," *China Quarterly*, no. 69 (March 1977), pp. 54–74.

These different perspectives on conflict and stratification suggest the range and variety of potential cleavage in Chinese politics. Among elites, the principal lines of cleavage may lie between different factions or "opinion groups" on major policy decisions; between governmental sectors, such as party, state, and army and their functional ministries or departments; between regional groupings and units, such as urban and rural or coastal and inland areas, or provinces and cities; between the central government and its subordinate administrative groupings, with the minority areas posing a special problem in the balancing of local autonomy against central direction; and between various elite strata — senior and junior cadres, party and nonparty cadres, "reds" and "experts," and so forth — with differing qualifications and experiences. Roughly comparable lines of cleavage may emerge at the basic level between groups who differ on the wisdom or means of implementing received policy; between local departments and offices; between local units, such as differently endowed or different types of collectives and enterprises; between the masses and local cadres; and between different classes or groups within local units such as regular and seasonal workers in factories, richer and poorer peasants in communes, politically favored and disfavored students in schools, and so forth.

All of these lines of cleavage, which delineate potential or latent interest groups, have been discussed in official writings and been involved visibly in the policy process. They have been most evident in "crisis" periods which have permitted or even encouraged latent conflicts to express themselves openly,[10] but the potential for group conflict is a given factor in Chinese politics at any point in time. To analyze all of these conflicts in detail, tracing their rise and fall over time, would require a volume in itself. The discussion here concentrates on the ways in which popular interests are articulated, stressing the crucial question of organization and offering a few illustrative examples of particular conflicts.

---

[10]The best analysis of conflict in the "great debate" of the mid-1950s is Schurmann, *Ideology and Organization in Communist China*, loc. cit and passim. On activation of "occupational groups" in the Cultural Revolution, see Michel Oksenberg, "Occupational Groups in Chinese Society and the Cultural Revolution," in Oksenberg, et al., *The Cultural Revolution: 1967 in Review* (Ann Arbor: University of Michigan, Center for Chinese Studies, 1968), pp. 1–39.

Unorganized Articulation. The CCP's desire to encourage expression of popular demands combines with its fear of organized competition or opposition to produce a substantial volume of unorganized, fragmented articulation of interests. By *unorganized* articulation, we mean articulation of interests by individuals or small numbers of people who have little opportunity to link up or communicate with others who might support the same demands. The public to whom these demands are known is normally quite limited, consisting essentially of immediate superiors and other members of the groups from which the demands come. The communications media may publicize them to a wider audience but usually only when higher elites have decided that the expression merits attention as a good or bad model. Selection as a good model may induce visits or communications from other units, but again this happens only with the stamp of official approval. The basic rule is that those expressing the demand have no independent means of expanding their audience and maintaining regular contact with those outside their own unit who might be interested.

The most frequent and effective unorganized articulation occurs precisely where the system provides for it — in the political processes of basic-level government. There is in the basic organization of Chinese society a rich variety of units, terminology, and organizational mechanisms; a multitude of changes over the years; and a number of questions about political relationships that remain unclear. As noted earlier, this organizational network performs many political functions including socialization, recruitment, and administration of state policy as well as interest articulation. It is not possible here to make precise distinctions about all these different functions and institutional varieties, but we can indicate the general considerations that relate most directly to the popular expression of demands.

Basic-level institutions operate at two sublevels, both open to popular inputs but in significantly different degrees. The first is basic-level government formally defined, that is, the basic level of state administration — primarily communes in the countryside and urban districts in the cities (the largest factories or industrial complexes may approximate this category). Before the Cultural Revolution these governments consisted of councils and committees supposedly chosen and supervised by popularly elected representative congresses. In practice the governments were cadre-dominated instruments of the state and party bureaucracies, the elections and representative congresses being largely a formality.[11]

In the years immediately after the Cultural Revolution, "revolutionary committees" replaced the old councils and congresses as a single governing body of basic-level government. These committees emerged from a process of discussion and negotiation designed to produce a "three-in-one" combination of representatives, a formula varying in its meaning but always including representatives of mass organizations or interests as one part of the triple alliance. The presence of mass representatives on the governing body, plus the sensitivity of the times to bureaucratism and popular needs, probably increased basic-level government responsiveness to constituent demands. However, administrative and party cadres gradually reasserted their control, and by 1975 the old division between representative congresses and administrative committees — the latter called revolutionary committees until 1979 reforms dropped even that name — was back in place. The post-1976 emphasis on socialist legality called for strengthening or at least regularizing basic-level elections and congresses, but their main function seems to be cooperation in implementation of higher-level policy rather than articulation of popular interests.

A different picture emerges at the second sublevel of primary units within basic-level government jurisdictions, that is, the level of production teams and brigades, workshops and factories, and residents' committees.[12] Here, several features

[11]James R. Townsend, *Political Participation in Communist China* (Berkeley: University of California Press, 1969). chap. 5.

[12]See Ibid, chap. 6, on pre-Cultural Revolution organization of primary units. More recent studies concentrating on and emphasizing the significance of political participation within primary units include Marc Blecher, "Leader-Mass Relations in Rural Chinese Communities: Local Politics in a Revolutionary Society" (Ph.D. University of Chicago, 1978); John P. Burns, "The Election of Production Team Cadres in Rural China, 1958–74," *China Quarterly*, no. 74 (June 1978), pp. 273–96; and Victor C. Falkenheim, "Political Participation in China," *Problems of Communism*, vol. 27, no. 3 (May–June 1978), pp. 18–32. For a description of the institutional context of primary units, with particular reference to more recent periods, see Gordon Bennett, *Huadong:*

encourage the regular expression of popular demands. First, the smallest groupings (production teams in the countryside, work teams in factories, and residents' small groups in cities) have frequent meetings and choose their own group leadership. Second, the masses also have a direct voice in the more inclusive groupings at this sublevel (production brigades, factorywide organization and residents' committees) through the selection of representatives to managing committees or, again, through meetings of the entire constituency. Selection of leaders and representatives may follow the path of discussion and consensus rather than contested elections and is not likely to produce individuals unacceptable to higher cadres. Nevertheless, those chosen come from within the unit itself and are in constant association with the mass membership; they are ordinary citizens serving in unpaid leadership posts, not cadres assigned to manage these units in the interests of the bureaucracy. In this context, popular interests can and do make themselves heard.

Third, primary units have responsibility for the management or consideration of many matters that are important to their memberships. The responsibilities vary according to the size and types of units but may include the following: allocation of work assignments and arrangements including nomination of candidates for advanced training and education; distribution of unit economic resources (within received guidelines) among worker remuneration, production costs and investment, and reserves for welfare and services, or participation in such decisions; establishment of pay scales and "work point" systems with the unit, again within certain guidelines; management of welfare and service programs for members and families, and participation in the management of attached schools and health care facilities; cooperation with state offices in public security activities and mediation of disputes; consultation with higher levels on planning, budgetary,

The Story of a Chinese People's Commune (Boulder: Westview Press, 1978); Stephen Andors, *China's Industrial Revolution: Politics, Planning, and Management, 1949 to the Present* (New York: Pantheon, 1977); and Janet Weitzner Salaff, "Urban Residential Communities in the Wake of the Cultural Revolution," in John Wilson Lewis, ed., *The City in Communist China* (Stanford: Stanford University Press, 1971), pp. 289–323.

and developmental decisions for the unit in question; resolution or transmission upward of mass grievances and suggestions concerning all of the above. In none of these activities are primary units free to reject policies or supervision of higher levels, nor can one claim that masses, leader-activists, and cadres are uniformly conscientious in fulfilling the opportunities for popular inputs that this system affords. Nonetheless, participation in primary units encourages regular articulation of popular interests relating to living and working conditions at the grass roots of society.

The articulation process just described has a consensual quality that obscures personal expressions, conflicts, and opposition. Does more individualized articulation occur, especially of an oppositional nature? It certainly does, primarily in the course of frequent meetings and discussions about unit affairs. At this level, given the restrictions on external organization and communications and the administrative guidelines which make serious deviation unlikely, expressions of difference and even opposition pose little threat.[13] The Chinese tendency to report decisions as consensus-building acts — "after thorough discussion and education, all agreed that this was the correct line" — does not mean that real give-and-take has no place in the process. The nature of the primary unit setting ensures a substantial variety of expression among its members.

Beyond this, there are other means of expressing individualized or deviant demands in a focused way. The writing of *dazibao* is a common means of placing one's views before the unit as a whole. Letters to communications media and personal visits to higher-level cadres and offices are encouraged. In rectification campaigns the masses have a special opportunity to reveiw and criticize the performance of local elites. All of these add to the scope of unorganized articulation but do not escape the restraints imposed by party leadership. The public debate of the winter of 1978–1979 was a case in point. Emboldened by the new "hundred flowers" atmosphere of 1978 and elite attacks on the Gang's violations of socialist

---

[13]Mao has said that even counterrevolutionaries should be tolerated on the principle of "don't kill a lone wolf," so long as they do no real harm; "On the Ten Great Relationships," in Ch'en, ed., op. cit., p. 80.

democracy, many citizens began to write letters and posters that questioned the Maoist legacy, criticized aspects of the socialist system, and called for fuller observance of democracy, legality, and human rights in China. The public expression of these views, often in full view of Western reporters and accompanied by discussion and rallies in the streets, soon brought official reaction. By the spring of 1979, authorities had arrested some of the leading dissidents and reminded all citizens that public debate must support the party and socialism. Socialist democracy was not to be confused with bourgeois democracy or to be used as a vehicle for weakening party leadership.

Finally, popular demands may express themselves through acts of noncompliance or resistance, such as absenteeism, slowdowns, concealed violations of regulations, capitalization on loopholes or ambiguities in policy, and so forth. The history of rural collectivization provides the best example. The first push to collectivization in the early and mid-1950s saw its share of peasant delay, slaughtering of livestock, and withdrawals from cooperatives and collectives. During the commune and retrenchment period, some peasants withheld personal implements from the communes, concealed or misreported harvests, and took advantage of the restoration of private plots and free markets.[14] This mode of articulation, unlike those discussed above, may have a quick and forceful impact on national elites, possibly resulting in policy change. However, it must be very widespread if it is to have that effect. Resistance to collectivization in the 1950s was noticeable but accomplished little more than short-run delays or adjustments. Resistance to the Great Leap did bring major policy changes but only in combination with a national political and economic crisis that involved far more than peasant discontent with the communes. Individualized noncompliance or resis-

[14]See Kenneth R. Walker, "Collectivisation in Retrospect: The 'Socialist High Tide' of Autumn 1955–Spring 1956," *China Quarterly,* no. 26 (April–June 1966), pp.1–43, and *Planning in Chinese Argiculture: Socialization and the private sector* (Chicago: Aldine, 1965); Peter R. Moody, *Opposition and Dissent in Contemporary China* (Stanford: Hoover Institution Press, 1977), provides other examples, detailing the regime's capacity to contain and/or manipulate oppositional tendencies.

tance, then, also has its limitations and is risky for those who engage in it.

Organized Articulation. Organized articulation occurs when the group making the demand has members drawn from many units or localities and some means of communication with its membership and the larger public. The most powerful and enduring organizations of this kind in China have been elite political structures — the state bureaucracies, the CCP, the PLA, and the Youth League. We are concerned here with those of a more popular character such as the Women's Federation, the trade unions, the democratic parties, and so forth. The question is: to what extent have these mass organizations advanced the interests of their members within the political system? Generally they have done so with regularity and effectiveness only when their demands have conformed to established policy and elite expectations. In this sense, they have served more as supportive agencies of the government than as articulators of popular demands; their loss of status during the Cultural Revolution was only the most dramatic proof of their lack of autonomy. Nonetheless, they have also served at times as spokesmen for the groups they represent. A few examples will indicate that organized articulation of popular interests does take place albeit with mixed results.

The women's movement, represented organizationally before the Cultural Revolution by the Women's Federation and its official publication *Zhongguo Funu* (*Chung-kuo Fu-nü, Chinese Women*) has probably been the most outspoken and effective articulator of particular group interests. It alone among the mass organizations has consistently criticized the social position of its membership and demanded that this situation be improved. It has, for example, called for election of more women representatives, advancement of more women into schools and the CCP, better enforcement of the marriage law, and elimination of inequalities between men and women in pay and employment opportunities. The CCP has frequently endorsed these demands, agreeing that women have not attained the full equality promised in the initial reconstruction reforms. To some extent, therefore, the vigor of the women's movement has rested on the support or receptivity of national elites. Nonetheless, elite support has been neither constant nor sufficient to realize the goals in question, so that women's organizations have had to push their demands aggressively and can claim much credit for gains in their constituents' status since 1949.[15] It is important to note that much of the effectiveness of women's organizations has been at the local level, pursuing their cause on specific policies and cases. Generally, the organized expression of popular demands seems more effective at the local than the national level, as long as it stays within the guidelines endorsed by the leadership.[16]

The All-China Federation of Trade Unions (ACFTU) offers a different example of the possibilities for organized articulation. Although workers' organizations have also enjoyed generalized elite support and have done much to improve their members' working and living conditions, the ACFTU illustrates the political hazards of explicit defense of group interests. On three occasions since 1949, trade unions have moved toward positions that provoked elite retaliation.[17] The first two in 1951 and 1957 involved demands by ACFTU leaders for some independence from the CCP and for greater attention to worker interests, as opposed to state or managerial interests. In both cases, the CCP removed the principal offenders from their ACFTU positions and reasserted the primacy of its policies as a guide for union action. The third occurred in the winter of 1966–1967, when some workers, encouraged by their union leaders and promises of economic benefits, entered the Cultural Revolution on the side of the

[15]The eclipse of the Women's Federation during the Cultural Revolution and the CCP's tacit toleration of some traditional marital practices (see Chap. V) are evidence of elite vacillation, although neither represents a denial of the principle of female equality. Useful sources on the women's movement in the PRC include Elisabeth Croll, *The Women's Movement in China: A Selection of Readings* (London: Anglo-Chinese Educational Institute, 1974); Delia Davin, *Woman-Work: Women and the Party in Revolutionary China* (Oxford: Clarendon Press, 1976); and Marilyn B. Young, ed., *Women in China* (Ann Arbor: University of Michigan, Center for Chinese Studies, 1973).

[16]Studies of local government reveal this balancing of central directives and popular interests. See Lewis, ed., op. cit., pp. 153–79, 325–70; Robert A. Scalapino, ed., *Elites in the People's Republic of China* (Seattle: University of Washington Press, 1972), pp. 199–377; and Ezra Vogel, *Canton Under Communism* (Cambridge: Harvard University Press, 1969).

[17]Paul Harper, "The Party and the Unions in Communist China," *China Quarterly*, no. 37 (January–March 1969), pp. 84–119.

Liuists and resisted extension of the revolution into the factories. Subsequently, the ACFTU was dissolved, its publications suspended, and its policies denounced as "economism" in the service of Liu Shaoqi's line. The demise of the ACFTU thus stems partly from its tendencies to offer a competing view of workers' interests but mainly from its close identification with the party bureaucracy that existed before the Cultural Revolution — an identification established, ironically, with some union resistance. For the ACFTU, organized articulation of interests that conflicted with CCP policy led to a quick reassertion of party control but not to organizational dismemberment; the latter came only with the unions' apparent entry into CCP factional struggle as an organizational base for one of the competitors.

Trade union experience suggests the dilemma that confronts organizations whose demands deviate from CCP policy. If the top leadership says that these demands represent a narrow, "selfish" interest contrary to the collective interest, the organization has little choice but to give in or to advance a different image of the collective interest. However, the latter course enters the field of aggregation and challenges the CCP's monopoly over the formulation of policy alternatives. Despite the obvious political hazards of this course, nonparty groups have moved towards it on occasion. One example is the "hundred flowers" campaign of 1957, in which a few intellectuals moved beyond complaints about their own role in socialist society to a broader attack on party leadership and line. The critics of 1957 had some of the rudiments of an oppositional organization in the democratic parties and their newspaper, *Guangming Ribao*, but entry into interest aggregation — if indeed it really went that far[18] — was bound to fail for lack of any real power base. A much more vigorous and formidable form of organized group conflict emerged in the Cultural Revolution.

Factionalism among mass organizations was a decisive fac-

[18]Party leaders probably overstated the political aspirations of the 1957 dissidents and may have even deliberately publicized the most extreme criticism to strengthen their hand for the coming counterattack on the rightists; Richard H. Solomon, *Mao's Revolution and the Chinese Political Culture* (Berkeley: University of California Press, 1971), pp. 314–15.

tor in the Cultural Revolution's shift from mass "power seizures" to restoration of order under PLA auspices.[19] That
influence alone indicates the importance of organizational
conflicts during the campaign, but these conflicts are also of
interest for their progression from a relatively narrow articulation of interests to a broader aggregation of multiple interests
in competition for local power. From mid-1966 to early 1967,
Red Guard and rebel groups proliferated, frequently along
discernible economic, political, or institutional lines. That is,
they tended to begin as small-scale organizations based on a
single school or factory; where organizational divisions
emerged within a unit, they were often between regular and
seasonal workers, between different classes within a school, or
between students of more or less privileged political and economic backgrounds.[20] Conflict centered on which group
would lead the movement in its unit, on how to go about
ridding the unit of its "capitalist-roaders," and on whether
students should "make revolution" in factories and enterprises.

However, these early organizational limitations evaporated
quickly. As the campaign continued, Red Guard and rebel
attention shifted to municipal and provincial offices where the
old "power holders" were still sitting tight. Citywide organizations of students and workers began to emerge, and when the
Maoists in Peking authorized "power seizures" in the winter
of 1966–1967, the way was open for the formation of federations of the new mass organizations. In most cities two major
coalitions loosely identifiable as "conservatives" and "radicals" (but each claiming support from cadres, workers, students and peasant groups) came to the fore. Although
economic and political interests probably influenced lines of
cleavage, each coalition claimed to speak for the "revolutionary masses" as a whole and wanted to control mass representation on the revolutionary committees that were then being

[19]Philip Bridgham, "Mao's Cultural Revolution in 1967: The Struggle to
Seize Power," *China Quarterly*, no. 34 (April–June 1968), pp. 6–37.
[20]See Alan P. L. Liu, *Political Culture and Group Conflict in Communist China*
(Santa Barbara: ABC-Clio Press, 1976), for thorough analysis of different
types of Cultural Revolution mass organizations and the divisions among
them.

formed. The principal issue was that conservatives tended to accept the trend toward compromise with old cadres, whereas radicals held out for a thorough cleansing of the system. In effect, these coalitions were aggregating local interests around the broader issue of consolidating or deepening the Cultural Revolution.[21] This was something the national leaders could not tolerate, and the ultimate victory of consolidation spelled the end for all of the larger-scale mass organizations, conservative and radical alike.

Bureaucratic Articulation. The foregoing discussion indicates that elite control of the articulation process is neither static nor absolute. Unorganized popular input at the lowest levels is substantial. Top elites have controlled organized articulation much more closely but have not prohibited it. Rather, their stance has been to support organized expression of popular demands in principle and then to take corrective action against those perceived as "erroneous" or "antagonistic." They have been unequivocal in their hostility to popular organization that appears to compete for legitimacy as the aggregator of interests. The Cultural Revolution was an extreme manifestation of this pattern in which an extraordinary level of popular political activity was followed by an attack on factionalism and a sharp reduction of organizational opportunities. It is significant, however, that popular demands do enter the political process. Even if mass organizations lack the autonomy and resources to present these demands effectively, elites may consider them and at times champion them in the decision-making process. Bureaucratic articulation of popular interests is, in fact, the key variable in determining their viability and effectiveness.

[21]For a close study of how one of these federations, the *Shengwulian* (short for Hunan Provincial Proletarian Revolutionary Great Alliance Committee), set forth a radical political program that challenged even the Maoist orthodoxy, see Klaus Mehnert, *Peking and the New Left: At Home and Abroad* (Berkeley: University of California,Center for Chinese Studies, 1969). On the growth and factionalization of mass organizations during the Cultural Revolution, see "Mass Factionalism in Communist China," *Current Scene,* vol. 6, no. 8 (May 15, 1968); Gordon A. Bennett and Ronald N. Montaperto, *Red Guard* (Garden City: Doubleday, 1971); Neale Hunter, *Shanghai Journal: An Eyewitness Account of the Cultural Revolution* (Boston: Beacon, 1971); and the sources cited in Chap. III, note 52.

The importance of bureaucratic articulation stems from the relative security, influence, and access to communications media that higher elites enjoy. Bureaucratic position is by no means invulnerable, as demonstrated by the Cultural Revolution, but its advantages over popularly based organizations and representatives are clear. Citizens have no significant means of pressuring decision makers above the basic level. If they or the organizations accessible to them persist in advancing disfavored demands, they risk political reprisals. Bureaucratic support is normally essential for popular demands to receive a hearing among higher officials. On the other hand, bureaucrats do not need a demonstration of public opinion to advance what they may perceive as popular interest; they may initiate, as well as screen, the articulation of popular demands. Our analysis of the Chinese political process turns logically, therefore, to elite recruitment and conflict.

POLITICAL RECRUITMENT

Three core political roles — activist, cadre, and party member — dominate the staffing of the Chinese political system. These roles may overlap (and each has its own important subdivisions), but the differences among them shed light on some basic characteristics of the recruitment process. Activists are ordinary citizens not holding full-time official positions who acquire a special interest, initiative, or responsibility in public affairs. Cadres are those who hold a formal leadership position, normally full-time, in an organization.[22] Party members are, of course, just what the term states.

Activists. Becoming an activist is generally the first step in the political recruitment process, and it is from the ranks of activists that most new cadres and CCP members are drawn. Local party organizations keep close track of activists within their jurisdiction, counting and labeling them as such and turning

---

[22]On the origins, definition, and ramifications of the "cadre" concept, see A. Doak Barnett, with a contribution by Ezra Vogel, *Cadres, Bureaucracy, and Political Power in Communist China* (New York: Columbia University Press, 1967), pp. 38–47; John Wilson Lewis, *Leadership in Communist China* (Ithaca, N.Y.: Cornell University Press, 1963), pp. 185–95 passim; and Schurmann, *Ideology and Organization in Communist China,* pp. 162–67. The discussion in this section draws heavily on these works.

to them when political campaigns and recruitment are under way. However, in practice there can be no rigid criteria for determining who merits this designation. Virtually every citizen is potentially eligible, the primary exclusions being the "five bad elements" — landlords, rich peasants, counterrevolutionaries, rightists, and miscellaneous "bad elements" — who constitute at most a few percent of the population. There are myriad considerations that may distinguish certain individuals from the mass. Personal qualities and community standing are particularly important, however.

Personal qualities leading to activism include motivational and skill elements. From an official point of view, "correct" motivation is the cardinal ingredient; selfless commitment and the desire to serve is by itself sufficient to establish activism. Some approximation of the ideal motivation no doubt infuses most activists, but personal ambition also enters in and may, as elites ruefully acknowledge, even be the decisive motivational factor at times. Moreover, some personal skills or ability are necessary to translate desire into operational activism. Literacy, intelligence, energy, and skill in human relations are obvious assets. Beyond these personal qualities, standing in the community is important since much of the activist's work involves mobilization of associates. The key factor here is not simply popularity but rather an expectation of informal leadership, a popular willingness to accept the activist's credentials. This may derive from the personal qualities mentioned above or from more generalized institutional considerations. Members of a unit may expect an individual to fill the activist's role because of his or her evident desire and ability, or because the individual is a PLA veteran, a party or league member known to be favored by local cadres, or even a "natural" leader through age or kinship determinants. A strong group feeling about an individual's fitness for the activist role may compensate for modest motivation or skills.

Local elites are by no means passive observers of this process. The party consciously recruits and even cultivates activists, particularly in the course of mass movements which are the single most important testing ground for the demonstration of activism, and it has the power to deny political recognition to individual candidates for the role. On balance, however, self-selection, personal ability, and group support tend to determine recruitment of activists, with local officials watching the process closely to veto undesirables and select for more important roles those deemed most promising.

Cadres. Recruitment to cadre status is quite a different matter. At the lowest levels, activist and cadre roles may overlap when an activist is selected for formal leadership responsibilities within a primary unit. For example, activists fill many posts in production teams and brigades, and to a lesser extent in commune government, which carry "local cadre" status. However, "local cadres" who receive their salary from the primary unit involved and whose recruitment reflects the considerations described above are a special group within cadre ranks. More influential and typical are "state cadres" who staff state, party, and mass organizational hierarchies above the primary level and receive their salaries from the government.[23] Recruitment to these posts is by appointment from within the bureaucracies through personnel sections of the state and organization departments of the CCP. Since party-member cadres dominate personnel sections within the government, owing to the obvious importance of this function, the CCP tends to control the appointment, promotion, transfer, and dismissal of all cadres above the primary level. Influences from outside enter the process through examination of a prospective appointee's motivation and relations with the masses; opportunities for mass criticism of cadres, especially during rectification campaigns, may also affect personnel decisons. With the shift from activist to cadre roles, however, the critical influence on recruitment shifts from individual motivation and community preferences to decision by party-member cadres within the bureaucracy.

The most serious problem in cadre recruitment is tension between political and professional criteria, the "red-expert" contradiction. Before 1949, party leaders thought of the cadre as a "combat leader fighting in the context of guerrilla war."[24] The role demanded direct leadership over and relationships

[23]On the distinction between "local" and "state" cadres, see Barnett, op. cit., pp. 39–41.

[24]Schurmann, *Ideology and Organization in Communist China*, pp. 164–65.

with the masses, a high degree of political consciousness, and an ability to apply central directives flexibly in the course of an acute political struggle. After 1949 many cadres became workers in state institutions and departments, in which job-oriented skills were of critical importance. The definition of a cadre expanded to accommodate the role's new requirements, but the old conception of ideal cadre qualities endured. Cadres were to be "both red and expert" — "red" to ensure the desired style of leadership and "expert" in the work assignments demanded of them. Unfortunately, there were simply not enough red-experts to staff the expanding bureaucracies. But if red and expert qualities could not be combined in each cadre, they could be balanced organizationally through the employment of some reds and some experts. The distinction between party and nonparty cadres is obviously relevant here.

Party-member cadres are not always red and lacking in expertise; nonparty cadres are not always experts and lacking in redness. But the CCP has relied on party-member cadres to maintain the redness of cadre ranks as a whole. That is, it has been willing to employ nonparty experts as cadres so long as party-member cadres occupy the leading positions or retain de facto control in each bureaucratic unit. The goal of "both red and expert" has never been abandoned, but in practice there has been a tendency to accept the priority of expert qualifications in the recruitment of nonparty cadres. For these cadres, insistence on redness shifts from the recruitment stage to their control and education in office. At the same time, the demand for redness in the recruitment of party members becomes more intense, since it is this role that must ensure the primacy of politics in the system as a whole.

Party Members. Admission to the CCP is the decisive act of political recruitment. For the activist, politics remains basically an avocation pursued within the primary unit. For the nonparty cadre, politics is a full-time job of broader scope, but the political status attaches to the position, not to the individual, and carries no presumption of permanent or growing political responsiblities; moreover, the nonparty cadre has no access to positions of supreme power and only limited opportunities for upward advancement. Party membership alone implies a life-long commitment to politics, confers a political status independent of work assignment, and provides entrance into a political career with significant opportunities for advancement and power. Of course, party membership is not necessarily permanent and does not lead inevitably to positions of power; members may withdraw or be expelled and many never become cadres. But the presumption of permanence and special political qualities remains, so that the party member is always in a position of relative political prominence. If an ordinary worker, the member is always a prime candidate for the activist role; among activists, the most likely to be selected as a cadre; and among cadres, superior in political status and opportunities to nonparty colleagues.

The CCP intends that recruitment to its ranks be carefully controlled and highly selective, admitting only those who are truly red and expert. It alone decides who shall enter its organization, vesting control of recruitment in the party branch subject to approval by higher party committees, although popular opinions on candidates may be solicited. Since competition for membership is keen, party recruitment is really at an advanced level, drawing heavily from the ranks of those who have already attained activist or cadre status. Nonetheless, there is nothing cut and dried about this process. Historically, political recruitment has been a constant source of concern for the CCP, shifting frequently in its intended and unintended consequences for the composition of political leadership. A survey of changing patterns of recruitment, with particular attention to the party itself, will help to clarify this point.

Recruitment Patterns to 1953. The CCP began to grow in the 1920s as an urban-oriented party of intellectuals and workers, but this pattern ended abruptly in 1927. Although the influence of these early years was crucial for the oldest Communists, Chiang Kai-shek's April 12th "coup" virtually eliminated the party's mass membership (see Table III) and drove the remnants to the countryside. From the late 1920s to the late 1940s, the CCP was a party of peasants and soldiers — the latter also of peasant origin — led by a small number of better-educated revolutionaries and occasionally infused with some

TABLE III. *Growth of the Chinese Communist Party, 1921–1977*

Period and year	Number of members	Years covered	Average annual increase or decrease
First revolutionary civil war			
1921 (1st Congress)	57	...	...
1922 (2nd Congress)	123	1	66
1923 (3rd Congress)	432	1	309
1925 (4th Congress)	950	2	259
1927 (5th Congress)	57,967	2	28,508
1927 (after "April 12")	10,000	...	...
Second revolutionary civil war			
1928 (6th Congress)	40,000	1	30,000
1930	122,318	2	41,159
1933	300,000	3	59,227
1937 (after the Long March)	40,000	4	−65,000
Anti-Japanese War			
1940	800,000	3	253,333
1941	763,447	1	−36,553
1942	736,151	1	−27,296
1944	853,420	2	58,635
1945 (7th Congress)	1,211,128	1	357,708

Third revolutionary civil war			
1946	1,348,320	1	137,192
1947	2,759,456	1	1,411,136
1948	3,065,533	1	306,077
1949	4,488,080	1	1,422,547
Under the People's Republic of China			
1950	5,821,604	1	1,333,524
1951	5,762,293	1	−59,311
1952	6,001,698	1	239,405
1953	6,612,254	1	610,556
1954	7,859,473	1	1,247,219
1955	9,393,394	1	1,533,921
1956 (8th Congress)	10,734,384	1	1,340,990
1957	12,720,000	1	1,985,616
1959	13,960,000	2	620,000
1961	17,000,000	2	1,520,000
1973 (10th Congress)	28,000,000	12	916,666
1977 (11th Congress)	more than 35,000,000	4	1,750,000

Sources: The figures for the years 1927–1961 are reprinted from John Wilson Lewis, *Leadership in Communist China*, pp. 110–111, copyright © 1963 by Cornell University, used by permission of the publisher, Cornell University Press; the 1973 figure, from Zhou Enlai's "Report" to the CCP Tenth National Congress of August 1973 in *The Tenth National Congress of the Communist Party of China* (Documents), (Peking: Foreign Languages Press, 1973) p. 8; and the 1977 figure, from *PR*, no. 35 (August 26, 1977), p. 6.

idealistic intellectuals. Recruitment was in a real sense self-recruitment. The CCP tested and screened its own membership, of course, but the very act of association with the revolution was a powerful, prior testing device. Most followers did not join the Communist movement casually for security, material, or opportunistic reasons. Hardship, danger, and the threat of execution by the Nationalists were risks faced by party members and followers alike, and there was little assurance of ultimate victory until very late in the game. A strong element of political commitment was implicit, therefore, in identification with the movement. The CCP, eager to expand and faced with steady losses from death and defection, was able to absorb most of the followers who applied.

Once members of the party, new recruits received a natural socialization in Maoist virtues. Life was frugal and rustic, organization simple and close to the masses, policy implementation decentralized, and the military experience always close-at-hand. Survival alone was almost sufficient to ensure upward mobility as the movement filled the places of departed comrades and tried to extend its influence. In short, environmental factors tended to resolve questions of recruitment and advancement in a way that produced a relatively homogeneous party of dedicated peasant-soldier revolutionaries.

A second pattern began to emerge in the late 1940s and lasted through 1953. This was the period when CCP military power spread rapidly over all of China, when the establishment of a new political structure to consolidate victory and implement reconstruction reforms became necessary, and, accordingly, when a burst of recruitment to activist, cadre, and party roles took place. Significantly, it was also a period when many of the earlier situational controls on recruitment disappeared. Although tense political struggle continued, particularly in land reform and suppression of counterrevolutionaries, the movement was now victorious. To join was to cast one's lot with a government in power whose future seemed secure and promising. Those who wanted to join no longer had to live in or travel to the red areas but could seek access to political positions in their own communities — although many were sent to other areas for actual service. The cities in particular became a major source of recruitment for the first time since the 1920s. The CCP recognized that the new circumstances made it easier for opportunists, careerists, and even "class enemies" to acquire political status and was relatively cautious in party recruitment. Although organizational growth was substantial during 1949–1953, it was modest and irregular relative to later years. Rectification campaigns in 1951–1952, designed to weed out the undesirables admitted during this fluid period, even brought a temporary halt to party growth (see Table III).

The need for activists and cadres could not be postponed, however. The great campaigns of 1949–1952 demanded and produced millions of new activists primarily from oppressed and outcast groups in the countryside with large numbers of students also rising to the call. These early rural activists, recruited in often violent campaigns against the old social order, became the foundation of Communist political power in the villages. They probably constitute even now a significant proportion of the "local cadres" in rural production units. The need for "state cadres" was no less urgent, and here the CCP was particularly short of talent. Intensive efforts raised the number of state cadres from 720,000 in 1949 to 3,310,000 in 1952, 5,270,000 in 1955, and 7,920,000 in 1958.[25] Of the 2,590,000 cadres recruited between 1949 and 1952, the majority (57.7 percent) were worker and peasant activists from the mass campaigns; 40.1 percent were members of the CCP and PLA or "progressive elements" among the retained personnel (former Nationalist officials) who had gone through short-term training; and 2.2 percent were graduates of higher schools.[26]

This early period was one of tremendous political mobility, both downward and upward. Most old officials were ruined, and many who stayed on as "retained personnel" were forced out later when more reliable cadres emerged. Some of the new recruits as well as old revolutionary cadres failed to pass the test when their qualifications and performance were reviewed in rectification campaigns. In the main, however, the period was one of relatively open recruitment and upward mobility in

[25]Ying-mao Kau, "Patterns of Recruitment and Mobility of Urban Cadres," in Lewis, ed., *The City in Communist China*, pp. 98–106; figures from p.106.
[26]Ibid., pp. 103–4.

which new activists and cadres entered the political system in its formative years, thereby establishing themselves within it. The CCP could take satisfaction in having met the immediate problem of numbers, but it was acutely aware of qualitative problems arising from the necessarily loose standards of the time. Party strength was still insufficient to supervise thoroughly the work of all offices, many filled with cadres of questionable "redness." In addition, the cultural and technical skills of most activists and low-level cadres were quite low; in fact, many were illiterate and totally untrained for administrative work.

Institutionalization of Recruitment, 1954–1965. Between 1954 and 1965 the CCP developed an institutionalized recruitment system that responded to the weaknesses and irregularities of the earlier period, changed significantly the determinants and compostion of party membership, and became an underlying cause of the Cultural Revolution. The central rationale for this transformation was to ensure CCP dominance over the process of socialist construction. If a large bureaucracy liberally staffed with experts was necessary for administering the transition to socialism, the CCP was determined that these experts be red or at least be under red leadership. This in turn required a vigorous expansion of the CCP and its organizational units and a movement of party members into other organizations. Beginning in 1954, the CCP added over a million new members in nearly every year down to 1961, at which time — the last year in which figures were reported before the Cultural Revolution — its membership reached 17,000,000 (see Table III). The number of basic-level party organizations increased from 250,000 in 1951 to 538,000 in 1956 and 1,060,000 in 1959.[27] The dominance of party members within state and mass organizations advanced so rapidly that by the time of the Great Leap, CCP committees were the effective governing bodies within all levels of administration.[28] Meanwhile, all cadres came under a regularized system of graded

[27]Schurmann, *Ideology and Organization in Communist China,* p. 134.
[28]See Barnett, op. cit., passim.

ranks and salaries, annual review, and bureaucratic stratification.[29]

The composition of the CCP changed as it grew into its increasingly intimate relationship with government departments. Although a majority of its members continued to come from peasant backgrounds and to work in rural areas (due to the overwhelmingly agrarian society and economy), urban influences increased sharply. By 1957 only 66.8 percent of members came from peasant backgrounds, whereas 14.8 percent were intellectuals, 13.7 percent workers, and 4.7 percent "other."[30] Sample data on major cities indicate that by 1959 4.4 percent of urban residents were party members, compared to only 2.2 percent of the total national population admitted to membership; urban members probably totaled about 4,-400,000 in that year, or nearly one-third of all party members.[31] Many of those recorded as working in agriculture — about 58 percent of CCP members in 1956[32] — were "local cadres" with administrative responsibilities in rural towns.

Where did the CCP find such large numbers of new recruits, and how did it satisfy itself that they were red and expert candidates who could work effectively in state administration and economic construction? Basically, it institutionalized the recruitment process through two organizations, the PLA and the Communist Youth League. The PLA historically had been a major supplier and employer of CCP members. From the late 1940s, with the influx of ex-Kuomintang troops and then younger conscripts, and with the increasing civilian orientation of the CCP, the proportion of party members in the army gradually declined. The officer corps retained a heavy concentration of members, who virtually monopolized the senior grades, but members became a minority among the rank and file.[33] On the other hand, as the PLA demobilized from its

[29]Ibid., pp. 41–43; and Ezra F. Vogel, "From Revolutionary to Semi-Bureaucrat: The 'Regularisation' of Cadres," *China Quarterly,* no. 29 (January–March 1967), pp. 36–60.

[30]Lewis, *Leadership in Communist China,* p. 108.

[31]Kau, op. cit., p. 109.

[32]Schurmann, *Ideology and Organization in Communist China,* p. 133.

[33]John Gittings *The Role of the Chinese Army* (London: Oxford University Press, 1967), pp. 110–11.

TABLE IV. _PLA Statistics, 1950–1958_[a]

	Strength	Demobilization	Recruitment
1950	5,000,000	...	...
1951	...		
1952	...	2,940,000	1,750,000
1953	3,500,000		
1954	...	1,820,000	830,000
1955	3,000,000		500,000
1956	2,750,000	740,000	500,000
1957	2,500,000	800,000	500,000
1958	2,500,000	500,000	500,000
1950–1958	...	6,800,000	4,580,000

[a] Reprinted by permission from John Gittings, _The Role of the Chinese Army_, p. 305, published by Oxford University Press under the auspices of the Royal Institute of International Affairs.

Korean War strength and entered into a conscription system with regular terms of service, it began to feed a steady stream of demobilized soldiers into civilian life—nearly seven million between 1950 and 1958 (see Table IV). Supplementing these were much smaller numbers transferred to duties in civilian organizations, usually as cadres, without being released from service. For a variety of reasons, demobilized and transferred soldiers have been prime candidates for activist, cadre, and party-member roles. Their term of service (according to the 1955 conscription law, three years for the army, four for the air force, and five for the navy) has given them disciplined organizational experience, regular political education, minimal literacy, and, in some cases, special technical skills. Moreover, the PLA's conscripts are an elite group to begin with, since only a fraction of those who reach the conscription age of eighteen are taken. Many are from peasant families, which gives them the added advantages of a favored class background, but they are the pick of China's rural youth.

The Youth League. The Youth League's importance in recruitment is obvious, since it received official recognition (until 1966) as the most appropriate organization in which youth demonstrate and acquire advanced political qualifications. The League's growth in the 1950's was impressive (see Table V). Starting from scratch in 1949, it matched the CCP in size

TABLE V. *Communist Youth League Membership, 1949–1959*[a]

Year	Members in millions	Branch units
1949 (April)	0.19	. . .
1949 (October)	0.50	. . .
1949 (December)	1.30	. . .
1950 (June)	3.00	. . .
1951 (September)	5.18	242,000
1952 (September)	6.00	. . .
1953 (June)	9.00	380,000
1954 (May)	12.00	520,000
1955 (December)	16.00	600,000
1956 (June)	20.00	700,000
1957 (May)	23.00	920,000
1958 (July)	23.20	. . .
1959 (May)	25.00	1,000,000

[a]Reprinted by permission of the author and the publisher from Klaus H. Pringsheim, "The Functions of the Chinese Communist Youth Leagues (1920–1949)," *China Quarterly*, no. 12 (October–December 1962), pp. 90–91.

by 1952 and was close to double the size of its parent organization by 1956. Its growth slowed during the Leap and its aftermath, but the CYL remained the largest activist political organization in the People's Republic. Membership apparently remained around the 25 million mark into the early 1960s, when pressures for growth resumed. One scholar estimates that membership rose to around 40 million by 1965, although Communist sources have confirmed only that a great recruitment drive in 1964–1965 brought in 8.5 million new members.[34] The League probably became the leading source of new party members about 1954, the time that the CCP began its own major growth period. Indeed, the CYL's emergence in the early 1950s as a substantial pool of organized, accessible, and presumably reliable activists was undoubtedly one factor encouraging the CCP to open up its recruitment drive. The precise number of League members entering the party is not known. One of the few direct references was a 1957 report that 2.8 million had done so between 1949 and

[34]Victor Funnell, "The Chinese Communist Youth Movement, 1949–1966," *China Quarterly*, no. 42 (April–June 1970), pp. 105–30, esp. pp. 115–16, 128.

the end of 1956.[35] This represented over 40 percent of CCP growth for the same period; in fact, since the League probably began to provide large numbers of party recruits only from 1954, the figures suggest that by the mid-1950s a solid majority of new party members were Youth Leaguers.[36] The last report on this topic before the Cultural Revolution stated that 600,000 league members joined the party in 1965, which must have been a very high proportion of those entering the CCP in that year.[37]

The CYL's centrality in recruitment before the Cultural Revolution is clarified by the distribution of its membership. In effect, the League was the key organizational linkage for China's incipient "new class," the subelite of activists and low-level cadres concentrated in urban settings — among students, industrial workers, and state employees — and in the PLA. A few figures will indicate how organizational membership in the League, with its direct political advantages, overlapped with and reinforced the opportunities of skilled occupational groups. In 1957, League membership was distributed as follows: 16.4 million in villages; 3.6 million in schools; 2.28 million in industry; 1.8 million in the army; 970,-000 in government offices; and 680,000 in commerce.[38] Village members constituted only 70 percent of total League membership, a figure well below the rural percentage of China's population and an indicator of the CYL's persistent and acknowledged weakness in the countryside. As late as 1964, the League had recruited only 13 percent of rural youth in the 15–25 age bracket and had major organizational gaps in production teams and brigades.[39] But League members consti-

[35]"What Has Happened to the Youth Corps?" *China News Analysis*, no. 633 (October 21, 1966), p. 2.

[36]In September 1956, CYL leader Hu Yaobang said that 2,150,000 Leaguers had joined the party to that time; if this and the 2.8 million figures are correct, then 650,000 League members joined the CCP in the last three months of 1956, supporting the statement in the text. See Hu Yaobang's speech in *Eighth National Congress of the Communist Party of China*, vol. 2 (Peking: Foreign Languages Press, 1956), p. 319.

[37]Funnell, op. cit., p. 116.

[38]"What Has Happened to the Youth Corps?" loc. cit. There is double counting here as the total of 25.7 million exceeds the announced membership of 23 million at that time; many included as "village" members probably fell into other categories as well.

[39]Funnell, op. cit., p. 116.

tuted major proportions of all the other categories given. Consider the following: 3.6 million in schools, when total secondary and higher school enrolment was about 5.6 million (and many in junior middle schools, the largest group of students in the total, would be underage); 2.28 million in industry, when the total of industrial workers was 7.9 million (and the majority overage for the CYL); 1.8 million in the PLA, when PLA strength was 2.5 million (with many overage); 1.65 million in "government offices" and "commerce," a very high percentage of employees under the age of twenty-five in such categories.[40]

Despite their limitations, these figures leave little doubt about the institutionalized character of recruitment in the 1954–1965 period. The CCP, seeking red and expert candidates with particular concern about redness, logically focused its search on the CYL, which was its own auxiliary and second only to the party in the assumed political activism and purity of its membership. To the extent that the party also wanted young candidates with somewhat advanced education or training (students and soldiers), or who were already acquiring valued work experience (low-level cadres, state employees, and industrial workers), it was also turning to institutions that were very much a part of the League's organizational domain. The CYL was probably enrolling from 60 to 90 percent of its age group in the PLA, the regular schools, the factories, and government offices. The League was relatively weak in the countryside, but even here it served as the logical provider of rural party recruits because so many of its rural members were village activists and cadres. As early as 1954, an estimated 6 million Leaguers were serving as basic-level officials in the countryside;[41] given a League membership of 12 million and estimating rural members as 70 percent of the total, about 70 percent of rural Leaguers held village "cadre" positions in 1954.

[40]School enrollment in 1957 from Leo A. Orleans, *Professional Manpower and Education in Communist China* (Washington, D.C.: Government Printing Office, 1961), pp. 35, 66. Industrial workers in 1957 from Nai-ruenn Chen, ed., *Chinese Economic Statistics* (Chicago: Aldine, 1967), pp. 474–75. PLA strength from Table IV. Chen, ed., op. cit., shows 2.88 million employees in "government administration" in 1956, and 3.7 million in "trade enterprises" in 1957, but I do not know if these categories match those referred to in the text.

[41]Funnell, op. cit., p. 144.

Standing astride the institutional channels of political re-cruitment, the League interposed itself as a crucial barrier between the young citizen and higher political status. Yet that citizen's access to the League was often dependent on earlier entry into institutions highly selective in their admissions pro-cess, e.g., the regular secondary schools and the PLA. More-over, all was not well with the League from a Maoist point of view. It was a huge bureaucracy, heavily oriented toward the cities and advanced schools, closely tied to the central party Secretariat and Propaganda Department, jealously guarding its power to pass judgment on the political qualifications of candidates, and filled with overage cadres making a career of "youth" work.[42] The implications were not lost on the political aspirant who recognized the institutional rules of the game that had to be played for the sake of a career.[43]

Finally, we should note that institutionalization of recruit-ment gave great weight to seniority and made upward mobility difficult for the post-1954 recruit. As shown in the next sec-tion, central leadership remained closed to all but the oldest of the party elite. A study of local leadership reveals that cadres recruited before 1949 or during land reform tended to hold on to their posts, steadily advancing the age of *xian* and district cadres in particular and blocking advancement for those at lower levels.[44] The weight of seniority was also evi-dent among top elites at the provicial level who tended to retain their positions or be replaced by cadres of roughly com-parable age, having the same result of a rising average age.[45]

[42]Cf. the previous chapter's discussion of the pre-Cultural Revolution crisis in socialization, and see Funnell, op. cit.; John Gardner, "Educated Youth and Urban-Rural Inequalities, 1958–1966," in Lewis, ed., *The City in Communist China*, pp. 276–86; and James R. Townsend, *The Revolutionization of Chinese Youth* (Berkeley: University of California, Center for Chinese Studies, 1967), esp. pp. 59–71.

[43]Michael Oksenberg, "The Institutionalization of the Chinese Communist Revolution: The Ladder of Success on the Eve of the Cultural Revolution". *China Quarterly*, no. 36 (October–December 1968), pp. 61–92.

[44]Michel Oksenberg, "Local Leaders in Rural China, 1962–65: Individual Attributes, Bureaucratic Positions and Political Recruitment," in A. Doak Barnett, ed., *Chinese Communist Politics in Action* (Seattle; University of Washington Press, 1969), pp. 155–215. This article analyzes local leadership and recruitment in detail, bringing out many dimensions of local recruitment not discussed here.

[45]Frederick C. Teiwes, *Provincial Party Personnel in Mainland China, 1956–1966* (New York: Columbia University, East Asian Institute, 1967), pp. 7, 31–33.

Reliance on old cadres is particularly important in view of the distribution of party members by date of admission. As early as 1961 only 20 percent were pre-1949 entrants, while those joining after 1953 constituted 70 percent of the party.[46] Those who entered the party after 1953 — that is, after the revolutionary wars and reconstruction struggles — probably constituted close to 80 percent of the party by 1965. By 1965 the CCP was an organization of recent recruits lacking revolutionary experience, led by a small stratum of old revolutionary cadres who held most of the responsible positions within it.

Table VI offers a simplified summary of the preceding discussion, emphasizing changes experienced by party organization between 1945 and 1965. Maoists recognized the shift from a revolutionary to a bureaucratic party and tried to combat it. There were attempts to reduce cadre numbers in the mid-1950s; initiation of movements to recruit more peasant CCP and CYL members, and repoliticization of the PLA in the late 1950s; socialist education and cultivation of revolutionary successor campaigns in the early 1960s; and a new CYL recruitment drive to add worker-peasant members and rejuvenate League organization in 1964–1965. These measures

TABLE VI. *Contrasts in the Chinese Communist Party of 1945 and 1965*

	1945	*1965*
Membership	1,211,128	Over 17,000,000
Age of top leaders	Forties	Sixties
Social background		
Percentage rural	Near 100	Over 60
Percentage urban	Near 0	Over 30
Primary work	Peasant or soldier	Cadre or office work
Style of political work	Generalist: mass mobilization and face-to-face relationships	Specialist: administrative in a bureaucratic setting
Remuneration	Nonsalaried	Salaried
Mobility	Open	Closed
Recruitment	Self-recruitment, screened by performance in revolutionary action	Competitive selection, screened by admission to feeder institutions (PLA, schools, Youth League)

[46]Lewis, *Leadership in Communist China,* pp. 111–13.

checked but did not reverse the institutionalization of recruitment. With the exception of the PLA, where Lin Biao's revival of the revolutionary political style had a marked impact,[47] none of the institutions involved turned decisively away from the post-1953 pattern. Maoist pressures simply created ambiguity and uncertainty in recruitment policy, possibly explaining the withholding of data on party and League membership after 1961.

"Fresh Blood" since the Cultural Revolution. The Cultural Revolution was replete with real and rhetorical attacks on the established recruitment process. The upsurge of Red Guards and rebels, purges of office holders, and suspension of the CYL cut sharply through existing routines and channels for political advancement. Maoist accounts commended the rise of millions of "previously unknown" activists who were appearing on the political scene. As the campaign shifted to its consolidation phase, an important editorial in *Hong-qi* forecast a more open and vigorous recruitment policy. Emphasizing the importance of recruitment in determining the future of the revolution, the editorial took its theme from a Mao quotation:

> A human being has arteries and veins through which the heart makes the blood circulate, and he breathes with his lungs, exhaling carbon dioxide and inhaling fresh oxygen, that is, getting rid of the stale and taking in the fresh. A proletarian party must also get rid of the stale and take in the fresh for only thus can it be full of vitality. Without eliminating waste matter and absorbing fresh blood the Party has no vigor.

The editorial continued in explanation:

> "Eliminating waste matter" means resolutely expelling from the Party the proven renegades, enemy agents, all counterrevolutionaries, obdurate capitalist roaders, alien class elements and degenerated elements. As for apathetic persons whose revolutionary will has declined, they should be advised to leave the Party.

[47]See Gittings, op. cit., pp. 225–62.

"Absorbing fresh blood" consists of two inter-related tasks: Taking into the Party a number of outstanding rebels, primarily advanced elements from among the industrial workers, and selecting outstanding Communist Party members for leading posts in the Party organizations at all levels.[48]

The preference for industrial workers is interesting, but the editorial made clear that recruitment criteria ought to be political and moral rather than socioeconomic: "boundless loyalty" to Mao; defense of his line during the Cultural Revolution; exercise of power for Mao and the proletariat, not for self-interest; vigorous study and propagation of Mao's thought with no pride, conceit, or halfway revolution; close ties with and service to the masses. The editorial attacked Liu Shaoqi for relying on the bourgeoisie and bourgeois intellectuals and inveighed against "conventional criteria," "old habits," and "blind faith in elections" as conservative influences used to exclude good comrades. "Direct action by the revolutionary masses" coupled with approval by the leadership was the editorial's approved formula for the constitution of new organs of power.

How far the CCP has actually gone in absorbing "fresh blood" and procedures is a complicated question to which several answers are possible — all of which are limited by insufficient data. One response is that the Cultural Revolution initiated another spurt of party growth, with membership rising to twenty-eight million by 1973 and over thirty-five million by August 1977 (see Table III). Assuming that growth must have been slow in the early 1960s, and stopped altogether for the 1966–1969 years, the 1970s were as heavy a recruitment period as the mid-1950s. The result was a substantial increase in the ratio of party members to total population, a ratio that rose from 1.72 per cent in 1956 to 3.68 per cent in 1977 (calculated from Table III and common population estimates.) By the late 1970s, the CCP was almost entirely an organization of post-1949 recruits; about half of them were recruited after the Cultural Revolution.

---

[48]"Absorb Fresh Blood from the Proletariat — An Important Question in Party Consolidation," *Hongqi*, no. 4 (October 14, 1968), in *PR*, no. 43 (October 25, 1968), pp. 4–7.

Second, there was a substantial radical influence on party recruitment in the first few years after the Cultural Revolution. The constitution adopted at the Ninth Party Congress in 1969 removed an earlier requirement for a year's probation before full membership and added a stipulation that popular opinions be solicited in assessing applicants' qualifications. Scattered reports indicated that admission in this period was simpler and quicker, generally favoring Cultural Revolution activists. The strongest evidence that post-1969ecruitment was under radical influence stems from later charges that the Gang of Four were stacking party rolls with their own supporters. In commenting on CCP membership at the Eleventh Party Congress in 1977, Ye Jianying observed, "There is the serious problem of impurity in ideology, organization and style of work among Party members as a result of the rather extensive confusion created by the 'gang of four' who in recent years vitiated the Party's line, undermined the Party's organizational principle and set their own standards for Party membership."[49] Yet clearly implied that the Gang's "crash admittance" efforts, bringing "political speculators" and "bad types" into the party, were the reason for the restoration of the one-year probation requirement and other disciplinary emphases adopted in the 1977 constitution. In general, the post-1976 assault on the Gang's intraparty activities testifies to the radicalization of recruitment procedures during 1969–1976.

A third point, following directly, is that post-1976 recruitment moved back toward the pattern of 1954–1965. The anti-Gang measures and positions cited suggest a preference for a more orderly, disciplined recruitment process. The reactivation of the old mass organizations — especially the Youth League, with its reported 1978 membership of forty-eight million and with explicit praise for its having "trained large numbers of outstanding cadres for the Party"[50] — provided the

[49]"Report on the Revision of the Party Constitution," *PR*, no. 36 (September 2, 1977), p. 36. "Radical-moderate" struggles over rehabilitation of cadres attacked during the Cultural Revolution were prominent throughout 1969–1976, suggesting similar conflict over recruitment; see Hong Yung Lee, "The Politics of Cadre Rehabilitation Since the Cultural Revolution," *Asian Survey,* vol. 18, no. 9 (September 1978), pp. 934–55.

[50]*PR*, no. 20 (May 19, 1978), p. 10.

screening institutions to implement it. A report that 72 percent of the new college students in 1978 were party or CYL members suggested resurgence of close relationships between higher education and political recruitment; indeed, the CCP adopted a specific policy of recruiting more scientists and technicians.[51] Given the size of the CCP — surely the world's largest bureaucracy, and one that attempts to maintain close control over every member — the routinization and institutionalization of recruitment must be difficult to resist. When the requirements of the "four modernization" policies are added, the evidence points strongly toward a recruitment process that will favor the more highly skilled and educated sectors of Chinese society, creating closer links between political status and socioeconomic status and fostering tendencies toward the emergence of a "new class" of technocratic party elites.

Recruitment to Top Leadership. Much more is known abut China's top political elite — commonly identified by membership in the CCP Central Committee (CC) — than about membership in the party generally or in any other stratum of Chinese society. Although information is still limited, it reveals significant facts about recruitment to the highest level of the political system.[52] These data illustrate broad trends in elite composition and more detailed shifts in intraparty struggles; attention here focuses on larger trends, with only a few observations on the relationship between CC composition and factional struggles.[53]

Table VII suggests several important changes in the CC over time. One of the more obvious is that the CC has grown steadily in size, making it less effective as a decision-making

[51] *PR*, no. 30 (July 28, 1978), pp. 19, 21–22.

[52] Major compilations of data on CCP elites include Donald W. Klein and Anne B. Clark, *Biographic Dictionary of Chinese Communism, 1921–1965* (Cambridge: Harvard University Press, 1971), 2 vols; *Chinese Communist Who's Who* (Taipei: Institute of International Relations, 1970–1971), 2 vols.; and *Who's Who in Communist China* (Hong Kong: Union Research Institute, 1969–1970), 2 vols.; See also Scalapino, ed., op. cit., especially Klein's chapter on "Sources for Elite Studies," pp. 609–56; and Paul Wong, *China's Higher Leadership in the Socialist Transition* (New York: Free Press, 1976).

[53] For close analysis of changing factional alignments within the CC, see the articles by Jürgen Domes cited in Table VII.

TABLE VII. *Changes in Composition of CCP Central Committees*

	8th Central Committee (1956–1958)	9th Central Committee (1969)	10th Central Committee (1973)	11th Central Committee (1977)
I. Number of members				
Full	97	170	195	201
Alternate	96[a]	109	124	132
Total	193	279	319	333
II. Turnover of members[b]				
Holdover from previous Central Committee	40%	19%	64%	56%
Newcomer	60%	81%	31%	38%
Returnee[c]	0%	0%	5%	6%
III. Occupational background[b]				
Civilian	81%	55%	63%	71%
Military	19%	45%	32%	29%
Unknown	0%	0%	5%	0%

264

IV. Occupational level[b]				
National	62%	33%	33%	35%
Provincial	38%	67%	62%	65%
Unknown	0%	0%	5%	0%
V. Average age of full members at election[d]	56.4	61.4	62.1	64.6

[a] Twenty-five alternate members were added to the 8th Central Committee at its second plenary session in 1958.
[b] Figures in II, III, and IV represent percentages of total (full and alternate) Central Committee membership.
[c] Returnees are those full and alternate members who were not elected to the immediately previous Central Committee but who were members of an earlier Central Committee.
[d] Data for 1969 based on 162 of 170 full members; data for 1977 based on 163 of 201 full members.

Sources: For I and II: *Who's Who in Communist China* (Hong Kong: Union Research Institute, 1966), pp. 703–7; Donald W. Klein and Lois B. Hager, "The Ninth Central Committee," *China Quarterly*, no. 45 (January–February 1971), pp. 37–56; Malcolm Lamb, *Directory of Central Officials in the People's Republic of China, 1968–1975* (Canberra: Australian National University, 1976), pp. 5–16; K'ung Te-liang, "An Analysis of the CCP's 10th National Congress," *Issues and Studies*, vol. 10, no. 1 (October 1973), pp. 17–30; Central Intelligence Agency, *China: A Look at the 11th Central Committee* (Rp 77–10276, October 1977).

For III and IV: *China: A Look at the 11th Central Committee*.
For V: Jurgen Domes, "The Ninth CCP Central Committee in Statistical Perspective," *Current Scene*, vol 9, no. 2 (February 7, 1971), pp. 5–14; Jurgen Domes, "China in 1977: A Reversal of the Verdict," *Asian Survey*, vol. 18, no. 1 (January 1978), pp. 6–9.

body but increasing its potential as a representative body for the party as a whole and strengthening its training and screening function for future Politburo service. Growth also means that the CC has had regular infusions of new members, the lowest percentage of newcomers being 31 on the Tenth CC elected in 1973; this is important to emphasize, since there are other ways in which elite change and mobility appears highly restricted. Moreover, Table VII points to three major consequences of the Cultural Revolution: first, there was a particularly heavy turnover of membership in the election of the Ninth CC in 1969; second, the campaign sharply increased military representation on the Ninth CC, followed by successive reductions of PLA influence on the Tenth and Eleventh committees; third, the upheavals of 1966–69 and the decentralizing policies associated with the Maoist model shifted the balance of power on the CC from those holding positions in central offices in Peking to those with primary responsibilities in the provinces (for example, secretaries of provincial party committees, heads of provincial revolutionary committees, or commanders of regional PLA forces), a shift that was not reversed in subsequent CC elections. Finally, this table documents the return of rehabilitated cadres to the Tenth and Eleventh CCs, the "reversal of verdicts" on older cadres purged in the Cultural Revolution that was such a potent issue between the "radicals" and "moderates" during 1969–76. Bear in mind that the relatively small percentages refer to sixteen returnees in 1973 and twenty more in 1977, representing a substantial component of the former purgees who were still alive to benefit from this reversal.

The last item in Table VII leads to another point more fully documented in Table VIII, namely, the iron grip of the "Long March generation" (people who had joined the CCP by the time of the epic Long March of 1934–35) on PRC political power. The average age of the CC rose from 46.8 on the Seventh CC elected in 1945[54] to 56.4 in 1956 and 61.4 in 1969; in other words, despite substantial turnovers of or additions to CC membership over these twenty-five years, most changes came from *within* the same increasingly elderly generation.

[54]References to Seventh CC data are from the first edition of *Politics in China* (Boston: Little, Brown, 1974), pp. 264–65.

TABLE VIII. *Background Data on Central Committee Members*

	9th Central Committee	10th Central Committee	11th Central Committee
Party seniority of full members			
Joined CCP:			
1921–1935	80.4%	63.2%	67.2%[a]
1936–1949	11.9%	15.4%	16.9%
After 1949	7.7%	21.4%	12.9%
Age distribution of full members			
Under 40	0.0%	3.6%	1.8%[b]
40 to 49	3.4%	4.4%	2.5%
50 to 59	37.3%	16.0%	6.1%
60 to 69	42.4%	54.7%	62.6%
Over 70	16.9%	21.1%	27.0%
Career background of full members			
Civilian cadres	31.0%	44.6%	52.2%[c]
Mass organizations	17.7%	17.9%	11.9%
Total PLA[d]	50.0%	37.5%	34.8%
PLA commanders	35.3%	25.9%	22.4%
PLA commissars	14.7%	11.6%	12.4%
Educational background of full members: highest level attained			
College or university	23.0%	27.6%	25.7%[b]
Military academy	35.7%	40.7%	30.1%
Normal school	16.7%	6.2%	8.6%
Secondary school	10.3%	8.9%	18.4%
Primary school	11.9%	8.3%	10.4%
No formal education	1.6%	8.3%	6.7%
Some foreign education	32.5%	20.9%	10.4%

[a] For 11th Central Committee, based on 195 of 201 members.

[b] For 11th Central Committee, based on 163 of 201 members.

[c] For 11th Central Committee, based on 199 of 201 members.

[d] A PLA career background is listed for all members who held a rank in 1955.

Source: Adapted and reprinted by permission of the author and the publisher from Jürgen Domes, "China in 1977: A Reversal of the Verdict," *Asian Survey*, vol. 18, no. 1 (January 1978), p. 8.

The average age of the two committees elected in the 1970s continued to increase, although (inevitably) not so rapidly as before. More specifically, 67 of the 77 members of the Seventh CC were reelected to the Eighth in 1956; and even though only 53 of the 193 members of the Eighth CC weathered the Cultural Revolution storm to serve on the Ninth, the Long March group continued to hold 80 per cent of the seats. The Long Marchers fell to 63 per cent of the Tenth CC then actually rose to 67 percent on the Eleventh CC elected in 1977. The percentage of post-1949 recruits on the CC rose sharply in 1973 but then fell in 1977, while the percentage of members over 60, and also over 70, rose steadily on the 1969, 1973, and 1977 committees. Although the Long March generation's dominance is obviously about to end, with nearly all its most prestigious representatives gone, its control of top leadership was still in place thirty years after 1949, even though the CCP had become essentially an organization of post-1949 recruits, with post-1965 recruits constituting about half the total. The disappearance of the Long Marchers in the 1980s will be a momentous change, providing both a challenge and an opportunity for the CCP and its younger cohorts.

The most significant aspect of the forthcoming change is the shift from leaders with substantial revolutionary experience to cadres whose main experience has been with PRC bureaucracies, But Table VIII suggests other trends that might affect it. For example, the 1970s saw a steady rise in civilian cadre strength on the CC, a steady fall in PLA representation — especially military commanders as contrasted to commissars — and a retreat from the modest mass representation that had emerged after the Cultural Revolution. If one assumes that the existing composition of the CC will have a strong influence on selection of new top leaders — a safe assumption barring another Cultural Revolution — then the successors to the Long March generation will be mainly civilian cadres with long bureaucratic experience. This is not to say that a better "fit" between top leaders and party masses will necessarily follow. The CC has always been dominated by a highly educated group (relative to Chinese educational attainment), which has not prevented sharp conflicts over the whole range of red-expert issues; curiously, the Long March generation actually had *more* foreign educational experience (due to the number of Chinese who studied abroad in the 1910s and 1920s) than its immediate successors, who may be responsible for guidance of large-scale cultural and educational exchanges with foreign countries. In general, however, the prolonged discrepany between old revolutionary leadership and the post-1949 rank and file will soon resolve itself in a closer match of elite and mass experience.

TABLE IX. *Changes in Composition of CCP Central Committee Politburos*

	8th Central Committee Politburo	9th Central Committee Politburo	10th Central Committee Politburo	11th Central Committee Politburo
Number of members				
Full	20[a]	21	21	23
Alternate	6	4	4	3
Total	26	25	25	26
Membership turnover				
Reelected to next politburo	9	16	15	...
Not reelected to next politburo	17[b]	9	10	...
Died before election of next politburo	3	2	5	...
Party seniority				
Joined 1921–1935	26	19[c]	17[d]	20[e]
Joined 1936–1949	0	2	4	2
Joined after 1949	0	0	2	1
Average age at election				
Full members	58	65	67	68
Alternate members	53	56	57	59
Professional background				
Civilian	19	14	16	14
Military	7	11	9	12

[a] Includes four full members added in 1958—Lin Biao, Ke Qingshi (K'o Ch'ing-shih), Li Jingquan (Li Ching-ch'uan), Tan Zhenlin (T'an Chen-lin).

[b] Includes two members of 8th Central Committee Politburo later elected to 11th Central Committee Politburo—Deng Xiaoping, Ulanhu (Ulanfu).

[c] Data available for 21 of 25 members only.

[d] Data available for 23 of 25 members only.

[e] Data available for 23 of 26 members only.

Sources: Donald W. Klein and Anne B. Clark, *Biographic Dictionary of Chinese Communism, 1921–1965* (Cambridge, Mass.: Harvard University Press, 1971); *Who's Who in Communist China* (Hong Kong: Union Research Institute, 1966); Malcolm Lamb, *Directory of Central Officials in the People's Republic of China, 1968–1975* (Canberra: Australian National University, 1976); Jürgen Domes, *China After the Cultural Revolution* (Berkeley: University of California Press, 1977); Jurgen Domes, "China in 1977: Reversal of Verdicts," *Asian Survey*, vol 18, no. 1 (January 1978), pp. 1–16; Central Intelligence Agency, *Chinese Communist Party Central Committee—Members Elected at the 11th Party Congress* (CR 77–14473, September 1977).

Changes in the Politburo (see Table IX) command special attention, since this body is the supreme decision-making elite. Recruitment to the Politburo mirrors the CC pattern of age and Long March domination; the average age of sixty-eight for full members of the 1977 Politburo gives the PRC an extremely elderly top national leadership. Turnover on the Politburo has also been about the same as on the CC, slightly higher overall due to more deaths but very close to the CC in purge percentages. In other ways, however, Politburo recruitment differs from the CC. Its size has been constant, reflecting the fact that it is a functioning committee, whereas the CC is more a representative assembly. Another difference is that PLA representation on the Politburo rose in 1969, fell in 1973, but then, in contrast to the CC, it rose again in 1977; this probably indicates PLA participation in the Hua-Deng coalition against the Gang of Four.

A fascinating question is what combination of qualifications and experiences creates access to CCP elitehood, but few solid generalizations can be formulated. By far the most important criterion for PRC leadership has been membership in the Long March generation plus a capacity to survive physically and politically; those who met these conditions simply *were* the elite down to the Cultural Revolution. That campaign revealed other considerations, however, with three new criteria emerging as particularly important recruitment assets. One was high military command, which seems to be a prime functional specialty for access to the top. A second was success as a provincial leader, with many new elite recruits capitalizing on their provincial bases; Hua Guonfeng was an example, although his Human experience was not the only factor in his ascent.[55] Finally, personal support from highest leaders was a very effective asset, the best example being the Gang of Four who benefitted from Mao's patronage in the late 1960s. These criteria overlap and must blend with other personal and political skills to produce a successful career, but they remain important — not exclusive — paths to the top. Post-1976 priorities suggest that some technocrats, highly skilled in the administration of

[55]Michel Oksenberg and Sai-cheung Yeung, "Hua Kuo-feng's Pre-Cultural Revolution Hunan Years, 1949–66," *China Quarterly,* no. 69 (March 1977), pp. 3–53.

modernization policies, will join military commanders, provincial leaders, and protégés in the 1980s as a fourth type of upwardly mobile cadres.

The 1970s transformed what Mao Zedong perceived to be the core problem of political recruitment. Mao was keenly aware of the necessity of "cultivating revolutionary successors" in large numbers to staff the burgeoning Chinese bureaucracies. His search was for cadres like himself who combined revolutionary ideology with intellectual or technical skills. The problem was that Chinese society seemed to offer relatively few recruits with these talents. Initially there were plenty of reds but their expertise was limited, whereas the available experts were contaminated by KMT influence or bourgeois education. When Mao saw that the new recruitment processes were not replicating his brand of revolutionary ideology, he began to fear that revisionist influences would overwhelm the party's revolutionary core. Hence his suspicion of the new elite, his promotion of the Cultural Revolution, and his continuing search for "fresh blood" that had escaped or renounced the influence of impure background or education.

By the late 1970s, two developments had changed this perception of the problem. Mao and his closest associates were gone, and although Long Marchers remained influential, the CCP was no longer dominated by a desire to replicate old revolutionary cadres. Moreover, the pool of potential recruits had expanded enormously due to increases in the number of activists, middle school graduates, members of mass organizations and the party, and cadres with substantial administrative experience. With this large and diverse body of potential recruits, nearly all products of socialist society and spread throughout that society, the danger of any particular group of recruits (such as intellectuals) transforming the party seemed small. Or perhaps it would be more accurate to say that the party was *already* transformed so that it could no longer perceive the problem in Mao's terms or with his sense of urgency.

The core recruitment problem for the 1980s, then, seems to be emerging as a mix of managerial and bureaucratic concerns: how to administer a process that requires review and examination of tens of millions of cases; how to balance priorities in the training of various specialties, ranging from rural to nuclear technology, from basic-level activists to computer experts, from foreign-language specialists to factory managers, and so forth; and how to prevent political recruitment processes, necessarily based on a great variety of institutional training and selection grounds, from producing enclaves of special interests that will breed factions and threaten the CCP's centralized organization and ideology.

ELITE CONFLICT

To summarize the discussion thus far, CCP theory recognizes the existence of multiple interests within Chinese society and maintains that nonantagonistic ones among the people should be expressed politically. The possibly competitive demands so legitimized emanate from a wide range of socioeconomic, institutional, and geographic groups. Popular articulation of demands occurs largely within basic-level government, especially within primary production and residential units, and is typically unorganized and fragmented. Organized articulation by nonparty groups is supervised closely by CCP elites to check competition with the party and to ensure that demands conform to its general line; deviations can and do occur but bring disciplinary and, if necessary, repressive responses from the CCP. "Bureaucratic articulation" in which office-holding elites champion selected interests is the primary means for injecting demands into the decision-making process, hence the importance of recruitment to higher political roles. The CCP hopes that its recruitment process will produce a unified elite of "red-experts" who will rise above partial interests in their aggregation of political demands. In fact, the party never has been monolithic in either ideology or organization. It maintained a relatively high degree of cohesion from the late 1930s into the early 1950s, but with its victory in 1949 it began to undergo major changes. It increased greatly in size; began to accept recruits of more varied motivation, skills, and backgrounds; expanded its control over, and then direct management of, the administrative processes of government; and bureaucratized its organization to cope with these new conditions. In the process the CCP absorbed the basic contradictions of Chinese society, and its organization became an arena for conflict between the demands of different strata, regions, generations, and institutions.

The resulting political process bears some similarity to the "bureaucratic politics" of traditional China,[56] but it operates in a much more encompassing and complicated governmental structure that opens the process to a greater variety of institutional and societal pressures. Closer to the mark is the concept of *cryptopolitics*, in which state direction of a tremendous range of activities creates an elaborate set of political institutions without permitting truly open, competitive politics in any of them; political conflict tends to be carried on in secretive or guarded ways throughout the governmental structure, in executive and administrative as well as nominally political institutions.[57] The Chinese brand of cryptopolitics is a volatile one which has encouraged a good deal of guided conflict resolution at the mass level and opened elite conflict to public view and even participation. In general, however, the definition and resolution of major political issues is the responsibility of party officials, whose conflicts are fought inside the bureaucracies in which they serve and are seldom exposed fully to public view. The process is political, but it does not lend itself to easy distinctions between articulation and aggregation, between decision making and administration.

Although elite conflict is normally handled with great discretion, partial evidence reveals something about the substance of important disputes and the principal actors in them. In the case of the Soviet Union, such evidence has led some scholars into an analysis of the structure and role of political interest groups in the Soviet system.[58] Are there political interest groups in the Chinese system? There are surely "group interests," but it is difficult to prove that "interest groups" exist as a regular means of advancing them. Critics of the interest group approach in Soviet and East European studies have argued that these groups have little legitimacy and autonomy within their systems.[59] This caution applies with great

---

[56]Cf. Chapter II, this book.

[57]T. H. Rigby, "Crypto-Politics," *Survey*, no. 50 (January, 1964), pp. 183–94.

[58]H. Gordon Skilling and Franklyn Griffiths, eds., *Interest Groups in Soviet Politics* (Princeton, N.J.: Princeton University Press, 1971), esp. Skilling, "Groups in Soviet Politics; Some Hypotheses," pp. 19–45.

[59]Andrew C. Janos, "Group Politics in Communist Society: A Second Look at the Pluralistic Model," in Samuel P. Huntington and Clement H. Moore, eds. *Authoritarian Politics in Modern Society: The Dynamics of Established One-Party Systems* (New York: Basic Books, 1970), pp. 437–50.

force to China, where the struggles of the 1960s and 1970s revealed the existence of factions but also their vulnerability to charges of illegitimacy. Further research may delineate more sharply the kinds of "interest groups" that operate and endure in the Chinese political process, or possibly what kinds will emerge in the more institutionalized system that seems to be taking shape, but the question remains a thorny one.[60]

In the absence of a strong interest-group theory to explain CCP conflict, debate has concentrated on two of its broadest dimensions: the number and defining characteristics of actors in intraparty conflict, and the evolution of conflict patterns over time. Debate on the first question has focused mainly on the merits of factional models versus "two-line struggle" models. The former sees multiple factions, based on complex personal and institutional loyalties, engaging in struggles that have little consistent or enduring relationship to broad policy lines; the latter seeks a higher level of generalization that divides antagonists in intraparty conflict into two major coalitions, each defined by broad agreement on sets of policy alternatives and having considerable continuity in personnel over time. The second question has produced a distinction between "constant conflict" models that emphasize the regularity of conflict (whether factional or two-line) over the course of CCP history, and evolutionary models that portray the CCP moving back and forth between more consensual and more conflictual modes of intraparty debate.[61] The following discus-

[60]The topic was thoroughly explored in papers at a conference on "The Pursuit of Political Interest in the People's Republic of China," sponsored by the Joint Committee on Contemporary China of the Social Science Research Council, and held at the University of Michigan, August 11–17, 1977. For analysis of formal and informal constituencies of Chinese elites, see Lowell Dittmer, "Base of Power in Chinese Politics: A Theory and Analysis of the Fall of the 'Gang of Four'," *World Politics,* vol. 31, no. 1 (October 1978), pp. 26–60.

[61]Andrew J. Nathan has argued the merits of factional models in "A Factionalism Model for CCP Politics," *China Quarterly,* no. 53 (January–March 1973), pp. 34–66, and has questioned the two-line model in "Policy Oscillations in the People's Republic of China: A Critique," Ibid., no. 68 (December 1976), pp. 720–33. An earlier and widely debated example of factional analysis is William Whitson, "The Field Army in Chinese Communist Politics," Ibid., no. 37 (January–March 1967), pp. 1–30. The two-line struggle model dominates official Chinese analyses of their conflicts and has been accepted by a majority of foreign analysts as a useful way of generalizing about the topic. A sophisticated interpretation of the two-line struggle concept, refining it to allow for changing lines of cleavage, is Lowell Dittmer, " 'Line Struggle' in Theory and Practice: The Origins of the Cultural Revolution Reconsidered," Ibid., no. 72

sion reflects all of these approaches, each of which advances important perspectives not always in conflict with each other, without trying to resolve the issues on which they divide.

Contained Conflict in the 1950s. Earlier discussions of "radical-conservative" and "Maoist-bureaucratic" conflicts have outlined the major issues of post-1949 politics. We now want to explore the changing patterns of elite cleavage produced by these issues. Franz Schurmann's distinction between "opinion groups" and "factions" within the CCP provides a useful point of departure.[62] An opinion group is an "aggregate of individuals" who have in common a "likeness of individual opinions" but no organizational basis for action. The CCP tends to tolerate such groups long as they accept majority decisions and avoid the temptation to organize around defense of their positions. A faction is an "opinion group with organized force behind it"; it has resources for action that can split the party along fixed lines and is viewed as an illegitimate form of intraparty conflict. The distinction between these two types of groups is not always clear in practice, but it seems to have been operative during the 1950s. During that period, the CCP contained intraorganizational conflict by practicing opinion group politics and restraining factional politics.

From 1949 into the early 1960s, the CCP maintained a relatively high degree of cohesion without repressing intraparty differences or resorting to extensive purges. The crucial decisions — those that marked the shift from the FFYP to the Geat Leap — emerged from a vigorous debate that addressed itself directly to issues and avoided open, personalized attacks on top leaders. "Conservatives" stated their positions, accepted their defeats, and continued to serve. "Radicals," too, ac-

---

(December 1977), pp. 675–712. The limits of factional analysis, and usefulness of line struggle as a generalization, are set forth in Tang Tsou, "Prolegomenon to the Study of Informal Groups in CCP Politics," Ibid., no. 65 (March 1976), pp. 98–114, and Edwin A. Winckler, "Policy Oscillations in the People's Republic of China: A Reply," Ibid., no. 68 (December 1976), pp. 734–50. The "constant conflict" model is argued in Richard C. Thornton, "The Structure of Communist Politics," *World Politics,* vol. 24, no. 4 (July 1972), pp. 498–517, and is implicit in the CCP view of two-line struggle. An evolutionary interpretation of post-1949 intraparty conflict is found in most foreign accounts of the origins of the Cultural Revolution.

[62]Schurmann, *Ideology and Organization in Communist China,* pp. 55–56.

cepted temporary setbacks without turning vindictively on colleagues who opposed them. Opinion group politics was thus the dominant mode of conflict. Leaders were able to differ on policy issues without forming permanently antagonistic groups. As new issues or stages arose, individuals might shift their positions or find themselves aligned with a new opinion group. Generally, elites were willing to maintain the appearance of unity in support of majority decisions.

Two purges of top elites occurred during the 1950s, neither clearly violating the principle of tolerance of opinion groups nor causing broad splits within the party. The first was the 1954 purge of Gao Gang (Kao Kang), Rao Shushi (Jao Shushih), and some lesser associates.[63] Gao was a Politburo member, the party leader of Northeast China, a vice chairman of the PRC, and head of the State Planning Commission; Rao was a leader in the East China region and director of the CC's Organization Department. The Gao-Rao clique was a faction, not simply an opinion group taking a distinctive stand on certain issues. Although Gao represented a Soviet-style approach (particularly in factory management) that was in conflict with Mao's, his group's fatal error was an attempt to capture control of the central apparatus using its organizational position as a base and trying to recruit additional followers within the CC. This factional power play was smashed in February 1954, although it was not made public until 1955.

The second case was the August 1959 purge of Peng Dehuai (minister of defense and Politburo member), along with Huang Kecheng (Huang K'o-ch'eng) (PLA chief of staff), Zhang Wentian (Chang Wen-t'ien) (vice minister of foreign affairs and an alternate member of the Politburo), and Zhou Xiaozhou (Chou Hsiao-chou) (first secretary of the Hunan Provincial Party Committee).[64] Peng's removal was a question-

[63]Frederick C. Teiwes, "A Review Article: The Evolution of Leadership Purges in Communist China," *China Quarterly,* no. 41 (January–March 1970), pp. 122–26; and Schurmann, *Ideology and Organization in Communist China,* pp. 56*n*, 267–78.

[64]Teiwes, "The Evolution of Leadership Purges in Communist China," op. cit., pp.126–29; David A. Charles, "The Dismissal of Marshall Peng Tehhuai," *China Quarterly,* no. 8 (October–December 1961), pp. 63–76; and *The Case of Peng Teh-huai, 1959–1968* (Hong Kong: Union Research Institute, 1968).

able decision in terms of the opinion group-faction distinction, as he and his associates ostensibly were promoting a debate on Great Leap economic policies. They did this mainly within organizational channels, in closed session, and without attacking Mao's leadership directly. There were two arguments for designating Peng's activities as factional and hence legitimizing his purge. One was his and Huang's powerful military position, their known dissatisfaction with Maoist pressures against military professionalism, and the possibility that Peng had communicated his unhappiness to Soviet Premier Khrushchev; the threat of organizational opposition was formidable even if the debate was cast in terms of policy issues. Beyond this, Mao apparently regarded the attack as a challenge to his own policies which had already been debated and approved; Peng was violating discipline and indulging in "right opportunism" by questioning Mao's leadership at a critical juncture and raising issues that he could have raised earlier.[65] These considerations were sufficient to secure Peng's dismissal as defense minister but not wholly persuasive. He was not denounced by name, retained his seat on the CC, and was even a candidate (albeit unsuccessful) for reinstatement in 1962. The unsettled status of Peng reflected the marginal nature of his "crimes" as seen by many on the CC and was a harbinger of the more open and divisive conflicts of the 1960s.

These two deviations from the dominant pattern of contained opinion group politics were exceptions that proved the rules of the game. The purges of Gao, Rao, and Peng demonstrated the party elite's ability to enforce its distaste for factional conflict without splitting the party. Both groups were small, isolated minorities facing an overwhelming majority willing to accept their purge in the interest of maintaining organizational cohesion. The two cases were quite different in character, of course. Action against the Gao-Rao clique was definitive, denouncing them publicly once the senior elite had agreed on their purge; whereas treatment of Peng was relatively moderate in keeping with the controversiality of his

[65]See Mao's statement at the Lushan (Eighth Plenum) meeting in *Chinese Law and Government,* vol. 1, no. 4 (Winter 1968–1969), pp. 25–51, 60–63, and esp. 45–46.

guilt. In both cases, however, the party elite kept the conflict closed until after if had made its decision and then supported with apparent unanimity the decision rendered.

Open Conflict in the 1960s. Just as the debate over the FFYP and Great Leap lines dominated the 1950s, so the Cultural Revolution dominated the politics of the 1960s. The former contained intraparty conflict in shifting opinion groups which blurred lines of cleavage and made political liquidation of opponents the exception rather than the rule. The latter opened conflict to public view, revealing hardened cleavages that led to sweeping purges. Factions in the earlier period were weak and vulnerable to a majority consensus against that style of politics. They grew stronger in the 1960s, providing protection for their members and serving as building blocks in the formation of coalitions of power. Behind this shift lay an intensification of conflict over fundamental issues, represented by the "struggle between two lines" of the two most powerful leaders, Mao Zedong and Liu Shaoqi.

It is not possible to review here the full range of differences between two men so deeply involved for so long in leadership of the Communist revolution. The record is not complete and has been distorted by the vilification of Liu that accompanied the Cultural Revolution. Still, the conflict between Mao and Liu was real, particularly in their general views of the worker-peasant relationship; of the relationship among party organization, leader, and masses; and of the proper attitude toward the Soviet Union and its example.[66] Briefly Liu tended toward a more orthodox Marxist admiration for the industrial worker and suspicion of the peasant's potential, whereas Mao had tremendous faith in the peasant's capacity for self-initiated political and economic advance. This difference found expression in Liu's skepticism about rapid agricultural collectivization and his belief that it ought to follow mechanization, industrialization, and close state guidance. Mao, in contrast, was the foremost advocate of rapid collectivization, arguing

[66]See the summary in Stuart R. Schram, "Mao Tse-tung and Liu Shao-ch'i, 1939–1969," *Asian Survey*, vol. 12, no. 4 (April 1972), pp. 275–93. The most thorough analysis is Lowell Dittmer, *Liu Shao-ch'i and the Chinese Cultural Revolution* (Berkeley: University of California Press, 1974).

that it could foster and even precede mechanization and industrialization, and that the peasants could carry this out largely on their own.[67]

Differences on the industrial-agricultural relationship spilled over into questions of organizational leadership. Liu was at heart an "organization man," dedicated to the principle of party above leader and to the maintenance of organizational discipline and authority. Although sensitive to the evils of bureaucracy, he saw no substitute for orderly, hierarchical administration and was inclined to defend higher cadres, including "experts," against what he saw as excessive mass democracy. Mao recognized the virtues of organization but placed his primary faith in the authority of the highest leader coupled with mass support and action; he was thus less inclined to defend the sanctity of the organization against the unsettling effects of mass movements and found it intolerable to subordinate his own views to those of his colleagues.[68] Finally, Liu was more inclined than Mao to see the Soviet Union as a positive model for China and possibly less inclined to see it as a real military threat.

Neither Mao nor Liu was totally consistent in articulation of these differences. Both tried at times to accommodate the other's views, or at least to conceal their divergence. The fascinating question is why their conflict, contained in the 1950s, should acquire sufficient virulence to split the party openly in the 1960s. The change was due partly to a natural hardening of views with age and experience. With each new round of debate each probably became more familiar with the other's arguments and more persuaded of his own correctness. With advancing age and Liu's apparent line on the succession (he had already replaced Mao as chairman of the PRC and was second in command within the party), resolution of the struggle acquired more urgency. Moreover, there were several trends in the Chinese governmental process that con-

[67]For an analysis of the complicated interplay of these issues, see Parris H. Chang, "Struggle Between the Two Roads in China's Countryside," *Current Scene,* vol. 6, no. 3 (Feb. 15, 1968); and Editor, "The Conflict Between Mao Tse-tung and Liu Shao-ch'i Over Agricultural Mechanization in Communist China," Ibid., vol. 6, no. 17 (Oct. 1, 1968).

[68]See Stuart R. Schram, "The Party in Chinese Communist Ideology," *China Quarterly,* no. 38 (April–June 1969), pp. 1–26.

tribute to an understanding of the split and why it took the factionalized form that it did. These trends underscore the point that political conflict in China pervades executive and administrative processes as well as articulation and aggregation. They are noted briefly here, with a fuller discussion reserved for the succeeding chapter.

Mao's declining role in the decision-making process was one trend that exacerbated his struggle with Liu Shaoqi. During the 1950s, Mao's vigor and prestige were usually sufficient to build a consensus on major decisions. As late as 1959 he was able to induce at least temporary and surface unity on the controversial dismissal of Peng Dehuai. However, at some point in the 1950s Mao had agreed to a division of highest leadership into a first and second front, placing himself in the second front and thus removing himself from direct supervision of party and government operations.[69] His relinquishment of the chairmanship of the PRC in late 1958 reinforced his isolation from administrative processes. Moreover, his refusal to retreat on such pivotal issues as the Great Leap and the Sino-Soviet conflict strained his relationship with some of his senior colleagues. By the early 1960s, Mao had lost his decisive authority within the top leadership, although his public stature was undiminished. This weakening of the authoritative voice of party consensus encouraged a growth of factionalism in which Mao himself participated.

Lines of potential cleavage also were expanded and complicated by the party's increasing assumption of governmental responsiblities, the differentiation of governmental structure, and the 1957 decentralization that strengthened the powers of provincial-level governments. The CCP's top elite no doubt retained their memories of more homogeneous experiences, but their contemporary roles had become distinctly heterogeneous. By the 1960s most had acquired responsibility for leadership in functionally defined governmental and party systems or in geographic units of administration. Inevitably they became preoccupied with their immediate responsibilities and sensitive to the interests of their constituencies. Inevitably, too, they acquired potential power bases in the bureaucracies they supervised.

[69]"Selections from Chairman Mao," *Translations on Communist China*, no. 90, JPRS-49826 (Feb. 12, 1970), pp. 13–15. See also Chapter VII, this book.

How far this compartmentalization of power had progressed by the time of the Cultural Revolution is uncertain, but it had at least created a situation in which no unitary bloc could control the party. Factions or potential factions were too numerous to be isolated and repressed by a unified majority. Power required a coalition of forces and invited coalition tactics on the part of opponents. The struggle that Mao forced on the CCP in 1965–1966 could not be contained, simply because the adversaries were too evenly matched and too well defended by their own institutional resources. Mao reestablished his leadership only by forging a coalition and mobilizing mass support for a public attack on his entrenched opponents. For the first time in post-1949 history, a purge was initiated and made public before the CC had worked out its own consensus decision.

No simple description does justice to the intricate factional maneuverings — demonstrable and alleged — that characterized elite behavior between 1965 and 1969.[70] In simplest terms, Mao defeated the Liu-Deng revisionists by seizing the initiative in coalition politics and playing it with great skill. His opponents were probably a majority of the top leadership, judging from what is known of CC meetings in 1965–1966 and from the extent of later purges, but they never succeeded in building a unified defense against the onslaught; their bases protected them for a time, but their fragmented organization was a fatal weakness. Mao, on the other hand, established early a coalition that gradually destroyed his opponents and emerged supreme at the Ninth Party Congress in 1969. This coalition was held together by a personal commitment to Mao's leadership and varying degrees of sympathy for his political stance, but it consisted of at least three factions. The most distinct of these was a "radical" faction, which favored a thoroughgoing Maoist position as enunciated early in the Cultural Revolution and which had its organizational base in the CC's Cultural Revolution Group as reconstituted in the summer of 1966. Its leaders were Chen Boda (Ch'en Po-ta), Kang Sheng (K'ang Sheng), and Jiang Qing, supported by other radical propagandists serving in the Cultural Revolution

[70]See Chong-Do Hah, "The Dynamics of the Chinese Cultural Revolution: An Interpretation Based on an Analytical Framework of Political Coalitions," *World Politics*, vol. 24, no. 2 (January 1972), pp. 182–220.

Group. It was close to Mao in personal terms, in that it included his wife, Jiang Qing, and his reputed son-in-law, Yao
Wenyuan; Chen and Kang also had histories of intimate association with Mao. Furthermore, it had a powerful regional base
in Shanghai, where Jiang and Yao were active and had gained
the support of Zhang Chunqiao, who rose to leadership in
Shanghai during that city's "January Revolution" of 1967.
Finally, the radical faction had a mass base in the Red Guards,
who looked to members of this group for authoritative indica-
tions of Mao's wishes. For obvious reasons, then, it held the
initiative during the early part of the Cultural Revolution.

The second faction was associated with Lin Biao, whose
strength rested on the PLA and his designation in the summer
of 1966 as Mao's "closest comrade-in-arms" and heir apparent. The Lin faction was by no means coterminous with the
PLA, which had its own internal divisions, but rested largely
on military officers closely associated with its leader. Still, Lin's
post as defense minister gave his faction tremendous leverage
within the organization that became the de facto government
during much of the Cultural Revolution. Premier Zhou Enlai
headed a third group of high-level cadres who survived the
first year's purges. The weakest and least distinct of these
three groups, it was perhaps a faction by default, a residual
category of leaders who held on due to Zhou's protection and
the need for some continuity in administrative leadership.

Tension within the Maoist coalition became evident as early
as the summer of 1967, when the slogan "drag out the handful
of capitalist-roaders in the army" was put forth.[71] Authority
for this slogan came from a Mao directive of May 16, 1966,
which had included the PLA among those institutions that had
to be purged of their capitalist-roaders — one of the few such
references to the PLA, which otherwise was accorded the privilege of conducting internal rectification on its own. Those
behind this attempt to turn the campaign on the army and
perhaps other leaders became known, from the date of the
directive, as the "May 16 Group" (or "516 Group"). More
accurately, only some of them were so labeled, because the

[71]On these events, see Barry Burton, "The Cultural Revolution's Ultraleft
Conspiracy: The 'May 16 Group'," *Asian Survey*, vol. 11, no. 11 (November
1971), pp. 1029–53.

slogan initially had widespread support particularly from the Cultural Revolution Group. The anti-PLA campaign peaked during the Cultural Revolution's most threatening military confrontation in Wuhan in July–August 1967.[72] In the aftermath of the Wuhan incident, however, a reaction set in. The top leadership retreated from the "drag out a handful" theme and laid the blame on the "May 16 Group," now identified as an "ultraleft conspiracy" aimed at Zhou Enlai as well as military figures. Purged as core elements of "May 16" were Wang Li, Qi Benyu (Ch'i Pen-yü), Guan Feng (Kuan Feng) Mu Xin (Mu Hsin), Zhao Yiya (Chao I-ya) and Lin Jie (Lin Chieh) — all members of the Cultural Revolution Group and the leading writers and propagandists of the early stages of the campaign. Although none of the radical faction's most prominent members was implicated at the time, the "May 16" purge marked a sharp decline of its influence within the Maoist coalition. Moreover, the "May 16" incident was to surface again in elite conflict after the Cultural Revolution.

Factional Conflict in the 1970s. Elite conflict in the 1970s combined elements of both earlier periods. Leaders tried in the main to contain conflict, to avoid open charges and full-scale mass mobilization in their struggles, and to keep purges secret until after the event; the two key purges, of Lin Biao and the Gang, brought mass criticism campaigns only after the victors had acted against their targets. On the other hand, factional groupings made use of organizational bases, communications media and popular activities — especially demonstrations and the writing of *dazibao* — in a way that belied any idea of elite consensus. Two- line struggle was at best a loose conceptuali-

---

[72]Thomas W. Robinson, "The Wuhan Incident: Local Strife and Provincial Rebellion During the Cultural Revolution," *China Quarterly*, no. 47 (July–Sept. 1971), pp. 413– 38. The Wuhan incident was a complicated affair, but it centered on the fact that Chen Zaidao (Ch'en Tsai-tao), Commander of the Wuhan Military Region, was backing a rebel federation labeled "conservative" by Peking rather than the opposing Red Guard and rebel organizations that Peking deemed "correct." When Xie Fuzhi (Hsieh Fu-chih) and Wang Li (sent by Peking to mediate the dispute) affirmed the central view, the Wuhan command and their "conservative" allies arrested the emissaries and took control of the city. Peking's dispatch of Zhou Enlai and loyal troops to the area reestablished its authority, but not without a very tense confrontation that involved some fighting between loyalist and regional forces.

zation of the resulting tensions. The Hua-Deng group claimed adherence to Mao's revolutionary line, initially branding Lin and the Gang as successors to Liu's rightist line; that was a political thrust requiring very agile argument, which later led to an "ultra-leftist" label for the Gang. Closer to the mark was the "radical-moderate" interpretation that the Gang was the successor to Cultural Revolution radicalism, with Zhou, Hua, and Deng successors to earlier revisionists. But the Gang was in some ways more Maoist than Mao and the "moderates" continued many policies associated with Mao. In other words, the radical- moderate cleavage of the 1970s was not identical to the Mao-Liu cleavage of the mid-1960s in either style or substance. Since discussion elsewhere in this book treats issues of the 1970s largely in terms of line struggle, the focus here is on key factional developments.

The Maoist coalition of radicals, Lin Biao and Zhou Enlai began to disintegrate shortly after the Ninth CCP Congress of 1969. Chen Boda, the highest-ranking radical, disappeared from view in August 1970; subsequent attacks on his "careerism" and on the "May 16 Group" indicated that his group was on the defensive for some of its campaign excesses.[73] Lin Biao fell shortly thereafter, accused of planning a coup against Mao.[74] The official version had Lin conspiring with Chen to seize power, planning the coup when his efforts were obstructed, and dying in an airplane crash in Mongolia, on September 13, 1971, when his attempt to assassinate Mao failed. Many observers doubted this story, but Lin had clearly split the coalition with his ambitions and probably his opposition to some policies favored by Mao and Zhou, such as rapprochement with the United States. The incident eliminated the Lin faction — five military members of the Politburo and several other CC and provincial figures fell with him — and led to a general decline of the administrative power acquired by the PLA during the Cultural Revolution.

By 1972 Zhou was the active governmental leader as Mao increasingly withdrew from public life. The next four years

[73] *Current Scene,* vol. 9, no. 11 (November 7, 1971), pp. 13–15; and Burton, op. cit.

[74] See the analysis and documents in Michael Y. M. Kau, *The Lin Piao Affair* (White Plains, N.Y.: International Arts and Sciences Press, 1975).

were full of tense debates as Zhou tried to institutionalize a new development program, while the radicals (now led by Jiang Qing, Zhang Chunqiao, Yao Wenyuan and their young Shanghai protégé Wang Hongwen) tried to weaken or dislodge him. Inhibited from overt attacks on the Gang by their close association with Mao, Zhou relied on his organizational base in the establishment, which he strengthened by sponsoring the rehabilitation of many experienced cadres purged in the Cultural Revolution.

The Gang engaged in more overt factional activities, capitalizing on their strongholds in the communications network, some universities and factories, and the Shanghai region. Through the media they urged militant struggle against the continuing threat of capitalist restoration, using several campaigns of the 1972–76 years as thinly veiled offensives against the moderates; particularly striking was their publication in Shanghai, beginning in September 1973, of a new theoretical journal titled *Xuexi yu Pipan* (*Hsüeh hsi yü P'i-p'an, Study and Criticism*) to carry more extreme attacks than those in the official CC publications in Peking, over which they also had considerable control.[75] They mobilized mass support to criticize industrial and educational cadres who were modifying Cultural Revolution reforms, giving national publicity to a few individuals willing to "go against the tide" with such criticism. Shanghai was a locale for organization of a model urban workers' militia that lent paramilitary support to their position.[76]

Zhou's death in January 1976 exposed the complexity and volatility of elite alignments.[77] The Gang struck quickly, with Mao's support, to open criticism of Deng Xiaoping (who had essentially taken over Zhou's duties during the premier's ill-

[75]Ting Wang, "Propaganda and Political Struggle: A Preliminary Case Study of *Hsüeh-hsi yü P'i-p'an,*" *Issues and Studies,* vol. 13, no. 6 (June 1977), pp. 1–14.

[76]James C. F. Wang, "The Urban Militia as a Political Instrument in the Power Contest in China in 1976," *Asian Survey,* vol. 18, no. 6 (June 1978), pp. 541–59.

[77]For detailed accounts of events of this period and of the complex factions and interests involved, see Jürgen Domes, "The 'Gang of Four' — and Hua Kuo-feng: Analysis of Political Events in 1975–76," *China Quarterly,* No. 71 (September 1977), pp. 473–497; and John Bryan Starr, "From the 10th Party Congress to the Premiership of Hua Kuo-feng: The Significance of the Colour of the Cat," Ibid., no. 67 (September 1976), pp. 457–88.

ness) and to block Deng's accession to the premiership. But others, possibly also including Mao, opposed radical claims to the post, resulting in a compromise choice of Hua Guofeng as acting premier. Growing tension in Peking climaxed with the Tiananmen Incident of April 5, in which popular protest against removal of memorial wreaths to Zhou from the great public square turned into an unruly demonstration of some one hundred thousand people, many expressing antiradical slogans and demands. Peking authorities finally broke up the demonstration late in the day, calling it a counterrevolutionary action staged by Deng's supporters. Politburo directives named Hua full premier, dismissed Deng from all his posts (but left him a party member), and defined his contradiction as "antagonistic."[78] Hua's position was not solid, however, despite profuse claims that he was Mao's personal choice. The Maoist umbrella now seemed to cover several actors (the Gang, Mao himself, Hua, and some military or security leaders), while the moderate spectrum included some cadres going along with Hua and others working for Deng's restoration. Great confusion marked the debates of the next several months, with Tiananmen-type incidents occuring in many provincial cities.

Hua's purge of the Gang soon after Mao's death in September 1976 rested on a broad coalition, with prominent support from the military-security apparatus, that necessarily included many who had taken different positions on events surrounding the Tiananmen Incident. Hua initially continued the criticism of Deng, but by the summer of 1977 he yielded to powerful pressures — publicized, like most conflicts of the 1970s, in both elite communications and popular *dazibao* — which favored Deng's second restoration as CCP Vice chairman and Vice premier of the government. For roughly a year, Hua and Deng maintained a working relationship, mediated by Ye Jianying as senior leader of the military cadres, in advancing the "four modernizations" policies. There were evident differences between them, however, with Deng less inclined to in-

---

[78]*PR*, no. 15 (April 9, 1976), pp. 3–7. See also the articles cited in note 77; and David S. Zweig, "The Peita Debate on Education and the Fall of Teng Hsiao-p'ing," *China Quarterly*, no. 73 (March 1978), pp. 140–59.

voke Maoist symbols and more emphatic about the need for economic, scientific, and technical revolution. [79]

Deng and his supporters became more aggressive in the latter part of 1978, pushing for further diminution of Mao's stature and demotion of several Politburo members associated with Deng's 1976 setback. In October this pressure brought dismissal of Wu De (Wu Teh) who, as mayor of Peking, had led the suppression of the Tiananmen demonstration and subsequent criticism of Deng. Other Politburo targets of pro-Deng *dazibao* were Chen Xilian (Ch'en Hsi-lien), commander of the Peking military region, Ji Dengkuei (Chi Teng-K'uei), commissar of the Peking region, and Wang Dongxing (Wang Tung-hsing), member of the Politburo Standing Committee and head of the security establishment. Since removal of these men would strip Hua of much of his Politburo support, the wall poster campaign suggested that Deng might be seeking Hua's positions for himself. Deng's supporters were increasingly open, too, in their insistence that the classification of the Tiananmen Incident as counterrevolutionary be reversed[80] and that its suppression be investigated, and they openly repudiated the Cultural Revolution. In attacking the 1965 article by Yao Wenyuan that led off the great campaign, they were very close to a repudiation of Mao's entire post-1965 career. These themes were also very threatening to Hua, whose own position rested very heavily on Mao's endorsement and the Tiananmen affair. The news reports on all these posters, articles, events, and rumored events included some references to physical violence in mass debates over the issues.

The Third Plenum of the Eleventh CC, held in December 1978, confirmed Deng's political ascendancy.[81] In addition to endorsing many demands associated with him — reversal of the Tiananmen verdict, continued rehabilitation of veteran cadres, and stronger criticism of the Cultural Revolution —

[79]See Kenneth Lieberthal, "The Politics of Modernization in the PRC," *Problems of Communism,* vol. 27, no. 3 (May-June 1978), pp. 1–17.

[80]See *PR,* nos. 47, 48 (November 24, December 1, 1978) for a new version of the incident, defining it as "completely revolutionary action."

[81]See "Communique of the Third Plenary Session of the 11th Central Committee of the Communist Party of China," *PR,* no. 52 (December 29, 1978), pp. 6–16.

the Plenum added several of Deng's supporters to the Politburo and to other high state and party posts. But there was
compromise, too, as Hua retained his leading positions and
considerable Politburo support. The general line of the new
period remained intact, suggesting consensus on the four
modernizations and on a desire to contain factional conflict.
The spread of wall posters and public debate that accompanied Deng's advance in the winter of 1978–1979 was sharply
curtailed in March 1979. Despite this evidence of efforts to
keep factionalism below the levels of 1966–1976, the potential
for future elite conflict remained high. The leadership faced
agonizing choices in its allocation of scarce resources for the
modernization drive; the Third Plenum began the process,
made public in early 1979, of reassessing and in some cases
cutting back the ambitious economic goals announced at the
Fifth NPC. Some elite instability was inevitable, given the advanced age of most Politburo members, and the long range
effects of the Maoist period on younger cadres' political orientations remained unclear. Adding to the uncertainty was the
role of popular participation in factional combat, a phenomenon present to some extent throughout the post-1965 period.
While much of this participation was solicited and even manipulated by elites, it also had elements of spontaneity that suggest mass support may be an unpredictable but significant
factor in the resolution of future elite conflicts.

CHAPTER VII

The Governmental Process

THE CHINESE GOVERNMENTAL PROCESS, through which authoritative decisions are translated into action, involves all the institutions discussed in earlier chapters. This chapter identifies several principles and problems that are prominent in the process without attempting to explore them in detail;[1] it is more in the nature of an essay, trying to bring together themes and material that have, for the most part, been introduced earlier. We begin with an overview of the governmental process and then turn to salient aspects of decision making, administration, the enforcement and adjudication of rules, and external influences on the process.

OVERVIEW OF THE PROCESS

Party leadership and mass line are the dominant principles of the Chinese governmental process. Although not inherently in conflict, they tend in practice to produce contradictory impulses that account for much of the complexity and instability of Chinese politics. The struggle to maintain a working balance between them has been perhaps the most persistent problem of the post-1949 government.

---

[1]The most thorough analyses of governmental institutions and processes for the pre-Cultural Revolution period are A. Doak Barnett, *Cadres, Bureaucracy and Political Power in Communist China* (New York: Columbia University Press, 1967); and Franz Schurmann, *Ideology and Organization in Communist China,* 2nd ed. enl. (Berkeley: University of California Press, 1968). Political upheavals and data limitations have frustrated comparable work on post-1966 administration.

Party Leadership. The principle of party leadership has a decisive impact on the organization and operation of formal government. It requires, above all, that authoritative leadership at the center be in the hands of the CCP elite. It thus ensures at least a minimal degree of ideological conformity and organizational continuity at the core of the political process. Elites may differ in their interpretation of the ideology, and the leading organization may undergo changes in composition and style; but there is no possibility, short of an overthrow of the system, that national elites will be chosen except through internal party processes or that any other political organization will capture control of the government.

The CCP itself is a centralized organization whose internal processes are essentially closed to and largely concealed from outsiders. Ordinary citizens may influence initial decisions on recruitment into the organization but from that point on have no significant participatory roles in CCP decisions. Even during the Cultural Revolution, when activists outside the party challenged some of its policies, procedures, and personnel, it was the surviving organizational leadership that made final decisions on the reconstitution of its membership and structure. Important meetings of the organization are closed affairs, frequently unannounced and unreported, their publicized results limited to those that the leadership wishes to disclose. Provisions for internal party democracy may encourage open discussion at meetings and result in infrequent, formalized elections of hierarchies of committees, but lower levels of the organization have no real control over higher levels; it is higher-level committees and organs, culminating in the Politburo, that can prescribe and overrule the actions of lower committees.

The Eleventh Party Constitution, like its predecessors, indicates that party leadership should apply throughout society. That is, all CCP committees and branches are to play a leading role at their respective levels, a role that all nonparty organizations are instructed to accept. In practice, the extent to which "leadership" constitutes direct control of governmental processes varies at different levels. At the center, the party elite monopolizes decision-making power and the controlling positions in state, party, and military bureaucracies that implement its decisions. At intermediate levels, the proportion of party members in leading positions is sufficient to ensure CCP dominance of governmental organs. At the basic level, party members may or may not constitute majorities on revolutionary committees; their role becomes that of a "leading core" which must realize CCP policy through persuasive cooperation with nonparty cadres and committee members. Within the smallest primary units, the CCP may have little representation. The extent of party leadership has also varied significantly over time, being most complete during the Great Leap and weakest during 1966–1968, and it sometimes differs among comparable administrative units in different geographic areas.

These variations notwithstanding, the primary locus of decision making in the Chinese system is the CCP, which establishes policy on the basis of alternatives and demands made known to it. At higher levels, administrative acceptance of party decisions is virtually automatic due to overlapping roles. At lower levels, where CCP members may not dominate governmental organs numerically, the members' role as a leadership core and the power of higher party-controlled bodies are normally sufficient to ensure compliance with CCP decisions. In general, then, the decision-making structure is a narrow one based on party committees acting in closed session. There is no open legislative process and relatively little issuance of public laws. Decisions tend to take the form of generalized statements on policy or doctrine, or emerge as administrative directives and regulations.[2]

The Mass Line. As noted at the outset of Chapter VI, Mao conceptualized the policy process as a dynamic pattern of reciprocating communication between leaders and followers. Despite the reluctance of some elites to practice the Maoist style of policy making,[3] the CCP has accepted the mass line as a cardinal point of its doctrine. In Mao's formulation, it assigns

[2]There is nonetheless great variety and subtlety in the directives and other communications that move through the Chinese bureaucracy; see Kenneth Lieberthal, *Central Documents and Politburo Politics in China* (Ann Arbor: University of Michigan, Center for Chinese Studies, 1978), esp. pp. 5–19; and Michel Oksenberg, "Methods of Communication Within the Chinese Bureaucracy," *China Quarterly,* no. 57 (January–March 1974), pp. 1–39.

[3]For an analysis of the differences between Mao and Liu Shaoqi on the policy-making process, see Harry Harding, Jr., "Maoist Theories of Policy-Making and Organization," in Thomas W. Robinson, ed., *The Cultural Revolution in China* (Berkeley: University of California Press, 1971), pp. 113–64.

the masses a continuous role in presenting their ideas to the party and in carrying out decisions rendered from above; the masses are to initiate as well as implement policy. Even in ideal form, the principle reserves for the party decision-making power and the right to distinguish between "correct" and "incorrect" ideas. Moreover, PRC institutions provide few opportunities, except within primary units, for popular influence on political decisions. But the mass line has a significant broadening effect on the postdecisional process, which leaves room for considerable local initiative, relies on popular action in the implementation of policy, and provides opportunities for feedback on cadre performance and policy effectiveness.

The mass line's influence on the policy process is closely related to and reinforced by the CCP's willingness to decentralize management responsibilities in many areas. Decentralization does not necessarily broaden the popular role in administration, nor is it always justified by the mass line concept. Management is not democratized simply by acquiring more powers from higher levels; and the transfer of powers from, say, a central ministry to a provincial or municipal department has little to do with either "coming from the masses" or "going to the masses." Decentralization is a political and administrative issue that merits discussion in its own right (a point to which we will return later in this chapter). Nonetheless, when decentralization extends to primary units which are organized for member participation, encouraging them to embark on projects of their own and to assist in the operation of schools, health facilities, and other social services, it provides the institutional opportunity for practice of the mass line's basic tenet: that the people must accept party policies as their own and demonstrate this in political action. There is, at least in Mao's view of decentralization, a direct linkage between the transferral of responsibilities to the lowest feasible level and the mass line's emphasis on direct popular action rather than bureaucratic administration.

The Mass Movement. Decentralization supports the mass line, but the mass movement is its most concrete manifestation. Major initiatives in Chinese politics do not always take the form of mass movements. For example, foreign policy shifts of the utmost importance, such as the Sino-Soviet conflict and the rapprochement with the United States, and most elite conflicts have been handled guardedly until after the die was cast. On many domestic problems, however, Chinese leaders have turned to the mass movement as a means of informing the population about policy objectives, of soliciting broad-based acceptance of the policy, and of mobilizing local units for action on central plans. As these movements have unfolded, the structures activated have moved in an ever-widening progression from party and state organs, through the communications media and experimental projects, and on into basic-level organizations, meetings, rallies, and discussion groups.

One of the consequences of this frequent reliance on mass movements has been irregularity in the pace and results of policy implementation. Local areas have varied in the speed with which they have carried out their preliminary organizing and testing as well as their extension of the campaign on a general scale. Different models have sometimes appeared in the course of a campaign, producing discrepancies between the results of its earlier and later stages. A policy applied through a mass movement simply does not follow a precise timetable or lend itself to a detailed set of regulations of uniform applicability. National elites may set target dates for completion of campaign stages, but they cannot be sure that targets will be met; they may establish guidelines for expected results, but they cannot be sure that a process relying so heavily on local performance will produce uniform results. Under these circumstances, it becomes difficult to say precisely what a policy is, when it has gone into effect, and what its operative consequences are. These answers may be clear only when the campaign is over. One has only to look at the general outlines of land reform, agricultural collectivization and communization, and the Cultural Revolution to recognize that the governmental process in China has a highly fluid and open-ended quality that is incompatible with a legalistic style of administration.

Experimentalism in Decisions. How can we reconcile the principle of party leadership with the flexibility that characterizes policy implementation? Part of the answer lies in a strong element of experimentalism in the Chinese elite's view of the policy process. Although the government issues some legalistic rules, implying implementation at a certain point in time with procedures to enforce compliance, its decisions on many important issues have a tentative and experimental quality. They are cast in the form of general statements, indicating models to be followed or goals to be attained but not specifying exact procedures, forms, and relationships. The meaning of such a decision emerges only in practice as lower levels carry out their preliminary work and begin to develop concrete responses to the tasks demanded of them. In the midst of this process, higher levels will begin to review and investigate the early results. On the basis of these reports, central organs may accelerate or decelerate the process, publicize new models, or even issue new directives that alter the initial thrust of the policy. Party elites seem to regard the attendant shifts and variations as healthy or at least necessary for the development of viable policies. It is their way of practicing the mass line, of testing mass consciousness and "objective reality," and of refining their views through practical experience.

Experimentalism in policy making does not necessarily weaken party leadership. It reduces the specificity and permanence of central decisions and increases the responsibilities of lower-level committees, but neither of these outcomes implies an abdication of the organization's leading role. It raises the possibility of deviation from central wishes, but only in the Cultural Revolution — and then only with the Maoists' initial blessing — did local actions take the form of outright defiance of CCP organizational authority. Probably the most important consequence of a reliance on mass movements and experimentalism is a tendency to blur the distinction between state and party organization. By attaching so much importance to the actions of lower levels, it leads the party to strengthen its leadership over local government. In its extreme form, as during the Great Leap, the phenomenon of party as government may mean the virtual displacement of state administration.

We turn now to a closer look at some of the problems suggested by these introductory comments. A section on decision making examines the central institutional framework, the role of Mao, and some enduring questions about the effectiveness of the process. Bureaucracy, political controls over it, and decentralization are discussed under the rubric of administration. The section on rule enforcement and adjudication deals with the formal legal system, coercion and voluntarism, and mechanisms of social control. A concluding section discusses briefly the importance of external influences on the governmental process.

DECISION MAKING

Institutional Considerations. Supreme decision-making power resides in the CCP Politburo and its Standing Committee. Politburo members are the core leadership of all major CCP meetings, and there is no regular mechanism by which other organs can overrule the Politburo's decisions. The decline of Politburo authority in the early part of the Cultural Revolution was made possible by a deep internal split within the body, not by an assertion of external control over it. Nonetheless, the Politburo does not monopolize decision making in the sense of excluding other elites and groupings from participation in the process. It is the authoritative locus of policy decisions; but if we look on decisions as inseparable from the policy-making process that accompanies them, then it is clear that the Politburo does not act alone. The history of the PRC indicates that top elites have regularly convened a great variety of larger and more representative meetings to assist in the formulation of national policies.[4]

The Central Committee, contrary to what one might expect, has not been a particularly important part of this expanded policy-making process. The CC was most active in 1956 to 1962 when it met in ten plenums; even so, these meetings were relatively brief and usually announced policies thrashed out in less formal gatherings preceding the plenums. The Eighth CC met only twice more after its Tenth Plenum of September 1962 before it was succeeded by the Ninth CC elected in 1969. The Ninth CC had only two plenums in its 1969 to 1973 span, the Tenth CC only three in its 1973 to 1977 tenure. The CC,

[4]Kenneth Lieberthal, *A Research Guide to Central Party and Government Meetings in China, 1949–1975* (White Plains: International Arts and Sciences Press, 1976).

then, has not been a regular instrument of policy making but rather a forum for ratifying and publicizing decisions reached elsewhere.

The substantive policy-making meetings have been diverse, ranging from slightly enlarged Politburo meetings; through middle-range gatherings of selected party, state, PLA and provincial elites; and including some conferences of several thousand participants, with even low-level cadres in attendance. The most significant conferences have been those of Politburo members with selected leaders of various functional and geographic hierarchies. Before 1966, there were several variations on these conferences. One was the "central work conference," common in the 1960s, that convened around a hundred people representing the Politburo and its administrative departments, the State Council, regional party organs, and the PLA. Another was the Supreme State Conference, a loose governmental advisory body authorized by the 1954 state constitution, that both Mao and Liu used in their capacity as chairman of the government. As party chairman, Mao also convened several meetings of provincial party secretaries, or mixed groups of central and provincial party elites. The Cultural Revolution and its factionalized aftermath upset this pattern of informal but somewhat institutionalized working conferences. Of 298 identified meetings of central party and state organs held between 1949 and 1975, 271 took place before August 1966, with the remaining 27 stretched out between August 1966 and January 1975.[5] While some of the difference in frequency of identified meetings may be due to nonreporting in the 1966 to 1975 period, it seems fair to conclude that the latter period saw a decline in the Politburo's convocation of consultative conferences.

The secrecy referred to above is an important aspect of the policy-making process. Only about 10 percent of the 298 meetings in question — and only 1–2 percent if CC plenums and party congresses are excluded — were given substantial coverage in Chinese media when they took place.[6] In general, both the format and substance of key policy meetings remain closed to public view until well after the event, if indeed they

[5]Ibid.
[6]Ibid., p. 7.

are ever announced. Finally, we should note that the informal and even ad hoc convocation of diversified conferences for policy debate and formulation has mixed implications for decision-making effectiveness. It injects far more variety, deliberation, and political give-and-take into the process than the formal structure shows. Precisely because it is irregular and informal, however, it may still leave information gaps, be manipulated by elites who want to exclude other positions. or succumb to the paralyzing effects of factional struggle within the Politburo.[7]

The Role of Mao. Mao Zedong was the central figure in the policy making process for most of PRC history. That fact alone justifies reflection on his influence, which has clearly posed continuing problems for his successors. Mao's roles between 1949 and 1966 were multiple, including initiating, deciding, and legitimating many of the most important policies adopted by the CCP. As initiator, he was the most vigorous and forceful advocate of new measures, presenting to his colleagues proposals that forced the decision-making process into action. His role as initiator included a willingness to promote his views before wider audiences — such as the provincial secretaries in the mid-1950s or the general public in the Cultural Revolution — thereby adding political pressure to the intrinsic force of his views. As decision maker, he was first among equals within the small group that bore ultimate responsibility for the direction of national affairs; more than any other individual, he was able to swing the judgment of his colleagues toward the decisions he favored. As legitimator, he served as a symbol of both elite and national unity, the figure whose support for a policy placed on it the stamp of authoritative approval.

Underlying these roles was a tremendous reservoir of personal ability, power, and prestige. Whatever his limitations, Mao displayed exceptional political capacities. His knowledge of personalities and issues, his self-confidence and determination, his persuasive abilities, and his sensitivity to both tactical and strategic maneuver made him a formidable politician. As

---

[7]Ibid., pp. 10–13, and Lieberthal, *Central Documents,* pp. 79–82.

party chairman he occupied a position that gave him ample power to influence the procedural and institutional context of elite politics. Above all, Mao held a uniquely prestigious place in contemporary politics. His personal identification with the success of the revolution and the guidance of postrevolutionary construction made him virtually invulnerable to removal. His policies were criticized, resisted, or altered at times, but direct challenges to his leadership were doomed to failure. How far Peng Dehuai, Liu Shaoqi and Lin Biao truly wanted to go or might have gone in their opposition to Mao may never be known. What is clear is that Mao's definition of the conflict as a choice between him and his antagonist brought a reaffirmation of his leadership.

Although Mao had a great influence on the policy-making process, he never shaped it wholly to his wishes. His overall impact was a function of serval variables, the most important of which seem to have been his own assertiveness, his relationship with his senior colleagues, the capacity of the party center to control the governmental structure, and the capacity of the system generally to realize centrally determined objectives.[8] The first two are discussed more thoroughly below, the basic point being that Mao was erratic in exercising his leadership potential, owing to his changing perceptions of political priorities and, perhaps, to variations in his health and vigor; and that his authority among his senior colleagues was much more fluid than his relatively constant popular prestige would indicate. The latter two points are also discussed in subsequent sections but require some comment here.

The CCP elite's monopoly of central decision making does not translate into a comparable monopoly of policy implementation; that is, the Politburo's power vis-à-vis the formulation of national goals and policies presents a misleading image of its control over the governmental structure. One reason for this is that the central government itself is a structure of con-

---

[8]This discussion draws liberally on Michel C. Oksenberg, "Policy Making Under Mao, 1949–68: An Overview," in John M. H. Lindbeck, ed., *China: Management of a Revolutionary Society* (Seattle: University of Washington Press, 1971), esp. pp. 80–88. See also Parris H. Chang, "Research Notes on the Changing Loci of Decision in the Chinese Communist Party," *China Quarterly*, no. 44 (October–December 1970), pp. 169–94.

siderable differentiation and complexity. Diverse interests are represented initially in Politburo decisions, through the involvement of provincial party secretaries, vice premiers of the functional sectors of the State Council, and directors of CC departments. These are elites who themselves head major bureaucratic structures, replete with their own conflicts and interests and fully capable of defending their positions. Moreover, it is these units that develop the actual targets and directives which represent the central will. Feedback and bargaining are unavoidable features of the process, if not in the formal decision then at least in the drafting of implemental rules.[9]

Once central decisions have been cast as central directives in a process already somewhat removed from the collective wisdom of the Politburo, the influence of decentralization and the mass line comes into play. Lower units may be permitted to draft their own rules or at least to interpret central directives flexibly with reference to their own circumstances, with much of the ultimate meaning of governmental outputs left to the actions of basic-level institutions. The actual capacity of central elites to control governmental performance was probably at its peak in the 1955–1958 period but declined thereafter. Reserving further commentary on decentralization, we simply note here that neither Mao nor any other central leader has been able to control consistently and thoroughly the substance of governmental output.

Perhaps the most fundamental restraint on Mao's and other elites' policy-making power has been the system's finite resources and capacities. Vagaries of weather, harvest, and popular morale, and the necessity for making hard choices among competing claims on scarce resources, have intruded constantly on the formulation of national goals. At times, as during the Great Leap, elite decisions have seemingly defied these limitations, but the realities of system capabilities have always been close at hand, forcing compromise and modification on the predispositions of the leadership.

When these variables are taken into account, the relativity

[9]On the way in which the central bureaucracy and its functional sectors may influence the policy process, see Barnett, op. cit., pp. 6–7, 71–84, 431–32.

and changeability of Mao's influence over the policy process become clearer. Mao alluded to this frequently in reference to policies that he did or did not approve and to his general command of governmental operations. His most revealing comment was at a Central Work Conference in October 1966, when he stated that he had approved division of the leadership into a first and second front, with himself in the second front and hence removed from supervision of the daily work of the government.[10] Mao identified the duration of the two fronts as seventeen years, presumably from 1949 to the Eleventh Plenum of August 1966. The precision of this reference is questionable, since Mao's second-front status was not rigorously observed throughout the 1949–1966 period; the years between 1959 and 1965 seem to mark his clearest performance of a second-line role. Nonetheless, the statement affirms Mao's willingness to restrict the scope of his political involvement, a willingness based, he said, on a desire to cultivate other leaders and to avoid the Stalin pattern of rule.[11]

More concretely, Mao's involvement in the 1949–1958 period was quite flexible. On the one hand, his political visibility was relatively low. He was absent from some key conferences,[12] let Liu and Deng take the lead at the Eighth National Congress of the CCP in 1956, and accepted the absence of reference to himself in the 1956 constitution. He was quite active, however, in the initiation and promotion of three crucial policies: accelerated collectivization in 1955; the "hundred flowers" episode of 1957; and the adoption of rectification, decentralization, and Great Leap policies in 1957–1958. In all three cases, Mao was able to secure favorable decisions and prompt governmental implementation. The mix of the variables discussed above permitted Mao to act with considerable freedom and effectiveness without assuming a dictatorial role.

[10]"Selections from Chairman Mao," *Translations on Communist China,* no. 90, JPRS-49826 (Feb. 12, 1970), pp. 13–15.

[11]Ibid., p. 13. In another reference, Mao also cited his health as a reason for the two fronts; ibid., p. 10.

[12]For example, Mao was absent from the Fourth Plenum of the Seventh CC in February 1954, which heard Politburo accusations against Gao Gang and Rao Shushi, and from a September 1957 conference that preceded and prepared for the Third Plenum of the Eighth CC; Chang, op. cit., pp. 183, 186.

However, as the Leap ran into difficulties, the mix shifted against Mao. In adopting decentralization and the Great Leap approach, the central leadership had stimulated local initiative and the mass movement but had also relinquished some of its control over governmental performance; its decisions became more controversial, less informed of local conditions, and more difficult to implement. Resource limitations, such as lowered output and popular morale, began to circumscribe the options open to decision makers. Mao stepped down as chairman of the PRC, accepted some criticism of the Leap and his role in promoting it, and threatened to form a new revolutionary movement if his colleagues repudiated him.[13] Subsequently, Mao's policy-making influence fell to its lowest ebb. Although his colleagues bolstered his public image with campaigns against the "rightists" of 1959 and in support of the wisdom of his "thought," their respect for his counsel seems to have declined. The veiled but sharp criticism of Mao that appeared in Peking publications in 1961–1962 was an accurate indication of his reduced authority at the center.[14] Retrenchment policies, oriented to restoration of governmental controls and accommodation of overstrained resources, left Mao little room for maneuver or initiative. When he began to assert his views again at the Tenth Plenum of September 1962, he found state and party bureaucracies much more resistant to compliance with his policies than in the 1950s.

Mao broke through in the Cultural Revolution, ending the two fronts and assuming undisputed leadership in central decision making. Once the Liu-Deng revisionists were purged, he seemed to hold more unqualified support from participants in the political process at all levels than ever before. Both the

[13]See Mao's speech at the Eighth (Lushan) Plenum in July 1959, in *The Case of P'eng Teh-huai, 1959–1968* (Hong Kong: Union Research Institute, 1968), pp. 15–30.

[14]I refer primarily to the writings of Wu Han ("The Dismissal of Hai Jui" and "Hai Jui Scolds the Emperor"), Deng Tuo (Teng T'o) ("Evening Talks at Yenshan"), and Wu, Deng, and Liao Mo-sha ("Notes from a Three Family Village"). These literary efforts by prominent Peking officials became the initial target of the Maoists in the late 1965–early 1966 beginnings of the Cultural Revolution. For a discussion of these writings and a survey of literary dissent in 1961–1962, see Merle Goldman, "The Unique 'Blooming and Contending' of 1961–62," *China Quarterly*, no. 37 (January–March 1969), pp. 54–83.

tone and substance of ensuing policy formulations reflected his ideas. But Mao's personal dominance at the center did not translate easily into governmental action. Over four years passed (January 1967 to August 1971) before revolutionary committees and new provincial party committees were established. The formalities of the state structure remained unsettled, despite repeated allusions to a forthcoming National People's Congress and the adoption of a new draft state constitution at the Second Plenum in August–September 1970. Efforts to reopen schools and establish Maoist educational reforms began as early as 1967 but had little visible effect for several years thereafter. The contrast with the 1950s, when central decision brought relatively prompt and thorough compliance throughout the country, was striking.

In any case, by the early 1970s Mao had entered the personal and political decline leading to his death. The "cult of Mao" receded as he moved into the background, leaving administrative leadership to Zhou Enlai and, as Zhou's health also failed, to the rehabilitated Deng Xiaoping. Deng's rapid rise in 1973–1975 was a prime indicator of Mao's declining capacity to control the process, as was his inability to resolve the debilitating factional conflict of this period. Yet his symbolic authority as legitimator held firm, and his support was crucial for some of the key decisions of his last years, such as rapprochement with the United States and the second purge of Deng in 1976. The power of Mao's symbolic authority was evident after his death, as Hua and Deng used it to legitimize the "four modernizations." It was also a source of conflict, however, since Hua used it to bolster his leadership, whereas Deng seemed intent on repudiating Mao's last decade — and necessarily reducing Mao's overall stature in the process — to serve Deng's personal and policy goals. It may be a long time before Chinese elites resolve the question of how to deal with Mao's substantive and symbolic legacy.

Problems of Decision Making. One conclusion following from this discussion is that Chinese decision making has involved far more than Mao Zedong's personal wishes or style. There is an understandable tendency to exaggerate Mao's impact on the system, to move from personality attributions to systemic characteristics. The fact that Mao the man stood out in bold relief, in contrast to the often murky workings of the system, encourages this tendency. But whatever the precise extent of Mao's influence, before and after his death,[15] it has been only one of many ingredients in Chinese decision making, and it would not have assumed the proportions it did without support from other sources. There are larger and more enduring questions that are of equal importance.

One concerns the effects of ideological commitments. It is clear that these commitments have not excluded elite consideration of alternative courses of action. Intraparty debate has been varied and vigorous, leading to policy shifts even on issues of high ideological sensitivity; witness, for example, the ebb and flow of degrees of agricultural collectivization, variations on central economic control, the fundamental alteration of relations with the Soviet Union and the United States, and the remarkable changes since 1976 with respect to Cultural Revolution policies and Mao's legacy. Chinese socialism places limits on what Chinese elites will consider, but practice demonstrates that these limits are not very restrictive.

The real problem of ideology is not rigidity, or the arbitrary rejection of alternative proposals, but rather the political hazards that follow from a system which is open to elite conflict but tends to label one set of competing demands as an "antagonistic" contradiction. Although the peak periods of Mao's dominance produced an unhealthy sycophancy among some of his supporters, the larger pattern is one of vigorous policy debate, with the decision-making process a high-risk enterprise for participants. Since the relative consensus of the 1950s, there has been a very high rate of turnover among Chinese top elites; indeed, the impact of dismissal or demotion has been so great that the Chinese bureaucracy has suffered at times from shortages of senior administrators and has had to devise ways for handling the special bureaucratic

---

[15]The issue is ably examined, from many points of view, in the essays in Dick Wilson, ed., *Mao Tse-tung in the Scales of History* (Cambridge: Cambridge University Press, 1977).

and political problem of rehabilitation and "reversal of verdicts."[16] As one analyst has observed, there is a possible inconsistency in some Western conceptualizations of Communist systems, in that the ideology is charged simultaneously with producing rigidity, sterility, and ossification among elites, and also great trauma and instability in the inevitable "succession crisis."[17] In the case of China, the problem lies more on the side of instability than ossification, and it is not simply a question of succession. Both with Mao and without, Chinese decision making has shown vigor and flexibility, coupled with a tendency to impose severe sanctions — at times damaging the system's effectiveness — on the backers of defeated alternatives.

A second question is whether the "red-expert" problem, with the prevailing Maoist insistence on "politics in command," has deprived decision makers of expert advice. The CCP's basic policy toward intellectuals and technical specialists has been to restrict their status and life-style, and to deny that their expertise is any claim to political authority. This approach has not precluded utilization of their services and advice. Most senior CCP decision makers have had ample access to staff experts, in addition to personal experience in one or more of the specialized administrative hierarchies.[18] On the other hand, the top elite has probably underutilized the intellectual resources available to them, mainly because the "red-expert" issue has been so vulnerable to extreme interpretation. In both the Great Leap and the period after the Cultural Revolution, hostility toward experts encouraged some ill-conceived policy experiments or caused a decline in the quality of specialized training. The marked post-1976 reversals in this area indicate that Mao's successors think China's experts can and should be better utilized in the future. Yet the PRC's overall development record disproves the notion that

---

[16]Michel Oksenberg, "The Exit Pattern from Chinese Politics and its Implications," *China Quarterly,* no. 67 (September 1976), pp. 501–18.

[17]Valerie Bunce, "Elite Succession, Petrification and Policy Innovation in Communist Systems: An Empirical Assessment," *Comparative Political Studies,* vol. 9, no. 1 (April 1976), pp. 3–42.

[18]See Lieberthal, *Central Documents,* pp. 26–49, for description of the extensive consultation, including technical review, that goes into the drafting of central documents, and for case studies of the process.

its leaders have been ignorant of the technical dimensions of their decisions.

Finally, one wonders if the weakness of popular representation at higher levels and the absence of independent communications media lead to an "information gap," so that elites are poorly informed on how policies will be or have been received at the grass roots. This is a real danger, since decision makers rely for their information largely on bureaucratic hierarchies, and what reaches the top is a very indirect and selective representation of the grass roots situation; as in all bureaucracies, tendencies to report data acceptable to superiors or data enhancing the position of the reporter are strong. There were spectacular misjudgments, for example, about the consequences of the "hundred flowers" experiment, the Leap, and the mobilization of the Red Guards. But again, Chinese elites have shown their awareness of the problem and adopted compensatory mechanisms, particularly in their experimentalism and in various mass line techniques. In assessing the overall effectiveness of Chinese decision making, and acknowledging the existence of these enduring problems, we must also recognize the leadership's efforts to consider alternative policy sets, its responsiveness to problems emerging in the course of implementation, and its willingness to alter policies in the face of widespread dissatisfaction or resistance at lower levels.

ADMINISTRATION

Bureaucracy. The Chinese political system entrusts the application of its rules to a variety of structures, including state, party, and army bureaucracies and the communications systems that they control; the management organs of primary units; and a multitude of popular committees, organizations, and meetings that mobilize the population for direct action on governmental programs. The national bureaucracies dominate the administrative process that brings central decisions to the local level. They are complex hierarchies, containing both territorial and functional divisions, but they share a common subordination to the authority of the central CCP leadership. They are staffed by full-time career cadres, appointed and assigned through internal processes. Their performance, too, is directed and supervised largely from within by party members in leading positions and by higher levels of their organizations. Institutionally speaking, they have a high degree of autonomy from society, being organized as agents of central decision-making organs.

There are important qualifications in this picture, however, because the Chinese Communists have made serious efforts to restrain the exercise of bureaucratic power. Although they accept the necessity of centrally directed organizational hierarchies that will implement the CCP's monopoly of political power, they have tried to ensure bureaucracy's responsiveness to political controls and to keep its structure relatively simple and efficient. As a result, the history of bureaucracy in post-1949 China has been one of recurring tendencies to expand and institutionalize, matched by counterpressures to limit and modify its role.

Bureaucratic institutions were not prominent in the pre-1949 movement. Environmental factors inhibited the growth of large-scale territorial units or of functionally sophisticated governmental departments. The major exception to this rule came in Yanan in the early 1940s, when United Front policies, assumption of a more complete governmental role, and an influx of intellectuals encouraged bureaucratization. This tendency was resisted successfuly by the rectification, "crack troops and simple administration," and "to-the-village" campaigns of 1942–1944.[19] After 1949, pressures for bureaucratization became much more formidable. The implementation of socialist reforms throughout the country not only required a governmental structure significantly larger and more complex than any the CCP had previously known but also encouraged co-optation of many cadres who had not experienced the socializing effects of the revolutionary movement. The path was opened for a flow of more traditional bureaucratic influences into the new government. The initiation of the Soviet-style economic plan, with its centralization of power in the state ministries, brought the rapid growth of an administrative structure that was almost a direct antithesis of the CCP's earlier organizational model.

[19]Mark Selden, *The Yenan Way in Revolutionary China* (Cambridge, Mass.: Harvard University Press, 1971), pp. 188–229.

The mid-1950s probably marked the peak of bureaucratic power in post-1949 China, but the new structure was not yet highly institutionalized. It proved vulnerable to the growing reaction against it which culminated in the Great Leap Forward. For a few years, an antibureaucratic tide was in ascendancy, only to give way in the early 1960s to a reassertion of official authority and prerogatives. The governmental system of 1961–1965 was less centralized and, in terms of its actual control over society, probably less powerful than that of the mid-1950s. On the other hand, it was more highly institutionalized, and it seemed to be creating a new establishment that made routinized concessions to mass line principles but was increasingly the preserve of bureaucratic interests and specialized skill groups. Its capacity to deflect and then resist the early thrusts of the Cultural Revolution was evidence of its strength and autonomy, even though ultimately it disintegrated under the Maoist attack.

Actually, the Cultural Revolution did not eliminate bureaucracy but rather replaced some bureaucratic sectors with others. The old state and party organs held on to their power until the winter of 1966–1967. It was only in the "seizure of power" stage that the country entered a period in which no bureaucratic apparatus seemed capable of providing effective government. Before long, however, the PLA began to fill this gap by taking over the basic administrative functions. The Maoists regarded the PLA as more "revolutionary" than its predecessors, owing to Lin Biao's reforms of the early 1960s, and had encouraged it to expand its political role as early as 1963–1965.[20] But even though the PLA entered the political arena under Maoist auspices, it was still a bureaucratic organization which displayed little enthusiasm for sharing its administrative duties with the radical mass organizations; the provincial revolutionary committees whose formation it supervised were dominated by military figures and included many former cadres.[21] With the reconstruction of the CCP after 1969, military administration gradually began to give way to the reviving civilian bureaucracies.

[20]Ellis Joffe, "The Chinese Army Under Lin Piao: Prelude to Intervention," in Lindbeck, ed., op. cit., esp. pp. 353–66.

[21]Ellis Joffe, "The Chinese Army in the Cultural Revolution: The Politics of Intervention," *Current Scene,* vol. 8, no. 18 (Dec. 7, 1970), pp. 1–25.

As noted repeatedly, the years between 1969 and 1976 brought intense struggle between administrative priorities oriented toward stabilization and economic development, and radical pressures for continuing "revolutionization" of the system. The post-1976 leadership resolved this debate with a forthright assertion of administrative prerogatives, stressing the need for central planning and controls, for technically competent management, and for regulations and labor discipline to ensure attainment of production targets. One lesson to be drawn from the Cultural Revolution experiment, therefore, is that bureaucratic administration is a given feature of Chinese politics, one that cannot be sacrificed even for goals that might have higher rhetorical priority. But it is also important to recognize the Chinese efforts to curb "bureaucratism" if not bureaucracy, to control what are seen as the negative aspects of the institutions they cannot do without. These efforts have been most evident in two principles — politicization of bureaucracy and decentralization — which were advanced vigorously in the Maoist period and which continue to influence post-Mao administration in less forceful ways.

Politicization of Bureaucracy. The Chinese Communists' mistrust of bureaucracy involves two basic principles. One views bureaucracy in basically negative terms as a nonproductive superstructure that is divorced from the front line of political struggle; it seeks to reduce the scope of bureaucracy and to transfer administrative powers to the lowest feasible level. (We discuss this impulse in the next section under the ruburic of "decentralization.") The other accepts some degree of bureaucratization as inevitable and potentially even positive in its provision of correct models and leadership; it focuses on the politicization of bureaucracy to ensure its subordination to political leadership and its acceptance of a mass line style of behavior. Although discussed separately, these two principles blend together in practice. Both reflect the CCP's hostility toward bureaucratic elitism and conservatism, its appreciation of earlier experience with mass mobilization and decentralized government, and its search for administrative relationships that will promote the all-around development of Chinese society.

One of the crucial issues in the politicization of bureaucracy is the relationship between the CCP and the state structure. Party and state have never been separated sharply in terms of personnel, due to the high proportion of party members serving in state organs. The very first step in establishing CCP rule was the placement of its members in controlling positions in the government. Although a fair number of nonparty officials were retained in the early years, their proportional representation fell steadily. By the late 1950s, party-member domination of state organs was virtually complete. Nonetheless, the CCP insisted that the two hierarchies were functionally and organizationally distinct; the state was responsible for administration of policy, especially in the economic realm, whereas the party was responsible for political and ideological affairs. Initially at least, the CCP tried to observe the distinction, so that its organizational control did not necessarily follow the placement of party members in governmental positions.

From the early 1950s to the Cultural Revolution, the Chinese leadership addressed this problem in terms of a choice between "vertical rule" and "dual rule."[22] Both types of rule assumed the existence of two parallel organizational hierarchies: one a bureaucratized network of branch agencies of the central ministries extending downward through subnational governments, the other a less bureaucratized hierarchy of party committees at each administrative level. Under vertical rule, which prevailed during the early part of the FFYP, the functional departments of local government were responsible to corresponding departments at higher levels leading up to the appropriate ministry in Peking. This system maximized central ministerial control over administration and encouraged the development of specialized bureaus at lower levels; but it also inhibited coordination across departmental lines within governmental levels and made local departments resistant to supervision by local party committees. The alternative of dual rule, which was endorsed by the Eighth Party Congress of 1956, strengthened local control by making departments responsible to local committees as well as to their higher administrative counterparts.

[22]See detailed analysis in Schurmann, op. cit., esp. pp. 188–219.

Dual rule, which came into its own with the decentralization of 1957 and the ensuing Leap, greatly increased the involvement of party committees in state administration. Indeed, for a brief period in the late 1950s, the central ministries simply lost much of their former control over lower levels. Local decisions were made by party committees, which became the effective agencies of subnational government. The phenomenon of party as government threatened to obliterate the distinction between state and party. However, the state regained some of its authority in the retrenchment period, and an approximation of dual rule resumed. The adoption of dual rule was a decisive step in asserting the primacy of politics, through the medium of CCP committees throughout the bureaucracy. But though it was successful in politicizing bureaucracy, in the sense of giving the CCP broad supervisory powers over administration, it had the unforeseen side effect of bureaucratizing politics. That is, as CCP organs intervened in the daily work of government departments, they began to absorb some of the interests and concerns of those departments. Nominally the organizational and functional distinction between state and party remained, but in practice the two came closer together. The contrast between the antibureaucratic impulse of 1955–1958 and that of the Cultural Revolution is instructive. The former viewed the state as the prime base of bureaucratic evils and sought a solution through increased party penetration of administrative functions; the latter saw the CCP itself as a stronghold of bureaucratism and turned to nonparty elements for assistance in rectifying it.

Following the Cultural Revolution, the CCP experimented briefly with the principle of "unified leadership," combining administrative and political tasks in a single organ — the revolutionary committee — which relied on the leadership of party members within it.[23] Ultimately, however, the organizational distinction between administrative and party organs returned, and with it an approximation of dual rule. That is, administrators were responsible for meeting goals set from above in the bureaucratic hierarchy, but they also operated under the supervision of the party committee within their own level or unit.

[23]Harding, op. cit., pp. 144–145.

After 1976, top leaders began to emphasize managerial authority and efficiency, suggesting, too, that party cadres should have some technical competence or experience in the line of work they supervised.[24] The implied effect was to give administrative and managerial organs much more responsibility than they had held during the Maoist era, although the basic principle of political (party) control of bureaucracy was maintained.[25]

The other major aspect of politicization of bureaucracy has been pressure to "revolutionize" cadre work style, that is, to get cadres to internalize the Maoist ethic and eradicate all the evils associated with "bureaucratism" — aloofness, privilege, corruption, commandism, conservatism, careerism, and so forth. The techniques for applying this pressure, and the ebb and flow of political emphasis on it, have already been discussed. There can be little doubt that the message of "serve the people" has penetrated the Chinese bureaucracy, making it sensitive to the issues involved and the dangers of ignoring them. Yet there is probably no area of Chinese political life where the contradictions are stronger.

On the one hand, cadres work in highly bureaucratized settings subject to complicated regulations and controls, have fixed pay scales and ranks that make them a privileged stratum, and hold considerable power over citizens with little access to the inner workings of the system.[26] The tradition of bureaucratic rule and authoritarian social relationships still reinforces these features. Since Mao's death, cadre status and prerogatives have been strengthened. On the other hand are all the mass line techniques applied to cadres, the memories of campaign criticism and sanctions, and a citizenry encouraged to develop high expectations about cadre responsiveness to mass needs and criticism. Here, too, the post-Mao period strength-

[24]See Hua's speech at the National Conference on Finance and Trade, *PR*, no. 30 (July 28, 1978), pp. 6–15, and Deng's speech at the National Science Conference, *PR*, no. 12 (March 24, 1978), pp. 9–18.

[25]A good case study of the CCP's efforts to maintain both competent management and political control in industrial management, with frequent shifts among different combinations of managerial responsibility, party power, and worker participation, is Stephen Andors, *China's Industrial Revolution: Politics, Planning, and Management, 1949 to the Present* (New York: Pantheon, 1977).

[26]Barnett, op. cit., passim.

ened existing features by extoling the virtues of socialist legality, making public examples of cadre deviations, and tolerating
public debate about democratic controls over all officials. How
this tension will be resolved is impossible to say. Maoist checks
on cadres address widely recognized problems of bureaucratization, yet do not deny the necessity, and even the advantages,
of many principles of bureaucratic government.[27] The tension
inherent in this approach may be healthy, in keeping administrators on their toes, or it may produce harsher conflict, if the
principles involved appear to be compromised or violated.

Decentralization. The relationship between national and subnational administrative units is one of the most complex problems of the Chinese political system.[28] The system is highly
centralized in its formal allocation of political authority. Central organs may assign certain functions and powers to lower
levels but retain the authority to reclaim them or to intervene
in their implementation; decentralization does not guarantee
lower levels the right to exercise their powers permanently or
autonomously. Yet decentralization is a principle of real operational importance that seems to be well established. Despite
its theoretical subordination to the principle of centralism, it
has gradually emerged since the late 1950s as one of the PRC's
primary administrative characteristics.

The influences that have prompted decentralization are diverse. They include desires to restrict the power of central
bureaucracy and thereby to give local units enough political
space to develop their own internal resources. Underlying this
view is the conviction that creation of a new political culture
requires opportunities for local action that cannot be realized
under a highly centralized system. More pragmatic consider-

[27]For sensitive analysis of how Maoism does and does not depart from
classical Western theories of bureaucratization, see Martin King Whyte, "Bureaucracy and Modernization in China: The Maoist Critique," *American Sociological Review*, vol. 38, no. 2 (April 1973), pp. 149–63; and "Iron Law Versus
Mass Democracy: Weber, Michels, and the Maoist Vision," in James Chieh
Hsiung, ed., *The Logic of "Maoism": Critiques and Explication* (New York: Praeger,
1974), pp. 37–61.

[28]For general discussion, see Schurmann, op. cit., passim; and the contrasting views of Parris Chang and Victor Falkenhein in "Peking and the Provinces," *Problems of Communism*, vol. 21, no. 4 (July–August 1972), pp. 67–83.

ations include efforts to rationalize the economic system by encouraging diversification and regional growth, cutting transport and distribution costs, and reducing the red tape and expense of a centralized planning apparatus. The size of the country and its uneven economic development provide powerful arguments for experimentation with decentralization. Decentralization may be in part a response to pressure from subnational elites, or at least a product of bargaining between central and local authorities. As noted earlier, Mao mobilized provincial support for his advocacy of the Great Leap, and in recent years decentralization has drawn support from influence acquired by subnational governments during the Cultural Revolution. Questions of national security and defense also affect elite thinking on some aspects of decentralization, particularly economic diversification and the development of regional or local self-sufficiency.

Decentralization impulses have taken the form of bureaucratic simplification and administrative decentralization. The former is that recurring wish, found in most political systems, to reduce the size and complexity of governmental structure. Motivated by desires for economy and efficiency, and by an innate suspicion that bureaucracies are always overweight, it tries to eliminate excess staff and departments. The CCP embarked on its first simplification campaign as early as 1941, in the context of its Yanan rectification movements.[29] Pressures for a repeat performance were not long in coming after 1949. by 1956, Mao had proposed a two-thirds cut in party and government organizations to correct "structural obesity."[30] Although his goal was unrealistic, a substantial reduction of administrative personnel and some simplification of lower-level administrative units took place over the next two years.[31] However, the CCP's greatest assault on bureaucratic proliferation came with the Cultural Revolution. According to one report, the forty ministries, eleven commissions, and twenty-one special agencies of the 1965 State Council had been re-

[29]Selden, op. cit., pp. 212–16.
[30]"On the Ten Great Relationships," in Jeron Ch'en, ed., *Mao* (Englewood Cliffs, N.J.: Prentice-Hall, 1969), p. 77.
[31]Rensselaer W. Lee, III, "The *Hsia Fang* System: Marxism and Modernisation," *China Quarterly,* no. 28 (October–December 1966), pp. 43–46.

duced in 1972 to seventeen ministries, three commissions, and fifteen special agencies.[32] The 1969 party constitution indicated that central CCP organization would be much less complicated than in the past. Model revolutionary committees were also noteworthy for their simplicity of administrative structure and staff.[33] There can be little doubt that the governmental apparatus of 1972 was significantly smaller and less top-heavy than it had been in 1965. But bureaucratization then resumed, so that be the late 1970s the general size and complexity of administration was not greatly different from the pattern before the Cultural Revolution. Perhaps the most that can be said is that Chinese leaders are sensitive to the problem of bureaucratic proliferation and that they can be expected to mount recurring attacks on it.

Administrative decentralization refers to a reordering of responsibilities within the government in which powers as well as personnel are shifted to lower levels. CCP historical experience was mainly with decentralized modes of government, a pattern continued in the 1949–1954 administrative system which gave a major role to regional units. Rapid centralization accompanied the FFYP, but in late 1957 the CCP adopted a decentralization policy that remained in effect, albeit with many twists and turns, through the 1970s. The initial 1957 decisions shifted control over many industrial and commercial enterprises, as well as financial resources, from the central ministries to provincial authorities.[34] This action, combined with dual rule, resulted in a marked increase in the powers of provincial party committees. Subsequently, a reverse process occurred in the countryside, as control over agriculture was pushed upwards from the cooperatives to the rural communes. The Great Leap was marked, therefore, by a concentration of power in the middle (provincial and commune levels) at the expense of the center and basic production units.

A different pattern emerged as Leap policies yielded to retrenchment policies. Further decentralization took place at lower levels as the communes were reduced in size and as rural

---

[32] *Current Scene,* vol. 10, no. 7 (July 1972), p. 12.

[33] Harding, op. cit., pp. 153–54.

[34] The following discussion draws on Schurmann, op. cit., pp. 175–78, 195–210.

production teams and individual enterprises acquired more autonomy. At higher levels, provincial dominance lessened with renewed emphasis on central planning and the reestablishment of regional party bureaus to oversee provincial activities. On the eve of the Cultural Revolution, the Chinese administrative system was thus highly diffuse. The central ministries retained direct control over some enterprises — largely those of most importance for national defense and heavy industry — and responsibility for overall planning of the economy. Provincial and municipal authorities managed the bulk of nonagricultural economic activities, subject to coordination with central plans. However, basic-level units also operated a variety of small-scale enterprises, and agricultural management essentially was decentralized to production units within the communes. Throughout this system, individual production units had some leeway in managing their activities either through negotiation with higher planning authorities or through setting their own targets and distribution arrangements.[35]

The Cultural Revolution brought little formal chnage in this system, but there have been some important shifts in relationships and emphasis. The weakening of CCP organization and the preoccupation with resolution of political disputes apparently gave units at all levels greater room for maneuver in performance of their routine activities. Second, decentralization has taken on a broader political significance due to the expansion of mass participation in basic-level decisions; powers that initially devolved to local elites are now at least partially shared with more representative bodies. Finally, the objectives of local development, self-reliance, and self-sufficiency that have been implicit in all decentralization decisions have received greater emphasis since the Cultural Revolution. Localities seem to have greater incentive and latitude to diversify through small-scale industry and to promote agricultural modernization within their areas.[36]

[35]On pre-Cultural Revolution industrial organization and management, see Barry M. Richman, *Industrial Society in Communist China* (New York: Random House, 1969), esp. chaps. 8–9.

[36]See Dwight Perkins, et al., eds., *Rural Small-Scale Industry in the People's Republic of China* (Berkeley: University of California Press, 1977).

Decentralization is not an unmixed blessing. It increases the possibility of real local autonomy, of the emergence of "independent kingdoms" from which subnational elites can defy the authority of the center. In a country still conscious of the disintegrative tendencies of the recent past, this is a serious concern. The central government has thus far been able to maintain its authority, but it was shaky during the Cultural Revolution and might become so again in future crises of comparable magnitude. Decentralization also creates problems for national planning and collection of data. The PRC's failure since the late 1950s to articulate a detailed economic plan or publish comprehensive statistics is due in part to the fact that much of China's economic activity takes place outside the center's purview. Although this does not seem to be a serious limitation on economic development at the present stage, it may become more critical as development proceeds. Finally, decentralization may have placed significant limits on the central government's capacity to control China's economic performance and direction. Since a large proportion of state revenue is collected and distributed by subnational governments, and since military and defense-related expenditures constitute a large fixed claim on centrally controlled resources, the central government does not have much flexibility in its allocation of investment funds.[37]

Despite their sensitivity to these problems, Chinese elites apparently remain committed to their pattern of diffused administrative responsibilities. It has served as a check on bureaucratic expansionism, prepared the country for resistance to foreign attack, and compiled a creditable record of economic growth. Most significantly, perhaps, it has created an administrative system that is sensitive to the growth potential of localities and encourages them to maximize the use of their own resources. This aspect of decentralization, in combination with mass line methods of work, supports political mobilization and community involvement among the population.

[37]Audrey Donnithorne, *The Budget and the Plan in China* (Canberra: Australian National University press, 1972).

RULE ENFORCEMENT AND ADJUDICATION

The Formal Legal System. Examination of how the political system enforces and adjudicates its rules logically begins with the formal legal system. The institutions concerned are the courts, whose function is to try cases, render verdicts, and assign sentences; the procuracy, which investigates and prosecutes possible violations of law; public security or police organs; and the CCP, which as a matter of practice is deeply involved in the entire legal process. The structure and activities of these institutions, and the relationships among them, set the general tone of law enforcement in China. However, it is also important to note that the formal legal system plays a relatively modest role in the broader function of social control in the PRC. The CCP approach to law enforcement and adjudication is not highly "legalistic," in the sense of reliance on statutes and institutionalized procedures for their application and interpretation. Rather, the party approaches this problem with perspectives derived from its ideology and the Chinese legal tradition, which tend to weaken legal formalities and to shift legal functions away from the specialized structures officially designed to perform them.

The party has little sympathy, for example, for the idea of judicial independence. Although the 1954 constitution stated that the courts should be independent in their administration of justice, there was little in Chinese legal history or previous Communist experience to support this principle. By the late 1950s, judicial independence was virtually a dead letter as police made heavy inroads on judicial functions and the party cast its controlling influence over all three arms of the legal structure.[38] Moreover, the CCP views the legal system in general as an agent of state power and has provided few safeguards against its potential arbitrariness. Regulatory acts often emerge as administrative edicts, subject to change and interpretation by cadres; a comprehensive criminal code, proposed in the mid-1950s, was not adopted. The right to legal defense

[38]Jerome Cohen, "The Party and the Courts: 1949–1959," *China Quarterly*, no. 38 (April–June 1969), pp. 120–57.

in a public trial, cited in the 1954 constitution, has not been practiced regularly. Determination of guilt and sanctions by police and procurators or by extralegal bodies has been common. "Law and legal institutions still serve principally as instruments for enhancing the power of the state and for disciplining the people to perform its bidding."[39]

Underlying these perspectives is an even more fundamental one which places primary emphasis on control of the man, not his performance.[40] Compliance is seen ideally as flowing from internal acceptance of rules rather than from external pressures or sanctions that enforce specified standards of behavior. The burden of control falls on political and ideological work and their socializing effects; if they are carried out properly, the formal legal system beomes a secondary aspect of social control necessary for dealing with recalcitrant members of society but hopefully employed infrequently in special cases that have not responded to "nonlegal" methods of control.

We should not exaggerate the uniqueness or consistency of the CCP's "antilegalism." Neglect or avoidance of legal formalities is pronounced in China but not unknown in other systems; judicial independence and due process are relative matters, even in societies which place a greater value on them than do the Chinese.[41] Moreover, "contradictions" exist in the CCP's approach to law just as they do in so many areas of Chinese politics. A useful conceptualization for appreciating this point is to view the legal system as influenced by two models, one "external" and one "internal."[42] In simplest terms, the external model calls for a highly codified and institutionalized system, specifying permissible conduct and procedures and enforced by specialized legal organs and

[39]Jerome Alan Cohen, "The Criminal Process in China," in Donald W. Treadgold, ed., *Soviet and Chinese Communism: Similarities and Differences* (Seattle: University of Washington Press, 1967), pp. 107–43, quotation from p. 109. For a more detailed analysis, see Cohen, *The Criminal Process in the People's Republic of China, 1949–1963: An Introduction* (Cambridge, Mass.: Harvard University Press, 1968).

[40]Schurmann, op. cit., pp. 309–15.

[41]Cohen, "The Party and the Courts: 1949–1959," pp. 125–28, 152–57; and Richard M. Pfeffer, "Crime and Punishment: China and the United States," in Jerome Alan Cohen, ed., *Contemporary Chinese Law: Research Problems and Perspectives* (Cambridge, Mass.: Harvard University Press, 1970), pp. 261–81.

[42]Victor H. Li, "The Evolution and Development of the Chinese Legal System," in Lindbeck, ed., op. cit., pp. 221–55.

personnel. Although compatible with some of the more legalistic elements of Chinese tradition, the external model derives
mainly from Western influences that were introduced into
China in the modern era and reinforced by Soviet legal practices. The internal model derives much more directly from the
Confucian tradition amplified by the CCP's mass line. It emphasizes education, internalization of norms, and societal resolution of conflict as the primary means of rule enforcement
and adjudication.[43]

The distinction between these two models is not always
sharp in practice, and both have contributed to the post-1949
evolution of the Chinese legal system. The external model was
particularly strong during the mid-1950s, encouraging the
general state institutionalization of those years and the more
specific regulations concerning courts and legal procedures
that appeared in the 1954 constitution and its supporting documents. However, the internal model was also developing in
the local infrastructure of China's government. With the post-
1957 movement away from the Soviet model, and the accompanying campaign against "rightists" and other bourgeois
influences, it emerged as the dominant element in the CCP
legal policy. The courts and procuracies declined, while party
and public security organs assumed a much wider and more
direct role in legal work. Codification, legal training and research, and elaboration of legal rights and obligations languished. The Cultural Revolution brought renewed attacks on
the external model coupled with unprecedented criticism of
the public security system for its alleged failure to follow the
Maoist line and with a general assumption of law-enforcement
duties by the PLA.

The post-1976 reaction against the Cultural Revolution involved a pronounced revival of the external model. Under the
rubric of upholding "socialist legality" — the phrase that had
sponsored the Soviet-influenced legalism of the mid-1950s —
the official press called for strict observance of legal principles, for promulgation of the long-postponed legal codes, and
for renewed study of law as an academic field. It also began to
publicize accounts of legal proceedings against criminals and
corrupt officials. The 1978 state constitution restored the

[43]Ibid.

procuracy, which had fallen by the wayside in the Cultural Revolution. In early 1979 attention turned to strengthening elections and representative congresses, which were acknowledged to have languished ever since the late-1950s, and to a general promotion of the legal foundations of "socialist democracy." These developments did not repudiate the internal model, nor were they likely to diminish CCP control of the legal system, but they constituted another significant political change from the Maoist period.

Coercion and Voluntarism. These introductory comments indicate that rule enforcement in the PRC emphasizes prevention of violations, through voluntary compliance or other deterrents, rather than legal processing and punishment of offenders. Even when the external model has been strong, formal legal action has been mainly a last resort or a means of publicizing "model" cases for deterrent or educational purposes. Control of deviance thus shifts away from formal legal institutions toward a great variety of other social institutions and pressures.[44] The emphasis on voluntarism does not, however, obviate the need for coercive instruments, which are an important part of the legal system.

The PRC's coercive apparatus is extensive. It centers on the state public security system, which is tightly controlled by the CCP and is particularly influential within local governments.[45] Public security organs are resourceful and powerful. They include administrative cadres, police, and secret police; they maintain extensive files based on both regular police reports and the numerous activities over which they have some supervisory powers (for example, rationing, census, travel, and the work of popular security and mediation committees); and they have de facto power to arrest, investigate, adjudicate, and sentence in many cases that never reach the courts or are subject to only nominal review and ratification by other arms of the legal structure. The police presence is not an oppressive

[44]An excellent introduction is Victor H. Li, *Law Without Lawyers: A Comparative View of Law in the United States and China* (Boulder: Westview Press, 1978).

[45]On the organization and activities of public security organs, see Barnett, op. cit., pp. 194–97, 219–41, 389–94; and Victor H. Li, "The Public Security Bureau and Political-Legal Work in Hui-yang, 1952–1964," in John Wilson Lewis, ed., *The City in Communist China* (Stanford, Cal.: Stanford University Press, 1971), pp. 51–74.

one in terms of numbers or display of force and arms; but it is backed by the militia and ultimately the PLA, which leaves little doubt about its capacity to employ force when it chooses to do so.

The coercive apparatus also includes certain structures of a quasi-legal or extralegal nature, which have acted episodically but with telling effect. The most prominent of these were the "struggle" and "speak bitterness" meetings, people's tribunals, and mass trials of the reconstruction era, which meted out "revolutionary justice" to landlords, counterrevolutionaries, and other enemies of the new regime. These instruments operated under varying degrees of governmental authority and supervision. For example, peasants' associations had legal authorization to redistribute land; the people's tribunals, to try counterrevolutionaries. All of the localized coercive measures of the early years had general party approval and leadership. At the same time, the party encouraged a degree of spontaneity and popular participation in their operations that blurred the lines of government control and made uniform standards and procedures impossible to maintain. The ad hoc measures of 1950–1952 have not been repeated on a comparable scale, but mass struggle meetings in campaigns have continued the policy of allowing extralegal institutions to bring real or threatened force to bear on political deviants. Red Guard activities, which had generalized support but not necessarily direct guidance from Maoist officials, included erratic acts of violence and property confiscation against suspected bourgeois or revisionist elements.

The sanctions imposed by the rule enforcement apparatus reflect its diversity. One scholar has distinguished between "administrative" sanctions, with "informal" and "formal" varieties, and "criminal" sanctions.[46] "Informal" sanctions are those imposed by what we have called quasi-legal or extralegal structures. During the "terror" of 1950–1952 they included severe penalties up to and including summary execution, but their normal range is varying degrees of criticism by local cadres and peers. The more moderate forms of criticism are constructive and nonthreatening, but the struggle meetings at the other end of the scale may include verbal abuse, physical

[46]Cohen, "The Criminal Process in China," op. cit., pp. 121–23.

intimidation, and physical attack. The Cultural Revolution brought an outburst of violent informal sanctions, resulting in some deaths (from suicide as well as assault), and evoked more formal demotions, dismissals, and labor sentences for large numbers of cadres and intellectuals charged with deviations from the Maoist road. "Administrative" sanctions of a "formal" nature are those imposed by public security organs without recourse to court proceedings. They include warnings, modest fines, and brief detention; "supervised labor," in which the offender remains in society but is subject to special supervision, indoctrination, and stigma; and "labor reeducation" or "rehabilitation," in which the offender is sent to a labor camp for an indefinite period. "Criminal" sanctions are those imposed by the courts, including "labor reform" (sentence to labor for a fixed period, considered a more severe sentence than "labor reeducation"), imprisonment, and death.[47]

The extent and effect of these coercive sanctions is difficult to gauge with precision (statistics are not available on such matters), but they have been applied on a scale sufficient to make a deep impression on the population. Those killed during land reform and suppression of counterrevolutionaries campaigns probably numbered in the millions, and virtually all Chinese are familiar with struggle meetings and the various kinds of labor reform that have been the most common sanctions since the reconstruction period. The threat and use of coercion must serve as a significant deterrent to resistance to or violation of state policies. It could not be otherwise for a regime that emerged from a bloody civil war, carried out a radical redistribution of wealth and status, sought to change many traditional social norms, and was to undergo serious internal upheavals in the postrevolutionary period. Opposition and noncompliance was inevitable, as was the impulse to attack it with force. That coercive sanctions were severe and arbitrary in the early years and have remained a ready response to serious deviations, particularly those of a political nature, is not surprising.

[47]On Chinese labor camps, see Martin King Whyte, "Corrective Labor Camps in China," *Asian Survey*, vol. 13, no. 3 (March 1973), pp. 253–69; and one inmate's story in Bao Ruo-wang (Jean Pasqualini) and Rudolph Chelminski, *Prisoner of Mao* (New York: Penguin, 1976).

Nonetheless, coercion is not the primary mechanism of social control in the PRC. There is no single mechanism that dominates the rule enforcement process, but there is a general approach that casts its influence over the entire process. Simply put, it is the view that citizens should be led to a voluntary acceptance of the system's goals and norms, that they should enforce them through their own actions, and that deviations should be corrected through education rather than punishment.[48] The ideal of voluntarism is not attained in practice, hence the need for the coercive apparatus. Still, the ideal is operative even within that apparatus. Trials seem to be valued more for their educational impact on the public than their punitive effect on the offender, and those on whom sanctions are imposed (whether "administratively" or "criminally") are told that the objective is reeducation rather than punishment. Without denying the harsh realities of labor reform, which is a form of penal servitude, we should note that the regime does try to realize reform as well as labor in its administration of this sanction. Voluntarism manifests itself most concretely, however, in forms of social control that encourage citizens to avoid offenses in the first instance and to develop cooperative orientations toward compliance with governmental rules.

Social Control. Despite the tension and outbreaks of violence that have accompanied political mobilizations, social life in the PRC has been relatively orderly and free of crime and corruption. One explanation for this is the government's success in reducing opportunities and temptations to violate its prescriptions. Chinese socialism, with its egalitarianism and austerity, is a factor here. Basic economic needs are met with few gross differentials in income and little conspicuous affluence. People know, in a general way, what others around them earn — peasant income is discussed collectively — and the rationale behind income differentials. There are few opportunities to increase one's income except by publicly known changes in employment status. In other words, perceptions of economic inequity are low, and illegal income is difficult to conceal and dangerous to display. Strict regulation of possession of fire-

<hr>

[48]See Ezra F. Vogel, "Voluntarism and Social Control," in Treadgold, ed., op. cit., pp. 168–84.

arms, rationing of scarce goods, controls on marketing activities, and close supervision of residence and travel present further obstacles to the commission of crimes and the evasion of authority.[49]

Moreover, the Chinese pattern of social organization leaves little space for individual privacy. Basic-level cadres and activists are close to the people and are able to engage in frequent face-to-face contact with the citizens whom they lead. Primary units are organized in small groups, each with an internal leadership structure that is necessarily familiar with individual activities and problems. The fact that many of these units are both work and residential groups adds to the fullness of knowledge that members have about each other. Group meetings and discussions provide a forum for direct solicitation and exchange of information about members' thoughts and behavior. Nor are officials free from supervision by subordinates, peers, and superiors, since the checks, reports, and discussion meetings required for cadres are more intense than those for ordinary citizens. *Xiafang* also exposes them to a special kind of public scrutiny. It is probably the case, as the CCP fears, that cadres are better able to manipulate the system to their advantage than are the masses, but the government makes serious efforts to counter the potential abuse of official position.

These conditions and controls cannot eliminate the possibility of deviant behavior. Their effectiveness has varied with the intensity of changes demanded by the government, with economic conditions, and with the stability of political authority. For example, there was considerable noncompliance with the marriage law and collectivization directives. The economic crises of 1959–1961 led to hoarding, black marketeering, and a revival of official corruption. Crimes of violence increased during 1967–1968, although it was difficult to distinguish in

[49]On rationing and residence controls and the control aspects of education and job assignments, see Lynn T. White, III, "Deviance, Modernization, Rations, and Household Registers in Urban China," in Amy Auerbacher Wilson, et al., eds., *Deviance and Social Control in Chinese Society* (New York: Praeger, 1977), pp. 151–72, and Lynn T. White, III, *Careers in Shanghai: The Social Guidance of Personal Energies in a Developing Chinese City, 1949–1966* (Berkeley: University of California Press, 1978). White's analysis of the way in which diverse government controls serve as positive guides to careers and community involvements, as well as deterrents to deviant behavior, is relevant to much of the following discussion.

those years between organized political violence and random criminal acts. Post-1976 criticism of the Gang's activities and influence involved many allegations about criminal behavior, profiteering, embezzlement, and so forth in 1974–1976. In 1978–1979, the press reported many current examples of crime and corruption to dramatize the need for stricter observance of law. Despite these variations in degrees of compliance, however, the Chinese pattern of control and supervision has been relatively effective in limiting rule violations.

The preceding comments have referred to controls that seek to minimize the use of coercive measures by denying opportunities for offenses or by making their consequences risky or unrewarding. In concluding this section, we want to emphasize the more positive and voluntaristic aspects of social control in the PRC. Two phenomena are of particular importance: popular participation in rule enforcement and adjudication, and the effects of political socialization.

The popular role in rule enforcement and adjudication includes some participation in formal legal organs.[50] The "people's tribunals" referred to above established early in PRC history the principle of mass participation in trials in both participant-observer and judicial roles. When state organs were formalized in 1954, a system of "people's assessors" was provided to continue this practice. People's assessors are mass representatives who sit with judges and theoretically participate equally with them in the hearing and deciding of a case. Popular exposure to court proceedings contributes to a better understanding of the judicial system and possibly lessens traditional fears of litigation; it may also inject some popular notions of equity into court decisions. However, the modest role of the courts and their general subordination to police and party organs limit the significance of this kind of participation.

Much more important as a means of involving the population are the "security and defense" committees and mediation committees that are organized within basic-level units. The former were, before the Cultural Revolution, the lowest arm of the public security system, operating under close police

---

[50]James R. Townsend, *Political Participation in Communist China* (Berkeley: University of Calfornia Press, 1967), pp. 137–42.

supervision. Their primary responsibilities were to watch for and report on illegal or suspicious activities, and to maintain surveillance over the "five bad elements" and other offenders sentenced to "supervised labor" in their home locale. Following attacks on police and the public security system during the Cultural Revolution, security committees evolved more diverse organizational arrangements with broader and possibly more autonomous law enforcement functions within their units.[51]

Mediation committees come close to representing the Maoist ideal of dispute resolution. As elected bodies, they add to the popular role in the local governmental process. As localized institutions composed of activists rather than full-time cadres, they are decentralized and nonbureaucratic in character. And in their mission of mediation, they display the Chinese preference for informal, persuasive, and voluntary modes of settlement over formal litigation and adjudication. Mediation is a preferred course of action for courts as well, with judges frequently advising disputants to work out settlements on their own or through intermediaries. Police, women's and labor organizations, cadres and activists, friends and relatives may also play mediating roles. But it is the mediation committees — which are charged with educating their fellow citizens about their social obligations and anticipating possible conflicts as well as mediating actual disputes — that perhaps symbolize best the ideal of a self-regulating society.[52] Although security and mediation committees are largely the domain of activists in close touch with political superiors, they shift much responsibility for social control from the state apparatus to mass-based community organizations.

Political socialization extends the development of voluntary social control to the entire population. As noted in Chapter V, socialization in the PRC stresses the citizen's obligation to

[51]See Ezra F. Vogel, "Preserving Order in the Cities," in Lewis, ed., op. cit., pp. 87–88; and Janet Weitzner Salaff, "Urban Residential Communities in the Wake of the Cultural Revolution," in ibid., pp. 307–12.

[52]For a discussion of the organization and philosophy of mediation, noting its linkages with traditional modes of dispute settlement, see Stanley Lubman, "Mao and Mediation: Politics and Dispute Resolution in Communist China," *California Law Review*, vol. 55, no. 5 (November 1967), pp. 1284–59; see also Jerome Alan Cohen, "Drafting People's Mediation Rules," in Lewis, ed., op. cit., pp. 29–50.

serve the community and creates multiple opportunities for the practice of this obligation in daily life. Participation in political study and discussion, in mass movements, in the management of primary unit affairs, in *Xiafang* and other forms of productive labor are all multifunctional activities. In them, the citizen gains a better understanding of the system's policies and norms and simultaneously takes part in their realization. Insistence on practice is of utmost importance, partly because it reinforces learning and individual commitment and partly because it creates a social milieu of collective effort toward attainment of community goals. Governmental pressures for compliance are intensified by the example of one's peers and by pressures for group conformity. There is nothing automatic about either group or individual acceptance of the system's prescriptions, but the PRC has made significant progress toward the development of a social ethic in which compliance with the demands of the political community is recognized as a legitimate obligation of every citizen.

EXTERNAL INFLUENCES ON THE PROCESS

One of the most striking changes brought about by the Chinese revolution is an altered relationship between state and society. The imperial political system, with its orientation toward maintenance of the status quo, accepted a certain isolation from society. It exchanged some of its capacity to mobilize the population in return for a high degree of autonomy from societal influences. The Communist system extends its influence and initiative to the mass level, magnifying greatly its capacity to mobilize social resources. In doing so it opens the political process to diverse societal pressures and demands which intrude constantly on the calculations of political elites. The welfare and morale of the population, the structure and leadership qualities of primary social units, the willingness of the population to comply with national programs, the distribution of resources among different regions and population groups — all constitute restraints as well as opportunities within the political process. In expanding the scope of governmental competence, the CCP also has expanded the range of societal influences that it must somehow accommodate. This point has, of course, been the subject of recurring analysis throughout our study.

A somewhat analogous change, which has not yet been discussed directly, has occurred in the system's external relations. Although foreign policy and relations fall outside the scope of this volume, a few observations on the impact of the external environment are in order. We begin with a brief review of changes in China's international role.

Changes in China's International Role. The PRC's early history was marked by a limited role in international affairs. The imperial political system — at least in Qing times — had been relatively aloof from the rest of the world, preserving in its foreign relations a degree of autonomy and self-sufficiency that more than matched its internal autonomy. There was little tradition of active participation in a system of nation-states. Western and later Japanese imperialism shattered China's isolationism, forcing late Qing and republican statesmen to enter into extensive contact and negotiation with representatives of foreign governments. China began to develop a foreign policy apparatus and to engage in a variety of international activities. However, the formalities of this shift were misleading, simply because China's "foreign policy" focused largely on internal problems. China's international role was that of a subject country whose demands on other countries dealt primarily with the power and privileges that those countries exercised within China. What its role might be after attainment of national independence and unification was an open question.

The CCP was in no position to reverse this position dramatically when it first came to power. Its own experience with other systems rested largely on its relationships with the Nationalists, Japanese, and Russians. Its immediate concerns were predominantly domestic, for obvious reasons, and it faced a Western world already caught up in cold war hostility to Communism. The PRC's intervention in the Korean War sealed an American policy of containment and isolation which, for two decades, placed American power behind efforts to restrict China's international role. For a few years after 1949, therefore, China's foreign contacts were mainly with other Communist systems.

In the mid-1950s, under the guidance of Zhou Enlai's "peaceful coexistence" policy, the PRC began to diversify its contacts with non-Communist countries, especially in Asia. Still, its foreign relations remained skewed toward the socialist bloc until the Sino-Soviet dispute initiated a fundamental shift, the evolution and consequences of which were to dominate PRC foreign policy (and to some extent domestic policy) throughout the 1960s and 1970s. China's adaptation to the schism was extraordinarily tortuous, but it can be divided into two general phases.

The first phase of the 1960s rested on strong opposition to both the United States and the USSR. In taking this stance, which placed it outside the two great global alliance systems, the PRC necessarily assumed a somewhat "isolationist" role. The Cultural Revolution reinforced this tendency by radical questioning of the foreign ministry — bringing the temporary recall of most PRC ambassadors at one point — and by creating a number of provocative incidents at home and abroad that strained bilateral relations with a number of countries. The effect was to exaggerate images of China as an "outlaw" country, intent on isolationist self-reliance. In fact Mao's strategy was not isolationist at all, but rather a search for new allies to bolster China's exceedingly hazardous position as the world's only serious enemy of both nuclear superpowers.

The search began with an effort to win over the socialist bloc, an effort that split the bloc but failed to create significant support for China. Among Communist states, only Albania became a real ally, the others remaining tied to the USSR or, as in the case of North Korea and North Vietnam, maintaining a shifting middle ground between the two rivals. Many pro-Chinese splinter groups formed in left-wing parties not in power, but again the results were mixed and gave the Chinese little real leverage. The PRC could not compete successfully with the Soviet Union for leadership of the world Communist parties.

Increasingly, then, Chinese opposition to the superpowers turned to the larger Third World arena. Portraying itself as the champion of resistance to colonialism and neocolonialism, and particularly of Third World liberation movements, the PRC adopted a militant posture on global revolution and channeled political and military aid to selected liberation movements. The combination of aid and rhetorical support, plus China's credentials as a Third World country, gave this strategy some substance, but as the 1960s wore on Vietnam became its key testing ground. As that conflict escalated and then moved toward North Vietnamese victory, the Chinese realized that American imperialism was a lesser threat than was the Soviet Union, whose border clashes with China in 1969 had raised the specter of a Sino-Soviet war, and that even in a country as close to China as Vietnam, the Russians could supply more material aid than could the PRC. The prospect of Soviet influence moving into Southeast Asia underscored China's fundamental military and economic weakness relative to the superpowers, a weakness that no amount of revolutionary rhetoric or Third World sympathy could counteract. In short, the strategy of the 1960s was an inadequate answer to the Soviet threat, and its anti-American rationale was dissipating as the United States absorbed its own bitter lessons from Vietnam and began to reconsider its long-standing containment policy.

With the 1970s, therefore, a new Chinese strategy took shape, one of building a global united front against Russian "social imperialism" with heavy reliance on cooperation with capitalist countries and a muting — although not an abandonment — of emphasis on world revolution. The crucial political event initiating the new phase was Sino-American rapprochement, signaled in July 1971 by Henry Kissinger's secret visit to Peking; followed by PRC admission to the United Nations later in the year, with tacit American support; and confirmed in February 1972 by Nixon's visit and the signing of the Shanghai Communiqué that opened the way for greatly improved relations between the two countries. Accompanying the breakthrough in United States-China relations were a sharp increase in diplomatic contacts with other countries, with the November 1972 normalization of Sino-Japanese relations perhaps the most significant development, and the beginnings of a marked expansion of foreign trade. Post-1976 policies accelerated China's economic ties with capitalist countries and made more explicit the desire to rally Western Europe, Japan, and the United States in common opposition to the Soviet Union. While China's relationship with these countries fell far short of a formal united front, resting largely on bilateral economic and cultural exchange, the Chinese openly advocated a strong anti-Soviet military posture for capitalist countries and were obviously deriving military benefits from their high-technology trade with them.

This brief survey underscores two major changes in the PRC's international role. The first has been in international alignments, with the PRC moving from reliance on the Sino-Soviet alliance in the 1950s, an alliance resting on mutual opposition to the United States as the primary enemy, to a united front strategy against the Soviet Union in the 1970s, involving close economic relations — and some shared military-security concerns — with Japan, Western Europe, and the United States. In the middle of this great reversal was a period of militant self-reliance and championship of Third World liberation movements which represented the Maoist response to China's precarious position between the superpowers. Yet the 1960s appear in retrospect as a transitional period in which economic movement toward the capitalist world was already underway. Whereas China's trade during the 1950s was mainly with Communist countries, especially the USSR, non-Communist countries moved into the lead as early as 1963 and increased their share steadily thereafter (see Appendix D). Japan became China's leading trade partner in 1965 and has held that position ever since; in 1966 the PRC's other leading partners, in order after Japan, were Hong Kong, the USSR, West Germany, Canada, the United Kingdom and France.[53] Although the most significant growth in trade began about 1972 (still well before Mao's death), the shift toward trade with capitalist countries occurred much earlier.

The second change has been increasing involvement in the international system. The PRC was never truly "isolated," securing diplomatic recognition from many European and Asian states — as well as all Communist states — soon after 1949. It maintained modest economic and cultural relations with a variety of countries around the world throughout its first two decades. Nonetheless, Chinese and American policies

---

[53]Nai-ruenn Chen, "China's Foreign Trade, 1950–1974," in US Congress, Joint Economic Committee, *China: A Reassessment of the Economy* (Washington: Government Printing Office, 1975), 648–50.

combined to limit the PRC's international contacts. As late as July 1971, the PRC held diplomatic recognition from only 54 countries, compared to 63 for the Republic of China(ROC) on Taiwan. Then the situation changed dramatically. By 1979 recognition had shifted to 118 for the PRC and 21 for the ROC. China's foreign trade increased sharply from 5.9 billion United States dollars in 1972 to a projection of nearly 20 billion for 1978. After its 1971 entrance to the United Nations, the PRC steadily expanded its participation in United Nations activities and other international meetings. Post-1976 policies led not only to accelerated growth of foreign trade, but also to increased tourism and cultural exchange, a Sino-Japanese peace treaty in 1978 that brought the two countries into a very close relationship, and extensive negotiations concerning capitalist investment in and loans to China. The diplomatic offensive of the 1970s culminated in normalization of diplomatic relations between the US and the PRC in January 1979.

National Security and Economic Development. These changing international roles reflect enduring problems of national security and economic development which have exerted a strong influence on domestic politics. Decades of foreign penetration and economic distress had given China's elite a sense of urgency about issues of security and development. This urgency intensified in the post-1949 international environment. Within its first year, the PRC became involved in the Korean War, which was fought close to its borders and produced threatened attacks on China itself. From then on, it faced an arc of American military power deployed around its eastern and southern perimeter and avowedly maintained to contain and isolate it; the threat of nuclear attack was explicit. The United States supported and defended the rival Nationalist government on Taiwan, which declared its intent to reconquer the mainland. While the PRC had little fear of the Nationalist government as such, its existence perpetuated the civil war and the possibility of military action that might attract American participation. In the 1960s, Vietnam raised the specter of another Korea-type confrontation with the United States, while the Sino-Soviet conflict created new military tension, again including nuclear threats, on the northern border. American pressure finally eased in the 1970s, but the Russians, with their pronounced military and technological superiority and their new influence in Southeast Asia, loomed as a closer and possibly less predictable adversary than the United States had been.

For much of PRC history, security concerns justified and reinforced the Maoist approach. They supported PLA political influence, the value of military virtues, and the idea of militia service for large portions of the population. They encouraged new applications of CCP historical experience with decentralized administration and dispersed production facilities. Especially during the Maoist period, when China confronted both superpowers, they buttressed the emphasis on self-sufficiency and self-reliance. Military encirclement, foreign intelligence activities, and the nearby presence of the ROC lent urgency to mobilization campaigns, intensified the secretive and coercive side of CCP rule, and heightened the tendency to view political opposition as "national betrayal" or "antagonistic contradiction." Perceptions of a hostile international environment helped to legitimate the ethic of austerity, sacrifice, and service for the national cause. In short, Maoism as practiced in 1958–1976 had strong support from and roots in the "war preparedness" themes of those years.

China's international position also placed sharp limits on its foreign policy options, reserving major commitments for border issues that were, from a Chinese point of view, inseparably linked to domestic affairs and internal security. PRC military ventures since 1949 have included the conquest of Tibet in 1950; the Korean intervention; intermittent hostilities in the Taiwan Straits in the 1950s; brief border wars or skirmishes with India and the Soviet Union; military and construction aid to Vietnam throughout that long war, followed by skirmishes and another brief war on the Sino-Vietnamese border in 1978–1979; and the occupation of the Paracel—*Xisha* (Hsisha)—Islands in the South China Sea in 1974. Without accepting the Chinese version of these disputes, it is evident that the PRC has reserved its military risk taking for issues that involved what its leaders perceived to be Chinese territory and to which they had at least some historical claim or to efforts to keep hostile powers away from sensitive border areas.[54]

This is not to minimize the PRC's other international involvements, which have included military and economic aid to a number of Communist states and other Third World countries and, of course, a program of political support and some military aid to Third World liberation movements.[55] These efforts have been modest compared to those of the United States and the USSR, and have not taken a large share of Chinese resources, but for a country with extraordinary economic needs of its own they have represented a significant commitment. Yet they have been chosen with great care to minimize risks and maximize publicity, have ranked below frontier and territorial issues in priority, and have frequently involved more rhetoric than substance. The primary commitments of Chinese leaders, including Mao, have been to the security of the Chinese revolution rather than to world proletarian revolution, and many of their actions in alleged support of the latter have been designed to preserve the former.[56] The PRC's dealings with countries like Pakistan and Iran, its opposition to almost every pro-Soviet movement or government, and its growing cooperation with capitalist countries all reflect the heavy influence of security considerations on the Chinese policy line.

The external environment has its greatest domestic impact on economic development policies and the competition for

[54]For contrasting analyses of these events and the general context of China's foreign relations, see A. Doak Barnett, *China and the Major Powers in East Asia* (Washington: Brookings, 1977); John Gittings, *The World and China, 1922–1972* (New York: Harper and Row, 1974); and Harold C. Hinton, *China's Turbulent Quest*, rev. ed. (New York: Macmillan, 1972). The Chinese invasion of Vietnam in February 1979 may challenge this generalization, since the PRC defined its action, in part, as "punishment" for the Vietnamese invasion of Cambodia. Nonetheless, some border territory was in dispute, and Peking's underlying concern was probably intensifying Soviet pressure on its southern flank through the medium of a Soviet-Vietnamese alliance.

[55]See Peter Van Ness, *Revolution and Chinese Foreign Policy: Peking's Support for Wars of National Liberation* (Berkeley: University of California Press, 1970); and Carol H. Fogarty, "China's Economic Relations with the Third World," in *China: A Reassessment of the Economy*, pp. 730–37.

[56]John Gittings, "The Statesman," in Wilson, ed., *Mao Tse-tung in the Scales of History*, pp. 246–71.

scarce resources. Although the Chinese military establishment has been relatively low-cost — due to its technological backwardness and its self-supporting or productive economic roles — it has still claimed 7–10 percent of the GNP or perhaps 40 percent of the state budget.[57] The development of nuclear capabilities, which the PRC undertook on its own after the rupture with the Soviet Union, has been a serious strain on national economic and technological resources. Yet direct military costs are only the most obvious indicator of international pressures on development priorities.

In 1949 the CCP faced a fundamental dilemma: long-term economic development, national security, and restoration of international power all required a program of rapid industrialization, but the base economy was too weak to generate easily the investment capital necessary for it. There were three possible responses to this dilemma. One was gradualism, to compromise on the goal of rapid development; historical, ideological, and security considerations opposed this option, which in fact has never had significant support in the PRC — fantasies about Mao's "anti-modernism" notwithstanding. A second was full-scale Stalinism, a forced-march industrialization based on coercive extractions, especially from the rural sector; although Chinese development has had elements of this approach, the lower margin of surplus in China — as compared to postrevolutionary Russia — and the CCP's stronger commitment to popular livelihood made it unacceptable. The third was to seek foreign capital and technical assistance to get industrialization underway; this was the course chosen, with the USSR the only logical provider in the cold war era. From the outset, then, as seen in the FFYP, PRC development strategy reflected strong external influences. Generally speaking, the plan worked to get industrialization started, although the PRC had to make major concessions to the Russians to get their aid.[58] It also revealed the dangers of dependence on a

---

[57]Barnett, *China and the Major Powers in East Asia,* p. 275.

[58]For a cost-benefit analysis of Sino-Soviet economic relations in the 1950s, see Alexander Eckstein, *Communist China's Economic Growth and Foreign Trade* (New York: McGraw-Hill, 1966), esp. chap. 5.

single foreign power, especially one whose national interests increasingly diverged from those of China.

The Sino-Soviet conflict forced the Chinese to choose again, this time under even greater constraints since there were no realistic foreign sources of aid and Mao had become highly suspicious of the Soviet model as a whole. The Maoist self-reliance extolled during 1958–1976 was an effort to continue rapid industrialization and simultaneously to strengthen the rural sector, in both production and provision of social services, by relying on fuller mobilization of domestic resources. It succeeded in maintaining strong industrial growth rates, in keeping agricultural growth abreast of population growth and in raising popular living standards. Yet it, too, had to adapt to international realities in two important respects. Self-reliance was qualified from the first by increasing trade with capitalist countries for grain and industrial equipment imports, which in turn required maintenance of export markets, especially those in Hong Kong, Singapore, and in other areas of Southeast Asia. Foreign trade remained low as a percentage of GNP, but its substance was crucial to China's development, and it forced the PRC to moderate, or compromise, some of its professed principles in order to get what it needed from the global economy.

The other and ultimately decisive liability of the Maoist approach was that it retarded technological development, preventing a breakthrough in agriculture and compromising long-term defense and security prospects. It is, of course, an open question as to whether this was really a consequence of Maoist development or of the factional difficulties that beset it. On this question, as on all issues discussed in this section, domestic politics interacted with external pressures in ways that obscure simple cause and effect relationships. What is clear is that some CCP elites realized that China was losing ground to the advanced countries — most importantly the Soviet Union — and that something like the "four modernizations" approach, with emphasis on science and technology, was essential if China were ever to secure its place as a major world power. Mao apparently shared some of these convictons, as seen in his doubts about Cultural Revolution extremism, and his desire to improve relations with the United States and other capitalist countries, but he was too closely identified with the earlier pattern to permit its reversal. The decisive change came only after his death, especially in the stunning events of 1978 that not only repudiated the Cultural Revolution but launched China on a new drive for economic development and technological revolution based heavily on foreign technology, trade, investments, and credits.

The purpose of this section is not to argue that external considerations determine domestic policies or that the three basic developmental decisions — "lean to one side" in 1949, Maoist self-reliance in the late 1950s, and the "four modernizations" after 1976 — were inevitable consequences of a changing international environment. It is rather to emphasize the contraints that follow from China's place in the global system and to suggest that explanations of domestic politics in terms of domestic considerations alone are inadequate. For example, the general line of the new period reflects factional and personal rivalries among the elites, popular dissatisfaction with the trauma of the Cultural Revolution, and even the influence of professional or revisionist interest groups. Yet none of these is a sufficient explanation for the new line, which rests on an elite consensus that a period of "learning from advanced countries" is the only way to score a breakthrough in economic development and guarantee China's security in the perilous decades ahead. Consensus may weaken on issues of timing and degree, and might even shatter in factional conflict, but the realities of power politics and China's developmental needs give the "four modernizations" line a persuasive power that will be difficult to refute.

CHAPTER VIII

The Maoist Model
and Chinese Development

THE DEATH OF MAO ZEDONG was a turning point in Chinese politics. Whatever his successors ultimately do with his legacy, however much of his thought they retain or reject, his departure opened the way for major policy changes. The end of the Maoist period, and of his long leadership within the CCP, also raised new questions about the Maoist model and how it relates to political development in contemporary China.

The introductory chapter pointed out that a wide range of images of totalitarian, Communist, and developing systems has influenced generalizations about contemporary China, particularly in shaping the emphases and values with which foreign scholars assessed the post-1949 system. Yet most studies recognized important differences between the PRC and these other models, preferring to talk about a "Chinese model" and to emphasize, at least implicitly, its assumed distinctiveness. In practice, the Chinese model usually meant the Maoist model, which in turn incorporated those aspects of Maoism that lent themselves most readily to differentiation from alternative models. Mao's death and subsequent policy changes alter this perspective in two important ways. They remind us that the Chinese model and the Maoist model are not identical, and they suggest that the Maoist model was stronger in theory than in practice.

The Maoist model has a secure place in theories of comparative development, owing to its articulation of a set of principles that contrast with standard Western ideas about the developmental process. To summarize points discussed throughout the text, the Maoist model emphasizes national independence and self-reliance over dependence on foreign aid, trade, and technology; it advances the idea of "walking on two legs" — that is, utilizing indigenous as well as foreign, traditional as well as modern methods — to compensate for the abstention from full-scale modernism. It emphasizes all-around development, particularly of the rural sector, over the specialized development of the heavy industrial, urban sector; its image of development is a push from the bottom, raising backward sectors and bringing local forces into play, rather than a pull from the top in which the leading sector forges ahead and benefits "trickle down" to the rest of society; its test of performance is the elimination of poverty and the wider distribution of social services rather than growth rates and increases in per-capita income. It emphasizes mobilization of the population, with campaign attacks on national problems and decentralized encouragement of local initiative over stability of bureaucratic controls and institutions. And it calls for "politics in command" in preference to "planning in command," an insistence that ideological purity and continuing revolution take precedence over technical or purely economic considerations.

This formulation of the Maoist model is an abstraction from Chinese reality; it isolates certain aspects of Mao's larger career and thought, and it ignores the compromises that intruded on their practice. But its appeal does not depend on its empirical application in China, resting more on the clarity with which it challenges concepts that dominated Western and Third World thinking about development for most of the period after World War II. During the 1960s, there was a growing realization among students of development that the gap between advanced and underdeveloped countries was growing, that the passing of colonialism had not ended Third World economic dependence on or subordination to the core capitalist powers, that economic development was lagging in much of the world, and that even substantial gains in GNP and per-capita income might conceal increasing impoverishment for large sectors of the population. The burgeoning critique of standard development ideas, with new stress on problems of poverty and dependence and calls for a new international economic order, coincided with the Cultural Revolution and its forceful presentation of the Maoist model. For those who sought an alternative developmental model that seemed to respond to emerging Third World problems as well as long-acknowledged problems in advanced societies, China was proof that such alternatives were at least posssible.[1]

The Maoist model would have been of little interest if it were purely theoretical; its practice, coupled with what could be seen of PRC development achievements, compelled people to take it seriously. Yet careful scholars were aware that the model had not proved its superiority, that its practice had been complicated and controversial. Its role was precisely what the role of a model ought to be: to sharpen generalizations and contrasts and to stimulate hypotheses about how and why developmental approaches differ in their consequences. In this sense, the Maoist model was and will remain useful, not only at the abstract level of an alternative image of development, but also as a test case in which the alternative was debated and practiced — albeit with many qualifications — in the world's most populous country.

As the tone of these remarks suggests, however, the practical viability of the Maoist model is unproven. The post-Mao leadership continued to stress all-around development, and to some extent mobilization and ideological themes, but it shifted to much greater reliance on foreign trade, technology, and capital coupled with more emphasis on expertise, planning, and institutionalization. In other words, the Chinese have moved away from a pure Maoist model, and reflection suggests the model was never as distinct in Chinese practice as it was in debates about its merits as a concept.

To illustrate the problem, consider one view of political development which asserts that structural differentiation (the emergence of increasingly specialized political roles and structure) and cultural secularization (the process of increasing orientations to cause-and-effect relationships associated with

---

[1]For reflective essays on these issues, citing China as an example of an alternative approach to development, see Mahbub ul Haq, *The Poverty Curtain: Choices for the Third World* (New York: Columbia University Press, 1976).

the development of science and technology) lead to the increased system capabilities that constitute political development.[2] The Maoist model as practiced in the Cultural Revolution was hostile in some ways to both differentiation and secularization; witness efforts to simplify state and party bureaucracies, the suspension of mass organizations, the assaults on experts and technicians, and the "cult of Mao" with its highly ideological and even mystical connotations. Yet over the Maoist period as a whole, the Chinese system seemed to be developing stronger capabilities for dealing with its domestic and international problems. The evidence was imperfect on both system development and Maoist hostility to differentiation and secularization, but it led, in the first edition of this book, to a tentative conclusion that "ever-increasing structural differentiation and specialization is not always necessary for development and that an ideological political culture is not always incompatible with secularization."[3] '

Given the revival of differentiation and secularization trends in 1972–1976, while Mao was still alive, and the acceleration of this tendency in 1976–1978 with some reference to supportive elements in Maoism, Maoism now appears as a weak challenge at best to the differentiation-secularization hypothesis. The problem is not that Cultural Revolution Maoism was a developmental failure, since it strengthened some capabilities as it weakened others. The problem is simply that the model's attack on diffferentiation and secularization was confined in practice to a brief campaign period in which radical rhetoric magnified the impact of what were temporary and controversial reforms. If one looks at the practice of the whole Maoist period, or at the full span of Mao's writings and career, one sees a very different pattern of increasing differentiation and secularization in Chinese society tempered by and interspersed with Maoist warnings about the possible consequences of this trend. The time span is too brief, and the evidence too ambiguous, to prove or disprove an hypothesis about long-term developmental tendencies.

We must remember that the Chinese system is still relatively

---

[2]Gabriel A. Almond and G. Bingham Powell, Jr., *Comparative Politics: System, Process, and Policy,* 2nd ed. (Boston: Little, Brown, 1978), pp. 19–21.

[3]James R. Townsend, *Politics in China* (Boston: Little, Brown, 1974), p. 338.

new and that the influence of the long revolutionary era extended well past 1949. It may be that Mao's death marked the end of the revolutionary era, but we are still left with the problem of trying to discern a "model" in a period characterized more by dramatic political shifts than by stable developmental patterns. Much the same problem would arise, perhaps, if one tried to describe an American, Russian, or French developmental model on the basis of the first two or three decades after their revolutions. The Maoist model can be conceptualized, but it has lost much of its clarity in the give-and-take of PRC political history.

In the context of that history, then, it seems best to think of Maoism not as a static model but as a strategy for negotiating China's transition from the revolutionary era to an era of accelerated modernization and economic development. The strategy focused on two key problems. One was the PRC's emergence as an independent global actor, its shift from dependence on the Soviet Union to a wide range of diplomatic, economic, and cultural relations with many countries. The other was the initiation of industrialization and modernization on a broad, national base, that is, the establishment of a developmental course that mobilized the country as a whole rather than limited economic, social, or geographic sectors within it. The Maoist period of 1958–1976 handled both transitional problems with considerable success. Because it did so, those who follow Mao are indeed in a new period that alters the perceptions of the late 1950s. China no longer stands alone against both superpowers, it has initiated rural industrialization and agricultural modernization, and it has broadened greatly the social and economic base for national development. The new policies of 1976–1978 build on these accomplishments of the Maoist strategy; in that sense, their difference from the specifics of the Maoist strategy are "post-Mao" rather than "anti-Mao."

To sum up these comments, the Maoist model is very useful as a concept, but its practical impact has been tempered by post-1976 changes, by doubts about how accurately it reflects Mao's ideas as a whole, and by the fact that its actual dominance in Chinese politics was limited. Hence, efforts to assess the model's developmental effectiveness, or to evaluate Chinese performance in terms of the model, are full of pitfalls. It is better to think of the Maoist period as advancing a strategy of initial industrialization that reflected Mao's concerns while attempting to change the circumstances that gave rise to them. Maoism's dynamic quality as a strategy frustrates efforts to cast it as a static model; it changed with the times while he was alive, and he would be the first to acknowledge the inevitability of continuing changes in the future.

For a more concrete assessment of development in the PRC, the central themes of China's revolutionary era provide a useful guide. Chapter II identified national independence and unification and socioeconomic development as the core concerns of the pre-1949 revolution. With establishment of a new state in 1949, national integration and political participation joined these older themes as targets of revolutionary change. These problems are not unique to China, matching closely the key developemental challenges faced by all political systems.[4] Since the problems in a long-term sense are much the same, interest lies in the timing, priorities, and results with which they are faced in different systems. What follows is an overview of PRC response, reflecting the particular features of the Chinese revolution and CCP efforts to build upon it.

National Independence and Unification. Challenges to the national independence and unification of modern China have taken three forms: foreign influence in Chinese affairs; the removal of Chinese territory from the control of the central government; and the existence within the political system of rival claimants to political authority. At issue here is state building in its most fundamental sense of maintaining unchallenged central contorl over what is regarded as national territory. Chinese governments from the mid-nineteenth century down to the 1940s were unable to accomplish this task. The defeat of Japan and CCP victory in the Civil War of 1946–1949 gave the new Communist government a greater measure of national control than had prevailed for several decades. Nonetheless, a vigorous expansion of its power was required to complete and secure its gains.

[4]Almond and Powell, op. cit., p. 22.

The defeat of Japan, postwar weakness of Europe, and American preoccupation with cold war issues facilitated the PRC's eradication of foreign penetration. Only the Soviet Union retained significant influence in Chinese affairs. Its aid program brought Soviet advisers into the Chinese government, established Russian language study and books in Chinese schools, and created a substantial Chinese debt to and economic dependence on the Soviet Union. The PRC also granted the Russians special privileges in Manchuria and Xinjiang (Sinkiang) that bore strong similarities to the foreign concessions extracted from China in earlier decades. However, the privileges were relinquished in the mid-1950s, aid ended in 1960, and the debt was repaid a few years later. There was a strong revival of foreign contacts in the late 1970s, with a resumption of foreign economic activity in and loans to China, but these contacts were diversified among a large number of countries, none likely to match earlier Soviet influence. The PRC entered into these relationships on its own terms, with much greater resouces than in the past for resisting foreign pressure.

The unification of national territory has proved to be a more enduring problem. The new central government quickly incorporated all significant areas of the mainland, occupying Tibet and erasing the last serious KMT resistance by the end of 1950. Territorial issues remained, however, in border areas, foreign colonies, and islands off the China coast. The key border disputes were with India and the USSR, and more recently with Vietnam. All involved armed clashes, demonstrating their seriousness in terms of PRC national security, but the areas in question are not integral to China's sense of national identity and unity. The two remaining colonies are Portugese Macao and British Hong Kong, both being small areas that were part of Guangdong province before their seizure in the mid-nineteenth century. There is little question about the PRC's capacity to retake them, but Macao is already under its influence and China finds it useful to leave Hong Kong separate for economic dealings and foreign exchange earnings. The island claims are to groups in the East and South China Seas, with many countries of the region advancing competing claims. Like the border issues, these claims carry the potential for international conflict and should not be taken lightly — possible oil reserves and control of shipping lanes make the islands very important — but their removal from PRC control is not really a problem of territorial unity.

The major problem, of course, is Taiwan. In one sense Taiwan, too, is peripheral to the territorial integrity of China. The island has never been well integrated into the mainland system, despite formal administrative ties before the Japanese annexation of 1895 and during a brief period of rule from Nanjing (Nanking) during 1945–1949; there is no loss of established relationships in its separation from the mainland. However, that perspective overlooks the multiple political considerations that make Taiwan the last major obstacle to complete national unification. Both governments regard the island as Chinese territory and reject the possibility of an independent Taiwan. The population, save for a few aborigines, is wholly Chinese ethnically, culturally, and linguistically. The Taiwanese, who constitute around 80 percent of the total population (about 17 million in 1978), are Chinese who emigrated from the southeastern provinces of the mainland over the past three centuries. Although distinct as a social group from the mainlanders who came to Taiwan with the Nationalist government in the postwar period, they are no less Chinese than those mainlanders or other distinctive groups among the Han Chinese under PRC control. Moreover, Taiwan received international recognition as Chinese territory during World War II and probably would have fallen to a Communist invasion in the early 1950s had not American intervention prevented the attempt.

Taiwan's role as an obstacle to unification is heightened by the Nationalists' claim to be the government of China. This is not simply a case of national territory removed from central control but a direct challenge as well to the PRC's authority over the mainland. Peking might be less concerned about the territorial issue if the authority issue were resolved; that is, it might be willing to accept a Taiwan removed from its actual control if the island's government did not offer itself as a rival candidate for the government of the mainland. Whatever the ultimate resolution of the residue of China's civil war, it seems likely that Taiwan will remain outside the effective control of the mainland government for some time to come, constituting the most important gap in the CCP's otherwise impressive strides toward national unification.

There have been other internal threats to national unity since 1949, but none has produced a rival claimant for political authority. The most serious of the scattered, localized uprisings that have occurred in the PRC was the Tibetan revolt of 1959, which was crushed promptly and thoroughly — although there was some guerrilla-type resistance both before and after 1959. The Tibetan rebels, like their counterparts in a few other minority areas, offered no challenge at all to the existence of the national government. Their maximum hope — futile at that — was to secure greater autonomy from Peking within their areas. The Cultural Revolution raised the specter of civil war and a revival of warlordism, but none of the competing groups offered itself as an alternative to or sought separation from the central government.

The PRC's creation and maintenance of national independence and unity marks a crucial developmental step for modern China. It is easy to take this step for granted, but one has only to consider the number of governments which have not made it or have had to retrace it to realize its significance. The Communist government's ability to establish its control over the full territorial extent of mainland China was direct evidence of capabilities which its predecessors had not possessed. Once in control of a unified and independent country, it gained access to resources denied to previous governments and could devote a much larger proportion of these resources to constructive purposes.

Economic and Social Development. As noted in earlier passages, economic development in the PRC has been erratic but cumulatively impressive. GNP nearly quadrupled between 1952 and 1976, with dramatic gains in major industrial items and steady diversification and modernization of the economy (see Appendix B). The estimates of Appendix B yield annual growth rates for 1952–1976 of 6 percent in GNP, 10 percent in industrial production and 2 percent in agricultural production. Some sources estimate slightly higher agricultural growth rates, but it has been the weak spot in Chinese economic development, barely keeping ahead of population growth. Preliminary reports on 1976–1978 show a sturdy economic revival following the slump of 1974–1976, indicating that Mao's successors were off to a good start in their efforts to accelerate both industrial and agricultural rates.

The discrepancy between industrial and agricultural growth indicates the high priority assigned to development of the industrial-military bases of state power, as well as the difficulties of transforming agriculture. Despite some impressions to the contrary, the Maoist strategy never abandoned the goal of rapid industrialization, which has remained at the core of all post-1949 developmental approaches. At the same time, the PRC has improved the living standards of its population. The "agriculture as the foundation" policy adopted in the wake of the Great Leap acknowledged the necessity of agricultural growth for sustaining industrial advance; it argued that industrial and investment policy must meet agricultural needs now to attain an industrialized society in the future. More generally, the policy expressed the Maoist concern that rural areas share in the benefits of modernization rather than serve simply as resource providers for industrial expansion. The effort to combine improved living standards with rapid industrialization has not been easy. The overhead costs of rural development have been enormous, requiring great investments of material and human resources in water control projects and other agricultural facilities even to accomplish the modest agricultural gains recorded. Per-capita production of key consumer items like grain and cotton cloth has increased only marginally since 1952 (see Appendix C).

Despite these problems and limitations, per-capita income nearly doubled betweeen 1952 and 1975. Even more significant, however, has been the system's increased distributive capacity which has enabled it to provide a larger share of goods and benefits, in a more secure and orderly way, to less privileged social sectors. Distribution policies have eradicated extreme wealth and alleviated poverty. By world standards the Chinese citizen's economic life is poor and austere, but the system has gradually moved toward fulfillment of the basic economic needs of its vast population. Improved transportation, marketing, and storage facilities permit better use of existing supplies. Public health, sanitation, education, and communications services have expanded greatly and have become more accessible to ordinary citizens. Housing and health care are cheap, and prices have remained relatively stable. In short, the political system's distribution policies have favored the development of state power but have been sufficiently balanced and responsive to provide a rising standard of living for the population.

Several factors account for the PRC's achievements in its economic development program. National independence and unity had a mutually reinforcing relationship with the capabilities of the system. That is, the strength of the Communist movement enabled it to unify the country, which immediately enhanced the resources at its command. The remarkable production increases of 1949–1952 did not represent new development as much as full utilization of existing or latent resources that the PRC's predecessors had not been able to exploit. CCP victory led to activation of unused or rundown facilities; reduction of the terrible costs of internal war and disorder; greater uniformity and effectiveness in regulatory policies, especially fiscal policy; acquisition of foreign assets or foreign-held territory; and, generally, the extension of governmental authority into areas that had been outside the previous system's control.

With the advent of the FFYP, the government began to extract a greater share of national resources and channel it into new investment. Socialization of the economy expanded the scope and ease of revenue collections, while the growth of political organization throughout society helped to enforce compliance with state demands. State expenditures in 1959 were almost eight times the 1950 level and in 1957 were running about 30 percent of national income.[5] Extractive capabilities fell off after the collapse of the Leap but remained sufficient to support economic recovery and renewed growth as well as expensive new ventures into nuclear and space technology. The most important change in extractive capabilities since the 1950s has been a shift of responsibility for many

[5]Nai-ruenn Chen, ed., *Chinese Economic Statistics* (Chicago: Aldine, 1967), pp. 141, 446–47. See also George N. Ecklund, *Financing the Chinese Government Budget: Mainland China, 1950–1959* (Chicago: Aldine, 1966).

economic activities away from the central government. While decentralization increased provincial powers, especially in economic management, it does not appear to have weakened significantly the central government's overall control over planning and resource allocation.[6]

Another change associated with the Maoist period was increased development of distributive and symbolic capabilities. Material and human resources were shifted to rural areas, which began to retain larger shares of production for stockpiling of grain, reinvestment in the rural economy, and distribution to commune members. The egalitarian ethic fostered by the Cultural Revolution accelerated leveling tendencies in society, evidenced in expanded opportunities for primary and middle school education and reduced differences in wages, symbols of status, and consumption patterns. Development of symbolic capabilites centered on the unifying theme of Maoism, including both the personal authority of the Chairman and the content of his ideas, which gave the PRC's self-image a clarity and autonomy lacking in the 1950s. The ideas of a self-reliant China, leading the world revolution in opposition to the two superpowers while building a truly socialist society on the basis of collectivist ideals and self-sacrifice, was a potent weapon for national mobilization.

The tradeoff here was a decline in regulatory capability, reflected in deviations from official norms in the early 1960s, and the episodic disruptions of the Cultural Revolution decade. Moreover, Maoist symbolism reached a point of diminishing returns owing to abuses committed in its name and the contradictory implications of more cooperative relations with capitalist countries. Accordingly, the post-Mao leadership has tried to strike a balance between the 1950s and the Maoist period. It seeks to expand its extractive capabilities through scientific and technological inputs and greater claims on international resouces, and its regulatory power through renewed emphasis on planning, administrative authority, labor discipline, and legal procedures. It is refining distributive mecha-

---

[6]Nicholas R. Lardy, "Economic Planning in the People's Republic of China: Central-Provincial Fiscal Relations," in US Congress, Joint Economic Committee, *China: A Reassessment of the Economy* (Washington: Goverment Printing Office, 1975), pp. 94–115.

nisms with greater use of material incentives and the granting of more benefits to the special groups that lead the modernization process. While it hopes to retain the symbolic benefits of Maoism, it is shifting the content away from revolutionary themes that encourage political struggle toward modernizing themes that promote economic development.

These shifts and tradeoffs should not obscure the overall expansion of system capabilities that has occurred since 1949. In addition to establishing a government with immense powers over national resources, the CCP has undertaken a thorough, grass-roots mobilization of human resources for economic and social development. The most important aspects of this include: intensive mobilization of the labor force, especially of previously underutilized groups such as women and youth, for productive activity; creation of new or stronger primary organizations that carry much of the responsibility for implementing state policy; co-optation of citizens into the regulatory system, so that voluntary compliance and peer group pressures supplement formal state controls; a general upgrading of educational and occupational skills among the working population, which has been an impressive achievement although less publicized than the sporadically negative treatment of the highly trained sectors of the population.

The PRC's ability to respond to the challenge of economic and social development during the initial stages of industrialization is no guarantee of future success. The post-Mao leadership has set very high developmental goals, especially in the target of 4–5 percent annual increases in agricultural production. The economy has not met this target consistently in the past, despite enormous labor-intensive investments and considerable rural modernization; it can do so in the future only with a technological revolution in agriculture. The system's capacity to reduce population growth will ease the long-run demand on agricultural resources but cannot solve the short-run need for marked increases in agricultural productivity. The industrial sector may meet its targets more easily, but there are many problems here, too, in inferior equipment, technological backwardness, and deficiencies in the transportation network. Increasing reliance on foreign trade, technology, and capital will raise new, possibly unforeseen, economic and political strains. Consumer demands are likely to rise as modernization proceeds, with more intense social competition for material rewards. The "four modernizations" policy offers hope that all of these demands can be met, but its very ambitiousness may exacerbate political tension over economic decisions. The political system faces socioeconomic developmental challenges that are, if anything, greater than those encountered thus far. One preliminary sign of the severity of these challenges was a sober reassessment of the economy in early 1979. There were cutbacks in the economic goals announced at the Fifth NPC in 1978, backtracking on planned purchases and loans from capitalist countries, and acknowledgements that living standards remained very low for large sectors of the population.

National Integration. The unification of modern China required not simply the consolidation of rival forces into a unitary national government but also the reintegration of society and polity. Once the revolution had begun, reintegration could only be on terms that would, in effect, create a new form of political community within the Chinese tradition. The leaders of the Communist movement understood well the integrative requirements of national unification. They came to power determined to break down the barriers that divided Chinese society within itself and the political system from society as a whole. Their objective was the creation of a modern, socialist nation-state that would eliminate cleavages between nationalities, communal groups, and classes and establish a national community based on primary identification with the political system. Progress toward this objective has been substantial, although key problems remain in each of the areas mentioned.

The PRC is a multinational state overwhelmingly dominated by the Han or Chinese people, who are said to constitute about 94 percent of the population. Chinese sources identify some fifty-four minority nationalities, of which ten have an estimated population in excess of one million.[7] Most reside in frontier or isolated areas which today tend to be designated as "autonomous" administrative units that will encourage preservation

[7]For thorough analysis of minority policy and problems, see June Teufel Dreyer, *China's Forty Millions* (Cambridge: Harvard University Press, 1976).

of the cultural tradition of the minorities who inhabit them. Historically most were poorly integrated into the Chinese system, although there were great variations among the minorities in their degree of contact with and assimilation into Han society. Minority membership is in a sense peripheral to creation of a Chinese political community, but the CCP is understandably concerned that the territories they inhabit be securely held by the central government. Moreover, it asserts emphatically that all citizens of the PRC — not just the dominant Han — must share in and contribute to the new Chinese political identity.

Since 1949, the integration of minority peoples and areas has been proceeding at a much more rapid rate than in the past. Han migration and resettlement threatens to overwhelm some minorities in their own areas, particularly those that are of strategic importance (Xinjiang and Inner Mongolia, for example). Economic and social change, new lines of transportation and communication, and the spread of educational themes approved by Peking are breaking down some of the barriers of the past. There has been a periodic resistance to this process, but none of the minorities has any realistic hope of stemming the tide. The real question is whether the process will ultimately lead to a total assimilation by the Han or whether the minorities will be able — as the CCP promises — to retain their national identities even as they become members of the new political community. It would be a mistake to assume that national identities will disappear simply because Chinese pressures for integration are so great and the current prospects for resistance so futile. Modernization probably will bring the minority nationalities ever more firmly into the Chinese system, and yet it may also encourage or revive a strong sense of community among themselves. Separatism is a doubtful alternative now or in the future, but the terms of integration will remain open and fluid for decades to come.

Communal cleavages are those within the major nationalities or ethnic groups. Our concern here is with subethnic groupings among the Han, the vertical lines of cleavage that have for centuries divided Chinese society into myriad smaller communities. The pattern of communal differentiation in pre-Communist society was rich and varied, but three general types of community were particularly important. One was the kinship group which identified itself on lines of descent from common ancestors. Best known, of course, were the great clans and lineages particularly dominant in southeastern China which were social organizations of considerable power in local settings.

Local territorial communities, based on an economic unit which tended to supply most of its residents' needs and to mark the effective limits of their activities and concerns, were extremely important throughout China. Exactly what this unit most commonly was and what determined its extent is a difficult question. Some have assumed that it was the natural village, although recent scholarship indicates that it was a supravillage marketing area.[8] The general point is that almost all Chinese had strong community attachments to a local territorial unit centered on the cellular network of peasant villages and market towns. They also might identify with the larger territorial units in which they lived or from which they came — county, large city, province, region — but the intensity of identification tended to decline with increasing size of the unit. Finally, there were distinct linguistic and cultural groupings among the Han Chinese which surpassed both kinship and territorial communities in scale. Most commonly identified by their different spoken "dialects" (Cantonese, Hakka, Hokkien, Shanghai, provincial variants of Mandarin, and so forth), they frequently produced sharp economic, social, and cultural rivalry when brought into contact with each other.

These various communal cleavages were a source of much suspicion, prejudice, rivalry, and even violent conflict in Qing China, and they tended to focus individual loyalties on localized or distinctive segments of the larger society. Nationalism had no significant claim on the population in this context, except for those elites whose activities and ambitions brought them into direct association with the imperial political system. One of the most fascinating problems of modern China is the way in which foreign penetration, economic change, and revo-

[8]G. William Skinner, "Marketing and Social Structure in Rural China," *Journal of Asian Studies,* vol. 24, nos. 1–3 (November 1964, February 1965, May 1965).

lutionary movements began to disrupt these communities, bring them into closer contact with each other, and create new lines of cleavage and identification.

Chinese Communism has accelerated this redefinition of community, trying to eradicate the inherited lines of division and to create a universal sense of membership in a national community defined in political terms. It has assaulted directly some of the organizational supports for traditional communalism, most notably in its destruction of clan organization and property holdings. Through its formal educational system and its multiple instruments of socialization, it has made Mandarin a national language[9] and has promoted new orientations toward the political system. Increased travel and mobility and a more extensive communication system have spread knowledge about the country as a whole among its citizens. Economic modernization has enlarged the basic territorial communities, bringing rural areas into the sphere of larger towns and creating new metropolitan and regional systems.

Although these efforts have not eradicated all of the old particularism — the preference for association with "insiders" of one's own group and the suspicion or resentment of "outsiders" — China unmistakably has developed a vigorous and growing mass nationalism. Perhaps the most interesting problem and possible limitation in the growth of nationalism is the fact that most Chinese experience political acitivity mainly within their primary units. So long as this is the case, it will be difficult to tell exactly how the development of generalized loyalties to the national system affects orientations toward intermediate communities. "Localism" has been a recurring problem in the PRC, usually identified with cadres who are, after all, the only ones in a positions to show much effective favoritism for their own kin, locality, or dialect group. Would the masses support "localist" movements and issues (Canton for the Cantonese, for example) if given the opportunity in a representative assembly of municipal, provincial, or national scale? Perhaps they might, and that may be one reason the

[9]Efforts to establish Mandarin as a national language began well before the Communists came to power; for non-Mandarin-speaking areas it is a second language that does not replace the native dialect.

CCP refrains from the direct election of representative bodies or elites except within the lowest units.

Traditional China's third overarching cleavage lines, along with nationality and communal divisions, were of a class character. The basic horizontal division of society was between elites and masses, between the gentry (in the broadest sense) and the peasantry. We will not attempt to unravel here the question of whether class or community was the most powerful determinant of social conflict in imperial China. Both found modes of expression, and their interrelationship was exceedingly complex. Suffice it to say that the Chinese Communists made class cleavage their initial point of attack and that they succeeded in destroying the social and economic base of the pre-Communist elite. The question that concerns us is whether the PRC has developed new lines of class distinction and, if so, what implications that has for the integration of society and polity.

In general, contemporary Chinese society is not marked by powerful class distinctions. There are, of course, differences in income, social status, and political influence among different strata of the population, but economic egalitarianism and the populist ethic give them a relatively moderate character. Yet class is by no means a dead issue in the PRC. The retention throughout the Maoist period of old class labels assigned during the 1950s, and the insistence that the basic conflict within society and party alike was that between proletarian and bourgeois forces, has made class analysis and labeling a potent weapon in Chinese politics. There has been a tendency to exaggerate or even manufacture class distinctions in interpreting social conflict.

This sensitivity to class relationships will become more important in the course of the four modernizations. During the Maoist period, the political leadership — itself the PRC's closest approximation of an elite class — deflected class struggle toward "bourgeois experts" and defeated factional leaders, insisting on its vanguard relationship with the working classes and promoting the PRC's image as a relatively egalitarian, if not literally classless, society. Since 1976, two important changes have occurred. One is the denial of a class distinction between mental and manual labor, the insistence that intellectuals and technicians are really workers whose different occupations represent no more than a necessary division of labor within socialist society. In effect, this liberates the only group in Chinese society that could reasonably be called bourgeois from that adverse category. In supporting this ideological switch, the new leaders have hinted that it is time to forget the old class labels that for so long stigmatized a significant proportion of China's more highly trained strata.

The other change is the thrust of new policies toward a merger of intellectual and political elitehood by recruiting experts into the party and insisting on more expertise from party cadres. The creation of a new technocratic elite is underway, an elite that is indeed "both red and expert" but hardly in the Maoist sense. If the old class labels weaken, if mental labor as such has no class character, and if class analysis continues to dominate Chinese political discourse, it is difficult to see how the emerging political-technocratic elite can escape identification as a politically defined "new class". In contrast to ethnic and communal cleavages, which may gradually yield to a new national identity, class cleavages are likely to itensify as Chinese look anew at the distribution of power and privilege in their modernizing society.

Political Participation. Given the difficult economic choices that lie ahead and the possible emergence of new class cleavages, participation becomes an increasingly complex developmental challenge for the political system. The Maoist period left a pattern of participation with three primary characteristics. First, it expanded popular participation in the affairs of primary units, thereby increasing mass involvement in the system but restricting it, in the main, to activities supportive of elite prescriptions. Second, it acknowledged intraelite conflict and encouraged factional rivalry while denying the legitimacy of political opposition; the result was to open elite conflict to public view and expand the arena in which it was fought but to make it a high-risk enterprise in which losers were charged with "antagonistic" contradictions. Third, through the combination of the first two characteristics, it created linkages between elite and popular participation when elites mobilized popular support as a weapon in factional conflict; the result was to draw some citizens into higher-level conflicts, sometimes in an organized way, and sometimes in support of issues or groups that were not necessarily those that their elite patrons favored.

These characteristics give Chinese participation a volatile quality not found in other Communist systems. It is a quality with strong roots in the popular base of the revolution, in the CCP's mass line, and in Mao's personal brand of populism that unleashed the Cultural Revolution's assault on party discipline and authority. It has remained strong in the first few years after Mao's death, as seen in continued popular involvement in elite struggles and new pressures for "democracy" and regular elections. Unless it is repudiated, it is likely to be increasingly important as a political outlet for economic and class tensions arising in the course of modernization. What does this mean for the future of political participation in China?

It does not mean that the PRC will cease to be a party dictatorship. The clampdown in March 1979 on the critical posters and public debate that flourished in the winter of 1978–1979 shows that the CCP is not ready to give up the principle of democratic centralism or accept the legitimacy of political opposition. In other words, elites will continue to determine and define the legitimate scope of participation in a system with substantial participatory orientations and pressures. This inherently dynamic situation might move toward any of three general patterns.

One rests on consensual leadership in which elites stop short of defining their differences as "antagonistic" contradictions. In this situation, popular participation can be vigorous within the prescribed institutions and limits of Chinese society. Basic-level elections and other participatory mechanisms, combined with a relatively open intellectual and cultural life, permit airing of popular tensions generated by modernization, interaction with foreign countries, and social stratification. This takes place within party-controlled institutions, however, so that popular dissent or conflict cannot command independent organizational resources. Moreover, the substance of debate depends on elite tolerance, a political fact that all participants understand; if leaders decide that a particular position or activity is "incorrect," its advocates retreat — save for a few stubborn deviants who suffer for their indiscretion. Generally, this pattern supports institutionalization and the interests of the better-educated strata who can best take advantage of the participatory opportunities it provides.

A second pattern emerges when elite consensus dissolves into "antagonistic" factional struggle. Here at least one faction — possibly more — tries to mobilize popular support as a weapon against its opponents. Organizations are politicized, some in common support of an elite position, but some possibly resisting the faction that has the initiative. Mass mobilization encourages some spontaneous action, with local issues or popular cleavages intermingling with elite cleavages. In extreme form, violent conflict arises between rival organizations, which go beyond what their patrons want; extensive purges, organizational reform or suppression, and lingering factional hostilities follow. In contrast to the first pattern, this one is more likely to activate worker and peasant groups, and to exacerbate latent class conflicts. It may produce social disorder and sharp policy fluctuations that interfere with economic development.

The third pattern is an authoritarian reaction, a kind of Chinese Stalinism, that supresses participation in the name of state interests and economic and security priorities. It might follow the second pattern as a Draconian response to the persistent tensions and uncertainties that characterize the effort to combine party controls with mass line. Although the momentum of CCP history, including the immediate post-Mao years, indicates the PRC will cling to the first two patterns, or variations between them, the last alternative cannot be excluded if the modernization effort produces severe factional conflict or social strains. Given the apparent legitimacy of Chinese-style mass participation, however, full-scale authoritarianism would require heavy coercive measures and run the risk of creating an underground opposition. Whatever the mix, variation, or sequence among these three hypothetical patterns, Chinese political development has reached a point where participatory pressures and elite response to them are an increasingly important component in policy decisions and processes.

Historical eras resist neat dividing lines, carrying with them elements of both preceding and succeeding stages. China's revolutionary era extended its influence well past 1949, contributing to rejection of the Soviet model and infusing the Maoist period with revolutionary rhetoric and themes. The Maoist period, in retrospect a transitional stage between revolutionary and modernization eras, dramatized its revolutionary credentials even as it anticipated some of the modernization policies to come. The modernization period is equally complex. From a Maoist perspective it seems revisionist, yet the Maoist legacy continues to act upon it. The political system of the modernization period appears initially, then, as a blend of Maoist and revisionist models. Inevitably, however, it will move beyond these old models, or any combination of them, as it responds to new challenges. The first major new challenge stems from China's entrance into full participation in the global order, and especially its increasing interaction and cooperation with capitalist countries. In responding to this challenge, the Chinese political system is opening itself to influences that transcend old categories, with consequences that will require new models to describe.

Appendixes

APPENDIX A

Provincial-Level Units: Area and Population

Province	Capital	Region	1970 area (thousand square miles)	Population (in thousands) 1953	Population (in thousands) 1965	Population (in thousands) 1976
Anhui	Hefei	East	54	30,663	37,442	45,000
Fujian	Fuzhou	East	48	13,143	17,823	24,000
Gansu	Lanzhou	Northwest	190	11,291	15,200	19,795
Guangdong	Canton [Guangzhou]	Central-south	83	34,770	42,684	54,100
Guizhou	Guiyang	Southwest	67	15,037	19,302	24,000
Hebei	Shijiazhuang	North	75	33,181	41,428	55,193
Heilongjiang	Harbin	Northeast	280	12,681	21,320	32,000
Henan	Zhengzhou	Central-south	65	43,911	54,829	67,468
Hubei	Wuhan	Central-south	72	27,790	35,221	43,848
Hunan	Changsha	Central-south	81	33,227	40,563	49,018
Jiangsu	Nanjing	East	40	38,329	48,523	61,504
Jiangxi	Nanchang	East	64	16,773	22,271	29,400
Jilin	Changchun	Northeast	110	12,609	17,177	23,000
Liaoning	Shenyang	Northeast	90	22,269	32,403	44,474
Qinghai	Xining	Northwest	280	1,677	2,644	3,858
Shaanxi	Sian [Xian]	Northwest	76	15,881	20,800	26,000
Shandong	Jinan	North	60	50,134	63,257	78,478

Shanxi	Taiyuan	North	61	14,314	18,349	23,000
Sichuan	Chengdu	Southwest	220	65,685	81,634	100,080
Yunnan	Kunming	Southwest	168	17,473	22,120	28,000
Zhejiang	Hangzhou	East	39	22,866	28,918	36,000
Autonomous regions						
Guangxi Zhuang	Nanning	Central-south	91	19,561	24,776	31,300
Inner Mongolia [Nei Monggol]	Hohhot	North	225	3,532	5,778	8,500
Ningxia Hui	Yinchuan	Northwest	40	1,637	2,253	3,000
Tibet [Xizang]	Lhasa	Southwest	470	1,274	1,458	1,700
Xinjiang Uygur	Urumqi	Northwest	640	4,874	7,119	10,000
Centrally administered cities						
Peking [Beijing]	...	North	6.6	4,591	7,730	8,490
Shanghai	...	East	2.2	8,808	10,966	12,312
Tianjin	...	North	1.2	4,622	6,386	7,226
Total	...	...	3,700	582,603	750,394	950,744

Sources: Theodore Shabad, *China's Changing Map* (New York: Praeger, 1972), p. 34; Central Intelligence Agency, *China: Economic Indicators* (ER 77–10508, October 1977), p. 9.

APPENDIX B

Selected Economic Indicators

	1952	1957	1965	1970	1971	1972	1973	1974	1975	1976
GNP (bil 1976 US $)	87	122	165	231	247	258	292	302	323	324
Population, midyear (mil persons)	570	640	750	840	860	880	899	917	935	951
Per capita GNP (1976 US $)	153	190	220	275	287	294	325	330	346	340
Agricultural production index (1957 = 100)	83	100	104	127	130	126	142	146	148	148
Total grain (mil metric tons)	161	191	194	243	246	240	266	275	284	285
Cotton (mil metric tons)	1.3	1.6	1.9	2.0	2.2	2.1	2.5	2.5	2.3	2.3
Hogs (mil head)	58	115	168	226	251	261	...	261	...	280
Industrial production index (1957 = 100)	48	100	199	316	349	385	436	455	502	502
Producer goods index (1957 = 100)	39	100	211	350	407	452	513	536	602	...
Machinery index (1957 = 100)	33	100	257	586	711	795	930	992	1,156	...
Electric generators (mil kW)	Negl	0.3	0.8	...	3.0	3.5	4.0	4.6	5.5	...
Machine tools (th units)	13.7	28.3	45.0	70.0	75.0	75.0	80.0	80.0	90.0	...
Tractors (th 15-hp units)	0	0	23.9	79.0	114.6	136.0	166.0	150.0	180.0	190.9
Trucks (th units)	0	7.5	30.0	70.0	86.0	100.0	110.0	121.0	133.0	...
Locomotives (units)	20	167	50	435	455	475	495	505	530	...

Freight cars (th units)	5.8	7.3	6.6	12.0	14.0	15.0	16.0	16.8	18.5	...
Merchant ships (th metric tons)	6.1	46.4	50.6	121.5	148.0	164.6	209.4	288.4	313.6	318.8

Other producer goods index (1957 = 100)

(1957 = 100)	**41**	**100**	**200**	**294**	**336**	**371**	**415**	**429**	**472**	**...**
Electric power (bil kWh)	7.3	19.3	42.0	72.0	86.0	93.0	101.0	108.0	121.0	...
Coal (mil metric tons)	66.5	130.7	220.0	310.0	335.0	356.0	377.0	389.0	427.0	448.0
Crude oil (mil metric tons)	0.4	1.5	11.0	28.2	36.7	43.1	54.8	65.8	74.3	83.6
Crude steel (mil metric tons)	1.3	5.4	12.5	17.8	21.0	23.0	25.5	23.8	26.0	23.0
Chemical fertilizer (mil metric tons)	0.2	0.8	7.6	14.0	16.8	19.8	24.8	24.9	27.9	...
Cement (mil metric tons)	2.9	6.9	16.3	26.6	31.0	38.1	41.0	37.3	47.1	49.3
Timber (mil m³)	11.2	27.9	27.2	29.9	30.7	33.2	34.2	35.2	36.2	...
Paper (mil metric tons)	0.6	1.2	3.6	5.0	5.1	5.6	6.0	6.5	6.9	...
Consumer goods index (1957 = 100)	**60**	**100**	**183**	**272**	**272**	**295**	**334**	**347**	**368**	**...**
Cotton cloth (bil linear meters)	3.8	5.0	6.4	7.5	7.2	7.3	7.6	7.6	7.6	...
Wool cloth (mil linear meters)	4.2	18.2	...	...	...	...	...	65.2	...	...
Processed sugar (mil metric tons)	0.5	0.9	1.5	1.8	1.9	1.9	2.2	2.2	2.3	...
Bicycles (mil units)	0.1	0.8	1.8	3.6	4.0	4.3	4.9	5.2	5.5	...
Foreign trade (bil current US $)	**1.9**	**3.0**	**3.8**	**4.3**	**4.7**	**5.9**	**10.1**	**14.0**	**14.4**	**12.9**
Exports, f.o.b.	0.9	1.6	2.0	2.0	2.4	3.1	5.0	6.6	7.0	6.9
Imports, c.i.f.	1.0	1.4	1.8	2.2	2.3	2.8	5.1	7.4	7.4	6.0

Source: Central Intelligence Agency, *China: Economic Indicators* (ER 77–10508, October 1977), p. 1.

Consumer Goods and Welfare

1. Production of Selected Consumer Goods

	1952	1958	1961	1965	1970	1975
Cotton cloth (million linear meters)	3,829	5,700	3,300	6,400	7,500	7,600
Processed sugar (thousand metric tons)	451	900	700	1,460	1,790	2,300
Bicycles (thousand units)	80	1,174	634	1,792	3,640	5,460
Television sets (thousand units)	. . .	. . .	2	5	15	205

Source: Central Intelligence Agency, *China: Economic Indicators* (ER 77–10508, October 1977), pp. 24–25, 43.

2. *Per-Capita Indicators of Consumer Welfare*

	1952	1958	1961	1965	1970	1975
GNP (1976 US $)	153	221	152	220	275	346
Grain output (kilograms)	283	315	242	259	289	304
Cotton cloth output (linear meters)	6.7	8.7	4.8	8.5	8.9	8.1
Consumer goods output (Index 1957 = 100)	67	115	74	156	208	252

Source: Central Intelligence Agency, *China: Economic Indicators* (ER 77–10508, October 1977), pp. 24–25, 43.

APPENDIX D

Foreign Trade

1. Balance of Foreign Trade (million U.S. $)

	Total trade				Communist countries				Non-communist countries			
	Total	Exports	Imports	Balance	Total	Exports	Imports	Balance	Total	Exports	Imports	Balance
1950	1,210	620	590	30	350	210	140	70	860	410	450	-40
1951	1,900	780	1,120	-340	980	465	515	-50	920	315	605	-290
1952	1,890	875	1,015	-140	1,315	605	710	-105	575	270	305	-35
1953	2,295	1,040	1,255	-215	1,555	670	885	-215	740	370	370	0
1954	2,350	1,060	1,290	-230	1,735	765	970	-205	615	295	320	-25
1955	3,035	1,375	1,660	-285	2,250	950	1,300	-350	785	425	360	65
1956	3,120	1,635	1,485	150	2,055	1,045	1,010	35	1,065	590	475	115
1957	3,055	1,615	1,440	175	1,965	1,085	880	205	1,090	530	560	-30
1958	3,765	1,940	1,825	115	2,380	1,280	1,100	180	1,385	660	725	-65
1959	4,290	2,230	2,060	170	2,980	1,615	1,365	250	1,310	615	695	-80
1960	3,990	1,960	2,030	-70	2,620	1,335	1,285	50	1,370	625	745	-120
1961	3,015	1,525	1,490	35	1,685	965	715	250	1,335	560	775	-215
1962	2,675	1,525	1,150	375	1,410	915	490	425	1,265	605	660	-55
1963	2,770	1,570	1,200	370	1,250	820	430	390	1,525	755	770	-15
1964	3,220	1,750	1,470	280	1,100	710	390	320	2,120	1,040	1,080	-40
1965	3,880	2,035	1,845	190	1,165	650	515	135	2,715	1,385	1,330	55
1966	4,245	2,210	2,035	175	1,090	585	505	80	3,155	1,625	1,530	95
1967	3,895	1,945	1,950	-5	830	485	345	140	3,065	1,460	1,605	-145
1968	3,765	1,945	1,820	125	840	500	340	160	2,925	1,445	1,480	-35
1969	3,860	2,030	1,830	200	785	490	295	195	3,075	1,540	1,535	5

1970	4,290	2,050	2,240	-190	860	480	380	100	3,430	1,570	1,860	-290
1971	4,720	2,415	2,305	110	1,085	585	500	85	3,635	1,830	1,805	25
1972	5,920	3,085	2,835	250	1,275	740	535	205	4,645	2,345	2,300	45
1973	10,090	4,960	5,130	-170	1,710	1,000	710	290	8,380	3,960	4,420	-460
1974	13,950	6,570	7,380	-810	2,435	1,430	1,010	420	11,515	5,140	6,375	-1,230
1975	14,385	7,025	7,360	-335	2,360	1,370	990	380	12,025	5,655	6,370	-715
1976[a]	12,885	6,915	5,970	945	2,340	1,270	1,070	200	10,545	5,645	4,900	745

2. Imports of Grain (mil metric tons)[b]

	Total	Argentina	Australia	Canada	United States	Other
1961	5.7	0.4	2.6	2.3	0	0.4
1962	4.5	0.5	1.2	2.0	0	0.8
1963	5.5	Negl	3.0	1.5	0	1.0
1964	6.3	1.4	2.2	2.1	0	0.6
1965	5.9	1.5	2.8	1.6	0	Negl
1966	5.6	1.6	1.3	2.6	0	0.1
1967	4.2	0.1	2.9	1.1	0	0.1
1968	4.4	0	1.6	2.2	0	0.6
1969	3.8	0	1.8	1.7	0	0.3
1970	4.6	0	2.2	2.0	0	0.4
1971	3.0	0	Negl	3.0	0	0
1972	4.8	0	0	3.9	0.9	0
1973	7.6	0.1	0.8	2.5	4.2	0
1974	7.0	0.7	1.4	1.9	2.8	0.2
1975	3.3	0.2	1.2	1.9	0	0
1976	2.0	0	0.9	1.1	0	0

[a] Preliminary.
[b] For the years in the table, imports vary between 1 and 3 percent of consumption.
Source: Central Intelligence Agency, China: Economic Indicators (ER 77-10508, October 1977), p. 37.

APPENDIX D (continued)

3. *Leading Trade Partners, 1959 and 1976 (total in million U.S. $)*

1959		1976	
Country	Total trade	Country	Total trade
USSR	2,054	Japan	3,052
East Germany	221	Hong Kong	1,620
Hong Kong	201	West Germany	952
Czechoslovakia	195	France	571
West Germany	191	Romania	453
United Kingdom	121	USSR	416
Indonesia	111	Australia	380
Poland	99	United States	351
Malaya and Singapore	88	Canada	309
Hungary	84	Singapore	294

Sources: 1959 data from Alexander Eckstein, *Communist China's Economic Growth and Foreign Trade* (New York: McGraw-Hill, 1966), pp. 94, 280–85, 291. 1976 data from Central Intelligence Agency, *China: International Trade, 1976–77* (ER 77–10674, November 1977), p. 2.

4. *Commodity Composition of Trade, 1976 (in percent)*

Exports, by sector of origin		*Imports, by end use*	
Manufacturing	52	Industrial supplies	59
Textile yarn and fabric	17	Iron and steel	24
Clothing and footwear	7	Chemicals	10
Other light manufactures	13	Textile fibers	5
Machinery and equipment	4	Nonferrous metals	4
Metals and metal products	4	Rubber	3
Chemicals	5	Metal products	1
Petroleum products	2	Other	12
Agricultural	36	Capital goods	31
Animals, meat, and fish	9	Nonelectric machinery	18
Grain	6	Transport equipment	8
Fruits and vegetables	5	Electric machinery	3
Textile fibers	4	Other	2
Crude animal materials	4		
Oilseeds	1	Foodstuffs	9
Other	7	Grain	5
		Sugar	3
Extractive	12	Other	1
Crude oil	9		
Crude minerals and metals	2	Consumer goods	1
Coal	1		

Source: Central Intelligence Agency, *China: International Trade, 1976–77* (ER 77–10674, November 1977), p. 3.

Index